Craig Hollaba

MW00997985

Embedded Linux: Hardware, Software, and Interfacing

✦Addison-Wesley

Boston • San Francisco • New York • Toronto • Montreal
London • Munich • Paris • Madrid
Capetown • Sydney • Tokyo • Singapore • Mexico City

Embedded Linux: Hardware, Software, and Interfacing

Many of the designations used by manufacturers and sellers to distinguish their products are claimed as trademarks. Where those designations appear in this book, and Addison-Wesley were aware of a trademark claim, the designations have been printed in initial capital letters or in all capitals.

The author and publisher have taken care in the preparation of this book, but make no expressed or implied warranty of any kind and assume no responsibility for errors or omissions. No liability is assumed for incidental or consequential damages in connection with or arising out of the use of the information or programs contained herein.

The publisher offers discounts on this book when ordered in quantity for special sales.

For more information, please contact:

Pearson Education Corporate Sales Division

201 W. 103rd Street

Indianapolis, IN 46290

(800) 428-5331

corpsales@pearsoned.com

Visit AW on the Web: www.awl.com/cseng/

ISBN 0-672-32226-9

Library of Congress Catalog Card Number 2001089582

Text printed on recycled paper

1 2 3 4 5 6 7 8 9 10—CRS—05 04 03 02

First printing, March 2002

Associate Publisher
Jeff Koch

Acquisitions Editor
Katie Purdum

Development Editor
Mark Cierzniak

Managing Editor
Matt Purcell

Project Editor
Andrew Beaster

Copy Editor
Kitty Wilson Jarrett

Indexer
Ken Johnson

Proofreader
Juli Cook

Technical Editor
Rob Savoye

Team Coordinator
Denni Bannister

Interior Designer
Anne Jones

Cover Designer
Aren Howell

Page Layout
Mark Walchle
Ayanna Lacey
Michelle Mitchell

Contents at a Glance

Table of Contents

Foreword

Embedded systems, the once-sleepy backwater of information technology, are now emerging as a multibillion-dollar industry that is already pervading our everyday existences and changing our lives. Around the world, "smart devices" are insinuating themselves into everyone's daily routine: You drive to work in your electronically controlled car or ride a digitally guided commuter train, take a call on your mobile phone, make copies at the office, sit in on a digital conference call, and then go home and watch a movie from your cable box or DVD player. If you look around you, you'll realize that 50 to 100 embedded computers touch your life every day.

Linux is taking this world of embedded and pervasive computing by storm. Once dominated by proprietary and obscure operating systems, tools, and applications, embedded designs today benefit from the transparency and functionality of open-source software, especially Linux. Even conservative estimates show embedded Linux garnering up to half of all new embedded designs by the end of 2002.

In my role at MontaVista Software, I have the pleasure of talking to thousands of embedded developers and of sneaking glimpses into their varied projects. In this context I first met Dr. Craig Hollabaugh at LinuxWorld in New York in 2001. In the course of his writing this book, I had the pleasure of his company several more times and numerous chats by phone.

I find Craig's approach both sensible and comprehensive. His choice of an application to run the fabled Silverjack winter resort both recalls the "meat and potatoes" of the embedded applications space (control and instrumentation) and launches into today's hot new areas of pervasive computing (embedded Web interfacing, multimedia, and messaging). His survey of available embedded hardware and key interface technologies and his step-by-step account of the embedded Linux development process provide invaluable signposts for aspiring system designers.

Craig's team of trailblazing engineers confronted the daunting task of acquiring and using embedded Linux development tools and deployment components. The Silverjack scenario and the details of the engineering effort mirror the experiences of many developers facing their first embedded Linux project. The slope is steep, but the rewards are very great. Books like *Embedded Linux*; organizations like the Embedded Linux Consortium, EMBLIX, and LinuxDevices; and the efforts of embedded Linux platform vendors clear a path to successful development and deployment of the next generation of smart, Linux-based devices.

William Weinberg
Director of Strategic Marketing/Embedded Linux Evangelist
MontaVista Software
San Jose, CA
January 2002

About the Author

Craig Hollabaugh has been fascinated by electronics since he bought an AM radio in elementary school. He was first exposed to Unix during a cross-country talk session in 1985. Later, he administered networked Sun and DEC workstations while pursuing a doctoral degree in electrical engineering at Georgia Institute of Technology.

Craig's first embedded SCADA (supervisory control and data acquisition) design, the PacMeister, remotely monitored the gasoline additive injection process and earned him a U.S. patent. His next embedded design, the Titan PAC-3, based on Intel x86 architecture, controlled this injection process, using a home-growth multitasking operating system written in C++, complete with boot code, communications ability, and field-downloadable application code.

In 1995 Craig co-founded Wireless Scientific, where he developed 20 spread-spectrum 900MHz ISM industrial telemetry products. Craig worked with more than 200 developers, systems integrators, and equipment manufacturers to incorporate wireless telemetry within their SCADA applications or product lines. In 1996 Wireless Scientific's Global Data Management project used Linux as a development platform to remotely monitor and control additive tank levels.

In 1997 Lanier Corporation charged Craig with architecting its next-generation VoiceWriter, a medical digital dictation and transcription system with revenues beyond $100 million. His responsibilities included ensuring that product development followed current/future technological trends, adhered to technical/medical information standards, and incorporated Lanier's legacy products.

Craig consults from his home in Ouray, Colorado. He developed the firmware for Antec's flagship cable distribution product, the Proteus Scalable Node. At Clifton, Weiss and Associates, Craig is a member of a carrier-class telecommunications network design team. His current responsibilities involve designing and analyzing wired and wireless voice and data networks for Dallas Area Rapid Transit, Metro North Railroad, New York City Transit, and Pittsburgh Area Transit. He's also designing FM, MP3, and Bluetooth headset electronics for Arriva.

The Ouray community benefits through Craig's system administration support of Ouraynet and his adult education classes in electronics and programming. Most recently, Craig co-founded The Silverjack Baking Company, where he will bake and sell scrumptious delights from a horse-drawn bakery wagon on Ouray's Main Street during the summer months. If there's snow flying, you'll most likely find him snowboarding at Telluride.

Dedication

For my support staff, the Spuds: Kathy and Chris Anderson, Caela and Steve Bova, Melanie and Scott Clemmons, Pam and Robert Cort, Tina Dittmar, Jonathan Fulford, Tanya and Kevin Hansel, Margaret Hollabaugh, Maureen and Steve Jett, Scott Kidner, Brian Kopp, Teresa Loconte, Michelle and Brad Lohrding, Darla and Alfred Lorber, Venita and Craig Lujan, Jean and John McLennan, Marce Miller, Lisa and Jim Olwine, Katie Purdum, Anna and Mike Sadler, Jennifer and Fritz Siegrist, Karen and John Totten, Karyn Young, and especially Melanie Kline.

Acknowledgments

The enthusiasm toward this book has been simply phenomenal. Everyone I mention it to has supported my efforts in some way. I'd like to start by thanking a few people who helped me to see my greatness: Katie Purdum, Angelo d'Amelio, Roger Smith, Gerri Spina, Eva Montibello, and Teresa Loconte. These day-to-day supporters then took over and continued the push: Melanie Kline, Josh Kline, Mouse and Harry Durgin, Paul Vallejos, Ben Blouse, Scott Kidner, Brian Kopp, and my little baby sister, Karen Totten. I attribute the book's readability to my editing team: John Hollabaugh, Rob Savoye, Kitty Jarrett, and Mark Cierzniak. A special thanks to Rick Lehrbaum, for his comprehensive embedded Linux Web site, linuxdevices.com. I want to thank these individuals at companies that offered their products and technical support for the book's examples: Doug Stead at Tri-M Systems, Stuart Adams at Brightstar Engineering, Ken Applebaum, John Havre, and Matt Hoover at Embedded Planet, Eugene Feng at Silicon Storage Technology, Juan Vazquez at ESPTech, Tom Barnum at VersaLogic, and Bill Weinburg at MontaVista Software. The work of these individuals also contributed to the examples: Thomas Oehser, Erik Mouw, Ori Pomerantz, Alessandro Rubini, Jonathan Corbet, Tim Waugh, Jan Axelson, Craig Peacock, Riku Saikkonen, Jens Gecius, Detlef Fliegl, Brad Hards, Mark Pilon, Daniel Smolik, Markus Schlup, Michael Hipp, David Beal, Wolfgang Denk, Mark Hatle, Dan Malek, Larry Doolittle, and Jim Ready. These open-source developers deserve a tremendous acknowledgement for their activities: all the kernel programmers, Debian, Apache Software Foundation, MySQL, and GNU. This book exists because of your contributions, support, and encouragement. I thank you.

Introduction

This is an exciting time. The proliferation of Internet technology has transformed our concept of information. 24 hours per day, people rely on network devices for business and personal use. Over time, this dependence will grow further. Today's network devices, such as servers, routers, and desktop computers, form the Internet's infrastructure. Tomorrow's devices will control your home's temperature, maintain inventory levels at your business, and monitor automobile traffic patterns. Only a handful of the billions of processors produced each year go into desktop or server computers. The remaining processors monitor and control other facets of the world.

Individuals and businesses want smart, network-connected, devices to improve their lives, their efficiency, and their bottom dollar. These devices must be simple to operate, reliable, and inexpensive. This is where Linux comes in. Advances in technology accompanied by competitive pricing allow Linux to move from the desktop and server environment to embedded devices. Linux offers reliability, features, open-source code, and a proven track record; these features make it perfectly suited for embedded system designs. In this book, you will find information to create an embedded Linux foundation. You can then extend this foundation in your own designs.

Benefits of This Book

When I first started researching material for this book, I assumed that online embedded Linux information was like other Linux information—plentiful and well documented. I quickly discovered that my assumption was wrong. I found embedded Linux documentation to be sparse, scattered, incomplete, and sometimes dated. This was discouraging and invigorating at the same time. Although I worried about being able to find adequate information, I was further convinced of the need for this book. People are designing embedded products with Linux, so the information and knowledge are out there; it just hasn't all been in one place until now.

As an instructor, I have determined that students best understand and retain theoretical concepts and ideas when accompanied by examples. When students see a concept in action—whether it is a robotic arm movement, a voltmeter reading, or an oscilloscope waveform—they're most likely to later apply that concept to solve their own problems. That's why this book is full of step-by-step examples. You will learn through the example and be able to apply that knowledge to your own designs.

What This Book Covers

This book includes a complete series of real-world interfacing examples designed to introduce embedded Linux from hardware and software perspectives. After you create an embedded Linux development environment, you will step through hardware and software interfacing examples, using asynchronous serial communication, the PC parallel port, USB, memory I/O, synchronous serial communication, and interrupts. All interfacing examples are then tied together using system integration. All this material is presented by using a winter resort automation project called Project Trailblazer. You can find the book's source code and scripts at www.embeddedlinuxinterfacing.com.

The following text briefly summarizes each chapter.

Chapter 1, "Introducing Embedded Linux," describes the brief history of Linux as an embedded operating system and the implications of using open-source software in product design.

Chapter 2, "System Architecture," introduces a winter resort automation project called Project Trailblazer and develops a series of project requirements. Project Trailblazer and its requirements form the basis for the book's interfacing examples.

Chapter 3, "Selecting a Platform and Installing Tool Sets," describes the process of platform selection. Four target boards—which use x86, StrongARM, and PowerPC processors—are selected for Project Trailblazer. This chapter then describes the creation of an embedded Linux development workstation called tbdev1. All the development tools are either installed or compiled, including the cross-compiled tool chain for the StrongARM and PowerPC processors.

Chapter 4, "Booting Linux," describes the Linux boot process, from power-on to the bash prompt. Using a minimum root filesystem, each target board is booted using Linux version 2.4.

Chapter 5, "Debugging," configures gdb and gdbserver for target board debugging over the Ethernet network. A cross-compiled version of helloworld is remotely executed and debugged.

Chapter 6, "Asynchronous Serial Communication Interfacing," describes the Linux serial port device driver for control of port signals and buffers. An RFID tag reader, an LCD display, and control circuitry are interfaced to the Linux serial port.

Chapter 7, "Parallel Port Interfacing," describes interfacing AC circuits to an x86 target board's parallel printer port. A custom device driver called helloworld_proc_module that uses a /proc directory entry is introduced.

Chapter 8, "USB Interfacing," describes connecting a camera and speakers for visual input and audio output to a target board's USB port.

Chapter 9, "Memory I/O Interfacing," describes interfacing AC circuits to the StrongARM and PowerPC target boards' CPU buses.

Chapter 10, "Synchronous Serial Communication Interfacing," describes SPI and I2C connections and communications. A low-cost SPI temperature sensor and I2C LED display driver are interfaced to the target boards.

Chapter 11, "Using Interrupts for Timing," describes Linux timing sources and the measurement of each target board's average interrupt latency. An event timer with 1ms accuracy is developed to measure race times.

Chapter 12, "System Integration," describes the creation of the Project Trailblazer database. Target and server `bash` scripts are developed, using this database for collection and distribution of temperature, image, and authentication data.

Chapter 13, "Final Thoughts," summarizes the interfacing projects and discusses embedded Linux topics that are not addressed elsewhere in the book.

Who This Book Is For

If you are a hardware engineer, software developer, system integrator, or product manager who's begun exploring embedded Linux for interfacing applications, then this book is for you. The book's comprehensive interfacing examples are simple, requiring only a basic understanding of digital logic design, C and `bash` programming, and Linux system administration.

Conventions Used in This Book

This book uses several common conventions to help teach embedded Linux.

The typographical conventions used in this book include the following:

- Commands and computer output appear in a `monospaced computer font`.
- Commands you type appear in a **`boldfaced computer font`**.
- *Italics* are used to introduce you to new terms.

In addition to typographical conventions, this book includes tips, which look like this:

TIP

Information that offers shortcuts and solutions to common problems is highlighted as a tip.

PART I

Getting Started

IN THIS PART

1

Introducing Embedded Linux

So you want to use Linux in your next embedded system design? Great! You're not alone: Thousands of developers worldwide are doing the same thing. Like you, they want to take advantage of countless hours of code creation to make their products reliable, feature packed, robust, and quick to market. *Embedded Linux*—using Linux as an operating system in embedded devices—is now commonplace. In 1999 not many developers considered Linux an option for embedded designs. Today, however, Linux is well poised to become the market leader for embedded operating systems.

In a couple years, it's likely that a fair percentage of the billions of processors produced every year will run Linux. The massive Internet adoption of Linux, combined with technology advances and price reductions in hardware (CPUs) and memory (both flash and RAM), finally make embedding Linux a viable option. Since 1999 use of embedded Linux has gone from zero adoption to taking second place, in terms of market share, behind Wind River.[1] Experts estimate that embedded Linux will take over the number-one market share position by the end of 2002[1]. This is very interesting, considering that Linux actually started as student project so many years ago. Linux can become number one, through the adoption of embedded Linux for designs that become products.

Why Linux, Why Now?

Microprocessor industry advances form the foundation for using Linux as an embedded operating system. Gone are the days of embedded designs that use 4- or 8-bit microprocessors; today it is just as easy and cost competitive to use 32-bit microprocessors with several megabytes of memory. The ever-changing pace of hardware innovation and obsolescence presents an enormous development challenge for real-time operating system (RTOS) vendors. With limited resources, these RTOS vendors make business decisions that often leave many developers unsupported. Developers always want the latest and greatest hardware and software for their new embedded designs while also requiring high reliability. Desktop operating systems provide the latest in software but lack reliability and require more memory and CPU resources. RTOS vendors offer reliability but struggle with software development in the ever-changing world of technology. This is where Linux comes in.

Linux offers reliability and efficiency, with a proven track record. Open-source code availability has spawned countless improvements, enhancements, and additions in terms of performance, functionality, driver development, and porting activities. Designers of embedded systems like open-source software because they often modify subsystem code for their designs. Linux supports Portable Operations System Interface (POSIX), which allows developers to easily port existing code. Linux is successfully ported to several microprocessors, including x86, SPARC, ARM, PowerPC, MIPS, and SuperH.

Initially, developers were apprehensive about considering Linux as an embedded operating system option because of its distributed development approach and a perceived lack of support structure. The support structure for embedded Linux has changed dramatically since 1999, thanks largely to the Embedded Linux Consortium (ELC), which was founded with 50 members in May 2000 and now has membership exceeding 125 companies. This consortium works toward standardizing and promoting Linux for use in embedded applications. In addition, several companies were founded solely for embedded Linux. These companies don't merely repackage distributions and sell CDs. They have a wide range of embedded Linux products as well as design and support services. Using embedded Linux, developers can design high-reliability products, using the latest and greatest hardware and software.

What Is an Embedded System?

If you ask a dozen engineers to define *embedded system,* you'll get a dozen different answers. Most embedded systems perform specific tasks. Let's assume that the simplest embedded system contains input and output capability, as well as control logic. This system performs some type of functionality, based on its configuration. Using these criteria, a discrete logic circuit that contains a 74123 counter that implements control logic with a state machine could be considered an embedded system. You might add that this system needs to be programmable, via software, and stored in the system firmware. This new definition for an embedded system consists of input/output (I/O) and control logic stored in system firmware. A desktop computer with a mouse, a keyboard, a network connection, and a multitasking operating system running a graphical user interface (GUI) fulfills these requirements, but is it considered an embedded system?

If you don't consider a desktop machine an embedded system, then what about handheld devices? They have I/O capability and can run control logic that's stored in firmware. Some say that desktop computers and handhelds are general-purpose computing devices that are capable of running software to perform many different tasks. An embedded system, on the other hand, is primarily designed for a specific task—for example, a dishwasher controller or flight navigation system. This specific functionality defines the sole purpose of the embedded design. If that's the case, why are some embedded systems designed with additional capability, such as program storage in nonvolatile memory and the capability of running multitasking operating systems that are capable of executing additional tasks beyond the original design?

In the past, it was much easier to distinguish an embedded system from a general-purpose computer than it is today. For example, you can easily tell that an 8051-based T1 framing card is an embedded system from a Sun Unix workstation. Today, in terms of functionality, a Sun workstation is hard to distinguish from a set-top box that contains a PowerPC with 32MB of memory and 16MB of Flash memory, that runs a multitasking operating system to control a set-top box with a GUI, that is field upgradable, that simultaneously runs multiple programs (such as a video controller, a digital VCR, and the Java Virtual Machine), and that makes secure Internet transactions. It's hard to say whether this set-top box is an embedded system. Clearly, the increase in hardware performance and the lower cost of that hardware has blurred the line between general-purpose computers and embedded systems. Technology advances have therefore made it hard to say what is embedded.

What Does *Real-Time* Mean?

If you ask engineers what *real-time* means, you'll get a number of different answers, filled with terms such as *guarantees, hard, soft, deterministic, preemptive, priority inversion, latency, interrupts,* and *scheduling.* Rick Lehrbaum of `linuxdevices.com` posed that question to seven experts.[3] These experts somewhat agreed that a *hard real-time system* guarantees a deterministic response to an event and that a late response is considered a system failure. They also somewhat agreed that *soft real-time systems* attempt to minimize event response time and don't consider late responses a system failure. The experts' opinions diverged when addressing real-time implementation and system performance characterization.

One performance aspect of Linux is clear: Stock Linux allows the kernel and device drivers to disable interrupts.[4] This could seriously affect a system's responsiveness. Fortunately, open-source code availability has allowed solutions to be developed to overcome this limitation. These solutions follow two approaches: Improve the Linux scheduler by making the kernel preemptive and run Linux as a thread within a small RTOS. Naturally, each approach has advantages, disadvantages, supporters, and opponents.

Implications of Open Source

Open-source software—with its accessibility, reliability, and means of support—clearly threaten the commercial software vendors who provide proprietary solutions. Using Linux for embedded development threatens the future market share for companies such as Microsoft and Wind River. It's in their best business interests to spread fear, uncertainty, and doubt within the embedded industry.[5,6] For many years, Microsoft didn't consider Linux a threat in the desktop, server, or embedded arenas. That situation has changed, as Microsoft has stated that Linux is now its number-one target.[7] Microsoft's attention to Linux further enhances Linux's position as a viable option for embedded development. Many developers see open source as a building block to create powerful products. Microsoft sees Linux as a threat to its future dominance of the embedded operating systems.

Use of open-source software has specific implications. In the context of using Linux for embedded design, open-source software has to do with a particular licensing model called the *General Public License (GPL).*[8] (The entire GPL is not covered here, but we will address some GPL requirements that affect you and your embedded Linux design.)

Linus Torvalds originally released the Linux kernel source under GPL. This means that you are free to use and redistribute Linux without royalty or licensing fees, but you must make the Linux source code available to your customers. You can't sell Linux, but you can sell any distribution media or enhancements that you develop. For example, when you purchase a Red Hat Linux product, you aren't buying Linux from Red Hat; you're buying Red Hat's enhancements to Linux. Red Hat's enhancements include a program that simplifies the installation process and some other goodies. GPL states that all "derived work" must also be released under GPL. This means that if you modify some piece of Linux kernel code, your modification is also covered under GPL. If you distribute a product based on your modified kernel code, you must make available not only the original kernel source but also your modifications to it, in source form. At this point, you may be asking, "If I never touch the kernel source code but just use Linux for a product, how does GPL affect me? Do I really have to make my product available in source form?" The answer depends on how your product is linked and what it is linked to.

Let's assume, for example, that your embedded product contains a device driver or kernel module that you developed. You have an option to include that device driver in the kernel binary code at compile time or deploy the driver as a loadable module.

If you build and distribute a kernel that includes your device driver, then your device driver code is automatically included under the GPL and you must make its source code available to your customers. Device drivers or modules that load dynamically after the kernel boot process are not included under the GPL, and you don't have to distribute your source code.

NOTE

Designing products with Linux and other open-source software doesn't mean you have to make your software open source. Use of loadable modules and LGPL libraries protects your intellectual property.

If an embedded product executes solely in the user space (that is, it has no kernel code or device drivers), it is not affected by the Linux kernel source code GPL. An embedded product running an application in the user space can be affected through linking to libraries that are included under the GPL or another licensing model, called *LGPL*. Originally called the Library General Public License, LGPL now stands for Lesser General Public License. This licensing model allows developers to link to code, such as libraries, without having their code automatically included under the GPL. GNU released `glibc` under LGPL.[9] If an embedded application statically or dynamically links to `glibc` for functionality, the application is not included under the GPL or LGPL, and you do not have to release your source code.

Use of open-source software promotes creativity and allows developers to quickly design embedded applications that are reliable and robust. Basing your embedded design on open source software doesn't automatically mean that you have to release your intellectual property in source form. It's quite possible that you can develop device drivers and kernel modules that load after the kernel boot process and your user space application code links to LGPL libraries.

Summary

Linux was created more than a decade ago. Since then, countless programmers have enhanced it, given it more features, and made it efficient, reliable, and robust. Today, thousands of businesses rely on Linux for daily client and server operations. Linux has a proven track record. Commodity pricing of microprocessors and memory devices will make future embedded designs using 32-bit architectures commonplace. Linux is already ported to these architectures and embedded Linux products exist in the marketplace. Embedded system designers adopting Linux enjoy open-source code availability, POSIX compliance, solid reliability, a large application base, and no licensing fees. These benefits, combined with commodity pricing, make Linux an excellent solution for an embedded operating system.

Additional Reading

1. "Developer interest in Embedded Linux skyrockets," `www.linuxdevices.com/news/NS2083407450.html`, 2001.

2. Fernando Ribeiro Corrêa, "Intelligent devices: A new arena for Linux," `www.olinux.com.br/artigos/279/1.html`, 2001.

3. Rick Lehrbaum, "Real-time Linux—What is it, why do you want it, how do you do it?" `www.linuxdevices.com/articles/AT9837719278.html`, 2000.

4. Kevin Dankwardt, "Fundamentals of real-time Linux software design," `www.linuxdevices.com/articles/AT5709748392.html`, 2000.

5. Mike Downing, "Revision 3.0 of open-source GPL stirs concern in embedded space," `http://icd.pennnet.com/Articles/Article_Display.cfm?Section=Articles&Subsection=Display&ARTICLE_ID=92350&KEYWORD=downing`, 2001.

6. Microsoft Corporation, "Prepared text of remarks by Craig Mundie, Microsoft senior vice president: The commercial software model," `www.microsoft.com/presspass/exec/craig/05-03sharedsource.asp`, 2001.

7. Paula Rooney, "Ballmer: Linux is top threat to Windows," `www.techweb.com/wire/story/TWB20010110S0006`, 2001.

8. "GNU General Public License," `http://www.gnu.org/copyleft/gpl.html`, 1991.

9. "GNU Lesser General Public License," `http://www.gnu.org/copyleft/lesser.html`, 1999.

2

System Architecture

A group of devices forming a network to distribute functionality that serve a common purpose defines a system. The initial system design phase creates a framework called the *system architecture*. The system architecture specifies, at a block level, the system components and their interconnection interfaces. Developers work within the system architecture, which provides a structure and an overall understanding of the project or product. System architectures provide the big picture. Furthermore, a set of high-level system requirements help to define the system architecture. Also, a system architecture does not address technical details of its blocks. Details, such as component specification and selection, are determined during a block's design phase.

This chapter introduces Project Trailblazer, a winter resort automation project. This project starts with the formation of the high-level system requirements, which will develop into a system architecture consisting of functional blocks and their interfaces. This chapter does not address any technical details concerning the functional block; it merely defines the Project Trailblazer system architecture. This book follows the Project Trailblazer development and the design and implementation of its functional blocks using embedded Linux.

Introducing Project Trailblazer

Silverjack Resort, located somewhere in the Rocky Mountains, is booming with activity. Guests from around the world travel to Silverjack to enjoy winter activities in a scenic location. Thanks to abundant natural and manufactured snow, the sporting season extends from November through April. Silverjack's 10 lifts offer guests access to a wide variety of terrain, whether they're skiers, snowboarders, or snowshoers. All these factors make Silverjack an attractive winter resort destination. Revenues have continually increased since the initial opening season, making the board of directors and investors happy. The forward-thinking Resort board members know that application of technology can make the mountain safer, the operations more efficient, and the guests' experience more enjoyable. They know that cutting-edge technology can help attract customers to Silverjack.

The board allocated funds for Project Trailblazer, which is a data acquisition and control system serving all of the Silverjack Resort. The board wants this information system to be reliable, robust, and low cost; to use off-the-shelf hardware; and to be designed, deployed, and tested within six months.

The Silverjack Engineering Department, with input from the Operations Department, developed a set of high-level requirements in three areas: safety, operations, and suppliers. These requirements don't contain any specific technical details. Rather, they offer guidelines to what needs to be developed. The board reviewed and approved these high-level requirements. They gave the Engineering Department a green light to start Project Trailblazer.

With great enthusiasm, the Engineering Department started designing Project Trailblazer. It quickly discovered that Project Trailblazer was basically a giant integration project with a short development timeframe. The department needs a flexible and reliable solution that connects serial, parallel, input/output (I/O) port, and universal serial bus (USB) devices to the operations center. After the department attended a conference on embedded systems, the answer was clear: It needed to use embedded Linux.

The Silverjack Resort Layout

Silverjack Resort consists of 10 lifts serving three mountain peaks, a racecourse, and an aerial acrobatic area called the AirPark. Snow-making equipment exists along Lifts 4, 5, and 10. Guests have access to Lifts 4, 7, and 10 from the village. The Operations Control Center (OCC) in the village houses the Operations, Information Technology (IT), and Engineering Departments. A hybrid fiber/copper network provides 10BaseT connectivity to all resort areas and facilities. All networking and computer equipment reside behind a firewall that uses private Class C addresses. The IT Department allocated the private Class C subnet 192.168.2.0 for Project Trailblazer's field equipment.

Figure 2.1 shows Silverjack's physical layout, which includes the OCC, 10 lifts, and Project Trailblazer's data acquisition and control electronics.

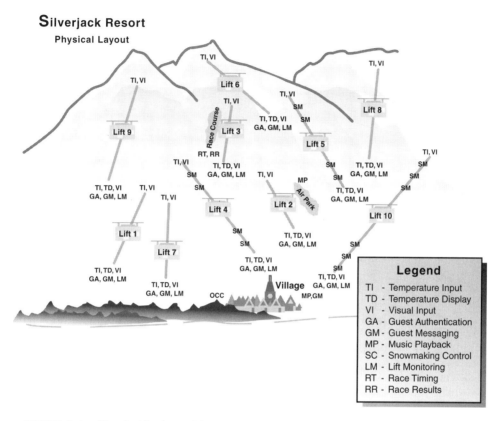

Silverjack Resort

Physical Layout

TI, VI

Lift 6

TI, VI

TI, VI

TI, VI

Lift 8

TI, VI

SM

SM

Race Course

TI, TD, VI
GA, GM, LM

Lift 3

Lift 9

Lift 5

RT, RR

TI, VI

TI, TD, VI
GA, GM, LM

SM

SM

TI, VI

MP

TI, TD, VI
GA, GM, LM

TI, VI

SM

SM

TI, TD, VI
GA, GM, LM

TI, VI

SM

SM

TI, TD, VI
GA, GM, LM

TI, VI

SM

Air Park

Lift 4

Lift 2

Lift 10

SM

Lift 1

SM

SM

TI, TD, VI
GA, GM, LM

Lift 7

TI, TD, VI
GA, GM, LM

SM

TI, TD, VI
GA, GM, LM

SM

TI, TD, VI
GA, GM, LM

Village

TI, TD, VI
GA, GM, LM

OCC

MP, GM

Legend	
TI	- Temperature Input
TD	- Temperature Display
VI	- Visual Input
GA	- Guest Authentication
GM	- Guest Messaging
MP	- Music Playback
SC	- Snowmaking Control
LM	- Lift Monitoring
RT	- Race Timing
RR	- Race Results

FIGURE 2.1   Silverjack's physical layout.

Figure 2.2 shows the Silverjack network. This hybrid copper/fiber network provides connectivity to the bottom and top of all lifts, the racecourse, the AirPark, and the village. This network provides Project Trailblazer field equipment with full 10BaseT connectivity and ample Internet Protocol (IP) address space.

Figure 2.3 details Silverjack's OCC, which is located in the village. The Silverjack router contains three interface cards that make connections to the Internet, Trailblazer mountain equipment, the Silverjack server, and the Engineering Department. The subnet and host addresses are shown in Figure 2.3.

You should examine these figures while reviewing the Project Trailblazer requirements in the following section.

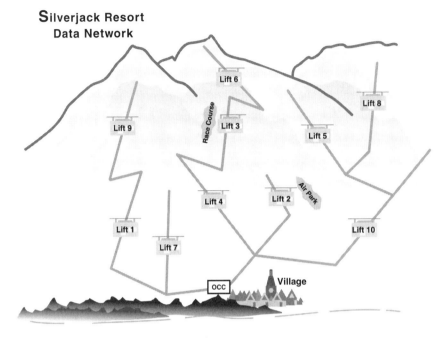

FIGURE 2.2   Silverjack's data network.

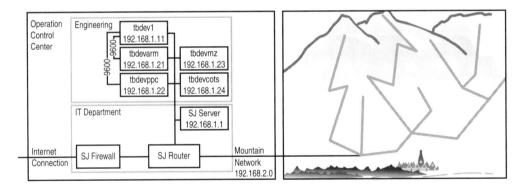

FIGURE 2.3   Silverjack's OCC.

Project Trailblazer Requirements

Project Trailblazer's high-level requirements are divided into three categories: safety, operations, and suppliers. Each requirement discussed here has a short title, a narrative describing the purpose of the requirement, and a reference to the chapter where the requirement is implemented.

Safety Requirements

Safety is a prime concern at Silverjack. Quickly changing weather conditions could pose a serious health threat to guests and employees. The mountain peaks' temperatures and visibilities always differ from those of the village. Project Trailblazer will collect and display various resort temperatures and visibilities.

Safety Requirement 1: Temperature Information

The temperature differential between the mountain base and peaks routinely exceeds 30 degrees. This differential could affect the health of guests, especially those who are inexperienced or unprepared. Project Trailblazer should collect and store the current temperatures for all key mountain locations. Project Trailblazer should display current temperature readings at the bottom of each lift. Project Trailblazer should provide a Web page displaying all the current temperatures.

Temperature information collection and display is addressed in Chapter 10, "Synchronous Serial Communication Interfacing." Web integration is addressed in Chapter 12, "System Integration."

Safety Requirement 2: Visual Information

Mountaintop visibility could affect the health of inexperienced or unprepared guests. Project Trailblazer should collect and store current visibility information in the form of still images for all key mountaintop locations. Project Trailblazer should provide Web pages that display recent still images.

Visual information collection is addressed in Chapter 8, "USB Interfacing." Visual information distribution is addressed in Chapter 12.

Operations Requirements

The Operations Department manages and maintains Silverjack's equipment. Operations seeks high efficiency at a low cost and achieves this through the effective use of manpower and low-cost equipment. Project Trailblazer addresses operations requirements in these areas: guest activities, snow-making control, lift monitoring, race timing, and music playback.

Operations Requirement 1: Guest Authentication

Project Trailblazer should allow lift access to guests who have proper authentication. Project Trailblazer must interface with the ticket office's point-of-sale system. Project Trailblazer should give the lift operator and guest a visual indication of proper authentication.

Guest authentication acquisition and permission are addressed in Chapter 6, "Asynchronous Serial Communication Interfacing."

Operations Requirement 2: Guest Messaging

Project Trailblazer should provide a mechanism to deliver personalized messages—of a personal or an emergency nature—to individual guests. A message should be delivered prior lift access. Project Trailblazer should have the capability to require the guest to acknowledge receipt of a message.

Patron messaging distribution and acknowledgement are addressed in Chapter 12.

Operations Requirement 3: Guest Tracking

Project Trailblazer should provide a mechanism to track guest movement. Operations will use this data in trend analysis for strategic planning. Guests might use this data for curiosity purposes.

Guest tracking distribution is addressed in Chapter 12.

Operations Requirement 4: Snow-Making Control

Project Trailblazer should provide a mechanism to control the snow-making equipment from the OCC. Primarily, this implies remote control of mountaintop-located water valves.

Snow-making control is addressed in Chapter 7, "Parallel Port Interfacing" and Chapter 9, "Memory I/O Interfacing."

Operations Requirement 5: Lift Monitoring

Project Trailblazer should monitor the operation of each lift and should provide instantaneous and historical lift operation data in a graphical form.

Lift monitoring acquisition is addressed in Chapters 7 and 9. Lift monitoring information distribution is addressed in Chapter 12.

Operations Requirement 6: Race Timing

Project Trailblazer should record and store race times, to 1-millisecond accuracy. Project Trailblazer should display intermediate and final race times at the racecourse finish line. Project Trailblazer should distribute race results through a Web interface.

Ski race timing acquisition is addressed in Chapters 11, "Using Interrupts For Timing." Race results distribution is addressed in Chapter 12.

Operations Requirement 7: Music Playback
Project Trailblazer should provide music playback functionality for the AirPark and the village. The OCC should control song selection and deliver songs to the music playback equipment via the network.

Music playback is addressed in Chapter 8 and song control is addressed in Chapter 12.

Supplier Requirements
Project Trailblazer can take two approaches to ensure lower equipment expenditures: Use no single-source supplier of equipment and do not design any complex circuit boards (that is, it should use low-cost commercial off-the-shelf hardware).

Supplier Requirement 1: No Single-Source Suppliers
Project Trailblazer should be designed with hardware and software that's available from multiple sources. Use of single-source suppliers results in loss of competitive pricing and alternative selection.

Supplier selection is addressed in Chapter 3, "Selecting a Platform and Installing Tool Sets."

Supplier Requirement 2: Low-cost Commercial Off-the-Shelf Hardware
Project Trailblazer should be designed with hardware that's available as part of a manufacturer's standard product line. No custom CPU boards should be designed.

Hardware selection is addressed in Chapter 3.

The Project Trailblazer System Architecture
The Project Trailblazer system architecture consists of functional blocks that acquire data (inputs), control equipment (outputs), store data, and distribute data. Figure 2.4 shows these blocks and their interconnection. Project Trailblazer's input, output, and data storage blocks exist on a private network to protect access to them. The data distribution block provides access to the stored data from a public network. Remember that a system architecture only specifies functional blocks and their interconnection. The design phase addresses implementation details, such as component specifications and selection. The Project Trailblazer architecture, although simple, provides the framework for design activities and shows the big picture for the project.

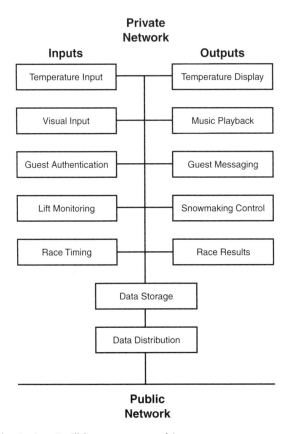

FIGURE 2.4   The Project Trailblazer system architecture.

Summary

This chapter introduced Project Trailblazer and the Silverjack Resort layout. The Engineering Department worked with the Operations Department to develop a set of high-level requirements. These requirements formed the basis for the Project Trailblazer system architecture. At this point, the Engineering Department understood the project from a block-level perspective. The functionality of the blocks was defined and their interconnection was established. The engineers are now ready to enter the design phase of Project Trailblazer and begin to specify components.

3

Selecting a Platform and Installing Tool Sets

Project Trailblazer commenced. The board of directors approved the project requirements and allocated funding. However, the engineers didn't know what hardware to choose, what software to use, what level of support would be needed, or even some of the performance requirements. They did know that embedded Linux would serve as the development platform because of its performance, reliability, open source, low cost, and support. They also know that Project Trailblazer's aggressive timeframe requires fast action. The engineers needed to choose a CPU architecture, off-the-shelf hardware, a kernel version, development tools, and a host development environment as soon as possible. There's a lot of work to do before the snow flies. In this chapter, we'll follow the engineers' progress in choosing and ordering hardware and building an embedded Linux workstation for multiprocessor development.

Sources of Information

The engineers started the hardware selection process by searching the Web for case studies, examples, and Web sites that discuss actual projects using hardware for embedded Linux applications. They wanted to select target hardware with which someone else had had success when using embedded Linux. Their first search returned a wealth of information, much of which was contained in the following Web sites:

- The Embedded Linux Consortium (ELC; www.embedded-linux.org) is a "nonprofit, vendor-neutral trade association whose goal is the advancement and promotion of Linux throughout the embedded, applied and appliance computing markets." The ELC, which has more than 125 member companies, actively promotes embedded Linux and endorses the ELC platform specification.[1] In the future, a developer using an ELC-certified embedded Linux product will be ensured of a common development application programming interface (API). Use of certified products reduces development time, lowers costs, and accelerates the use of Linux in embedded applications. The engineers decided to do business with ELC member companies if possible. These companies are active and support the embedded Linux movement.

- Linux Devices (www.linuxdevices.com), which is created and maintained by Rick Lehrbaum, is an embedded Linux Portal that contains daily news updates on embedded Linux, a complete series of quick reference guides, numerous articles written by key developers, a "Cool Devices" section, numerous links to other Linux sites, and an interactive discussion forum. The engineers find this site to be unbelievable in terms of content coverage, variety, and depth. The quick reference guides "Embedded Linux: An Introduction and Overview,"[2] "Embedded Distributions," "Real-time Linux Software," and "Linux-friendly Embedded Single Board Computers"[3] provide invaluable information for Project Trailblazer.

- *Embedded Linux Journal* (*ELJ*; embedded.linuxjournal.com) focuses on Linux and other open-source software for use in embedded systems. *ELJ* offers complimentary bimonthly subscriptions. The Web site contains the magazine's complete article archive. Industry leaders write excellent, thorough, and pertinent articles on embedded Linux for *ELJ*.

ELC, Linux Devices, and *ELJ* (and their links to other sites) provide comprehensive information on practically all aspects of embedded Linux. This encouraged the engineers, but the amount of information and the huge number of options in architectures, single-board computers, software distributions, and tools was overwhelming. The engineers were now educated, but they still didn't know where to start in the hardware selection process. They summarized their research and then formulated a strategic direction, as discussed in the following section.

The Project Trailblazer Strategic Direction

The engineers' research exposed them to kernel ports, tool chain ports, development/product single-board computers, various ongoing embedded Linuxprojects, software repositories, commercial and open-source embedded Linux distributions, and the advantages of using kernel version 2.4. The engineers were able to summarize all their research and develop a strategic direction consisting of three areas: kernel porting, source code, and kernel version.

Kernel ports must exist for all CPU architectures under consideration. The Trailblazer engineers don't have the expertise or time to port the kernel to a new architecture. Several architectures' ports exist and can be found within the kernel source tree. Checking the kernel version 2.4.0 source, the engineers found port information in the arch directory for the following processors: Alpha, ARM, i386, IA-64, m68k, MIPS, MIPS64, PA-RISC, PowerPC, S390, SuperH, SPARC, and SPARC64.

Wherever possible, the engineers wanted to use and compile open-source codefor the kernel, applications, and tools. Embedded Linux is a new industry. In the coming years, the current landscape will change due to mergers, buyouts, and failures. Adopting a product or distribution introduces a potential risk if support becomes unavailable in the future. By learning how to compile the tools, the kernel, and the applications from their open-source code repositories, the developer and projects become immune to changes in the industry. Compiling open-source code promotes a better understanding of Linux—including its kernel, the boot process, necessary applications, and library interaction.

NOTE

Learning to compile open-source code protects your projects from changes in the embedded Linux industry.

Linux kernel version 2.4.0, released in January 2001, represents a major technological leap forward.[4,5] Developers are pushing Linux into new areas and concentrating their efforts on 2.4 code. No reason exists to consider using an older kernel version. Project Trailblazer requires the following version 2.4 technologies: improved process scheduler, memory technology devices (support for ROM and Flash memory devices), and universal serial bus (USB) support.

Developing this three-area strategic direction allowed the engineers to take a couple steps toward choosing hardware. They required off-the-shelf boards with processors that have kernel 2.4.x or greater ports. They also required open-source code availability for the kernel, applications, and tools. Hardware and software selection remained wide open for the engineers. Should they select the popular x86 or look at other processors, such as ARM, PowerPC, or MIPS? Should they use a commercial open-source product, a noncommercial open-source embedded Linux distribution, or downloaded source code? Should they buy a support package? These were tough questions, each of which had answers that imply different levels of risk, development time, and cost. Time was ticking away.

After much research and thought, as well as conversations with board suppliers and software distribution suppliers, the engineers decided on architecture, boards, and software.

The engineers chose the following hardware architectures and vendors/boards:

- **x86**—Standard desktop 586 CPU with a Flash memory Integrated Drive Electronics (IDE) drive (that is, no moving parts)

- **x86**—Tri-M MZ104 with MachZ embedded PC-on-a-chip 486 microprocessor with Flash memory IDE drive

- **PowerPC**—Embedded Planet RPX-CLLF with Motorola MPC860 microprocessor and 16MB Flash memory

- **ARM**—Brightstar Engineering MediaEngine with Intel SA-1110 microprocessor and 16MB Flash memory

For the software kernel, the engineers chose Version 2.4 or greater. They decided to go with the GNU Tool chain, including the compiler, assembler, libraries, debugger, and utilities.

While waiting for their hardware to arrive, the engineers constructed their development workstation, called tbdev1. They planned to use this workstation to compile the tools, kernel, and applications for the x86, PowerPC, and ARM processors.

The remaining sections of this chapter address tbdev1 configuration for x86 compiling and PowerPC and ARM processor cross-compiling. The engineers want to use tbdev1 to compile the kernel, applications, and libraries for the Trailblazer target platforms. Chapter 4, "Booting Linux," addresses unique configuration and booting of the target platforms. Chapter 5, "Debugging," covers remote debugging of helloworld on each board.

Building tbdev1, the Embedded Linux Development Workstation

The Silverjack engineers decided to consolidate all the Project Trailblazer development tools in a single place. They devoted a single computer to act as a development workstation, hosting all the compilers, cross-compilers, debuggers, libraries, and kernel and application source code. This consolidation simplified the development activities because the engineers didn't have to spend time configuring each engineer's workstation for cross-development. This section outlines the steps for building tbdev1, the Project Trailblazer development workstation:

1. Getting started

2. Installing the Linux operating system

3. Installing the native GNU tool chain and other applications

4. Building the GNU tool chain for cross-compiling

After these four steps have been completed, `tbdev1` will be capable of compiling C code for the x86 using `gcc`. Cross-compilers for PowerPC (`powerpc-linux-gcc`), and ARM (`arm-linux-gcc`) processor will also be created. All the examples in subsequent chapters utilize the `tbdev1` workstation. The remaining sections in this chapter help you to create your own `tbdev1` workstation that's identical to Project Trailblazer's `tbdev1`.

> **TIP**
>
> Creating a cross-development environment generates a set of libraries for another CPU architecture, such as PowerPC or ARM. During the installation process, you have an opportunity to overwrite the existing x86 libraries with a PowerPC or ARM version. Devoting a computer to act as the cross-development workstation eliminates the possibility of destroying your personal desktop workstation x86 libraries.

Getting Started

In this section we'll build the `tbdev1` development workstation, using the Debian distribution potato, which is Debian version 2.2r5 (kernel 2.2.19). You can download potato and install it on `tbdev1` using a LAN Internet connection and three floppy disks. The resultant workstation will contain only the software required to build the cross-development environment. Other programs, such as `sendmail`, Web servers, and X Windows, will not be installed, thus lowering hardware requirements for `tbdev1`. Here's what you need to get started:

- An x86 computer with 32MB RAM and 1.5GB or larger drive, with a master drive on the primary IDE controller and an Ethernet card
- Three 1.44 floppy disks
- A LAN Internet connection
- A keyboard and a monitor

To start, you need to download three floppy image files from the Debian Web site (`www.debian.org`). At this point, you might not have a Linux machine running. Therefore, Microsoft Windows instructions are included here, but only to the point where you get Linux up and running. After that, only Linux instructions are given because Project Trailblazer is, after all, a Linux project.

You need to download three images files, using your browser, FTP, `wget`, or `lynx`. You should download the files into a temporary directory called `/tmp` or `c:\tmp`, which you might need to create. Here's the base URL for the image files:

```
http://ftp.us.debian.org/debian/dists/stable/
➥main/disks-i386/current/images-1.44/idepci/
```

Download these three image files: `rescue.bin`, `root.bin`, and `driver-1.bin`.

If you are a Windows user, you need to also download a program called `rawrite2.exe` from `ftp://ftp.debian.org/debian/tools`.

Now you need to create the installation disks. To do so, Unix users should use the following commands:

```
holla@taylor[501]: cd /tmp
holla@taylor[502]: dd if=rescue.bin of=/dev/fd0 bs=1024 conv=sync ; sync
holla@taylor[503]: dd if=root.bin of=/dev/fd0 bs=1024 conv=sync ; sync
holla@taylor[504]: dd if=driver-1.bin of=/dev/fd0 bs=1024 conv=sync ; sync
```

Windows users should open a DOS window by choosing Run from the Start menu, entering **command** and pressing Enter. Then in the DOS window enter following:

```
C:\> cd c:\tmp
C:\tmp> rawrite2 -f rescue.bin -d a:
C:\tmp> rawrite2 -f root.bin -d a:
C:\tmp> rawrite2 -f driver-1.bin -d a:
```

Label the disks "rescue," "root," and "drivers." You are now ready to start the potato installation on `tbdev1`.

Installing the Linux Operating System

The instructions in the following sections step through the potato network installation process. The steps include a portion of what you'll see on your installation screen and the action you should take. The intention here isn't to teach you about the Debian installation; please read Debian's detailed install guides at `www.debian.org/releases/stable/#new-inst` for more information. In this section you'll quickly build a Linux workstation to compile the cross-compiler and libraries. The numbered lines in the steps below match what you should see on your workstation monitor during the Debian installation process.

Step 1: Boot `tbdev1`

In this step, you boot your workstation, using the floppy disks that you just created. The rescue disk contains the Linux kernel. The root disk contains a compressed filesystem that this kernel uses during the installation process. Follow these steps:

1. Insert the floppy disk marked rescue and turn on your workstation.

2. The Welcome screen should appear, with a `boot:` prompt. Press Enter.

3. The Linux kernel on the rescue disk loads into memory and begins executing. You should see about 50 lines showing the status of the boot process. The boot

process stops when the kernel needs access to the root filesystem. You see this: VFS: Insert root floppy to be loaded into RAM disk and press ENTER:. Remove the rescue disk and insert the root floppy and press Enter.

4. The Release Notes Screen appears. Read through the notes if you want, and then press Enter.

Step 2: Partition the Hard Disk

In this step, you remove the existing partitions on the master drive on your primary IDE controller. Then you create a swap and root partition on that drive. This operation destroys all the information on that disk. Make sure that you have the correct disk installed, and then follow these steps:

> **TIP**
>
> If you have multiple drives in your computer, you might want to disconnect all of them except the one you're installing Linux on. This ensures that you don't accidentally install Linux on the wrong drive.

1. The Debian installation screen has an option Partition a Hard Disk. Use the arrow keys to highlight this option and then press Enter.

2. The Select Hard Drive screen allows you to select a hard disk drive to partition. Select /dev/hda and press Enter.

3. The LILO Limitations screen appears. Read about the limitations and then press Enter.

4. At this point you're about to repartition the master drive on your primary controller. Make sure you have the correct disk installed. The cfdisk screen presents you with a list of current partitions and a menu along the bottom. Use the up and down arrows to select from the partition list. Use the right and left arrows to select a menu item. Select the first partition, and then select Delete and press Enter. Continue until you have deleted all the drive partitions.

5. Make a new 64MB swap partition by first selecting the New menu and pressing Enter. Then select Primary and press Enter, set the size to 64 and press Enter, and select Beginning and press Enter.

6. The partition list should now have an hda1 entry. With it selected, select the Type menu and set the type to 82 (Linux Swap). At this point, the partition list should show a 64MB swap partition called hda1.

7. Select Free Space from the partition list.

8. Make new partition by first selecting the New menu and then selecting Primary. Set the size to use the remainder of the drive space, and then select Beginning.

9. The partition list should now have an hda2 entry. With it selected, select the Type menu and set the type to 83 (Linux). At this point, the partition list should show a 64MB swap partition called hda1 and another partition with filesystem, FS type, Linux.

10. Select hda2 from the partition list, and then make hda2 bootable by selecting the Bootable menu.

11. Finalize this partitioning by selecting Write and confirm the write operation with by typing **yes**.

12. Exit from the cfdisk screen by selecting Quit.

Step 3: Configure the Keyboard and Activate the Partitions

In step 3 you configure and activate the hda1 and hda2 partitions you just created. Remember that hda1 is the 64MB swap partition. Follow these steps:

1. Select the Configure Keyboard menu and press Enter. Select the keyboard that best fits your situation and press Enter.

2. Activate the swap partition by selecting the Initialize and Activate a Swap Partition menu, and then select /dev/hda1. When you're asked to skip the scan for bad blocks, select No. When you're asked whether you are sure, confirm by selecting Yes.

3. Activate the Linux partition by selecting the Initialize a Linux Partition menu, and then select /dev/hda2. When asked about Pre-2.2 Linux kernel compatibility, select No. When asked to skip the scan for bad blocks, select No. When asked whether you are sure, confirm by selecting Yes.

4. Finalize the activation by mounting /dev/hda2 as the root file system. When asked "Mount As Root Filesystem?" select Yes.

Step 4: Install the Operating System Kernel and Modules

Now that the hard disk is partitioned, initialized, and mounted, it's time to copy the Linux kernel and modules. To do so, follow these steps:

1. Start copying by selecting the Install Operating System Kernel and Modules menu.

2. At the Select Installation Medium screen, select /dev/fd0 and press Enter.

3. Insert the rescue disk and then select Continue. The installation program copies the kernel file contained on the rescue disk to the hard disk.

4. When asked to insert Driver Disk 1, remove the rescue disk and insert the drivers disk and then select Continue. The drivers are then copied to the hard disk.

5. Select Configure Device Driver Modules from the main menu.

6. When asked about skipping the additional drivers floppy, select Yes.

7. Configure the workstation's Ethernet card. The driver's floppy disk contains Ethernet drivers for a wide variety of Ethernet cards. Start by selecting Net: Drivers for Network Interface Cards and Network Protocols.

TIP

Drivers for these Ethernet cards—3COM, Western Digital/SMC, Racal-Interlan, AMD PCnet32, DECchip Tulip, EtherExpressPro/100, PCI NE2000, and VIA Rhine—are already built in to the potato kernel.[6] If you have one of these cards, you can skip to the section "Step 5: Configure the Network."

8. Select your Ethernet card from the list. For example, select ne for a NE2000 compatible. Select OK by pressing Enter.

9. When asked to install this module in the kernel, confirm by selecting Yes.

10. Some Ethernet cards require additional configuration. When asked to enter command-line arguments, enter your Ethernet card's I/O address and IRQ if necessary. For this example, you might enter **io=0x300 irq=5**.

11. The installation program loads the Ethernet driver, and the driver attempts to find the Ethernet card. If the driver finds the card, a screen announces successful loading of the driver. If the card is not found, you have the option to restart and correct the Ethernet card configurations. Your ethernet card needs to be functioning correctly to complete the installation.

12. Exit the module configuration by selecting Exit from the Select Net Modules menu, and then select Exit from the Category menu.

Step 5: Configure the Network

Now that the kernel is installed and the Ethernet driver has found the Ethernet card, it is time to configure the network. Later, you'll need the network to install the various applications that you download from the Debian Web site. Follow these steps to configure the network:

1. Select Configure Network from the main menu.

2. When asked to choose the host name, enter **tbdev1** and press Enter.

3. When asked about automatic network configuration, select No. No DHCP or BOOTP server exists. You are going use static IP addressing.

4. When asked to choose the IP address, type **192.168.1.11** and press Enter.

5. When asked to choose the network mask, type **255.255.255.0** and press Enter.

6. When asked what your IP gateway address is, type **192.168.1.254** or your network gateway address and press Enter.

7. When asked to choose the domain name, leave the name blank and press Enter.

8. When asked to choose the DNS name addresses, enter **192.168.1.1** or your DNS server address and press Enter.

9. Next, you need to install a collection of programs called the *base system*. Select Install Base System and press Enter.

10. You will be downloading the base system from the Debian Web site. Select Network: Retrieve from Network and press Enter.

11. The installation program announces that it is about to fetch the base2_2.tgz installation over the network using HTTP. Select Continue.

12. At the Select installation server screen, use the Tab key to select OK, and then press Enter.

13. The installation program downloads the 16MB Base2_2.tgz file from the Debian Web site. This is a perfect time to take a break.

Step 6: Configure the Base System

The installation program finishes the download of Base2_2.tgz, decompresses it, and installs various applications and files on your hard disk. There's not much involved in configuring the base system other than setting the time zone. Follow these steps:

1. Select Configure Base System from the main menu and press Enter.

2. Scan through the list and select your time zone. Then use the Tab key to select OK.

3. When asked to set your clock to GMT, select Yes.

Step 7: Make Linux Bootable Directly from the Hard Disk

With the kernel, device drivers, and base system installed, one more step remains: making Linux bootable directly from the hard disk. In this step, you write the Linux Loader (LILO) bootloader to the hard disk's master boot record (MBR). When the computer boots, the bootloader code executes first and loads the Linux kernel from the hard disk to memory. Then the kernel executes. Follow these steps:

1. At the main menu, select Make Linux Bootable Directly From Hard Disk and press Enter.

2. Choose `/dev/hda` from the Where Should the LILO Bootloader Be Installed? menu and press Enter.

3. Select Reboot the System at the main menu and confirm by selecting Yes. Eject the disk. The computer reboots from the hard disk and the installation process continues.

Step 8: Set Passwords, Accounts, and PPP

After rebooting, the installation process continues: You configure passwords, accounts, and point-to-point protocol options. To do so, follow these steps:

1. When asked "Shall I enable MD5 Passwords?", select No.

2. When asked "Shall I install shadow passwords?", select No.

3. When prompted "Enter a password for root", type **p** or something you'll remember and press Enter.

4. When prompted to re-enter password to verify, retype the password you just entered and press Enter.

5. When asked, "Shall I create a normal user account?", select No. You can add user accounts later, with the `adduser` command.

6. When asked, "Shall I remove pcmcia packages?", select Yes.

7. When asked, "Do you want to use a PPP connection to install the system?", select No.

Step 9: Configure `apt`

All major Linux distributions support a software package management system that ensures clean and easy software installations through dependency and conflict checking. The Debian package system, `apt`, works with packages called *debs*, and its command-line interface program is called `apt-get`. System administrators use apt-get to install and remove software packages. The apt package management system requires updated package lists. In this step, you use the installation program to configure apt and download the current package lists from the Debian Web site:

1. At the Apt Configuration menu, select http and press Enter.

2. When asked, "Use non-US software?", select Yes.

3. When asked, "Use non-free software?", select Yes.

4. When asked, "Use contrib software?", select Yes.

5. When asked to select a country, select your country and press Enter.

6. When asked to choose the Debian mirror to use, select http.us.debian.org or the mirror closest to you.

7. When asked to enter http proxy information, leave a blank or fill in your HTTP proxy information.

8. At this point, the install program downloads apt package information from the Debian site.

9. When asked to add another apt source, select No.

10. When asked, "How do you want to choose additional software to install?", select Advanced and then select OK.

11. A program called dselect starts. Don't install any software with dselect at this time. At the Start dselect screen, select OK.

12. Exit from dselect by selecting Quit.

Step 10: Have Fun!

The potato installation is now complete. Follow these steps:

1. The installation program instructs you to have fun. So select OK and start having some fun!

2. You now get a tbdev1 login prompt. Log in as root, with the password you set earlier. This logs you in to tbdev1 as root, running the bash shell.

3. Check the disk filesystem space usage with the df command. This shows the hard disk space requirement for a clean potato installation. Here's a sample of df output:

```
Filesystem          1k-blocks      Used Available Use% Mounted on
/dev/hda2            4854520      67496  4540428   1% /
```

You have now completed the potato installation. Next, you need to use apt-get to install a few packages that are required to build the GNU tool chain.

Installing the Native GNU Tool Chain and Other Applications

The potato base system that was installed in the section "Step 6: Configure the Base System" does not contain many development tools. You need to install a few packages to build the GNU tool chain. At the prompt, type these apt-get commands to install additional development tools:

```
root@tbdev1[501]: apt-get -y install gcc
root@tbdev1[502]: apt-get -y install make
root@tbdev1[503]: apt-get -y install file
root@tbdev1[504]: apt-get -y install flex
root@tbdev1[505]: apt-get -y install bison
root@tbdev1[506]: apt-get -y install patch
root@tbdev1[507]: apt-get -y install libc6-dev
root@tbdev1[508]: apt-get -y install perl
root@tbdev1[509]: apt-get -y install bzip2
root@tbdev1[510]: apt-get -y install wget
root@tbdev1[511]: apt-get -y install libncurses4-dev
root@tbdev1[512]: apt-get -y install telnetd
```

You're now ready to build the GNU tool chain for cross-compiling. The gcc compiler you just downloaded is the native x86 compiler that generates x86 executables. You are going to use this x86 compiler to compile two new versions of gcc—powerpc-linux-gcc and arm-linux-gcc—that create PowerPC or ARM executables. The next section discusses cross-compiling and the creation of powerpc-linux-gcc and arm-linux-gcc, the cross-compilers and their appropriate glibc library files, and gdb.

Building the GNU Tool Chain for Cross-Compiling

A cross-compiler runs on a processor but generates executable code for a different processor. For example, an ARM cross-compiler running on an x86 processor generates code for an ARM processor, and a PowerPC cross-compiler generates code for a PowerPC.

Why does Project Trailblazer require a cross-compiler? Typically embedded systems don't have the RAM or storage resources to compile their own executables. A host processor, in this case tbdev1, can cross-compile code to create an executable. This executable is then transferred and executed on the target board. The GNU tool chain is capable of cross-compiling, but not as a command-line option. The entire tool chain requires compiling for operation as a cross-compiler. This is not a simple make, make install, apt-get, or rpm process. The cross-compiler build process is not completely documented or kept current.

The Trailblazer engineers are using the Embedded Planet RPX-CLLF (PowerPC MPC860) and the Brightstar MediaEngine (ARM SA-1110). They found two HOWTOs that explain building the GNU tool chain for the ARM and PowerPC processors:

- The GNU Toolchain for ARM targets HOWTO: `www.armlinux.org/docs/ toolchain`

- The Linux for PowerPC Embedded Systems HOWTO: `http://penguinppc.org/ usr/embedded/howto/PowerPC-Embedded-HOWTO.html`

Reading through these HOWTOs, the engineers discovered that building a cross-compiled version of the GNU tool chain is quite an operation. They first manually built the tool chain. Later, they switched kernel versions and found that they had to rebuild the tool chain because `gcc` and `glibc` depend on kernel header files. Manually building the tool chain is tedious and prone to mistakes, so the engineers automated the process by developing a `bash` script called `buildtoolchain`.

`buildtoolchain` can build either PowerPC and ARM cross-compiled versions of `gcc`, `glibc`, `gdb`, GNU utilities, and a `helloworld` test program. The `buildtoolchain` script simplifies compiling of `powerpc-linux-gcc` and `arm-linux-gcc`, the appropriate `glibc` library files, and `gdb`. `buildtoolchain` isn't a monolithic script with 12 steps; rather, it is a collection of 14 scripts. First, there's `buildtoolchain` itself, which merely calls 13 other scripts. Because `buildtoolchain` is broken into steps, the build process can be restarted in case of failure. `tbdev1` (which is a 400MHz Celeron) requires more than an hour to completely run `buildtoolchain`.

`buildtoolchain` starts by executing the script called `buildtoolchain-environment`, which sets a series of environment variables. `buildtoolchain` continues by executing additional scripts that perform these steps:

1. Checks for the required source files:

    `buildtoolchain-step01-check`

2. Cleans up old builds:

    `buildtoolchain-step02-clean`

3. Makes build directories:

    `buildtoolchain-step03-makebuilddirectories`

4. Builds `binutils`:

    `buildtoolchain-step04-binutils`

5. Sets up the kernel source and headers:

   ```
   buildtoolchain-step05-kernelsourceheaders
   ```

6. Builds a cross-compiled version of gcc:

   ```
   buildtoolchain-step06-gcc
   ```

7. Builds a cross-compiled version of `glibc`:

   ```
   buildtoolchain-step07-glibc
   ```

8. Builds a cross-compiled version of gdb:

   ```
   buildtoolchain-step08-gdb
   ```

9. Checks the version of gcc:

   ```
   buildtoolchain-step09-gccversion
   ```

10. Checks the tool chain build by cross-compiling `helloworld`:

    ```
    buildtoolchain-step10-helloworld
    ```

11. Rebuilds gcc:

    ```
    buildtoolchain-step11-rebuildgcc
    ```

12. Rebuilds `glibc`:

    ```
    buildtoolchain-step12-rebuildglibc
    ```

The following text explains each script in greater detail.

Let's use `buildtoolchain` to build the GNU tool chain for the PowerPC.
`buildtoolchain` version 0.8 compiles the following versions of `binutils`, `gcc`, `glibc`,
and `gdb` for PowerPC:

```
BINUTILSVERSION=binutils-2.11.2
GCCVERSION=gcc-2.95.3
GLIBVERSION=glibc-2.2.3
GLIBCTHREADSVERSION=glibc-linuxthreads-2.2.3
KERNELVERSION=linux-2.4.7
GDBVERSION=gdb-5.0
```

Start by logging on to tbdev1 as root. Make a directory called /root/cross and change directory into it. Use wget to fetch buildtoolchain and tar to extract all the bash scripts. Finally, run buildtoolchain with powerpc as the command-line parameter. Here are the bash commands to get started:

```
root@tbdev1[526]: mkdir /root/cross
root@tbdev1[527]: cd /root/cross
root@tbdev1[528]: wget http://www.embeddedlinuxinterfacing.com/
➥chapters/03/buildtoolchain/buildtoolchain.tar.gz
root@tbdev1[529]: tar zxvf buildtoolchain.tar.gz
root@tbdev1[530]: ./buildtoolchain powerpc
```

The command buildtoolchain powerpc executes the buildtoolchain-environment script and the 12 other scripts listed in the steps above. The buildtoolchain script, shown in Listing 3.1, completely creates the cross-development environment for the PowerPC. Each script prints out information concerning the build process. The remainder of this chapter describes the buildtoolchain scripts and provides source code listings and relevant script output.

> **TIP**
>
> The buildtoolchain script generates more than 8MB of output. You might want to execute buildtoolchain in the background and redirect its output to a file. Then use tail -f to view your output file as it is being created.

LISTING 3.1   The buildtoolchain Script

```
#!/bin/bash
# buildtoolchain v0.8 10/30/01
# www.embeddedlinuxinterfacing.com
#
# The original location of this script is
# http://www.embeddedlinuxinterfacing.com/chapters/03/buildtoolchain
#
# Copyright (C) 2001 by Craig Hollabaugh
#
# This program is free software; you can redistribute it and/or modify it
# under the terms of the GNU Library General Public License as published by
# the Free Software Foundation; either version 2 of the License, or (at your
# option) any later version.
#
# This program is distributed in the hope that it will be useful, but WITHOUT
# ANY WARRANTY; without even the implied warranty of MERCHANTABILITY or
```

LISTING 3.1   Continued

```
# FITNESS FOR A PARTICULAR PURPOSE. See the GNU Library General Public
# License for more details.
#
# You should have received a copy of the GNU Library General Public License
# along with this program; if not, write to the Free Software Foundation,
# 59 Temple Place, Suite 330, Boston, MA 02111-1307 USA
#
#
# Files needed and source locations
# binutils             ftp://ftp.gnu.org/gnu/binutils/
# kernel               ftp://ftp.kernel.org/pub/linux/kernel
# gcc                  ftp://ftp.gnu.org/pub/gnu/gcc/
# glibc                ftp://ftp.gnu.org/pub/gnu/glibc/
# glibc-linuxthreads ftp://ftp.gnu.org/pub/gnu/glibc/
# gdb                  ftp://ftp.gnu.org/pub/gnu/gdb/
#
# ARM specific patches
#  Toolchain ftp://ftp.armlinux.org/pub/toolchain
#  Kernel    ftp://ftp.arm.linux.org.uk/pub/armlinux/source/kernel-patches/
#  Kernel    ftp://ftp.netwinder.org/users/n/nico/
#
#
# references
# The GNU Toolchain for ARM targets HOWTO
#    http://www.armlinux.org/docs/toolchain/
# The Linux for PowerPC Embedded Systems HOWTO
#    http://penguinppc.org/usr/embedded/howto/PowerPC-Embedded-HOWTO.html
#
# Change Log
#
# v0.5
#    a. added $SRCFILELOC to filenames in Step 1
#    b. made helloworld.c do a little counting
#    c. now saving linux/.config in tmp then restoring in Step 5
#
# v0.6
#    a. changed clean to remove
#    b. fixed *PATCH being undefined and file check for it
#
# v0.7
#    a. split steps into files, so you can tinker in middle and not
```

LISTING 3.1   Continued

```
#       have to start over from the beginning
#       b. added targetboard in step5, this keeps you from running make
#          menuconfig
#       c. added KERNELPATCH3 for arm mediaengine needs 3 patches
#       d. kernel patches are now done in the linux directory with patch -p1
#
# v0.8
#       a. added wgets to step01 to get sources except for patches
#          (arch dependent)
#       b. changed command line parameter ppc to powerpc


set -e


. ./buildtoolchain-environment $1


buildtoolchain-step01-check
buildtoolchain-step02-clean
buildtoolchain-step03-makebuilddirectories
buildtoolchain-step04-binutils
buildtoolchain-step05-kernelsourceheaders
buildtoolchain-step06-gcc
buildtoolchain-step07-glibc
buildtoolchain-step08-gdb
buildtoolchain-step09-gccversion
buildtoolchain-step10-helloworld
buildtoolchain-step11-rebuildgcc
buildtoolchain-step12-rebuildglibc
```

The buildtoolchain script is simple; it merely calls the buildtoolchain-environment script and the scripts for the 12-step build process.

The buildtoolchain-environment script, shown in Listing 3.2, either sets environment variables for PowerPC/ARM builds or removes a previous installation. If you want to use different versions of the GNU tools or the kernel, you can modify the buildtoolchain-environment script and then run buildtoolchain.

LISTING 3.2   The buildtoolchain-environment Script

```
#!/bin/bash
# buildtoolchain-environment 10/30/01
# www.embeddedlinuxinterfacing.com
#
```

LISTING 3.2   Continued

```
# The original location of this script is
# http://www.embeddedlinuxinterfacing.com/chapters/03/buildtoolchain
#
# Copyright (C) 2001 by Craig Hollabaugh
# See buildtoolchain script for General Public License statement


export SRCFILELOC=/root/cross
export BUILDLOC=/root/cross/builds
export PREFIX=/usr

case "$1" in
"powerpc" )
export ARCH=ppc
export TARGET=powerpc-linux
export TARGETBOARD=rpxcllf
#export TARGETBOARD=bseip
export BINUTILSVERSION=binutils-2.11.2
export GCCVERSION=gcc-2.95.3
export GCCPATCH=
export GLIBVERSION=glibc-2.2.3
export GLIBCTHREADSVERSION=glibc-linuxthreads-2.2.3
export KERNELVERSION=linux-2.4.7
export KERNELPATCH1=
export KERNELPATCH2=
export KERNELPATCH3=
export GDBVERSION=gdb-5.0
;;
"arm" )
export ARCH=arm
export TARGET=arm-linux
export TARGETBOARD=mediaengine
export BINUTILSVERSION=binutils-2.11.2
export GCCVERSION=gcc-2.95.3
export GCCPATCH=gcc-2.95.3-diff-010218.bz2
export GLIBVERSION=glibc-2.2.3
export GLIBCTHREADSVERSION=glibc-linuxthreads-2.2.3
export KERNELVERSION=linux-2.4.2
export KERNELPATCH1=patch-2.4.2-rmk1.gz
export KERNELPATCH2=diff-2.4.2-rmk1-np2.gz
```

LISTING 3.2   Continued

```
export KERNELPATCH3=patch-2.4.2-rmk1-np2-bse.gz
export GDBVERSION=gdb-5.0
;;
"remove-arm" )
TARGET=arm-linux
echo Removing $TARGET files
rm -rf $BUILDLOC/$TARGET*
rm -rf $PREFIX/bin/$TARGET*
rm -rf $PREFIX/$TARGET
rm -rf $PREFIX/src/$TARGET
rm -rf $PREFIX/lib/gcc-lib/$TARGET
rm -rf /usr/man/man1/$TARGET
exit 0
;;
"remove-powerpc" )
TARGET=powerpc-linux
echo Removing $TARGET files
rm -rf $BUILDLOC/$TARGET*
rm -rf $PREFIX/bin/$TARGET*
rm -rf $PREFIX/$TARGET
rm -rf $PREFIX/src/$TARGET
rm -rf $PREFIX/lib/gcc-lib/$TARGET
rm -rf /usr/man/man1/$TARGET*
exit 0
;;
* )
    echo "Usage $0 arm|powerpc|remove-arm|remove-powerpc"
    exit 1
;;
esac

echo buildtoolchain environment setup complete
echo

export BUILDTOOLCHAINENV=1
```

The following sections describe the steps in the process of building `buildtoolchain`.

Step 1: Check for Required Source Files

Before you start building the GNU tool chain, you need the source code for
binutils, gcc, glibc, glibc-linuxthreads, the kernel source, gdb, and any patches.
You can download the source from the following locations or have buildtoolchain-
step01-check do it for you:

Needed File	Locations
binutils	ftp://ftp.gnu.org/gnu/binutils
kernel	ftp://ftp.kernel.org/pub/linux/kernel
gcc	ftp://ftp.gnu.org/pub/gnu/gcc
glibc	ftp://ftp.gnu.org/pub/gnu/glibc
glibc-linuxthreads	ftp://ftp.gnu.org/pub/gnu/glibc
gdb	ftp://ftp.gnu.org/pub/gnu/gdb

You also need the ARM-specific patches if you are compiling for the ARM processor:

Patch	Location
Toolchain	ftp://ftp.armlinux.org/pub/toolchain
Kernel	ftp://ftp.arm.linux.org.uk/pub/armlinux/source/ kernel-patches
Kernel	ftp://ftp.netwinder.org/users/n/nico

The buildtoolchain-step01-check script, shown in Listing 3.3, determines whether
the required files exist. If any are missing, this script downloads them, by using wget.

LISTING 3.3   The buildtoolchain-step01-check Script

```
#!/bin/bash
# buildtoolchain-step01-check v0.2 10/30/01
# www.embeddedlinuxinterfacing.com
#
# The original location of this script is
# http://www.embeddedlinuxinterfacing.com/chapters/03/buildtoolchain
#
# Copyright (C) 2001 by Craig Hollabaugh
# See buildtoolchain script for General Public License statement


if [ ! $BUILDTOOLCHAINENV ]
then
. ./buildtoolchain-environment $1
fi
```

LISTING 3.3 Continued

```
#
# Step 1 - Check for required src files
#
echo Step 1 - Check for required src files
if [ ! -f $SRCFILELOC/$BINUTILSVERSION.tar.gz ]
then
    echo Missing $BINUTILSVERSION.tar.gz
    wget ftp://ftp.gnu.org/gnu/binutils/$BINUTILSVERSION.tar.gz
fi


if [ ! -f $SRCFILELOC/$GCCVERSION.tar.gz ]
then
    echo Missing $GCCVERSION.tar.gz
    wget ftp://ftp.gnu.org/pub/gnu/gcc/$GCCVERSION.tar.gz
fi


if [ $GCCPATCH ]
then
    if [ ! -f $SRCFILELOC/$GCCPATCH ]
    then
        echo Missing $GCCPATCH
        exit 1
    fi
fi


if [ ! -f $SRCFILELOC/$GLIBVERSION.tar.gz ]
then
    echo Missing $GLIBVERSION.tar.gz
    wget ftp://ftp.gnu.org/pub/gnu/glibc/$GLIBVERSION.tar.gz
fi


if [ ! -f $SRCFILELOC/$GLIBCTHREADSVERSION.tar.gz ]
then
    echo Missing $GLIBCTHREADSVERSION.tar.gz
    wget ftp://ftp.gnu.org/pub/gnu/glibc/$GLIBCTHREADSVERSION.tar.gz
fi


if [ ! -f $SRCFILELOC/$KERNELVERSION.tar.gz ]
then
```

LISTING 3.3   Continued

```
    echo Missing $KERNELVERSION.tar.gz
    wget ftp://ftp.kernel.org/pub/linux/kernel/v2.4/$KERNELVERSION.tar.gz
fi


if [ $KERNELPATCH1 ]
then
    if [ ! -f $SRCFILELOC/$KERNELPATCH1 ]
    then
        echo Missing $KERNELPATCH1
        exit 1
    fi
fi


if [ $KERNELPATCH2 ]
then
    if [ ! -f $SRCFILELOC/$KERNELPATCH2 ]
    then
        echo Missing $KERNELPATCH2
        exit 1
    fi
fi


if [ $KERNELPATCH3 ]
then
    if [ ! -f $SRCFILELOC/$KERNELPATCH3 ]
    then
        echo Missing $KERNELPATCH3
        exit 1
    fi
fi


if [ ! -f $SRCFILELOC/$GDBVERSION.tar.gz ]
then
    echo Missing $GDBVERSION.tar.gz
    wget ftp://ftp.gnu.org/pub/gnu/gdb/$GDBVERSION.tar.gz
fi


echo Step 1 - Complete
echo
```

Step 2: Clean Up Old Builds

The `buildtoolchain-step02-clean` script removes old versions of the build directories, previously created versions of the tool chain binaries, any cross-compiled libraries, temporary kernel source files, and any *man pages* (that is, online versions of manuals) for the cross-compiled tools. Listing 3.4 shows the `buildtoolchain-step02-clean` script. When `buildtoolchain-step02-clean` script completes, the workstation is clean and ready to compile the tool chain.

LISTING 3.4   The `buildtoolchain-step02-clean` Script

```
#!/bin/bash
# buildtoolchain-step02-clean v0.1 8/16/01
# www.embeddedlinuxinterfacing.com
#
# The original location of this script is
# http://www.embeddedlinuxinterfacing.com/chapters/03/buildtoolchain
#
# Copyright (C) 2001 by Craig Hollabaugh
# See buildtoolchain script for General Public License statement


if [ ! $BUILDTOOLCHAINENV ]
then
. ./buildtoolchain-environment $1
fi

# Step 2 - Clean Up
#
#clean up from before we start, this only cleans for TARGET
echo Step 2 - Clean Up
echo Removing previous $TARGET files
rm -rf $BUILDLOC/$TARGET*
rm -rf $PREFIX/bin/$TARGET*
rm -rf $PREFIX/$TARGET
rm -rf $PREFIX/lib/gcc-lib/$TARGET
rm -rf /usr/man/man1/$TARGET*

echo Step 2 - Complete
echo
```

Step 3: Make Build Directories

The `buildtoolchain-step03-makebuilddirectories` script creates build directories for binutils, gcc, glibc, and gdb (see Listing 3.5). These directories will contain the intermediary object files created during the compilation process. When buildtoolchain completes execution, you can remove these build directories.

LISTING 3.5   The `buildtoolchain-step03-makebuilddirectories` Script

```
#!/bin/bash
# buildtoolchain-step03-makebuilddirectories v0.1 8/16/01
# www.embeddedlinuxinterfacing.com
#
# The original location of this script is
# http://www.embeddedlinuxinterfacing.com/chapters/03/buildtoolchain
#
# Copyright (C) 2001 by Craig Hollabaugh
# See buildtoolchain script for General Public License statement

if [ ! $BUILDTOOLCHAINENV ]
then
. ./buildtoolchain-environment $1
fi


#
# Step 3 - Make Build Directories
#
echo Step 3 - Make Build Directories
echo Making build directories in $BUILDLOC

if [ ! -e $BUILDLOC ]
then
    mkdir $BUILDLOC
fi

mkdir $BUILDLOC/$TARGET-binutils
mkdir $BUILDLOC/$TARGET-gcc
mkdir $BUILDLOC/$TARGET-glibc
mkdir $BUILDLOC/$TARGET-gdb

echo Step 3 - Complete
echo
```

Step 4: Build binutils

The buildtoolchain-step04-binutils script builds the cross-compiled versions of the binary utilities (see Listing 3.6). These programs are used in the cross-compile process to create executables. The buildtoolchain-step04-binutils script performs the following:

1. It extracts the binutils source from the tar file in the build directory.

2. It runs the configuration from the build directory.

3. It makes the binary utilities.

4. It installs the binary utilities. These binutils are x86 executables that manipulate PowerPC binary files. They are installed in /usr/bin but have the prefix powerpc-linux.

5. It cleans the build directory.

6. It lists what was built and installed in the /usr/bin directory.

LISTING 3.6   The buildtoolchain-step04-binutils Script

```
#!/bin/bash
# buildtoolchain-step04-binutils v0.1 8/16/01
# www.embeddedlinuxinterfacing.com
#
# The original location of this script is
# http://www.embeddedlinuxinterfacing.com/chapters/03/buildtoolchain
#
# Copyright (C) 2001 by Craig Hollabaugh
# See buildtoolchain script for General Public License statement

if [ ! $BUILDTOOLCHAINENV ]
then
. ./buildtoolchain-environment $1
fi


#
# Step 4 - Build binutils
#
echo Step 4 - Build binutils
echo Building $BINUTILSVERSION for $TARGET
cd $BUILDLOC
tar zxf $SRCFILELOC/$BINUTILSVERSION.tar.gz
```

LISTING 3.6   Continued

```
cd $TARGET-binutils
../$BINUTILSVERSION/configure --target=$TARGET --prefix=$PREFIX -v
make
make install

cd $BUILDLOC
rm -rf $TARGET-binutils
rm -rf $BINUTILSVERSION

ls -1 $PREFIX/bin/$TARGET-*

echo Step 4 - Complete
echo
```

Here's buildtoolchain-step04-binutils output, which lists the powerpc-linux binutils:

```
/usr/bin/powerpc-linux-addr2line
/usr/bin/powerpc-linux-ar
/usr/bin/powerpc-linux-as
/usr/bin/powerpc-linux-c++filt
/usr/bin/powerpc-linux-gasp
/usr/bin/powerpc-linux-ld
/usr/bin/powerpc-linux-nm
/usr/bin/powerpc-linux-objcopy
/usr/bin/powerpc-linux-objdump
/usr/bin/powerpc-linux-ranlib
/usr/bin/powerpc-linux-readelf
/usr/bin/powerpc-linux-size
/usr/bin/powerpc-linux-strings
/usr/bin/powerpc-linux-strip
Step 4 - Complete
```

Step 5: Set Up the Kernel Source and Headers

Cross-compiling gcc and glibc requires kernel headers. The buildtoolchain-step05-kernelsourceheaders performs the following steps to prepare the kernel headers (see Listing 3.7):

1. It extracts the kernel in the build directory.

2. It applies any patches.

3. It preserves the preexisting kernel configuration file, .config.

4. It removes the preexisting kernel source directory.

5. It moves the newly created kernel directory from the build directory to
   /usr/src.

6. It copies the saved .config file to config.original in the new kernel source
   directory.

7. It modifies the top-level kernel makefile, changing the ARCH and CROSS_COMPILE
   statements for the architecture that is being built.

8. It configures the kernel source and headers, using a default target board configuration from the arch directory.

9. It makes mrproper and dep.

10. It creates kernel headers that include directories for the cross-compiling
    process.

LISTING 3.7   The buildtoolchain-step05-kernelsourceheaders Script

```
#!/bin/bash
# buildtoolchain-step05-kernelsourceheaders v0.1 8/16/01
# www.embeddedlinuxinterfacing.com
#
# The original location of this script is
# http://www.embeddedlinuxinterfacing.com/chapters/03/buildtoolchain
#
# Copyright (C) 2001 by Craig Hollabaugh
# See buildtoolchain script for General Public License statement

if [ ! $BUILDTOOLCHAINENV ]
then
. ./buildtoolchain-environment $1
fi


#
# Step 5 - Setup Kernel Source and Headers
#
echo Step 5 - Setup Kernel Source and Headers
echo Setting up $KERNELVERSION source and headers for $TARGET
cd $SRCFILELOC

echo Removing $SRCFILELOC/linux
rm -rf $SRCFILELOC/linux
```

LISTING 3.7   Continued

```
echo Extracting $KERNELVERSION.tar.gz
tar zxf $KERNELVERSION.tar.gz

cd linux
if [ $KERNELPATCH1 ]
then
    echo Patching with $KERNELPATCH1
    gzip -cd ../$KERNELPATCH1 | patch -p1
fi
if [ $KERNELPATCH2 ]
then
    echo Patching with $KERNELPATCH2
    gzip -cd ../$KERNELPATCH2 | patch -p1
fi
if [ $KERNELPATCH3 ]
then
    echo Patching with $KERNELPATCH3
    gzip -cd ../$KERNELPATCH3 | patch -p1
fi

# save the existing kernel configuration if it exists
cd $SRCFILELOC
if [ -f $PREFIX/src/$TARGET/.config ]
then
    echo Saving $PREFIX/src/$TARGET/.config
    mv $PREFIX/src/$TARGET/.config /tmp/config.original
fi

# remove all the exist kernel source code for this target
echo Removing $PREFIX/src/$TARGET
rm -rf $PREFIX/src/$TARGET

echo Creating $PREFIX/src/$TARGET
mv linux $PREFIX/src/$TARGET

cd $PREFIX/src/$TARGET

if [ -f /tmp/config.original ]
then
 echo Saving $PREFIX/src/$TARGET/.config as $PREFIX/src/$TARGET/config.original
 mv /tmp/config.original $PREFIX/src/$TARGET/config.original
fi
```

LISTING 3.7   Continued

```
make mrproper

sed "s/ARCH :=.*$/ARCH := $ARCH/1" Makefile > /tmp/Makefile
cp /tmp/Makefile Makefile
sed "s/CROSS_COMPILE.*=.*$/CROSS_COMPILE = $TARGET-/1" Makefile > /tmp/Makefile
cp /tmp/Makefile Makefile

make mrproper

# use the target board defconfig if defined,
# otherwise have the user go through make menuconfig
if [ $TARGETBOARD ]
then
    make $TARGETBOARD"_config"
    make oldconfig
else
    make menuconfig
fi

make dep

if [ ! -e $PREFIX/$TARGET ]
then
    mkdir $PREFIX/$TARGET
fi

mkdir $PREFIX/$TARGET/include
cp -dR $PREFIX/src/$TARGET/include/asm-$ARCH $PREFIX/$TARGET/include/asm
cp -dR $PREFIX/src/$TARGET/include/linux $PREFIX/$TARGET/include/linux

echo Step 5 - Complete
echo
```

Step 6: Build a Cross-Compiled Version of gcc

With the binary utilities cross-compiled and installed and the kernel headers prop-
erly configured and installed, it's time to build a cross-compiled version of gcc.
Before we start, you need to know about a little problem that's about to happen.
Generating a cross-compiled version of gcc requires that a cross-compiled version of
glibc and headers be installed. glibc has not been created yet; that occurs in step 7.
Generating a cross-compiled version of glibc requires a cross-compiled version of

gcc. So gcc requires glibc, which requires gcc. This situation occurs on the first-time build of a cross-compiler. The organization of the gcc and glibc source code enables this interdependency situation to exist. The libchack[7] solution permits the initial building of gcc without glibc headers. Having gcc enables successful cross-compiling of glibc in step 7. Later, steps 11 and 12 rebuild gcc and glibc without libchack. The buildtoolchain-step06-gcc script performs the following steps to build a cross-compiled version of gcc (see Listing 3.8):

1. It extracts the gcc source in the build directory.

2. It applies any patches.

3. It applies the libchack solution.

4. It makes a cross-compiled version of gcc.

5. It installs the cross-compiled version of gcc.

6. It lists what was built and installed in the /usr/bin directory.

LISTING 3.8 The buildtoolchain-step06-gcc Script

```
#!/bin/bash
# buildtoolchain-step06-gcc v0.1 8/16/01
# www.embeddedlinuxinterfacing.com
#
# The original location of this script is
# http://www.embeddedlinuxinterfacing.com/chapters/03/buildtoolchain
#
# Copyright (C) 2001 by Craig Hollabaugh
# See buildtoolchain script for General Public License statement

if [ ! $BUILDTOOLCHAINENV ]
then
. ./buildtoolchain-environment $1
fi


#
# Step 6 - Building a Cross-Compiler Version of gcc
#
echo Step 6 - Building a Cross-Compiler Version of gcc
echo Building $TARGET-$GCCVERSION
cd $BUILDLOC

tar zxf $SRCFILELOC/$GCCVERSION.tar.gz
```

LISTING 3.8   Continued

```
if [ $GCCPATCH ]
then
    cd $GCCVERSION
    bzip2 -cd $SRCFILELOC/$GCCPATCH | patch -p0
    cd ../$TARGET-gcc
fi


cd $BUILDLOC/$TARGET-gcc

# this is called the libchack

if [ $ARCH = "arm" ]
then
    sed "s/TARGET_LIBGCC2_CFLAGS.*$/TARGET_LIBGCC2_CFLAGS =
➥-fomit-frame-pointer -fPIC -Dinhibit_libc -D__gthr_posix_h/1"
➥../$GCCVERSION/gcc/config/arm/t-linux > /tmp/libchack
    cp /tmp/libchack ../$GCCVERSION/gcc/config/arm/t-linux

    ../$GCCVERSION/configure --target=$TARGET \
                             --prefix=$PREFIX \
                             --with-headers=$PREFIX/src/$TARGET/include \
                             --enable-languages=c \
                             --disable-threads
fi

if [ $ARCH = "ppc" ]
then
    sed "s/TARGET_LIBGCC2_CFLAGS.*$/TARGET_LIBGCC2_CFLAGS =
➥-fomit-frame-pointer -fPIC -Dinhibit_libc -D__gthr_posix_h/1"
➥../$GCCVERSION/gcc/config/t-linux > /tmp/libchack
    cp /tmp/libchack ../$GCCVERSION/gcc/config/t-linux

    ../$GCCVERSION/configure --target=$TARGET \
                             --prefix=$PREFIX \
                             --with-headers=$PREFIX/src/$TARGET/include \
                             --enable-languages=c \
                             --disable-threads
fi

make
make install
```

LISTING 3.8   Continued

```
ls -1 $PREFIX/bin/$TARGET-*

echo Step 6 - Complete
echo
```

Here's the listing output from the buildtoolchain-step06-gcc script; notice that /usr/bin/powerpc-linux-gcc now exists:

```
/usr/bin/powerpc-linux-addr2line
/usr/bin/powerpc-linux-ar
/usr/bin/powerpc-linux-as
/usr/bin/powerpc-linux-c++filt
/usr/bin/powerpc-linux-gasp
/usr/bin/powerpc-linux-gcc
/usr/bin/powerpc-linux-ld
/usr/bin/powerpc-linux-nm
/usr/bin/powerpc-linux-objcopy
/usr/bin/powerpc-linux-objdump
/usr/bin/powerpc-linux-protoize
/usr/bin/powerpc-linux-ranlib
/usr/bin/powerpc-linux-readelf
/usr/bin/powerpc-linux-size
/usr/bin/powerpc-linux-strings
/usr/bin/powerpc-linux-strip
/usr/bin/powerpc-linux-unprotoize

Step 6 - Complete
```

Step 7: Build a Cross-Compiled Version of glibc

The buildtoolchain-step07-glibc script performs the following steps to build glibc (see Listing 3.9):

1. It extracts the glibc source in the build directory.

2. It extracts glibc-threads in the build directory.

3. It configures the build.

4. It makes a cross-compiled version of glibc.

5. It installs the cross-compiled version of glibc.

LISTING 3.9   The `buildtoolchain-step07-glibc` Script

```
#!/bin/bash
# buildtoolchain-step07-glibc v0.1 8/16/01
# www.embeddedlinuxinterfacing.com
#
# The original location of this script is
# http://www.embeddedlinuxinterfacing.com/chapters/03/buildtoolchain
# See buildtoolchain script for General Public License statement

if [ ! $BUILDTOOLCHAINENV ]
then
. ./buildtoolchain-environment $1
fi

# Step 7 - Build a Cross-Compiled Version of glibc
#
echo Step 7 - Build a Cross-Compiled Version of glibc
echo Building $GLIBVERSION for $ARCH
cd $BUILDLOC
tar zxf $SRCFILELOC/$GLIBVERSION.tar.gz
cd $GLIBVERSION
tar zxf $SRCFILELOC/$GLIBCTHREADSVERSION.tar.gz


cd ../$TARGET-glibc



if [ $ARCH = "arm" ]
then
CC=$TARGET-gcc ../$GLIBVERSION/configure $TARGET
➥--build=i586-linux --prefix=$PREFIX/$TARGET --enable-add-ons
fi

if [ $ARCH = "ppc" ]
then
# need to remove memset.S for 8xx processors
rm -rf $BUILDLOC/$GLIBVERSION/sysdeps/powerpc/memset.S

CC=$TARGET-gcc  ../$GLIBVERSION/configure $TARGET
➥--build=i586-linux --prefix=$PREFIX/$TARGET --enable-add-ons

fi
```

LISTING 3.9   Continued

```
make
make install

echo Step 7 - Complete
echo
```

Step 8: Build a Cross-Compiled Version of gdb

The GNU debugger, gdb, is used to debug executables. If you're debugging PowerPC or ARM executables, you need a cross-compiled version of gdb. The buildtoolchain-step08-gdb script performs the following steps to build gdb (see Listing 3.10):

1. It extracts the gdb source in the build directory.

2. It configures the build.

3. It makes a cross-compiled version of gdb.

4. It installs the cross-compiled version of gdb.

5. It lists what was built and installed in the /usr/bin directory.

LISTING 3.10   The buildtoolchain-step08-gdb Script

```
#!/bin/bash
# buildtoolchain-step08-gdb v0.1 8/16/01
# www.embeddedlinuxinterfacing.com
#
# The original location of this script is
# http://www.embeddedlinuxinterfacing.com/chapters/03/buildtoolchain
# See buildtoolchain script for General Public License statement

if [ ! $BUILDTOOLCHAINENV ]
then
. ./buildtoolchain-environment $1
fi

#
# Step 8 - Build Cross-Compiled Version of gdb
#
echo Step 8 - Build Cross-Compiled Version of gdb
echo building $GDBVERSION
cd $BUILDLOC
rm -rf $GDBVERSION
```

LISTING 3.10   Continued

```
tar zxf $SRCFILELOC/$GDBVERSION.tar.gz

cd $TARGET-gdb
../$GDBVERSION/configure --target=$TARGET --prefix=$PREFIX -v
make
make install

ls -1 $PREFIX/bin/$TARGET-*

echo Step 8 - Complete
echo
```

Here's the listing output from the buildtoolchain-step08-gdb script; notice that /usr/bin/powerpc-linux-gdb now exists:

```
/usr/bin/powerpc-linux-addr2line
/usr/bin/powerpc-linux-ar
/usr/bin/powerpc-linux-as
/usr/bin/powerpc-linux-c++filt
/usr/bin/powerpc-linux-gasp
/usr/bin/powerpc-linux-gcc
/usr/bin/powerpc-linux-gdb
/usr/bin/powerpc-linux-ld
/usr/bin/powerpc-linux-nm
/usr/bin/powerpc-linux-objcopy
/usr/bin/powerpc-linux-objdump
/usr/bin/powerpc-linux-protoize
/usr/bin/powerpc-linux-ranlib
/usr/bin/powerpc-linux-readelf
/usr/bin/powerpc-linux-run
/usr/bin/powerpc-linux-size
/usr/bin/powerpc-linux-strings
/usr/bin/powerpc-linux-strip
/usr/bin/powerpc-linux-unprotoize
Step 8 - Complete
```

Step 9: Check the Version of gcc

The buildtoolchain-step09-gccversion script executes the new cross-compiler and outputs the version (see Listing 3.11).

LISTING 3.11   The buildtoolchain-step09-gccversion Script

```
#!/bin/bash
# buildtoolchain-step09-gccversion v0.1 8/16/01
# www.embeddedlinuxinterfacing.com
#
# The original location of this script is
# http://www.embeddedlinuxinterfacing.com/chapters/03/buildtoolchain
# See buildtoolchain script for General Public License statement
#


if [ ! $BUILDTOOLCHAINENV ]
then
. ./buildtoolchain-environment $1
fi


#
# Step 9 - gcc Version Check
echo Step 9 - gcc Version Check
echo -n "$TARGET-gcc version is "
$TARGET-gcc --version

echo Step 9 - Complete
echo
```

Here's the buildtoolchain-step09-gccversion script output:

```
Step 9 - gcc Version Check
powerpc-linux-gcc version is 2.95.3
Step 9 - Complete
```

Step 10: Check the Tool Chain Build

buildtoolchain-step10-helloworld creates a helloworld.c source code file and
then cross-compiles it (see Listing 3.12). If the helloworld.c file successfully
compiles, then gcc, glibc and its headers files were properly configured, compiled
and installed. The script then calls the Linux file program that displays the architecture of the new helloworld executable. If helloworld.c doesn't successfully
compile, then an error occurred in the buildtoolchain execution. You'll have to find
the error in the buildtoolchain output and correct the situation.

LISTING 3.12   The `buildtoolchain-step10-helloworld` Script

```bash
#!/bin/bash
# buildtoolchain-step10-helloworld v0.1 8/16/01
# www.embeddedlinuxinterfacing.com
#
# The original location of this script is
# http://www.embeddedlinuxinterfacing.com/chapters/03/buildtoolchain
#
# Copyright (C) 2001 by Craig Hollabaugh
# See buildtoolchain script for General Public License statement

if [ ! $BUILDTOOLCHAINENV ]
then
. ./buildtoolchain-environment $1
fi

#
# Step 10 - Checking Tool Chain Build by Cross-Compiling Helloworld
#
echo Step 10 - Checking Tool Chain Build by Cross-Compiling Helloworld
echo creating helloworld.c

cd $BUILDLOC
rm -rf helloworld.*

cat > helloworld.c << ENDOFINPUT
#include <stdio.h>

int main(void)
{
    int i;

    for (i = 1; i < 10; i++)
    {
        printf("Hello world %d times!\n",i);
    }
}

ENDOFINPUT

$TARGET-gcc -g -o helloworld-$TARGET helloworld.c
file helloworld-$TARGET
```

LISTING 3.12 Continued

```
echo Step 10 - Complete
echo

Here's actual Step 10 output.

Step 10 - Checking Tool Chain Build by Cross-Compiling Helloworld
creating helloworld.c
helloworld-powerpc-linux: ELF 32-bit MSB executable, PowerPC or cisco 4500,
version 1, dynamically linked (uses shared libs), not stripped
Step 10 - Complete
```

The output `ELF 32-bit MSB executable for PowerPC` verifies a successful tool chain build.

Step 11: Rebuild `gcc`

Now that `glibc` and its header files exist, the `libchack` solution is no longer necessary. The `buildtoolchain-step11-rebuildgcc` script configures, makes, and installs `gcc` again without the `libchack` (see Listing 3.13).

LISTING 3.13 The `buildtoolchain-step11-rebuildgcc` Script

```
#!/bin/bash
# buildtoolchain-step11-rebuildgcc v0.1 8/16/01
# www.embeddedlinuxinterfacing.com
#
# The original location of this script is
# http://www.embeddedlinuxinterfacing.com/chapters/03/buildtoolchain
#
# Copyright (C) 2001 by Craig Hollabaugh
# See buildtoolchain script for General Public License statement

if [ ! $BUILDTOOLCHAINENV ]
then
. ./buildtoolchain-environment $1
fi

#
# Step 11 - rebuilding a Cross-Compiler Version of gcc
#
echo Step 11 - rebuilding the Cross-Compiler Version of gcc
echo Re-building $TARGET-$GCCVERSION
```

LISTING 3.13   Continued

```
cd $BUILDLOC
rm -rf $GCCVERSION

tar zxf $SRCFILELOC/$GCCVERSION.tar.gz

if [ $GCCPATCH ]
then
    cd $GCCVERSION
    bzip2 -cd $SRCFILELOC/$GCCPATCH | patch -p0
    cd ../$TARGET-gcc
fi

cd $BUILDLOC/$TARGET-gcc

if [ $ARCH = "arm" ]
then
        ../$GCCVERSION/configure --target=$TARGET \
                            --prefix=$PREFIX \
                            --with-headers=$PREFIX/src/$TARGET/include \
                            --enable-languages=c
fi

if [ $ARCH = "ppc" ]
then

"CFLAGS=-msoft-float" ../$GCCVERSION/configure --target=$TARGET \
                        --prefix=$PREFIX \
                        --with-headers=$PREFIX/src/$TARGET/include \
                        --enable-languages=c \
                        --without-fp
fi

make
make install

ls -l $PREFIX/bin/$TARGET-*

echo Step 11 - Complete
echo
```

Step 12: Rebuild glibc

With gcc properly rebuilt, the buildtoolchain-step12-rebuildglibc script
recompiles glibc for the final time. Step 12 differs significantly from step 7. The
buildtoolchain-step12-rebuildglibc script, as shown in Listing 3.14, configures
the prefix command-line option differently. Look back at buildtoolchain-step07-
glibc's configuration line. If you do a little environment variable substitution for
this PowerPC example, the buildtoolchain-step07-glibc script configuration
prefix command-line option expands to this:

--prefix=/usr/powerpc-linux

LISTING 3.14   The buildtoolchain-step12-rebuildglibc Script

```
#!/bin/bash
# buildtoolchain-step12-rebuildglibc v0.1 8/16/01
# www.embeddedlinuxinterfacing.com
#
# The original location of this script is
# http://www.embeddedlinuxinterfacing.com/chapters/03/buildtoolchain
#
# Copyright (C) 2001 by Craig Hollabaugh
# See buildtoolchain script for General Public License statement

if [ ! $BUILDTOOLCHAINENV ]
then
. ./buildtoolchain-environment $1
fi

# Step 12 - Build a Cross-Compiled Version of glibc
#
echo Step 12 - Build a Cross-Compiled Version of glibc
echo Building $GLIBVERSION for $ARCH

cd $BUILDLOC
cd $GLIBVERSION

cd ../$TARGET-glibc

if [ $ARCH = "arm" ]
then
```

LISTING 3.14   Continued

```
CC=$TARGET-gcc  ../$GLIBVERSION/configure $TARGET --build=i586-linux \
                                          --prefix=/ \
                                          --enable-add-ons
fi


if [ $ARCH = "ppc" ]
then


CC=$TARGET-gcc CFLAGS="-msoft-float -D_SOFT_FLOAT -mcpu=860" \
../$GLIBVERSION/configure $TARGET --build=i586-linux \
                                  --prefix=/ \
                                  --enable-add-ons \
                                  --without-fp
fi


#don't do a make install here, the prefix is /,
#installing will trash this computer's /lib directory


make


mkdir $BUILDLOC/$TARGET-lib
make install_root=$BUILDLOC/$TARGET-lib install



echo Step 12 - Complete
echo
```

The prefix option prefixes a path to /lib; in this case, buildtoolchain-step07-glibc compiles and installs glibc and other libraries, using /usr/powerpc-linux/lib instead of just /lib. The path /usr/powerpc-linux/lib is actually hard-coded into step 7's PowerPC version of glibc and other libraries. The buildtoolchain-step07-glibc script configures this prefix so that the glibc installation script doesn't overwrite the x86 glibc library on tbdev1. Overwriting the x86 glibc with a PowerPC version would cause substantial problems for tbdev1.

Think about running programs on the target PowerPC board, the RPX-CLLF. The library loader, ld.so, expects glibc and other common libraries to exist in the /lib directory. Using the cross-compiled version of glibc from step 7 on the target system with the hard-coded path /usr/powerpc-linux/lib in glibc would cause havoc. The library loader would have problems finding various libraries. The buildtoolchain-step12-rebuildglibc script doesn't merely recompile glibc: It configures with the prefix command-line option to /, it makes glibc, and then it installs glibc in a special build library directory. In this PowerPC example, when buildtoolchain-step12-rebuildglibc completes, /root/cross/builds/powerpc-lib contains glibc libraries for use on the PowerPC target system.

In summary, the buildtoolchain-step07-glibc script generates cross-compiled glibc libraries for use on the host workstation tbdev1 in the /usr/powerpc-linux/lib directory. Using a prefix reduces the chance of overwriting the x86 glibc. Step 7 cross-compiled glibc library files can't be used on the target system; the prefix /usr/powerpc-linux is hard-coded in the library files themselves. The buildtoolchain-step12-rebuildglibc script generates an additional set of libraries with the prefix / for use on the target system.

At this point, the PowerPC cross-compiler, powerpc-linux-gcc, exists in the /usr/bin directory. The PowerPC cross-compiled libraries are located in /usr/powerpc-linux/lib. The buildtoolchain script, using powerpc-linux-gcc and the PowerPC glibc libraries, compiles /root/cross/builds/helloworld.c using the following command:

```
powerpc-linux-gcc -g -o helloworld-powerpc-linux helloworld.c
```

The PowerPC executable helloworld-powerpc-linux exists in /root/cross/builds. If you execute helloworld-powerpc-linux on your x86 development station, you should get the following error because helloworld-powerpc-linux is not an x86 executable:

```
root@tbdev1[530]: cd /root/cross/builds
root@tbdev1[531]: ./helloworld-powerpc-linux
bash: ./helloworld-powerpc-linux: cannot execute binary file
```

In Chapter 5, you'll transfer this helloworld-powerpc-linux executable to the Embedded Planet RPX-CLLF target board. You'll also execute it and remotely debug it.

Congratulations on building the GNU tool chain for cross-compiling! If you need to build the tool chain for the ARM processor, run buildtoolchain arm, sit back, and watch tbdev1 configure, compile, and install an ARM version of the GNU tool chain.

Summary

The Silverjack engineers researched embedded Linux and found a wealth of online information on ports, tools, boards, distributions, tools, and kernel versions. They summarized their findings by developing the Project Trailblazer strategic direction, which consists of three areas: kernel porting, source code, and kernel version. After research, thought, and discussions with vendors and suppliers, they decided on target hardware. They ordered target boards from Tri-M, Embedded Planet, and Brightstar Engineering. While they waited, they learned about cross-compiling the GNU tool chain and developed the `buildtoolchain` scripts. The engineers are now ready and anxious to boot their target systems when they arrive.

Additional Reading

1. Embedded Linux Consortium, "Unified Embedded Platform Specification Established and Promoted by Embedded Linux Consortium Board," `www.embedded-linux.org/pressroom.php3?type=0#66`.

2. "The Linux-friendly Embedded SBCs Quick Reference Guide," `www.linuxdevices.com/articles/AT2614444132.html`, 2001.

3. "The Embedded Linux Distributions Quick Reference Guide," `www.linuxdevices.com/articles/AT2760742655.html`, 2001.

4. Joe Pranevich, "Wonderful World of Linux 2.4—Final Candidate #3—4/10/00," `http://linuxtoday.com/mailprint.php3?action=pv&ltsn=` `2000-04-11-003-04-NW-LF`, 2000.

5. Jerry Epplin, "Linux 2.4 Unmasked (Including the Embedded Perspective)," `www.linuxdevices.com/articles/AT8294600687.html`, 2000.

6. "The Debian Potato IDEPCI Kernel Configuration," `http://ftp.us.debian.org/debian/dists/stable/main/disks-i386/current/` `images-1.44/idepci/kernel-config`.

7. "The -Dinhibit_libc hack," `www.armlinux.org/docs/toolchain/toolchHOWTO/` `x183.html#DIN`.

4

Booting Linux

Project Trailblazer was off and running. The Silverjack Engineering Department ordered the development target platforms and other hardware: the Embedded Planet RPX-CLLF, the Brightstar Engineering MediaEngine, the Tri-M MZ104 x86 single-board computer, and the solid-state hard disk hardware to boot a commercial off-the-shelf (COTS) PC. The staff then had a few days to learn about the Linux boot process and the root filesystem for the four target platforms. Fortunately, Linux's code commonality simplifies development and deployment, regardless of platform. This chapter chronicles the team's booting journey. The team wanted to ultimately run its version of helloworld on all the target platforms.

The engineers developed a small set of platform boot requirements (PBRs) for all the incoming target boards. These requirements are simple and are shown in the following section. When the boards are successfully booted, they will form the baseline development system, shown in Figure 4.1, on which to build Project Trailblazer.

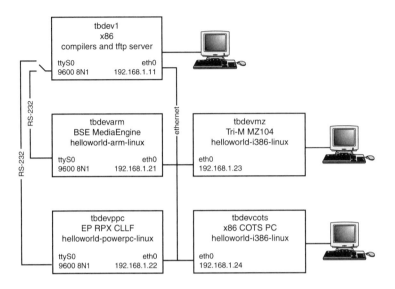

FIGURE 4.1   The Project Trailblazer development layout.

The Target PBRs

Each target platform will need to fulfill all of the following requirements in order to be used for Project Trailblazer designs:

- **PBR-1**—The target board will use Linux kernel 2.4 or greater. Running the same kernel version across all target platforms would be nice, but it is not necessary. The engineers discovered that the i386, ARM and PowerPC kernel development occurs at different paces. ARM and PowerPC kernel patches don't always exist for the most recent version of the kernel.

- **PBR-2**—The target board will execute the bash shell. Exiting from the bash shell causes the bash shell to re-execute.

> **TIP**
>
> Defining boot requirements and evaluating target boards forms a development system base-line. Having a bash prompt on all your targets means Linux is running. This simplifies porting code and scripts from one architecture to another.

- **PBR-3**—The target board will execute the bash shell without security authentication. This reduces development time but leaves open a future security hole. Later, the engineers will add security, such as the login process.

- **PBR-4**—The target board will boot, initialize the Ethernet hardware, set a static IP address, and be configured to use the Domain Name Service (DNS).

- **PBR-5**—The target board will contain the ping program to debug network programs.

- **PBR-6**—The target board will be capable of executing the cross-compiled version of helloworld.

- **PBR-7**—The target board will use a current version of GNU glibc. The selected target platforms contain sufficient RAM and storage resources to use GNU glibc. Projects such as BusyBox, sglibc, uClibc, dietlibc, newlib, and libc5 will not be considered.

Awaiting hardware and armed with these seven target PBRs, the engineers proceeded to learn about the Linux boot process, the root filesystem, whether to compile or download the root filesystem binaries, target platform similarities and differences, kernel compilation, and some i386 hard disk booting specifics. We'll come back to these boot requirements later in this chapter.

The Linux Boot Process

A target board booting Linux proceeds through several steps after reset to get to a system prompt. The initial steps, such as ROM startup code and register configuration, are microprocessor hardware dependent. The kernel itself contains microprocessor architecture–dependent initialization code that is executed first. This initialization code configures the microprocessor registers for protected-mode operation and then invokes the architecture-independent kernel starting point called start_kernel. From this point on, the kernel boot process is identical for all architectures. The Linux boot process involves the following steps:

1. After a processor is reset, it executes ROM startup code.

2. The ROM startup code initializes the CPU, memory controller, and on-chip devices, and it configures the memory map. The ROM startup code then executes a bootloader.

3. The bootloader decompresses the Linux kernel into RAM from Flash memory or a TFTP server transfer. It then executes a jump to the kernel's first instruction. The kernel first configures microprocessor registers and then invokes start_kernel, which is the architecture-independent starting point.

4. The kernel initializes its caches and various hardware devices.

5. The kernel mounts the root filesystem.

6. The kernel executes the init process.

7. The executing init process loads shared runtime libraries.

8. init reads its configuration file, /etc/inittab, and executes scripts. Typically, init executes a startup script, /etc/rc.d/rcS, which configures and starts networking and other system services.

9. init enters a runlevel where system duties can be performed or the login process can start, allowing for user sessions.

The Project Trailblazer engineers learned from the board manufacturers' documentation that steps 1, 2 and 3 are fairly easy to understand, configure, and execute. Step 4 is dependent on kernel compilation configuration. Step 5 presents a wide range of options, including mounting a local disk drive, mounting a network drive, and using a RAM disk. Step 7 requires proper compilation of glibc and other libraries.

The engineers read about replacing the init program with bash directly in step 6. They opted to use init for two reasons. First, init can handle initialization of networking and system services via scripts. Second, in step 9 the engineers will use init to call bash directly instead of using the login process. init can respawn processes that terminate. This means that if bash terminates, init will re-execute it. Use of init fulfills PBR-2. Having bash execute directly instead of login allows console operations without security. The engineers intend to add the login process prior to placing the target board in field operations.

> **TIP**
>
> Having init call bash directly instead of login saves time because you don't have to log in during development. In a secure lab, convenience outweighs security. When you deploy designs, you should modify /etc/inittab so that init calls login, to provide the first level of authentication.

The Linux root Filesystem

The Linux root filesystem contains files and executables that the kernel requires, as well as executables for system administration. In a desktop workstation installation, the kernel mounts a hard disk partition on the / directory. The following directories exist beneath the / directory:

- /bin and /sbin contain system executables such as init, ifconfig, mount, cd, mkdir, and ping.

- /lib contains the shared libraries (libc and others) and the Linux dynamic loader.

- /etc contains system configuration files and scripts.

- /dev contains special device files.

- The kernel dynamically creates the /proc directory in memory to provide system information.

- /usr contains additional programs and libraries.

- /var contains files that change during runtime, such as lock and log files.

The Trailblazer engineers began to understand the root filesystem contents by examining tbdev1 (the Debian distribution development computer, which is described in Chapter 3, "Selecting a Platform and Installing Tool Sets"). They found that the root filesystem contained 10,734 files and used 67.428MB of hard disk space. They found that a default Red Hat installation contains 29,296 files and uses 382.020MB. Clearly, taking the simple approach of merely copying the contents from a default Debian or Red Hat disk exceeds the storage capability of the engineers' four target platforms, which ranges from 4MB to 16MB. The engineers needed to decide what files are really necessary to boot Linux and execute a bash prompt.

TIP

Developing a root filesystem by examining the Linux boot process from start_kernel to the bash prompt results in a minimum set of required files and gives you an understanding of Linux's interaction with programs and libraries.

Someone suggested that they could just start deleting files and see what happens. That hit-or-miss approach was quickly dismissed. The engineers learned from the Linux boot process that the kernel starts the init process that executes network and system initialization scripts and then executes bash. The engineers then wondered what files are required for init, the network and system initialization, and bash. Then, concern surfaced about this init/bash file approach and the four target platforms. The engineers wondered if they could determine what files are necessary for init and bash, would those same files be required for all architectures? Or would some architecture-based files be missing? No one had an answer other than to say that after the kernel boots, all architectures shared the same source code for init, bash, and the shared libraries. This means that if the engineers determine a root filesystem for one architecture, it should work for the others.

Required Files for init

After the kernel initializes its caches and various hardware devices, it executes the first user process, init, which spawns all other process. In order for init to run, it needs certain files and libraries to be present in the filesystem. On tbdev1, the engineers used a program called ldd to discover init's shared library dependencies. This is the output of ldd:

```
root@tbdev1[514]: ldd /sbin/init
        libc.so.6 => /lib/libc.so.6 (0x40015000)
        /lib/ld-linux.so.2 => /lib/ld-linux.so.2 (0x40000000)
```

The first file the new root filesystem needs is /sbin/init, which requires /lib/libc.so.6 and /lib/ld-Linux.so.2. By reading the man page for init, the engineers determined that init uses a configuration file called /etc/inittab that contains instructions for init. On a desktop or server Linux workstation, the init process initializes the networking and system services, and then it enters a runlevel—typically the login process. On the target systems, the engineers are not concerned with runlevels per se; rather, they want to boot the system and get bash running. So they aren't using a predefined runlevel, as in the Unix/Linux world. They are configuring init to simply initialize the network. Then they are configuring init to execute bash without authentication and to respawn bash if bash terminates.

> **TIP**
>
> The kernel completes booting by executing the first user process, init. init's scripts start all the system services. You can configure init to start programs and then to restart them if they terminate.

The engineers examined the /etc/inittab file on the tbdev1 workstation. They then created a simplified version that initializes the network and then executes bash. Here's their simplified inittab file:

```
id:2:initdefault:
l2:2:wait:/etc/init.d/rcS
1:2435:respawn:/bin/bash
2:6:wait:/etc/init.d/umountfs
```

In this version of the /etc/inittab file, id:2:initdefault: tells init the default level to enter. l2:2:wait:/etc/init.d/rcS tells init to run the /etc/init.d/rcS script before entering runlevel 2, and then to wait for completion. 1:2435:respawn:/bin/bash tells init to run /bin/bash and respawn it if bash terminates. 2:6:wait:/etc/init.d/umountfs tells init that upon entering runlevel 6, someone is rebooting the target board, to run the umountfs script and wait for its completion.

Required Files for bash

The bash shell requires libraries to execute. On tbdev1, the engineers again used ldd to discover bash's shared library dependencies. Here is the output of ldd:

```
root@tbdev1[516]: ldd /bin/bash
        libncurses.so.5 => /lib/libncurses.so.5 (0x40016000)
        libdl.so.2 => /lib/libdl.so.2 (0x40055000)
        libc.so.6 => /lib/libc.so.6 (0x40059000)
        /lib/ld-linux.so.2 => /lib/ld-linux.so.2 (0x40000000)
```

In addition to init, inittab, rcS, umountfs, ld-linux.so.2, and libc.so.6, the new
root filesystem needs bash, libdl.so.2, and libncurses.so.5. The engineers poked
around in the /bin, /sbin, and /usr/bin directories and found that the following
programs would also be necessary in order to have a functional system: cat, ls,
mount, umount, ps, df, kill, ping, chmod, touch, rm, ifconfig, route, telnet, and
gdbserver. They checked for shared library and configuration file dependencies,
and after a little trial and error, they compiled the root filesystem file list shown in
Table 4.1. These files exist in a directory structure that consists of these directories:
/bin, /dev, /etc, /etc/init.d, /lib, /proc, /sbin, /tmp, /usr, and /usr/bin. With
this root filesystem, the kernel calls init, which initializes the network and then
executes bash. A user can then ping other network computers and run helloworld.
This booted system will fulfill all seven PBRs.

TIP

The Linux program ldd outputs a list of shared libraries required by a program or library.
When adding programs to the root filesystem, you should use ldd to determine whether
additional libraries are required.

TABLE 4.1 The Project Trailblazer Target root Filesystem Files

/bin	/dev	/etc	/lib	/sbin	/usr/bin
bash	Console	fstab	ld.so.1	ifconfig	gdbserver
cat	null	inittab	ld-2.2.3.so	init	telnet
chmod	ram	protocols	libc.so.6	route	
echo	tty	resolv.conf	libc-2.2.3.so		
df	tty0	services	libdl.so.2		
kill	ttyS0		libdl-2.2.3.so		
ls			libm.so.6		
mount			libm-2.2.3.so		
ping			libncurses.so.5		
ps			libncurses.so.5.2		
rm			libnss_dns.so.2		
sh			libnss_dns-2.2.3.so		
touch			libnss_files.so.2		
umount			libnss_files-2.2.3.so		
			libproc.so.2.0.7		

TABLE 4.1   Continued

/bin	/dev	/etc	/lib	/sbin	/usr/bin
			libpthread.so.0		
			libpthread-0.0.so		
			libresolv-2.2.3.so		
			librt.so.1		
			librt-2.2.3.so		
			libstdc++-3-libc6.1-2-2.10.0.so		
			libstdc++-libc6.1-2.so.3		
			libutil.so.1		
			libutil-2.2.3.so		

The root Filesystem Binary Files: Compile or Download?

The engineers determined that it would be easy to find all these files for the i386 platforms. They could just copy them from the tbdev1 computer. The ARM and PowerPC versions would require cross-compiling. Although this list is short compared to the Debian base installation of 10,734 files, cross-compiling all these executables would require significant effort. The most current source code would have to be located and downloaded. The individual makefiles would require modification for cross-compiling and library linking. Finally, the code would need to be compiled. The engineers thought that there must be an easier way, that someone else had probably already done this ARM and PowerPC cross-compiling. During their initial research, the engineers found that the Debian Linux site (www.debian.org) contains source and compiled binaries for Alpha, ARM, i386, m68k, PowerPC, and SPARC processors. This availability of compiled binaries looked promising, until the engineers investigated the source code versions. The Debian software distribution lags behind current versions of open-source software. Debian publicly acknowledges this and distributes software "when it's time." In addition, the Debian versions of PowerPC binaries are compiled for microprocessors that have floating-point units. The Trailblazer RPX-CLLF target board uses a Motorola MPC860 that doesn't have a floating-point unit. They decided to look elsewhere.

Recently, MontaVista software released Hard Hat Linux (HHL), version 2 using kernel version 2.4.2.[1] MontaVista distributes two varieties of HHLv2: the Journeyman and the Professional editions. The Journeyman edition caught the engineers' attention because it supports i386, ARM, and PowerPC, specifically the MPC8xx processors—and it's free. The Journeyman CD contents as well as CD images are publicly available at the MontaVista FTP site (ftp.mvista.com/pub/Journeyman).

TIP

Some PowerPC microprocessors don't have a floating-point unit and don't execute floating-point instructions gracefully. When executing PowerPC programs, you should make sure they have been compiled correctly for your microprocessor.

MontaVista's HHLv2 isn't just a repackaging of the open-source GNU software. MontaVista's engineers are considered leading developers in architecture porting issues and development activities. They have incorporated much of their work (via patches) into the MontaVista distribution. All their architecture-specific work for the kernel and other GNU software is incorporated into the HHLv2 source and binaries. The Project Trailblazer engineers, who aren't architecture experts, were excited that they wouldn't have to become experts just to get their target platforms booted. The engineers decided that instead of reinventing the wheel, they could use MontaVista's Journeyman product, including the Journeyman cross-compiled versions of the programs for their ARM and PowerPC root filesystem. After a successful booting of both the ARM and PowerPC target platforms, they decided to use Journeyman for i386 root filesystem as well. This decision simplified their lives in ways they didn't imagine. Building a root filesystem for all the target platforms eventually involved running a script that would download the Journeyman Red Hat Package Management (RPM) binaries, extract the files, copy various binary programs to the new root filesystem, and create all the configuration files. This script, called buildrootfilesystem, is shown in Listing 4.1 and can be found at www.embeddedlinuxinterfacing.com/chapters/04/buildrootfilesystem.

LISTING 4.1   The buildrootfilesystem Script

```
#!/bin/bash
# buildrootfilesystem v0.2 10/23/01
# www.embeddedlinuxinterfacing.com
#
# The original location of this script is
# http://www.embeddedlinuxinterfacing.com/chapters/04/buildrootfilesystem
#
# Copyright (C) 2001 by Craig Hollabaugh
#
# This program is free software; you can redistribute it and/or modify it
# under the terms of the GNU Library General Public License as published by
# the Free Software Foundation; either version 2 of the License, or (at your
# option) any later version.
#
# This program is distributed in the hope that it will be useful, but WITHOUT
# ANY WARRANTY; without even the implied warranty of MERCHANTABILITY or
```

LISTING 4.1   Continued

```
# FITNESS FOR A PARTICULAR PURPOSE. See the GNU Library General Public License
# for more details.
#
# You should have received a copy of the GNU Library General Public License
# along with this program; if not, write to the Free Software Foundation,
# 59 Temple Place, Suite 330, Boston, MA 02111-1307 USA
#

umask 022

SRCFILELOC=/root/cross
BUILDLOC=$SRCFILELOC/builds

case "$1" in
"ppc" )
ARCH=powerpc
TARGET=powerpc-linux
MVRPMLOC=ftp://ftp.mvista.com/pub/Journeyman/cd2/ppc_8xx/apps/
#MVRPMLOC=http://www.embeddedlinuxinterfacing.com/ftp.mvista.com/pub/
➥Journeyman/cd2/ppc_8xx/apps/
TEMPFSLOC=$BUILDLOC/$ARCH-rootrpms/opt/hardhat/devkit/ppc/8xx/target/
;;
"arm" )
ARCH=arm
TARGET=arm-linux
MVRPMLOC=ftp://ftp.mvista.com/pub/Journeyman/cd1/arm_sa_le/apps/
#MVRPMLOC=http://www.embeddedlinuxinterfacing.com/ftp.mvista.com/pub/
➥Journeyman/cd1/arm_sa_le/apps/
TEMPFSLOC=$BUILDLOC/$ARCH-rootrpms/opt/hardhat/devkit/arm/sa_le/target/
;;
"i386" )
ARCH=i386
TARGET=i386
MVRPMLOC=ftp://ftp.mvista.com/pub/Journeyman/cd1/x86_586/apps/
#MVRPMLOC=http://www.embeddedlinuxinterfacing.com/ftp.mvista.com/pub/
➥Journeyman/cd1/x86_586/apps/
TEMPFSLOC=$BUILDLOC/$ARCH-rootrpms/opt/hardhat/devkit/x86/586/target/
;;
* )
    echo -n "Usage " `basename $0`
    echo " i386|arm|ppc [ramdisk]"
```

LISTING 4.1   Continued

```
    exit 1
;;
esac

#
# Step 1 - Determine what packages to download
#
echo Step 1 - Determine what packages to download

PACKAGES="glibc-2 bash procps textutils fileutils shellutils sysvinit
➥ netbase libncurses libstdc mount telnet-client net-tools
➥ ping gdbserver modutils"

echo packages are $PACKAGES
echo Step 1 - Complete
echo

#
# Step 2 - Create build and new target root filesystem directories
#
echo Step 2 - Create build and new target root filesystem directories

if [ ! -e /tftpboot ]
then
    mkdir /tftpboot
fi

if [ ! -e $SRCFILELOC ]
then
    mkdir $SRCFILELOC
fi

if [ ! -e $BUILDLOC ]
then
    mkdir $BUILDLOC
fi

ROOTFSLOC=/tftpboot/$ARCH-rootfs

echo Creating root file system for $ARCH
```

LISTING 4.1   Continued

```
rm -rf $ROOTFSLOC
mkdir  $ROOTFSLOC

if [ ! -e $BUILDLOC/$ARCH-rootrpms ]
then
    mkdir  $BUILDLOC/$ARCH-rootrpms
fi

cd $ROOTFSLOC
mkdir      dev etc etc/init.d bin sbin lib usr usr/bin proc tmp
chmod 755 . dev etc etc/init.d bin sbin lib usr usr/bin proc tmp

echo Step 2 - Complete
echo

#
# Step 3 - Download the packages
#
echo Step 3 - Download the packages

cd $BUILDLOC/$ARCH-rootrpms

lynx -dump $MVRPMLOC | grep ftp > /tmp/rpmlist
for i in $PACKAGES
do
    a=`grep $i /tmp/rpmlist`
    rpmurl=`echo $a | cut -d " " -f 2`
#    echo $rpmurl
    rpm=`basename $rpmurl`
#    echo $rpm

    if [ ! -f $BUILDLOC/$ARCH-rootrpms/$rpm ]
    then
        echo Getting $rpm
        wget $rpmurl
    else
        echo Have $rpm
    fi

done
```

LISTING 4.1   Continued

```
echo Step 3 - Complete
echo


#
# Step 4 - Extract the package's contents into a temporary directory
#
echo Step 4 - Extract the package\'s contents into a temporary directory
cd $BUILDLOC/$ARCH-rootrpms

# this is the old way, too slow because it converts RPMs everytime
#alien -t *rpm
#find . -name "*tgz" -exec tar zxvf {} \;
#rm -rf *tgz


IFS='
'

for rpm in `ls *rpm`
do
    if [ ! -f $rpm.extracted ]
    then
        alien -t $rpm
        tgz=`ls *tgz`
        tar zxvf $tgz
        rm -rf $tgz
        touch $rpm.extracted
    fi
done


echo Step 4 - Complete
echo


#
# Step 5 - Copy the required programs
#
echo Step 5 - Copy the required programs

echo
```

LISTING 4.1   Continued

```
#lib files
cd $TEMPFSLOC/lib
cp -av ld*                    $ROOTFSLOC/lib
cp -av libc-*                 $ROOTFSLOC/lib
cp -av libc.*                 $ROOTFSLOC/lib
cp -av libutil*               $ROOTFSLOC/lib
cp -av libncurses*            $ROOTFSLOC/lib
cp -av libdl*                 $ROOTFSLOC/lib
cp -av libnss_dns*            $ROOTFSLOC/lib
cp -av libnss_files*          $ROOTFSLOC/lib
cp -av libresolv*             $ROOTFSLOC/lib
cp -av libproc*               $ROOTFSLOC/lib
cp -av librt*                 $ROOTFSLOC/lib
cp -av libpthread*            $ROOTFSLOC/lib


#libm and libstdc are needed by telnet-client
cp -av libm*                  $ROOTFSLOC/lib

cd $ROOTFSLOC/usr
ln -s ../lib lib

cd $TEMPFSLOC/usr/lib
cp -av libstdc*               $ROOTFSLOC/usr/lib

#sbin files
cd $TEMPFSLOC/sbin
cp -av init ifconfig route    $ROOTFSLOC/sbin

#bin files
cd $TEMPFSLOC/bin
cp -av bash cat ls mount umount ps $ROOTFSLOC/bin
cp -av df kill ping chmod touch rm $ROOTFSLOC/bin
cp -av echo                   $ROOTFSLOC/bin

cd $ROOTFSLOC/bin
ln -s bash sh

#usr/bin files
cd $TEMPFSLOC/usr/bin
cp -av telnet gdbserver       $ROOTFSLOC/usr/bin
```

LISTING 4.1   Continued

```
#helloworld
cd $ROOTFSLOC/tmp

cat > helloworld.c << ENDOFINPUT
#include <stdio.h>

int main(void)
{
    int i;

    for (i = 1; i < 10; i++)
    {
        printf("Hello world %d times!\n",i);
    }
}

ENDOFINPUT

if [ $ARCH == "i386" ]
then
    gcc -g -o helloworld-$TARGET helloworld.c
else
    $TARGET-gcc -g -o helloworld-$TARGET helloworld.c
fi
file helloworld-$TARGET


chown -R root.root $ROOTFSLOC/*


echo Step 5 - Complete
echo

#
# Step 6 - Strip the required programs
#
echo Step 6 - Strip the required programs
echo

# strip it, strip it good
if [ $ARCH == "i386" ]
```

LISTING 4.1   Continued

```
then
    strip -s -g $ROOTFSLOC/lib/*
    strip -s -g $ROOTFSLOC/bin/*
    strip -s -g $ROOTFSLOC/sbin/*
    strip -s -g $ROOTFSLOC/usr/bin/*
    strip -s -g $ROOTFSLOC/usr/lib/*
else
    $TARGET-strip -s -g $ROOTFSLOC/lib/*
    $TARGET-strip -s -g $ROOTFSLOC/bin/*
    $TARGET-strip -s -g $ROOTFSLOC/sbin/*
    $TARGET-strip -s -g $ROOTFSLOC/usr/bin/*
    $TARGET-strip -s -g $ROOTFSLOC/usr/lib/*
fi


echo Step 6 - Complete
echo

#
# Step 7 - Create configuration files
#
echo Step 7 - Create configuration files
echo

#etc files
cd $TEMPFSLOC/etc
cp -av protocols services              $ROOTFSLOC/etc

cd $ROOTFSLOC/etc
cat > fstab << endofinput
# <file system>       <mount point>    <type>  <options> <dump>  <pass>
proc                  /proc            proc    defaults  0       0
endofinput

if [ $# == 2 ] && [ $2 == "ramdisk" ]
then
  echo "/dev/ram              /                ext2 defaults  0   0" >> fstab
else
  echo "192.168.1.11:/tftpboot/$ARCH-rootfs / nfs defaults  1   1" >> fstab
fi
```

LISTING 4.1 Continued

```
cat > inittab << endofinput
id:2:initdefault:
l2:2:wait:/etc/init.d/rcS
1:2:respawn:/bin/bash
2:6:wait:/etc/init.d/umountfs
endofinput


cat > init.d/rcS << endofinput
#!/bin/bash
/bin/mount -n -o remount,rw /

# clear out mtab
>/etc/mtab

/bin/mount -a
echo Starting Network

/sbin/ifconfig lo 127.0.0.1 netmask 255.0.0.0 broadcast 127.255.255.255
/sbin/route add -net 127.0.0.0 netmask 255.0.0.0 lo
endofinput


case "$ARCH" in
"powerpc" )
cat >> init.d/rcS << endofinput
/sbin/ifconfig eth0 192.168.1.22 netmask 255.255.255.0
/sbin/route add default gw 192.168.1.254 eth0
endofinput
;;
"arm" )
cat >> init.d/rcS << endofinput
/sbin/ifconfig eth0 192.168.1.21 netmask 255.255.255.0
/sbin/route add default gw 192.168.1.254 eth0
endofinput
;;
"i386" )
cat >> init.d/rcS << endofinput
/sbin/ifconfig eth0 192.168.1.23 netmask 255.255.255.0
/sbin/route add default gw 192.168.1.254 eth0
endofinput
```

LISTING 4.1   Continued

```
;;
esac

chmod 755 init.d/rcS

cat > init.d/umountfs << endofinput
/bin/echo umounting filesystems and remounting / as readonly
/bin/umount -f -a -r
/bin/mount -n -o remount,ro /
endofinput

chmod 755 init.d/umountfs

cat > resolv.conf << endofinput
domain trailblazerdev
nameserver 192.168.1.1
endofinput
echo Step 7 - Complete
echo

#
# Step 8 - Create devices in /dev directory
#
echo Step 8 - Create devices in /dev directory

#dev files
cd $ROOTFSLOC/dev
mknod -m 0666 tty c 5 0
mknod -m 0666 tty0 c 4 0
mknod -m 0666 ttyS0 c 4 64
ln -s ttyS0 console
mknod -m 0666 null c 1 3
mknod -m 660 ram b 1 1
chown root.disk ram

echo Step 8 - Complete
echo

#
# Step 9 - Prepare the root filesystem for operation on the target board
#
```

LISTING 4.1 Continued

```
echo Step 9 - Prepare the root filesystem for operation on the target board


if [ $# == 2 ]
then
  if [ $2 == "ramdisk" ]
  then
    echo Building $ARCH root filesystem ramdisk
    rm -rf /tmp/tmpmnt
    mkdir /tmp/tmpmnt
    rm -rf /tmp/ramrootfs
    dd if=/dev/zero of=/tmp/ramrootfs bs=1k count=8192
    mke2fs -F -m 0 -i 2000 /tmp/ramrootfs
    mount -o loop -t ext2 /tmp/ramrootfs /tmp/tmpmnt
    cd /tmp/tmpmnt
    cp -av $ROOTFSLOC/* .
    cd /tmp
    umount /tmp/tmpmnt
    cat /tmp/ramrootfs | gzip -9 > /tftpboot/$ARCH-ramdisk.gz

    if [ $ARCH == "powerpc" ]
    then
      cp /tftpboot/$ARCH-ramdisk.gz
➥         /usr/src/$TARGET/arch/ppc/boot/images/ramdisk.image.gz
      echo Copying /tftpboot/$ARCH-ramdisk.gz to
➥                  /usr/src/$TARGET/arch/ppc/boot/images/ramdisk.image.gz
      fi

      rm -rf /tmp/ramrootfs
      rm -rf /tmp/tmpmnt

      echo Your $ARCH root filesystem ramdisk is /tftpboot/$ARCH-ramdisk.gz
    fi
fi


if [ $ARCH == "i386" ]
then

    echo
    echo -n This script is about to work with your /dev/hdc1 partition,
```

LISTING 4.1   Continued

```
    echo is this OK? yes/no?" "

    read hdc1ok

    if [ $hdc1ok == "yes" ]
    then


    mkdir $ROOTFSLOC/boot

    #dev files
    cd $ROOTFSLOC/dev
    rm -rf console
    mknod console c 5 1
    chmod 666 console
    mknod hda b 3 0
    mknod hda1 b 3 1
    mknod hda2 b 3 2
    chmod 666 hda*

    #/boot files
    cp /boot/boot.b $ROOTFSLOC/boot
    cp /usr/src/linux/arch/i386/boot/bzImage $ROOTFSLOC/boot/bzImage

    TMPMOUNT=/tmp/tmpmnt

cat > /tmp/lilo.conf.1 << ENDOFINPUT
# this is a special lilo.conf file used to install lilo on the /dev/hdc drive
# when the machine is booted from the /dev/hda drive. Don't run lilo with this
# conf file if you booted the machine from this second drive.

disk=/dev/hdc bios=0x80        # This tells LILO to treat hdc as hda

boot=/dev/hdc                  # install boot on hdc
map=$TMPMOUNT/boot/map         # location of the map file
install=$TMPMOUNT/boot/boot.b  # boot file to copy to boot sector

prompt                         # show LILO boot: prompt

timeout=10                     # wait a second for user input
```

LISTING 4.1   Continued

```
image=$TMPMOUNT/boot/bzImage     # kernel location
label=linux                      # kernel label

root=/dev/hda1                   # root image location after you
                                 # finalize disk location

read-only                        # mount root as read only


ENDOFINPUT

cat > $ROOTFSLOC/etc/fstab << endofinput
# <file system> <mount point> <type> <options>                <dump> <pass>
/dev/hda1          /            ext2   defaults,errors=remount-ro  0      1
proc            /proc          proc   defaults                   0      0
endofinput

   e2fsck -y /dev/hdc1

   rm -rf $TMPMOUNT
   mkdir $TMPMOUNT
   mount /dev/hdc1 $TMPMOUNT

   echo -n "Do you want to erase the /dev/hdc1 partition, continue yes/no? "
   read deleteall

   if [ $deleteall == "yes" ]
   then
       # this deletes everything on your partition, WATCH OUT!!
       rm -rf $TMPMOUNT/*
       mkdir $TMPMOUNT/lost+found
   fi

   cp -av $ROOTFSLOC/* $TMPMOUNT

   /sbin/lilo -C /tmp/lilo.conf.1

   cd /
   umount $TMPMOUNT
   rm -rf $TMPMOUNT
```

LISTING 4.1   Continued

```
    e2fsck -y /dev/hdc1
fi


#hdc1ok
fi

echo Step 9 - Complete
echo

echo Your $ARCH root filesystem        is  $ROOTFSLOC
```

Creating the `root` Filesystem

The Project Trailblazer engineers' decision to use the MontaVista compiled versions of the binary, library, and configuration files that are required in order for the kernel to execute `init` and `bash` was just the beginning. Many Linux programs aren't distributed singly; rather, they're grouped by functionality and distributed as a package. For example, the `ls` program doesn't exist as the `ls` package, nor does the `ls` source code exist on its own. The GNU developers bundled `ls` and other file utilities into the `fileutils` package, which contains `chgrp`, `chmod`, `chown`, `cp`, `dd`, `df`, `dir`, `dircolors`, `du`, `install`, `ln`, `ls`, `mkdir`, `mkfifo`, `mknod`, `mv`, `rm`, `rmdir`, `touch`, `vdir`, and `sync`. If you want only the `ls` program, you have to extract it from the `fileutils` package.

You should extract files from packages into a temporary directory. After all the packages are extracted, the required binaries from Table 4.1 should be copied from the temporary directory to a new `root` filesystem directory. Linux distribution packages, whether they're Red Hat Package Management (RPMs[2]) files or Debian Package Management (debs[3]) files, contain extra files, such as man pages, that may not have any application in the new `root` filesystem. These extra files just take up space. When you build the `root` filesystem, the contents of a package are extracted to a temporary directory and then you can copy required files to the new `root` filesystem directory. Later, this new `root` filesystem directory can be used to create the actual `root` filesystem that the target systems will mount.

Deciding Which Package to Use

The engineers used the Debian Web site (www.debian.org) to determine what packages contained the programs the new `root` filesystem requires. They searched the Debian package section (www.debian.org/distrib/packages) for the program they wanted, using the "search on descriptions" option. For example, they found that the ls program is contained in the fileutils package. If they couldn't determine which package to use for a program, they explored the MontaVista Journeyman FTP site (ftp.mvista.com) to find it. Table 4.2 shows the engineers' list of files from Table 4.1 and the packages in which these programs are contained.

TABLE 4.2 Packages Required for the Target root Filesystem

MontaVista Journeyman Package	File
netbase	/etc/protocols
	/etc/services
bash	/bin/bash
textutils	/bin/cat
shellutils	/bin/echo
fileutils	/bin/ls
	/bin/df
	/bin/chmod
	/bin/touch
	/bin/rm
mount	/bin/mount
	/bin/umount
procps	/bin/ps
	/bin/kill
	/lib/libproc.so.2.0.7
netkit-ping	/bin/ping
sysvint	/sbin/init
net-tools	/sbin/ifconfig
	/sbin/route
glibc-2.2.3	/lib/ld-2.2.3.so
	/lib/ld.so.1
	/lib/libc-2.2.3.so
	/lib/libc.so.6
	/lib/libutil-2.2.3.so
	/lib/libutil.so.1
	/lib/libdl-2.2.3.so
	/lib/libdl.so.2
	/lib/libnss_dns-2.2.3.so
	/lib/libnss_dns.so.2
	/lib/libnss_files-2.2.3.so
	/lib/libnss_files.so.2
	/lib/libresolv-2.2.3.so
	/lib/libresolv.so.2
	/lib/libpthread-0.9.so

TABLE 4.2   Continued

MontaVista Journeyman Package	File
	/lib/libpthread.so.0
	/lib/libm-2.2.3.so
	/lib/libm.so.6
	/lib/librt-2.2.3.so
	/lib/librt.so.1
libncurses	/lib/libncurses.so.5
	/lib/libncurses.so.5.2
libstdc++	/lib/libstdc++-3-libc6.1-2-2.10.0.so
	/lib/libstdc++-libc6.1-2.so.3
netkit-telnet-client	/usr/bin/telnet
gdbserver-5.0	/usr/bin/gdbserver

The Process for Building the `root` Filesystem

The procedure for building a `root` filesystem consists of the two steps: Edit the `buildrootfilesystem` script PACKAGES line, incorporating the package information from Table 4.2, and then execute the `buildrootfilesystem` script. The `buildrootfilesystem` script performs the following operations:

1. It determines what packages to download.

2. It creates the build and new target `root` filesystem directories.

3. It downloads the packages defined in the PACKAGES script line.

4. It extracts the packages' contents into a temporary directory.

5. It copies the required programs (see Table 4.2) from the temporary directory to the new target `root` filesystem directory.

TIP

Do you want the `buildrootfilesystem` script to add another program to your `root` filesystem? If so, determine which package contains the program you want. Edit the `buildroot-filesystem` script, add the package name to the PACKAGES line, add the program name to the script's step 5 section and re-run the script.

---

6. It strips the required programs of their debugging information. (Many programs are compiled with the `-g` debugging flag, which creates executables that have larger file sizes. You're probably not going to debug these particular executables, so you can strip the debugging information to get more file space.)

7. It creates the extra configuration files, such as `inittab` and `rcS`.

8. It creates devices in the /dev directory.

9. It prepares the new root filesystem for operation on the target board.

Running buildrootfilesystem

buildrootfilesystem simplifies the creation of the root filesystem for the ARM, PowerPC, and i386 target boards. This script downloads the current versions of packages, extracts their contents, copies required programs, strips these programs of their debugging information, creates configuration files, creates devices, and prepares the root filesystem for target board operation. Before you run the buildrootfilesystem script, you need to add two additional packages to the tbdev1 workstation that you built in Chapter 3: lynx and alien. The buildrootfilesystem script uses lynx in dump mode to get the contents of an FTP directory. alien converts packages from one format to another (for example, it converts an RPM file to a compressed tar archive). You can start building the root filesystem by installing lynx and alien and then downloading the buildrootfilesystem script from the Web site. On tbdev1, log in as root and execute these commands:

```
root@tbdev1[501]: apt-get -y install lynx
root@tbdev1[502]: apt-get -y install alien
root@tbdev1[503]: cd /root/cross
root@tbdev1[504]: wget http://www.embeddedlinuxinterfacing.com/chapters/04/
➥buildrootfilesystem/buildrootfilesystem
root@tbdev1[505]: chmod 755 buildrootfilesystem
```

The following sections describe the buildrootfilesystem script steps.

Step 1: Determine What Packages to Download
The Project Trailblazer engineers determined what packages are required for the root filesystem. They edited the PACKAGES line in the buildrootfilesystem script. Step 1 sets the PACKAGES variable:

```
PACKAGES="glibc-2 bash procps textutils fileutils shellutils sysvinit netbase
➥ libncurses libstdc mount telnet-client net-tools ping gdbserver"
```

Step 2: Create the Build and New Target root Filesystem Directories
Step 2 of the buildrootfilesystem script creates the build and the new target root filesystem directories. You can use the same build directory from Chapter 2: /root/cross/build. A separate directory, one per architecture within /root/cross/build, holds the downloaded RPMs. buildrootfilesystem then creates a separate root filesystem directory in /tftpboot for each architecture—in the case of Project Trailblazer, /tftpboot/powerpc-rootfs, /tfpboot/arm-rootfs, and

/tftpboot/i386-rootfs. In Chapter 5, "Debugging," targets use the /tftpboot directories to mount their root filesystems using Network File System (NFS).

Within the root filesystem, buildrootfilesystem creates these directories: dev, etc,
etc/init.d, bin, sbin, lib, usr, usr/bin, proc, and tmp.

Step 3: Download the Packages

Step 3 of the buildrootfilesystem script uses lynx to download the current list of
files at the MontaVista FTP site. From this list, buildrootfilesystem scans PACKAGES
and downloads the package RPM file by using wget.

Step 4: Extract the Packages' Contents into a Temporary Directory

The MontaVista binaries are contained within an RPM file. You don't want to install
the entire RPM file contents; you just want to extract the contents to a temporary
directory. The program alien converts the RPM into a compressed tar archive
(called a tarball). Using tar decompresses the archive and extracts the contents
into a temporary directory. This seems like a lot of work, but this extraction instead
of installation into a temporary directory will make step 5 easier.

Step 5: Copy the Required Programs to the New Target root Filesystem Directory

The tar command from step 4 extracts the MontaVista binaries in the temporary
directory, for example /root/cross/builds/powerpc-rootrpms/opt/hardhat/
devkit/ppc/8xx/target. Step 5 of the buildrootfilesystem script changes into that
directory, and then copies the required binaries from lib, usr, sbin, bin, and
usr/bin to the new root filesystem directory.

In step 5, the script also creates helloworld.c in the /tmp directory and then
compiles it. We'll use this cross-compiled version of helloworld to verify PBR-6.

Step 6: Strip the Required Programs of Their Debugging Information

Step 6 of the buildrootfilesystem script uses the cross-compiled version of strip to
remove the debugging symbols from libraries and other binary executables within
the new target root filesystem. How can you tell if a binary contains debugging
symbols? You use the file command, as in the following example:

```
root@tbdev1[515]: cd /root/cross/builds/powerpc-rootrpms/
root@tbdev1[516]: cd opt/hardhat/devkit/ppc/8xx/target/

root@tbdev1[517]: file bin/bash
bin/bash: ELF 32-bit MSB executable, PowerPC or cisco 4500, version 1,
➥dynamically linked (uses shared libs), not stripped

root@tbdev1[518]: ls -l bin/bash
```

```
-rwxr-xr-x   1 5003     510         702350 May 23 15:16 bin/bash*

root@tbdev1[519]: powerpc-linux-strip -s -g bin/bash

root@tbdev1[520]: file bin/bash
bin/bash: ELF 32-bit MSB executable, PowerPC or cisco 4500, version 1,
➥dynamically linked (uses shared libs), stripped

root@tbdev1[521]: ls -l bin/bash
-rwxr-xr-x   1 5003     510         605480 Aug 23 15:08 bin/bash*
```

Step 7: Create Extra Configuration Files

Step 7 of the buildrootfilesystem script creates the following files:

File	Description
/etc/services	Provides a mapping between textual names for Internet services and their underlying assigned port numbers and protocol types
/etc/protocols	Describes Internet protocols within the TCP/IP subsystem
/etc/fstab	Provides information about various file systems used by mount
/etc/inittab	Describes processes that are started at bootup and during normal operation
/etc/init.d/rcS	Functions as a startup script that is run by init
/etc/init.d/umountfs	Functions as a shutdown script that is run by init to unmount filesystems
/etc/resolv.conf	Provides configuration information to the DNS resolver

Step 8: Create the Devices in the /dev Directory

Step 8 of the buildrootfilesystem script creates the tty, tty0, ttyS0, console, null, and ram devices in the /dev directory. These are the minimum devices needed for Linux to run.

Step 9: Prepare the root Filesystem for Operation on the Target Board

When step 8 completes, the new target root filesystem, located in /tftpboot /powerpc-rootfs, is almost ready for use. Step 9 of the buildrootfilesystem script prepares the root filesystem for the target board. The ARM and PowerPC target boards in field operation will extract the contents of their root filesystem into a RAM disk. The i386 platforms won't use a RAM disk; instead, they will use their flash memory as an IDE hard disk. During debugging in Chapter 5, this root filesystem won't exist as a RAM disk or hard disk. The platforms will mount their root filesystem over the Ethernet network via NFS, which makes remote debugging of code more efficient.

In summary, the preparation of the root filesystem is dependent on the field application and target board architecture. The specific preparations for Project Trailblazer are as follows:

- A. Field ARM and PowerPC target boards require a root filesystem for RAM disk use.

- B. Field i386 target boards require the root filesystem to exist on their Flash IDE disk drives.

- C. For debugging, the root filesystem will be mounted over the network, using NFS.

Each preparation requires different procedures, as described in the following sections.

Step 9, Preparation A: The root **Filesystem on a RAM Disk**
If it is configured with RAM disk support, the kernel contains code to create a disk drive in RAM memory, extract the contents of this RAM disk from another location, and then mount this RAM disk as its root filesystem. This common procedure allows embedded system operation without a hard disk. Keep in mind that the RAM disk exists only until the power cycles or the machine reboots. The contents of the RAM disk are not typically stored across reboots. (Project Trailblazer accepts this limitation because no field unit will store information locally.)

To prepare a RAM disk, the buildrootfilesystem script implements these steps:

1. It creates a file, called ramrootfs, that is the same size as the final RAM disk.

2. It fills ramrootfs with zeros.

3. It makes a filesystem in ramrootfs.

4. It mounts ramrootfs using a loopback device.

5. It copies the contents of the target root filesystem directory to ramrootfs.

6. It unmounts ramrootfs.

7. It compresses ramrootfs.

Step 9 of the buildrootfilesystem script contains the commands to create, fill, and compress ramrootfs. See the section "Booting the Embedded Planet RPX-CLLF," later in this chapter for specific instructions on getting the PowerPC board booted using ramrootfs. See the section "Booting the Brightstar Engineering MediaEngine," later in this chapter, for specific instructions to boot the ARM board.

Step 9, Preparation B: The root Filesystem on a Flash IDE Drive

The buildrootfilesystem script can completely configure an IDE drive to boot an i386 platform. With a partitioned drive, either hard disk or Flash disk, located as the master on tbdev1's secondary IDE controller (that is, /dev/hdc1), step 9 in the script creates additional devices, creates lilo and mount configuration files, copies the root filesystem to the drive, and executes lilo and installs lilo in the master boot record (MBR) of the second drive. When step 9 completes, you can place this second drive on the primary IDE controller, and Linux will boot from it. See the section "Booting i386 Platforms," later in this chapter for specific instructions to boot the i386 boards.

TIP

buildrootfilesystem gives you the option to erase all the files in /dev/hdc1 to effectively make a clean minimum root filesystem. Make sure that you have your disk drives connected properly before you erase all the files.

Step 9, Preparation C: The root Filesystem for NFS Mounting

Chapter 5 addresses mounting the target root filesystem using NFS. See that chapter for more information.

Installing the TFTP Server

TheMediaEngine and RPX-CLLF bootloaders can download files over Ethernet using Trivial File Transfer Protocol (TFTP). The bootloader configures the target board's Ethernet hardware and can download the kernel and RAM disk files into specific RAM locations. The user can then execute the kernel located in memory. The target specific commands for doing this are covered in the following sections. This section shows how to configure the tbdev1 workstation as a TFTP server.

TFTP is a simple file transfer protocol that doesn't require authentication. TFTP servers primarily serve boot images over a network to diskless workstations (such as Project Trailblazer's MediaEngine and RPX-CLLF boards). Follow these steps to install and configure a TFTP server on tbdev1:

1. Install the TFTP server and the client on the tbdev1 workstation by using these commands:

```
root@tbdev1[520]: apt-get install tftpd
root@tbdev1[521]: apt-get install tftp
```

/etc/rc.d/init.d/xinetd resTarT

/etc/xinetd.d/Tftp

Red Hat 7.2

dgram

udp

yes

rooT

/usr/sbin/in.TftPd

-s /tftpbooT

no

Red Hat 7.3

dgram

udp

yes

rooT

/usr/sbin/in.tftpd

-s /tftpbooT

no

11

100,2

2. Configure the server by modifying its configuration file, /etc/inet.conf. Edit /etc/inet.conf, and then search for tftp. Make the tftp line look like this:

```
tftp dgram udp wait  nobody  /usr/sbin/tcpd  /usr/sbin/in.tftpd /tftpboot
```

This tells the TFTP server what directory (/tftpboot) to use for TFTP client requests.

3. Change the permissions on /tftpboot to 755 by using this command:

```
root@tbdev1[525]: chmod 755 /tftpboot/
```

4. Changing /etc/inet.conf requires that you signal the inetd program to reload its configuration file. Use the ps command to get the process ID, and then use the kill command to send the HUP signal:

```
root@tbdev1[526]: ps x | grep inetd
147  ?        S    0:00 /usr/sbin/inetd
root@tbdev1[527]: kill -HUP 147
```

5. Test the TFTP server installation. As root, create the file /tftpboot/test and put something in it (for example, "This is a test"); make this test file readable by all users:

```
root@tbdev1[509]: echo "This is a test" > /tftpboot/test
root@tbdev1[510]: chmod 666 /tftpboot/test
```

6. Change directory into /tmp and type the command tftp 192.168.1.11. You should get a TFTP prompt. Type get test, and the test file should transfer. Then type quit. The transfer occurs via TFTP to the /tmp directory. You should have a file called /tmp/test. Here are the commands that implement this test:

```
root@tbdev1[528]: cd /tmp
root@tbdev1[529]: tftp 192.168.1.11
tftp> get test
Received 16 bytes in 0.0 seconds
tftp> quit
root@tbdev1[530]: cat /tmp/test
This is a test
```

-p30 "PC computers IP

Booting the ARM and PowerPC targets requires a TFTP server, and tbdev1 workstation now has a configured and tested TFTP server.

Installing `minicom`

The ARM and PowerPC bootloaders communicate with the host over a serial line at 9600 baud. The bootloader commands are issued over this serial link. The `tbdev1` workstation requires a serial terminal emulation program called `minicom` to issue boot commands to the target boards. Here are the commands to install `minicom` on `tbdev1`:

```
root@tbdev1[531]: apt-get install minicom
```

After `minicom` is installed, you need to configure `minicom`'s serial port by following these steps:

1. Run `minicom`:

   ```
   root@tbdev1[532]: minicom
   ```

2. Configure `minicom` by typing CTRL-a o, select "Serial port setup", and then change your settings to match these:

   ```
   A -     Serial Device      : /dev/ttyS0
   B - Lockfile Location      : /var/lock
   C -    Callin Program      :
   D -   Callout Program      :
   E -     Bps/Par/Bits       : 9600 8N1
   F - Hardware Flow Control : No
   G - Software Flow Control : No
   ```

   Exit from this screen.

3. Select "Save setup as dfl", and then exit from this screen.

4. Exit from `minicom` by typing CTRL-a q.

Now that the `root` filesystem is created and properly prepared, the TFTP server is configured, tested, and running, and `minicom` is installed, you are now ready to boot the target boards.

Booting the Embedded Planet RPX-CLLF

Before you can boot the RPX-CLLF, you need to compile the kernel for it. The `buildtoolchain` script in Chapter 3 configured the kernel and its kernel headers but didn't compile the kernel. This section describes how to compile the 2.4.7 kernel for the RPX-CLLF, create an image file consisting of the kernel and a RAM disk, download the image file to the RPX-CLLF, and boot the RPX-CLLF. Here are the steps for booting the RPX-CLLF:

1. Change directory to the PowerPC kernel source:

   ```
   root@tbdev1[501]: cd /usr/src/powerpc-linux
   ```

2. A default configuration file for RPX-CLLF exists in `arch/ppc/configs/`
   `rpxcllf_defconfig`. Configure the kernel using this default config file, with
   two `make` commands:

   ```
   root@tbdev1[502]: make rpxcllf_config
   root@tbdev1[503]: make oldconfig
   ```

3. You need to change one setting in the kernel configuration. The default RAM
   disk size is too small. The PowerPC `root` filesystem requires more than 4096KB
   of disk space. Run `make menuconfig`, select `"Block devices"`, and then change
   the default RAM disk size to 8192. Then, exit twice and select Yes to save the
   new kernel configuration.

4. Use these commands to compile the kernel and make an image file with a RAM
   disk for the RPX-CLLF.

   ```
   root@tbdev1[504]: make dep
   root@tbdev1[505]: make zImage.initrd
   ```

   You're likely to get this error:

   ```
   powerpc-linux-objcopy: cannot stat: ../images/ramdisk.image.gz:
   ➥No such file or directory
   ```

   This error means `make` couldn't find the RAM disk file. You need to rerun
   `buildrootfilesystem` script again, with the `ramdisk` option:

   ```
   root@tbdev1[506]: cd /root/cross/buildrootfilesystem
   root@tbdev1[507]: buildrootfilesystem ppc ramdisk
   ```

   This creates a PowerPC RAM disk file in two locations: `/tftpboot/` and
   `/usr/src/powerpc-linux/arch/ppc/boot/images`:

   ```
   root@tbdev1[512]: cd /tftpboot/
   root@tbdev1[514]: ls -l powerpc-ramdisk.gz
   -rw-r--r-- 1 root     root      1791234 Aug 24 01:15 powerpc-ramdisk.gz
   root@tbdev1[515]: cd /usr/src/powerpc-linux/arch/ppc/boot/images
   root@tbdev1[516]: ls -l ramdisk.image.gz
   -rw-r--r-- 1 root     root      1791234 Aug 24 01:15 ramdisk.image.gz
   ```

5. Change directory back to the kernel directory and rerun `make zImage.initrd`:

```
root@tbdev1[517]: cd /usr/src/powerpc-linux/
root@tbdev1[518]: make zImage.initrd
```

This time you should be successful in creating the `zImage.initrd` file called `zImage.initrd.embedded` in the `arch/ppc/boot/images` directory.

6. Copy `zImage.initrd.embedded` to `/tftproot/powerpc-zImage`:

```
root@tbdev1[520]: cp arch/ppc/boot/images/zImage.initrd.embedded
➥/tftpboot/powerpc-zImage
```

The RPX-CLLF kernel and RAM disk image combination file called `powerpc-zImage` that is located in `/tftpboot` is ready to be downloaded and booted.

7. Connect RPX-CLLF's serial port `ttyS0` to tbdev1's `ttyS0` (COM1) port. Run minicom and reboot the RPX-CLLF. Look for the PlanetCore `Bootloader` banner:

```
PlanetCore Boot Loader v1.02
Copyright 2000 Embedded Planet.  All rights reserved.
DRAM available size = 16 MB
wvCV
DRAM OK
Autoboot in 2 seconds.
ESC to abort, SPACE or ENTER to go.
PlanetCore Diagnostics and Utilities - Release 2.01
pcd#q
>
```

If the PlanetCore Diagnostics program starts running (at the `pcd` prompt), exit the program by typing q `return`; this gives you the bootloader prompt (>).

8. Use the `tftp` program to download `powerpc-zImage`. Downloading the image to address offset of 400000 puts the image in the middle of the RAM space. The kernel and RAM disk decompression should occur without errors. Here are the RPX-CLLF `TFTP` commands and the go instruction to boot the kernel:

```
>tftp
Load using tftp via Ethernet
Enter server IP address <192.168.1.11> : 192.168.1.11
Enter server filename   <powerpc-zImage> : powerpc-zImage
Enter (B)inary or (S)record input mode <S> : B
Enter address offset  : <FFF80000 hex> : 400000
.1.2.4.8.16.32.64.128.256.512.1024.2048.4096
Total bytes = 2313209 in 4136171 uSecs
```

```
Loaded addresses 00400000 through 00634BF8.
Start address = 00400000
>
>go
[Go 00400000]
loaded at:     00400000 0040B580
relocated to:  00180000 0018B580
board data at: 001801C0 001801DC
relocated to:  00200100 0020011C
zimage at:     00408000 0047DE2D
initrd at:     0047DE2D 0063332F
avail ram:     00634000 01000000

Linux/PPC load: root=/dev/ram
Uncompressing Linux...done.
Now booting the kernel
Linux version 2.4.7 (root@tbdev1) (gcc version 2.95.3 20010315 (release)) #3
➡ Fri Aug 24 01:22:07 MST 2001

On node 0 totalpages: 4096
zone(0): 4096 pages.
zone(1): 0 pages.
zone(2): 0 pages.
Kernel command line: root=/dev/ram
Decrementer Frequency = 180000000/60
Calibrating delay loop... 47.82 BogoMIPS
Memory: 13016k available (920k kernel code, 332k data, 52k init, 0k highmem)
Dentry-cache hash table entries: 2048 (order: 2, 16384 bytes)
Inode-cache hash table entries: 1024 (order: 1, 8192 bytes)
Mount-cache hash table entries: 512 (order: 0, 4096 bytes)
Buffer-cache hash table entries: 1024 (order: 0, 4096 bytes)
Page-cache hash table entries: 4096 (order: 2, 16384 bytes)
POSIX conformance testing by UNIFIX
Linux NET4.0 for Linux 2.4
Based upon Swansea University Computer Society NET3.039
Starting kswapd v1.8
Starting kswapd v1.8
CPM UART driver version 0.03
ttyS00 at 0x0280 is a SMC
ttyS01 at 0x0380 is a SMC
ttyS02 at 0x0100 is a SCC
ttyS03 at 0x0200 is a SCC
```

```
pty: 256 Unix98 ptys configured
block: queued sectors max/low 8554kB/2851kB, 64 slots per queue
RAMDISK driver initialized: 16 RAM disks of 8192K size 1024 blocksize
eth0: CPM ENET Version 0.2 on SCC1, 00:10:ec:00:26:41
fec.c[1367] mii_link_interrupt: unexpected Link interrupt
eth1: FEC ENET Version 0.2, FEC irq 3, addr 00:10:ec:80:26:41
loop: loaded (max 8 devices)
NET4: Linux TCP/IP 1.0 for NET4.0
IP Protocols: ICMP, UDP, TCP, IGMP
IP: routing cache hash table of 512 buckets, 4Kbytes
TCP: Hash tables configured (established 1024 bind 1024)
NET4: Unix domain sockets 1.0/SMP for Linux NET4.0.
RAMDISK: Compressed image found at block 0
Freeing initrd memory: 1749k freed
VFS: Mounted root (ext2 filesystem).
INIT: version 2.78 bootingry: 52k initú
INIT: Entering runlevel: 2
Starting Network
bash-2.04#
```

You are now at the bash prompt.

9. Try out the network connection and check for proper DNS configuration:

```
bash-2.04# ping yahoo.com
PING yahoo.com (216.115.108.243): 56 data bytes
64 bytes from 216.115.108.243: icmp_seq=0 ttl=246 time=72.5 ms
64 bytes from 216.115.108.243: icmp_seq=1 ttl=246 time=91.8 ms
64 bytes from 216.115.108.243: icmp_seq=2 ttl=246 time=139.2 ms

--- yahoo.com ping statistics ---
3 packets transmitted, 3 packets received, 0% packet loss
round-trip min/avg/max = 72.5/101.1/139.2 ms
```

TIP

The ping program's output tells whether DNS is working. When you ping a host by name, its IP address is returned in the output, meaning that DNS is configured properly and is operational.

Pinging yahoo.com returns the IP address 216.115.108.243, which confirms proper DNS configuration. Pings are returned, so you know the network is running.

10. Run helloworld, which is located in the /tmp directory:

```
bash-2.04# cd /tmp
bash-2.04# ls -l
total 31
-rwxr-xr-x 1 0    0        28931 Aug 24  2001 helloworld-powerpc-linux
-rw-r--r-- 1 0    0          120 Aug 24  2001 helloworld.c
bash-2.04# ./helloworld-powerpc-linux
Hello world 1 times!
Hello world 2 times!
Hello world 3 times!
Hello world 4 times!
Hello world 5 times!
Hello world 6 times!
Hello world 7 times!
Hello world 8 times!
Hello world 9 times!
```

The Embedded Planet RPX-CLLF is now up and running.

Embedded Planet RPX-CLLF Target PBR Review

In this section, the seven PBRs are reviewed for the RPX-CLLF. The output from the "Booting the Embedded Planet RPX-CLLF" section earlier in the chapter provides all the information necessary for this review. Remember that each target board needs to fulfill the seven PBRs in order to be used in Project Trailblazer.

PBR-1 for the RPX-CLLF

The target board should use Linux kernel 2.4 or greater. Here's the RPX-CLLF console output during the boot process:

```
Now booting the kernel
Linux version 2.4.7 (root@tbdev1) (gcc version 2.95.3 20010315 (release)) #3
➥Fri Aug 24 01:22:07 MST 2001
```

PBR-1 is fulfilled because Linux version 2.4.7 boots.

PBR-2 for the RPX-CLLF

The target board will execute the bash shell. Exiting from the bash shell re-executes the bash shell. On the RPX-CLLF console, exit from the bash shell by using the exit command:

```
bash-2.04# exit
exit
bash-2.04#
```

PBR-2 is fulfilled because exiting from bash respawns bash. init is properly configured.

PBR-3 for the RPX-CLLF

The system should execute the bash shell without security authentication. Here's the RPX-CLLF console output during the boot process:

```
INIT: version 2.78 bootingry: 52k initú
INIT: Entering runlevel: 2
Starting Network
bash-2.04#
```

PBR-3 is fulfilled because init starts bash without authentication.

PBR-4 for the RPX-CLLF

The system should boot, initialize the Ethernet hardware, set a static IP address, and be configured to use DNS. At the bash prompt, use ifconfig to display Ethernet hardware configuration and use ping to verify proper DNS configuration:

```
bash-2.04# ifconfig
eth0      Link encap:Ethernet  HWaddr 00:10:EC:00:26:41
          inet addr:192.168.1.22  Bcast:192.168.1.255  Mask:255.255.255.0
          UP BROADCAST RUNNING MULTICAST  MTU:1500  Metric:1
          RX packets:44 errors:0 dropped:0 overruns:0 frame:0
          TX packets:7 errors:0 dropped:0 overruns:0 carrier:0
          collisions:0 txqueuelen:100
          Base address:0x3c00
bash-2.04# ping yahoo.com
PING yahoo.com (216.115.108.243): 56 data bytes
64 bytes from 216.115.108.243: icmp_seq=0 ttl=246 time=72.5 ms
```

PBR-4 is fulfilled because the Ethernet hardware is initialized. The target board's resolver translated yahoo.com to 216.115.108.243. This verifies proper DNS configuration.

PBR-5 for the RPX-CLLF

The system should contain the ping program to debug network programs.

```
bash-2.04# ping yahoo.com
PING yahoo.com (216.115.108.243): 56 data bytes
64 bytes from 216.115.108.243: icmp_seq=0 ttl=246 time=72.5 ms
```

PBR-5 is fulfilled because the yahoo.com ping is successful.

PBR-6 for the RPX-CLLF

The system should be capable of executing the Project Trailblazer compiled version of helloworld. At the bash prompt, execute the cross-compiled helloworld program.

```
bash-2.04# ./helloworld-powerpc-linux
Hello world 1 times!
Hello world 2 times!
Hello world 3 times!
. . .
```

PBR-6 is fulfilled because the cross-compiled version of helloworld executes.

PBR-7 for the RPX-CLLF

The system should use the current version of GNU glibc. At the bash, list the library directory and confirm current versions:

```
bash-2.04# ls /lib
ld-2.2.3.so       libncurses.so.5.2      libresolv.so.2
ld.so.1           libnss_dns-2.2.3.so    librt-2.2.3.so
libc-2.2.3.so     libnss_dns.so.2        librt.so.1
libc.so.6         libnss_files-2.2.3.so  libstdc++-3-libc6.1-2-2.10.0.so
libdl-2.2.3.so    libnss_files.so.2      libstdc++-libc6.1-2.so.3
libdl.so.2        libproc.so.2.0.7       libutil-2.2.3.so
libm-2.2.3.so     libpthread-0.9.so      libutil.so.1
libm.so.6         libpthread.so.0
libncurses.so.5   libresolv-2.2.3.so
```

PBR-7 is fulfilled because the target boots with the current version of GNU glibc.

The Embedded Planet RPX-CLLF fulfills all the PBRs.

Booting the Brightstar Engineering MediaEngine

Before you can boot the MediaEngine, you need to compile the kernel for it. The buildtoolchain script in Chapter 3 configured the kernel and the kernel headers but didn't compile the kernel. This section describes how to compile the 2.4.2 kernel for the MediaEngine, generate a RAM disk, download the kernel and RAM disk using TFTP, and then boot the MediaEngine. Booting the MediaEngine differs from booting the RPX-CLLF in that the kernel and RAM files are downloaded separately.

Here are the steps for booting the MediaEngine:

1. Change directory to the ARM kernel source:

   ```
   root@tbdev1[553]: cd /usr/src/arm-linux
   ```

2. The MediaEngine and Brightstar Engineering's nanoEngine share the same default configuration file: `arch/arm/def-config/nanoengine`. Configure the kernel by using this default config file and two `make` commands:

```
root@tbdev1[554]: make nanoengine_config
root@tbdev1[555]: make oldconfig
```

3. The RAM disk defaults to 8192KB, so you don't need to change that with `make menuconfig`.

4. Compile the kernel:

```
root@tbdev1[555]: make zImage
```

5. The new kernel image is `arch/arm/boot/zImage`. Copy it to the `/tftpboot` directory:

```
root@tbdev1[556]: cp arch/arm/boot/zImage /tftpboot/arm-zImage
```

6. Make the ARM target `root` filesystem by using the `buildrootfilesystem` script:

```
root@tbdev1[557]: cd /root/cross/buildrootfilesystem
root@tbdev1[558]: buildrootfilesystem arm ramdisk
buildrootfilesystem will create the ARM target root filesystem file
➥called /tftpboot/arm-ramdisk.gz
```

7. Connect the MediaEngine's serial port to `tbdev1`'s COM1 port. Run `minicom` and then reboot the MediaEngine. Look for the Brightstar Engineering (BSE) banner

```
Boot: BSE 2001 R1.0 SN# 00:50:15:03:00:19
>
```

8. Set the MediaEngine's IP address, TFTP server, and netmask addresses by using these commands:

```
>set myip 192.168.1.21
>set serverip 192.168.1.11
>set netmask 255.255.255.0
```

9. Download the ARM RAM disk file:

```
>load arm-ramdisk.gz c0800000
loading ... 1699015 bytes loaded cksum 0000D9C8
 done
```

10. Download the ARM kernel file:

```
>load arm-zImage c0008000
loading ... 646240 bytes loaded cksum 00004DF2
 done
```

11. Boot the kernel by executing go at memory address c0008000:

```
>go c0008000
```

12. The MediaEngine should boot, and you should see this:

```
Uncompressing Linux........................ done, booting the kernel.
Linux version 2.4.2-rmk1-np2-bse (root@tbdev1) (gcc version 2.95.3 20010315
➥(release)) #1 Fri Aug 24 14:53:14 MST 2001

Processor: Intel StrongARM-1110 revision 6
Architecture: BSE nanoEngine
On node 0 totalpages: 8192
zone(0): 8192 pages.
zone(1): 0 pages.
zone(2): 0 pages.
Kernel command line: root=/dev/ram
Calibrating delay loop... 194.15 BogoMIPS
Memory: 32MB = 32MB total
Memory: 26496KB available (1268K code, 260K data, 60K init)
Dentry-cache hash table entries: 4096 (order: 3, 32768 bytes)
Buffer-cache hash table entries: 1024 (order: 0, 4096 bytes)
Page-cache hash table entries: 8192 (order: 3, 32768 bytes)
Inode-cache hash table entries: 2048 (order: 2, 16384 bytes)
POSIX conformance testing by UNIFIX
Linux NET4.0 for Linux 2.4
Based upon Swansea University Computer Society NET3.039
Starting kswapd v1.8
pty: 256 Unix98 ptys configured
block: queued sectors max/low 17530kB/5843kB, 64 slots per queue
RAMDISK driver initialized: 16 RAM disks of 8192K size 1024 blocksize
Uniform Multi-Platform E-IDE driver Revision: 6.31
ide: Assuming 50MHz system bus speed for PIO modes; override with idebus=xx
cerf89x0:cerf89x0_probe()
cerf89x0.c: (kernel 2.3.99) Russell Nelson, Andrew Morton
eth0: cs8900 rev J Base 0xF0000300<6>, IRQ 0, MAC 00:50:15:03:00:19
bad dev id: got 0x19001900, expected 0x12098086 (0)
bad dev id: got 0x19001900, expected 0x12098086 (0)
```

```
RAMDISK: Compressed image found at block 0
Freeing initrd memory: 4096K
loop: loaded (max 8 devices)
Serial driver version 5.02 (2000-08-09) with no serial options enabled
Testing ttyS0 (0x0300, 0x0000)...
ttyS03 at 0x0300 (irq = 10) is a 16550A
SA1100 serial driver version 1.3
ttyS0 on SA1100 UART1 (irq 15)
ttyS1 on SA1100 UART2 (irq 16)
ttyS2 on SA1100 UART3 (irq 17)
SA1100 Real Time Clock Driver v0.02
PPP generic driver version 2.4.1
PPP Deflate Compression module registered
PPP BSD Compression module registered
Linux PCMCIA Card Services 3.1.22
  options:  none
SA-1100 PCMCIA (CS release 3.1.22)
NET4: Linux TCP/IP 1.0 for NET4.0
IP Protocols: ICMP, UDP, TCP
IP: routing cache hash table of 512 buckets, 4Kbytes
TCP: Hash tables configured (established 2048 bind 2048)
IP-Config: Incomplete network configuration information.
NET4: Unix domain sockets 1.0/SMP for Linux NET4.0.
NetWinder Floating Point Emulator V0.95 (c) 1998-1999 Rebel.com
VFS: Mounted root (ext2 filesystem).
Freeing init memory: 60K
INIT: version 2.78 booting
INIT: Entering runlevel: 2
Starting Network
bash-2.04#
```

You are now at the bash prompt on the MediaEngine.

13. Try out the network connection and check for proper DNS configuration:

```
bash-2.04# ping yahoo.com
PING yahoo.com (216.115.108.245): 56 data bytes
64 bytes from 216.115.108.245: icmp_seq=0 ttl=246 time=49.7 ms
64 bytes from 216.115.108.245: icmp_seq=1 ttl=246 time=55.5 ms
64 bytes from 216.115.108.245: icmp_seq=2 ttl=246 time=57.8 ms
64 bytes from 216.115.108.245: icmp_seq=3 ttl=246 time=100.8 ms
```

```
--- yahoo.com ping statistics ---
4 packets transmitted, 4 packets received, 0% packet loss
round-trip min/avg/max = 49.7/65.9/100.8 ms
```

Pinging yahoo.com returns the IP address 216.115.108.245, which confirms proper DNS configuration. Pings are returned, so you know the network is running.

14. Run helloworld, which is located in the /tmp directory:

```
bash-2.04# cd /tmp
bash-2.04# ls -l
total 24
-rwxr-xr-x    1 0         0     22266 Aug 24  2001 helloworld-arm-linux
-rw-r--r--    1 0         0       120 Aug 24  2001 helloworld.c
bash-2.04# ./helloworld-arm-linux
Hello world 1 times!
Hello world 2 times!
Hello world 3 times!
Hello world 4 times!
Hello world 5 times!
Hello world 6 times!
Hello world 7 times!
Hello world 8 times!
Hello world 9 times!
```

The Brightstar Engineering MediaEngine is now up and running.

Brightstar Engineering MediaEngine Target PBR Review

In this section, the seven PBRs are reviewed for the MediaEngine. The output from the "Booting the Brightstar Engineering MediaEngine" section earlier in the chapter provides all the information necessary for this review. Remember that each target board needs to fulfill the seven PBRs in order to be used in Project Trailblazer.

PBR-1 for Brightstar Engineering MediaEngine

The target board should use Linux kernel 2.4 or greater. Here's the MediaEngine console output during the boot process:

```
Linux version 2.4.2-rmk1-np2-bse (root@tbdev1) (gcc version 2.95.3 20010315
➡(release)) #1 Fri Aug 24 14:53:14 MST 2001
```

```
Processor: Intel StrongARM-1110 revision 6
Architecture: BSE nanoEngine
```

PBR-1 is fulfilled because Linux version 2.4.2 boots.

PBR-2 for Brightstar Engineering MediaEngine

The target board will execute the bash shell. Exiting from the bash shell re-executes
the bash shell. On the MediaEngine console, exit from the bash shell by using the
exit command:

```
bash-2.04# exit
exit
bash-2.04#
```

PBR-2 is fulfilled because exiting from bash respawns bash. init is properly configured.

PBR-3 for Brightstar Engineering MediaEngine

The system should execute the bash shell without security authentication. Here's the
MediaEngine console output during the boot process:

```
INIT: version 2.78 booting
INIT: Entering runlevel: 2
Starting Network
bash-2.04#
```

PBR-3 is fulfilled because init starts bash without authentication.

PBR-4 for Brightstar Engineering MediaEngine

The system should boot, initialize the Ethernet hardware, set a static IP address, and
be configured to use DNS. At the bash prompt, use ifconfig to display the Ethernet
hardware configuration and use ping to verify proper DNS configuration:

```
bash-2.04# ifconfig
eth0      Link encap:Ethernet  HWaddr 00:50:15:03:00:19
          inet addr:192.168.1.21  Bcast:192.168.1.255  Mask:255.255.255.0
          UP BROADCAST RUNNING MULTICAST  MTU:1500  Metric:1
          RX packets:5 errors:0 dropped:2 overruns:0 frame:0
          TX packets:0 errors:0 dropped:0 overruns:0 carrier:0
          collisions:0 txqueuelen:100
          Base address:0x300
bash-2.04# ping yahoo.com
PING yahoo.com (216.115.108.243): 56 data bytes
64 bytes from 216.115.108.243: icmp_seq=0 ttl=246 time=66.3 ms
64 bytes from 216.115.108.243: icmp_seq=1 ttl=246 time=68.8 ms
```

PBR-4 is fulfilled because the Ethernet hardware is initialized. The target board's resolver translated yahoo.com to 216.115.108.243. This verifies proper DNS configuration.

PBR-5 for Brightstar Engineering MediaEngine

The system should contain the ping program to debug network programs:

```
bash-2.04# ping yahoo.com
PING yahoo.com (216.115.108.243): 56 data bytes
64 bytes from 216.115.108.243: icmp_seq=0 ttl=246 time=66.3 ms
64 bytes from 216.115.108.243: icmp_seq=1 ttl=246 time=68.8 ms
```

PBR-5 is fulfilled because the yahoo.com ping is successful.

PBR-6 for Brightstar Engineering MediaEngine

The system should be capable of executing the Project Trailblazer compiled version of helloworld. At the bash prompt, execute the cross-compiled helloworld program:

```
bash-2.04# ./helloworld-arm-linux
Hello world 1 times!
Hello world 2 times!
Hello world 3 times!
. . .
```

PBR-6 is fulfilled because the cross-compiled version of helloworld executes.

PBR-7 for Brightstar Engineering MediaEngine

The system should use the current version of GNU glibc. At the bash prompt, list the library directory and confirm the current versions:

```
bash-2.04# ls /lib
ld-2.2.3.so libncurses.so.5.2 libresolv.so.2
ld-linux.so.2 libnss_dns-2.2.3.so librt-2.2.3.so
libc-2.2.3.so libnss_dns.so.2 librt.so.1
libc.so.6 libnss_files-2.2.3.so libstdc++-3-libc6.1-2-2.10.0.so
libdl-2.2.3.so libnss_files.so.2 libstdc++-libc6.1-2.so.3
libdl.so.2 libproc.so.2.0.7 libutil-2.2.3.so
libm-2.2.3.so libpthread-0.9.so libutil.so.1
libm.so.6 libpthread.so.0
libncurses.so.5 libresolv-2.2.3.so
```

PBR-7 is fulfilled because target boots with the current version of GNU glibc.

The Brightstar Engineering MediaEngine fulfills all the PBRs.

Booting the Tri-M MZ104 and the COTS PC with a Flash IDE Drive

The x86 CPU powers the final two targets: the Tri-M MZ104 and COTS PC. These targets boot from and use Flash IDE drives. This section presents the flash IDE technology selected and shows how to compile the kernel, create the target root filesystem, and prepare the flash drive for booting.

Flash IDE Technology

Flash technology has matured and provides a "no moving parts" solution for embedded designs. Flash ATA IDE drive capacity ranges from 8MB to 384MB, with single-piece pricing starting at $25 (as of fall 2001). The smallest size, 8MB, provides ample capacity for the Project Trailblazer root filesystem. The following components were selected for evaluation:

- SanDisk 8MB Compact Flash Card ($24.99, www.sandisk.com)

- SST58SD/LD32 32MB ATA-Disk Chip ($50.00, www.ssti.com/ata_disk/atabrief.pdf)

- PCEngines IDE to Compact Flash Adapter ($20.00, www.pcengines.com/cflash.htm)

- VersaLogic VL-CFA-1 CompactFlash Adapter ($70.00, www.versalogic.com)

TIP

Connecting a Compact Flash memory card to an IDE controller requires an adapter. Using Compact Flash IDE drives eliminates moving parts from your design.

Pricing shown here reflects the manufacturer's suggested retail price in fall 2001. The SanDisk Compact Flash Card and SST ATA-Disk chip claim 100% ATA IDE compatibility. This means the Project Trailblazer engineers should be able to treat it like a regular drive (that is, they should be able to use fdisk, format, copy, and so on). The engineers also discovered that removable IDE drive bays, such as the StarTech SNT127A (www.startech.com), ease swapping IDE drives during development.

Preparing the Tri-M MZ104 and the COTS PC

Installing Linux with a distribution CD, such as Debian or Red Hat, on a commercial off-the-shelf PC is easy. Just put in the CD, boot, and install. As you saw earlier in this chapter, a minimum Debian installation requires 67MB and Red Hat requires 382MB, both of which are beyond the capacity of the Project Trailblazer Flash IDE drives.

During these installations, what actually happens? The distribution installation program partitions the destination drive, and if necessary, formats the drive, creates directories, extracts files from an archive file into these directories, configures various systems and subsystems, prepares the drive to be bootable, and then reboots. Sounds simple enough, doesn't it?

Preparing the root filesystem presents the largest challenge for distribution vendors. They have to select from among the thousands of existing programs. The Project Trailblazer engineers decided earlier in this chapter what their target Linux machines require. They also know what configuration files are necessary to boot the target root filesystem. Therefore, they now have to partition and format the Flash IDE drive, compile the x86 kernel, build the target root filesystem on the IDE drive, and boot the target board.

Partitioning and Formatting the Flash IDE Drive
The Tri-M MZ104 or the COTS PC will boot from and mount its root filesystem from a Flash IDE drive. Here are the steps in partitioning and formatting the Flash IDE drive using tbdev1:

1. Using an IDE-to-Compact Flash adapter, connect the Compact Flash IDE drive to tbdev1's secondary controller. Set its jumper to master. Note that partitioning the Compact Flash IDE drive will destroy all data on it.

2. Boot tbdev1 and log in as root.

3. Use the dmesg command to get a report on the Compact Flash drive:

> **TIP**
>
> If your PC doesn't recognize the Compact Flash IDE drive, you might have to upgrade your PC BIOS.

```
root@tbdev1[506]: dmesg
Linux version 2.2.19pre17-idepci (root@oink) (gcc version 2.7.2.3) #1
BIOS-provided physical RAM map:
. . .
    ide0: BM-DMA at 0xf000-0xf007, BIOS settings: hda:pio, hdb:pio
    ide1: BM-DMA at 0xf008-0xf00f, BIOS settings: hdc:pio, hdd:pio
hda: Maxtor 85120 A8 -, ATA DISK drive
hdb: probing with STATUS(0x00) instead of ALTSTATUS(0x50)
hdb: probing with STATUS(0x00) instead of ALTSTATUS(0x50)
hdc: SunDisk SDCFB-40, ATA DISK drive
ide0 at 0x1f0-0x1f7,0x3f6 on irq 14
ide1 at 0x170-0x177,0x376 on irq 15
```

```
hda: Maxtor 85120 A8 -, 4884MB w/256kB Cache, CHS=622/255/63
hdc: SunDisk SDCFB-40, 38MB w/1kB Cache, CHS=612/4/32
```

The dmesg output shows that the SunDisk SDCFB-40 is located on hdc, which is the 40MB Flash disk.

4. Partition the drive with the cfdisk command on /dev/hdc:

TIP

fdisk and cfdisk both partition hard disks. cfdisk is easier to use.

```
root@tbdev1[507]: cfdisk /dev/hdc
```

5. The cfdisk screen presents a list of current partitions and a menu along the bottom. Use the up and down arrow keys to select from the partition list. Use the right and left arrow keys to select a menu item. Select the first partition, and then select Delete and press Enter. Continue until you have deleted all the drive partitions.

6. Select Free Space from the partition list.

7. Make a new partition by selecting the New menu, and then select Primary. Set the size to use the remainder of the drive space, and then press Enter.

8. The partition list should now have an hdc1 entry. With hdc1 selected, select the Type menu and set the type to 83 (Linux).

9. Select hdc1 from the partition list, and then make hdc1 bootable by selecting the Bootable menu.

10. Finalize this partitioning by selecting Write and confirm the write operation by typing **yes**.

11. Exit from the cfdisk screen by selecting Quit.

12. The partition you just created is /dev/hdc1. Format it with this command:

```
root@tbdev1[510]: mke2fs /dev/hdc1
```

13. Mount the drive on /mnt and check disk usage with these commands:

```
root@tbdev1[515]: mount /dev/hdc1 /mnt

root@tbdev1[516]: df

Filesystem          1k-blocks      Used Available Use% Mounted on
```

```
/dev/hda2              4854280    1838440    2769244    40% /

/dev/hdc1                37910         13      35940     0% /mnt
```

14. Unmount /dev/hdc1 by using this command:

```
root@tbdev1[517]: umount /dev/hdc1
```

The flash IDE drive is now ready for the kernel, the root filesystem, and booting preparation.

Compiling the i386 Kernel

Before you can boot the Tri-M MZ104 or COTS PC, you need to compile the kernel for it. This section describes how to compile the 2.4.10 kernel for the x86 target boards. Here are the steps to compile the x86 kernel:

1. Download the kernel source from www.kernel.org into the /usr/src directory. This example uses version 2.4.10:

```
root@tbdev1[503]: cd /usr/src
root@tbdev1[504]: wget  http://www.kernel.org/pub/linux/
➥kernel/v2.4/linux-2.4.10.tar.gz
```

2. Extract the kernel source from the downloaded compressed tar file:

```
root@tbdev1[505]: tar zxvf /root/cross/linux-2.4.10.tar.gz
```

3. You should now have a directory /usr/src/linux. Configure the kernel by using these commands:

```
root@tbdev1[506]: cd /usr/src/linux
root@tbdev1[507]: make mrproper
root@tbdev1[508]: make menuconfig
```

NOTE

For more kernel compiling information, please see "The Linux kernel HOWTO: Compiling the kernel."[4]

---

4. Scan through the menus and exclude (by using [ ]) anything you don't require, such as SCSI support, sound, plug-and-play, or USB. The more items you exclude, the smaller the kernel. For now, don't compile anything as modules. Items you do want built in (marked by [*]) include the following:

- Processor type and features (select your processor family, the MZ104 has a 486 processor)

- Network device support

    - Select Ethernet (10Mbps or 100Mbps)

    - Select Other ISA cards

    - Select NE2000/NE1000 support, the MZ104 has an NE2000 ISA card.

    - Remember to select built-in[*], not module [M]

5. Exit from make menuconfig and save the new kernel configuration:

```
root@tbdev1[509]: make dep
root@tbdev1[510]: make bzImage
```

This should create a compressed kernel image called bzImage in the arch/i386/boot directory. The buildrootfilesystem script requires this file.

Building the Target root Filesystem on the Compact Flash IDE Drive

The target root filesystem can now be placed on the flash IDE drive. The drive has been partitioned, formatted, and checked, and the kernel has been compiled. MontaVista's Journeyman FTP site provides the RPMs for root filesystem required programs. The buildrootfilesystem script also works for x86 platforms. The script performs the following steps:

1. It downloads RPMs and extracts their contents into a temporary directory.

2. It then copies the required target root filesystem programs and creates various system configuration files in the /tftpboot/i386-rootfs directory.

3. It installs the Linux loader (LILO) into the master boot record of the flash drive, /dev/hdc. Installing LILO makes the drive boot to Linux.

4. It copies the target root filesystem to the drive and checks the filesystem for integrity. See the script section "Step 9: Prepare the root Filesystem for Operation on the Target Board," earlier in this chapter.

5. Run buildrootfilesystem to create and prepare the flash IDE drive for Linux boot and operation:

```
root@tbdev1[511]: cd /root/cross
root@tbdev1[512]: buildrootfilesystem i386
```

6. You can check the flash IDE drive by mounting it and examining the file contents:

```
root@tbdev1[513]: mount /dev/hdc1 /mnt
root@tbdev1[514]: cd /mnt
root@tbdev1[515]: ls
bin/  boot/  dev/  etc/  lib/  lost+found/  proc/  sbin/  tmp/  usr/
root@tbdev1[516]: ls -l boot/bzImage
-rw-r--r--   1 root     root       876986 Aug 25 00:53 boot/bzImage
root@tbdev1[517]: umount /dev/hdc1
```

7. Shut down tbdev1 with the init 6 command, power down, and remove the flash IDE drive from the secondary IDE controller.

Booting the Tri-M MZ104 Target

The Flash IDE drive contains the kernel and the root filesystem for the x86 target boards. Connect the Flash IDE drive to the x86 target primary IDE controller and power up. The target BIOS should find the flash IDE drive. LILO starts by showing the boot prompt then the kernel loads. The kernel mounts the root filesystem. The kernel then executes init, which executes bash. Here's the console output for the MZ104 power-up to bash prompt boot sequence:

```
LILO boot:
Loading linux..............
Linux version 2.4.10 (root@tbdev1) (gcc version 2.95.2 20000220
➥(Debian GNU/Linux)) #1 Fri Dec 7 02:28:38 MST 2001
BIOS-provided physical RAM map:
 BIOS-e820: 0000000000000000 - 000000000009f400 (usable)
 BIOS-e820: 000000000009f400 - 00000000000a0000 (reserved)
 BIOS-e820: 00000000000d0000 - 00000000000d4000 (reserved)
 BIOS-e820: 00000000000e5c00 - 0000000000100000 (reserved)
 BIOS-e820: 0000000000100000 - 0000000002000000 (usable)
 BIOS-e820: 00000000fff80000 - 0000000100000000 (reserved)
On node 0 totalpages: 8192
zone(0): 4096 pages.
zone(1): 4096 pages.
zone(2): 0 pages.
Kernel command line: auto BOOT_IMAGE=linux ro root=301
➥BOOT_FILE=/tmp/tmpmnt/boot/bzImage
Initializing CPU#0
Console: colour VGA+ 80x25
Calibrating delay loop... 39.83 BogoMIPS
```

Memory: 30020k/32768k available (1098k kernel code, 2360k reserved,
➡313k data, 180k init, 0k highmem)
Checking if this processor honours the WP bit even in supervisor mode... Ok.
Dentry-cache hash table entries: 4096 (order: 3, 32768 bytes)
Inode-cache hash table entries: 2048 (order: 2, 16384 bytes)
Mount-cache hash table entries: 512 (order: 0, 4096 bytes)
Buffer-cache hash table entries: 1024 (order: 0, 4096 bytes)
Page-cache hash table entries: 8192 (order: 3, 32768 bytes)
CPU: Before vendor init, caps: 00000000 00000000 00000000, vendor = 1
CPU: After vendor init, caps: 00000000 00000000 00000000 00000000
CPU: After generic, caps: 00000000 00000000 00000000 00000000
CPU: Common caps: 00000000 00000000 00000000 00000000
CPU: Cyrix Cx486DX4
Checking 'hlt' instruction... OK.
POSIX conformance testing by UNIFIX
PCI: PCI BIOS revision 2.10 entry at 0xfd99e, last bus=0
PCI: Using configuration type 1
PCI: Probing PCI hardware
PCI: Cannot allocate resource region 0 of device 00:00.0
 got res[1040:107f] for resource 1 of PCI device 1078:0400 (Cyrix Corporation)
Linux NET4.0 for Linux 2.4
Based upon Swansea University Computer Society NET3.039
Starting kswapd
Detected PS/2 Mouse Port.
pty: 256 Unix98 ptys configured
Serial driver version 5.05c (2001-07-08) with MANY_PORTS SHARE_IRQ
➡SERIAL_PCI enabled
ttyS00 at 0x03f8 (irq = 4) is a 16550A
ttyS01 at 0x02f8 (irq = 3) is a 16550A
block: 64 slots per queue, batch=8
Uniform Multi-Platform E-IDE driver Revision: 6.31
ide: Assuming 33MHz system bus speed for PIO modes; override with idebus=xx
PCI_IDE: unknown IDE controller on PCI bus 00 device 92, VID=1078, DID=0402
PCI_IDE: chipset revision 1
PCI_IDE: not 100% native mode: will probe irqs later
    ide0: BM-DMA at 0x1000-0x1007, BIOS settings: hda:pio, hdb:pio
    ide1: BM-DMA at 0x1008-0x100f, BIOS settings: hdc:pio, hdd:pio
hda: SunDisk SDCFB-40, ATA DISK drive
ide0 at 0x1f0-0x1f7,0x3f6 on irq 14
hda: 78336 sectors (40 MB) w/1KiB Cache, CHS=612/4/32
Partition check:
 hda: hda1

```
Floppy drive(s): fd0 is 1.44M
FDC 0 is a National Semiconductor PC87306
ne.c:v1.10 9/23/94 Donald Becker (becker@scyld.com)
Last modified Nov 1, 2000 by Paul Gortmaker
NE*000 ethercard probe at 0x300: 00 40 33 55 3d c7
eth0: NE2000 found at 0x300, using IRQ 5.
loop: loaded (max 8 devices)
Linux Kernel Card Services 3.1.22
  options:  [pci] [cardbus]
NET4: Linux TCP/IP 1.0 for NET4.0
IP Protocols: ICMP, UDP, TCP, IGMP
IP: routing cache hash table of 512 buckets, 4Kbytes
TCP: Hash tables configured (established 2048 bind 2048)
NET4: Unix domain sockets 1.0/SMP for Linux NET4.0.
ds: no socket drivers loaded!
VFS: Disk change detected on device ide0(3,1)
 hda: hda1
VFS: Mounted root (ext2 filesystem) readonly.
Freeing unused kernel memory: 180k freed
INIT: version 2.78 booting
INIT: Entering runlevel: 2
Starting Network
bash-2.04#
```

You're now at the bash prompt on the COTS PC.

Tri-M MZ104 Target Platform Boot Requirements Review

In this section, the seven PBRs are reviewed for the MZ104. Remember that each target board needs to fulfill the seven PBRs in order to be used in Project Trailblazer.

PBR-1 for the MZ104

The target board should use Linux kernel 2.4 or greater. Here's the MZ104 console output during the boot process:

```
Linux version 2.4.10 (root@tbdev1) (gcc version 2.95.2 20000220
➥(Debian GNU/Linux)) #1 Fri Dec 7 02:28:38 MST 2001
```

PBR-1 is fulfilled because Linux version 2.4.10 boots.

PBR-2 for the MZ104

The target board will execute the bash shell. Exiting from the bash shell re-executes the bash shell. On the MZ104 console, exit from the bash shell by using the exit command:

```
bash-2.04# exit
exit
bash-2.04#
```

PBR-2 is fulfilled because exiting from bash respawns bash. init is properly configured.

PBR-3 for the MZ104

The system should execute the bash shell without security authentication. Here's the
MZ104 console output during the boot process:

```
INIT: version 2.78 booting
INIT: Entering runlevel: 2
Starting Network
bash-2.04#
```

PBR-3 is fulfilled because init starts bash without authentication.

PBR-4 for the MZ104

The system should boot, initialize the Ethernet hardware, set a static IP address, and
be configured to use DNS. At the bash prompt, use ifconfig to display the Ethernet
hardware configuration and use ping to verify proper DNS configuration:

```
bash-2.04# ifconfig
eth0      Link encap:Ethernet  HWaddr 00:40:33:55:3D;C7
          inet addr:192.168.1.23  Bcast:192.168.1.255  Mask:255.255.255.0
          UP BROADCAST RUNNING MULTICAST  MTU:1500  Metric:1
          RX packets:17 errors:1 dropped:0 overruns:0 frame:0
          TX packets:14 errors:0 dropped:0 overruns:0 carrier:0
          collisions:0 txqueuelen:100
          Interrupt:5 Base address:0x300
bash-2.04# ping yahoo.com
PING yahoo.com (216.115.108.245): 56 data bytes
64 bytes from 216.115.108.245: icmp_seq=0 ttl=246 time=49.2 ms
64 bytes from 216.115.108.245: icmp_seq=1 ttl=246 time=48.8 ms
64 bytes from 216.115.108.245: icmp_seq=2 ttl=246 time=53.0 ms
```

PBR-4 is fulfilled because the Ethernet hardware is initialized. The target board's
resolver translated yahoo.com to 216.115.108.245. This verifies proper DNS configuration.

PBR-5 for the MZ104

The system should contain the ping program to debug network programs:

```
bash-2.04# ping yahoo.com
PING yahoo.com (216.115.108.245): 56 data bytes
64 bytes from 216.115.108.245: icmp_seq=0 ttl=246 time=49.2 ms
64 bytes from 216.115.108.245: icmp_seq=1 ttl=246 time=48.8 ms
64 bytes from 216.115.108.245: icmp_seq=2 ttl=246 time=53.0 ms
```

PBR-5 is fulfilled because a yahoo.com ping is successful.

PBR-6 for the MZ104

The system should be capable of executing the Project Trailblazer compiled version of helloworld. At the bash prompt, execute the helloworld program:

```
bash-2.04# /tmp/helloworld-i386
Hello world 1 times!
Hello world 2 times!
Hello world 3 times!
. . .
```

PBR-6 is fulfilled because the i386 version of helloworld executes.

PBR-7 for the MZ104

The system should use the current version of GNU glibc. At the bash prompt, list the library directory and confirm the current versions:

```
bash-2.04# ls /lib
ld-2.2.3.so       libncurses.so.5.2       libresolv.so.2
ld-linux.so.2     libnss_dns-2.2.3.so     librt-2.2.3.so
libc-2.2.3.so     libnss_dns.so.2         librt.so.1
libc.so.6         libnss_files-2.2.3.so   libstdc++-3-libc6.1-2-2.10.0.so
libdl-2.2.3.so    libnss_files.so.2       libstdc++-libc6.1-2.so.3
libdl.so.2        libproc.so.2.0.7        libutil-2.2.3.so
libm-2.2.3.so     libpthread-0.9.so       libutil.so.1
libm.so.6         libpthread.so.0
libncurses.so.5   libresolv-2.2.3.so
```

PBR-7 is fulfilled because the target boots with the current version of GNU glibc.

The Tri-M MZ104 fulfills all the PBRs.

Boot Comparison

The Project Trailblazer engineers developed a target comparison table shown in Table 4.3. This table compares the "power on to bash prompt" timing and target root filesystem size for the four platforms involved in Project Trailblazer.

TABLE 4.3   Project Trailblazer Target Comparison

Platform	Power On to bash **Prompt Time**	**Target** root **Filesystem Size**
Embedded Planet RPX-CLLF, PowerPC 860	27 seconds, including 6-second TFTP download of the kernel and RAM disk	4612KB
Brightstar Engineering MediaEngine, StrongArm1100	13 seconds, including 6-second TFTP download of the kernel and RAM disk	4232KB
Tri-M MZ104, Pentium (100MHz)	29 seconds, including 17-second PC BIOS completion time	4888KB
Micron COTS PC, Celeron (400MHz)	27 seconds, including 20-second PC BIOS completion time	4888KB

All the target platforms power up and boot to a bash prompt in under 30 seconds. The fastest is the MediaEngine, at 13 seconds. The RPX-CLLF and MediaEngine boot times include a 6-second TFTP kernel transfer time. This time would be eliminated if the on-board Flash memory stored the kernel image. The x86 MZ104 and COTS PC boot times include the mandatory PC BIOS completion time. The filesystem size similarity shows that the compiled binary files are roughly the same size for x86, ARM, and PowerPC microprocessors.

Summary

This chapter covered a lot of ground. The Project Trailblazer engineers started with their known platforms: the Embedded Planet RPX-CLLF, the Brightstar Engineering MediaEngine, the Tri-M MZ104 x86 single-board computer, and the COTS PC. They developed seven target platform boot requirements, and then they learned about the Linux boot process and developed the target root filesystem. Instead of compiling the root filesystem programs themselves, the engineers decided to use the MontaVista Journeyman product, which contains compiled binaries for all the target platforms. They developed the buildrootfilesystem script, which generates the target root filesystem and prepares it for use. On the way to booting their platforms, the engineers installed, configured, and started a TFTP server on `tbdev1`. This enabled them to boot the RPX-CLLF and MediaEngine. The MZ104 and COTS PC were also booted using a Flash IDE drive. Each target platform successfully booted and passed the seven target platform boot requirements. The engineers are ready to move on to remote debugging.

Additional Reading

1. Monta Vista Corporation, "Hard Hat Linux Overview," `www.mvista.com/products/hhl.html`.

2. Red Hat Corporation, "RPM software packaging tool," `http://rpm.redhat.com`.

3. Debian, "Basics of the Debian package management system," `www.debian.org/doc/FAQ/ch-pkg_basics.html`.

4. "The Linux kernel HOWTO: Compiling the kernel," `www.linux.org/docs/ldp/howto/Kernel-HOWTO-5.html`.

5

Debugging

Regardless of their talent or expertise, all programmers need to debug code. The Project Trailblazer engineers know that they'll need to do some debugging and that the time they spend on debugging will affect their schedule.

The Project Trailblazer engineers want a reliable and robust solution for their remote debugging needs. They want this solution to span the project's target processors (x86, ARM and PowerPC), communicate over the Transmission Control Protocol/Internet Protocol (TCP/IP) network, and be non-proprietary. The GNU debugging tools gdb and gdbserver provide this solution.

In this chapter, you'll debug the helloworld program both locally and remotely, using gdb and gdbserver. Then you'll reduce the compile/run/debug iteration cycle time by configuring the project target boards to mount their root filesystems via Network File System (NFS). This chapter is by no means a comprehensive explanation of debugging; other sources of information already exist.[1,2] Nor does it use graphical user interface (GUI) debugging tools, such as xxgdb,[3] DDD,[4] and insight,[5] which are built on gdb. This chapter presents information on remotely debugging a simple program across the network. You can then use this debugging knowledge and other tools to enhance your environment and decrease your development time.

Introducing gdb

The GNU tool chain debugger, gdb, allows you to control program execution, view and change program variables, examine program internals, and examine core files of crashed programs. You can use gdb to start an executable, debug an already running executable, or make a network connection to gdbserver. gdb and gdbserver handle and correct cross-processor issues such as big endian and little endian addressing and integer size. gdb runs as a console text application, without a GUI. Its open-source nature permits enhancements; you can get GUI tools that provide the integrated development environment (IDE) functionality that programmers have become accustomed to.

This chapter does not dive into a complete discussion of gdb's features, capabilities, and functionality. Rather, it shows you how to list an executable's source code, set a breakpoint, print a variable value, and set a variable value. You can then debug the cross-compiled executable over a network, using one of the Project Trailblazer target platforms. Table 5.1 shows the basic gdb commands that are used in this chapter.

TABLE 5.1   gdb Commands

Command	Shortcut	Description
list	l	Lists the program file
run	r	Starts a debugged program
break	b	Sets a breakpoint
next	n	Steps a program without entering subroutines
continue	c	Continues the program that is being debugged
print	p	Prints a variable's value

gdb's online help provides additional command information. For example, within gdb, here's the help section for the command next:

```
(gdb) help next
Step program, proceeding through subroutine calls.
Like the "step" command as long as subroutine calls do not happen;
when they do, the call is treated as one instruction.
Argument N means do this N times (or till program stops for another reason).
(gdb)
```

> **TIP**
>
> You can start exploring gdb's commands by typing help at the (gdb) prompt.

Local Debugging

Let's start by compiling and debugging helloworld solely on the host system, tbdev1. The script buildrootfilesystem generates helloworld.c in /root/cross/builds and cross-compiles it for the target system. Let's use that source code file and compile it for the x86 processor using tbdev1. Here are the steps to install gdb and compile and debug helloworld.c for the x86 on tbdev1:

1. Install gdb on tbdev1:

   ```
   root@tbdev1[508]: apt-get install gdb
   ```

2. Change into the /root/cross/builds directory and compile helloworld.c
   with the debugging flag -g:

   ```
   root@tbdev1[509]: cd /root/cross/builds
   root@tbdev1[510]: gcc -g -o helloworld-i386-linux helloworld.c
   ```

3. You need to check a couple things. Using the file program, you can determine
   the executable's architecture and see whether it contains debugging symbol
   tables:

   ```
   root@tbdev1[512]: file helloworld-i386-linux
   helloworld-i386-linux: ELF 32-bit LSB executable, Intel 80386, version 1,
   ➥dynamically linked (uses shared libs), not stripped
   ```

   stripped means the executable contains no debugging symbol tables, and not
   stripped means the executable contains debugging symbol tables.

   As you can see, this compiled version of helloworld is for the Intel 80386, x86,
   and is not stripped. You can later use the strip program to remove debugging
   symbol tables and then use file to see that helloworld doesn't contain debugging symbol tables.

4. Execute helloworld, to check for proper compilation:

   ```
   root@tbdev1[516]: ./helloworld-i386-linux
   Hello world 1 times!
   Hello world 2 times!
   Hello world 3 times!
   Hello world 4 times!
   Hello world 5 times!
   Hello world 6 times!
   Hello world 7 times!
   Hello world 8 times!
   Hello world 9 times!
   ```

5. Use gdb to debug helloworld:

   ```
   root@tbdev1[521]: gdb helloworld-i386-linux
   GNU gdb 19990928
   Copyright 1998 Free Software Foundation, Inc.
   GDB is free software, covered by the GNU General Public License,
   and you are welcome to change it and/or distribute copies
   of it under certain conditions.
   ```

```
Type "show copying" to see the conditions.
There is absolutely no warranty for GDB.  Type "show warranty" for
details.
This GDB was configured as "i686-pc-linux-gnu"...
(gdb)
```

NOTE

Don't forget about the oldest debugging tool, the print statement. C programs can use `printf` while kernel modules use `printk`. You can use `printk` while debugging kernel module code because kernel drivers can't link to the standard C library.

6. Debug `helloworld`. List the `helloworld-i386-linux` executable source code by using the `list` command, and then run the `helloworld-i386-linux` executable:

```
(gdb) list
1       #include <stdio.h>
2
3       int main(void)
4       {
5               int i;
6
7               for (i = 1; i < 10; i++)
8               {
9                       printf("Hello world %d times!\n",i);
10              }
(gdb) run
Starting program: /root/cross/builds/helloworld-i386-linux
Hello world 1 times!
Hello world 2 times!
Hello world 3 times!
Hello world 4 times!
Hello world 5 times!
Hello world 6 times!
Hello world 7 times!
Hello world 8 times!
Hello world 9 times!

Program exited with code 025.
(gdb)
```

Without breakpoints, `helloworld-i386-linux` executes to completion while printing Hello world and variable `i`'s value to the screen.

7. Set a breakpoint at line 9, by using the break command:

```
(gdb) break 9
Breakpoint 1 at 0x80483f8: file helloworld.c, line 9.
(gdb)
```

8. Start helloworld-i386-linux again, by using run:

```
(gdb) run
Starting program: /root/cross/builds/helloworld-i386-linux

Breakpoint 1, main () at helloworld.c:9
9                       printf("Hello world %d times!\n",i);
(gdb)
```

This means you're about to execute line 9.

9. Execute the line by using the next command:

```
(gdb) next
Hello world 1 times!
7                  for (i = 1; i < 10; i++)
(gdb)
```

"Hello world 1 times!" is the output from line 9's printf statement.

10. Use continue to continue. The program should break again at line 9. Examine the value of i by using the print command:

```
(gdb) continue
Continuing.

Breakpoint 1, main () at helloworld.c:9
9                       printf("Hello world %d times!\n",i);
(gdb) print i
$1 = 2
(gdb) next
Hello world 2 times!
7                  for (i = 1; i < 10; i++)
(gdb)
```

As expected, i = 2 because this is the second time through the for loop. You could continue like this, examining i eight more times. Instead, change i to 8 to speed things along. Use the set variable command, and then use continue:

```
(gdb) set variable i = 8
(gdb) continue
Continuing.
Hello world 8 times!

Breakpoint 1, main () at helloworld.c:9
9                       printf("Hello world %d times!\n",i);
(gdb)
```

Use continue again, and helloworld continues to execute and then exits:

```
(gdb) continue
Continuing.
Hello world 9 times!

Program exited with code 025.
(gdb)
```

NOTE

You can use a watchpoint to stop program execution whenever a variable value changes. Watchpoints slow program execution but really help to determine what's going on in a program. You can use the backtrace command to examine stack frames. backtrace shows a nested list of calling functions.

11. You are done debugging helloworld-i386-linux, so use the quit command:

```
(gdb) quit
root@tbdev1[525]:
```

In this section, you compiled helloworld with the debugging flag -g. Using the file program, you determined helloworld's architecture and found that it contains debugging symbol tables. Then you executed helloworld within gdb, listed its source code, ran helloworld, set a breakpoint, examined a variable value, and set a variable. You did all this on the Project Trailblazer development workstation, tbdev1. In the next section, you will learn how to remotely debug a cross-compiled version of helloworld on Project Trailblazer's ARM target board over the network.

Remote Debugging

In *remote debugging*, the executable being debugged and the debugger run on different computers. The executable runs on the target computer, and the debugger runs on the host computer. Remote debugging requires a debugging server running on the target computer. The debugging server, gdbserver, interfaces the target executable with the host debugger, gdb. The debugging server and the debugger converse over a communications link. You are using the TCP/IP Ethernet network, but serial links can also be used. After link establishment, the debugging process proceeds like a local debugging session.

In this section, you'll boot the MediaEngine, tbdevarm, as you did in Chapter 4, "Booting Linux," and then you'll run gdbserver on it. (In Chapter 4, the buildrootfilesystem script copied gdbserver and helloworld-arm-linux to the target's root file system.) You can run gdb on the tbdev1 host and establish a TCP connection to tbdevarm's gdbserver. Then, you can debug helloworld-arm-linux running on the tbdevarm.

Figure 5.1 shows tbdev1 and tbdevarm, with a serial connection and a network connection. You are again using minicom on tbdev1 to boot the tbdevarm (see Chapter 4) and gain access to bash. Remember that tbdevarm's console is routed through its serial port, ttyS0.

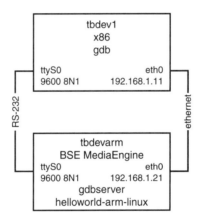

FIGURE 5.1   The remote debugging computer configuration.

Here are the steps to remotely debug helloworld-arm-linux running on the MediaEngine and gdb running on tbdev1:

1. Run minicom on tbdev1 and boot tbdevarm. Start gdbserver on tbdevarm, telling gdbserver to accept a TCP/IP connection from tbdev1 and start executing helloworld-arm-linux:

```
bash-2.04# cd /tmp
bash-2.04# gdbserver 192.168.1.11:2345 helloworld-arm-linux
Process helloworld-arm-linux created; pid = 17
```

tbdevarm's gdbserver is now executing helloworld-arm-linux and will accept
a connection on port 2345 from 192.168.1.11 (that is, tbdev1).

2. In a different console window on tbdev1, start gdb. (You can use Alt+F2 on
tbdev1 to switch to the second virtual console window.) You need to be in the
correct directory, /root/cross/builds, where the helloworld source code
exists. If helloworld-arm-linux doesn't exist, compile it by using the -g debugging flag. You also need to run the processor-specific cross-compiled version of
gdb that was compiled in Chapter 3. In this case, it's arm-linux-gdb. Here are
the commands to cross-compile helloworld.c with the debugging option and
start gdb:

```
root@tbdev1[530]: cd /root/cross/builds
root@tbdev1[531]: arm-linux-gcc -g -o helloworld-arm-linux helloworld.c
root@tbdev1[532]: arm-linux-gdb helloworld-arm-linux
GNU gdb 5.0
Copyright 2000 Free Software Foundation, Inc.
GDB is free software, covered by the GNU General Public License, and
you are welcome to change it and/or distribute copies of it under
certain conditions.

Type "show copying" to see the conditions.
There is absolutely no warranty for GDB.  Type "show warranty" for
details.
This GDB was configured as "--host=i686-pc-linux-gnu
➥--target=arm-linux"...
(gdb)
```

3. Tell gdb to establish the remote connection to tbdevarm, by using the target
extended-remote command. Using extended-remote allows for the target
executable to restart without restarting tbdevarm's gdbserver.

```
(gdb) target extended-remote 192.168.1.21:2345
Remote debugging using 192.168.1.21:2345
0x40002a50 in ?? ()
(gdb)
```

4. Switch to the minicom console (by pressing Alt+F1), and you'll see that remote
debugging has begun:

```
Process helloworld-arm-linux created; pid = 17
Remote debugging using 192.168.1.11:2345
```

Sunday
January
2002

6

9:00	
9:30	
10:00	
10:30	
11:00	
11:30	
12:00	
12:30	
1:00	
1:30	
2:00	
2:30	
3:00	
3:30	
4:00	
4:30	

January						2002	February						2002
S	M	T	W	T	F	S	S	M	T	W	T	F	S
		1	2	3	4	5						1	2
6	7	8	9	10	11	12	3	4	5	6	7	8	9
13	14	15	16	17	18	19	10	11	12	13	14	15	16
20	21	22	23	24	25	26	17	18	19	20	21	22	23
27	28	29	30	31			24	25	26	27	28		

006   **Sunday, January 6**   **359**

:v1, is now connected to tbdevarm's
·ld-arm-linux. Any tbdev1 gdb
y execute on tbdevarm.

ıg session described in the preceding
. Switch back to tbdev1's second console:

tarted already.
  y
helloworld-arm-linux

.loworld's printf went to tbdevarm's
his by switching back to the minicom

  pid = 21

```
hello world 5 times.

Child exited with retcode = 15

Child exited with status 0
Killing inferior
GDBserver restarting
Process helloworld-arm-linux created; pid = 22
```

The cross-compiled version of helloworld has successfully executed on the
ARM processor of tbdevarm.

6. Set a breakpoint at line 9 and then step through the program, examine the
value of variable i, change the value, and view the program's output on the
tbdevarm console:

```
(gdb) break 9
Breakpoint 1 at 0x83cc: file helloworld.c, line 9.
(gdb) run
The program being debugged has been started already.
Start it from the beginning? (y or n) y
Starting program: /root/cross/builds/helloworld-arm-linux

Breakpoint 1, main () at helloworld.c:9
9                         printf("Hello world %d times!\n",i);
(gdb) print i
$1 = 1
(gdb) next
7                 for (i = 1; i < 10; i++)
(gdb) set variable i = 8
(gdb) continue
Continuing.

Breakpoint 1, main () at helloworld.c:9
9                         printf("Hello world %d times!\n",i);
(gdb) continue
Continuing.

Program exited with code 025.
(gdb)
```

7. Switch back to the minicom console to see the expected printf result of variable i being changed from 1 to 8:

```
GDBserver restarting
Process helloworld-arm-linux created; pid = 34
Hello world 1 times!
Hello world 9 times!

Child exited with retcode = 15

Child exited with status 0
Killing inferior
GDBserver restarting
Process helloworld-arm-linux created; pid = 35
```

You have now completed your first multi-architecture remote debugging session. Wasn't that easy? You now have a functional multiarchitecture system to build on. From here, you can investigate the use of the tools that are built on gdb, such as ddd and insight, to make your debugging life easier. See the "Additional Reading" section at the end of this chapter for more information.

Network-Mounting the root Filesystem

tbdevarm's root filesystem, generated by the buildrootfilesystem script, contains the cross-compiled version of helloworld and gdbserver. Changing the helloworld source code would require completely rebuilding the root filesystem, rebooting the MediaEngine, and then downloading the kernel and root filesystem again. Even though the MediaEngine boots quickly, taking this approach over time would become tedious and time-consuming.

Instead of transferring the root filesystem, you can mount it over the Ethernet network by using NFS. With a network-mounted root filesystem, you can generate the ARM cross-compiled version of helloworld.c on tbdev1. Then you can directly execute it or remotely debug it without regenerating the MediaEngine root filesystem or rebooting. The buildrootfilesystem script creates the minimum root filesystem in the /tftpboot directory and can be NFS-mounted directly.

The Unix world commonly uses NFS to mount hard disks on remote computers. For example, a server can share its /home directory for user workstations or the /tftpboot directory for diskless workstations to mount their root filesystem. (Note that diskless workstations and the Project Trailblazer target platforms use TFTP, not NFS, to download their kernels.) The Linux kernel itself contains NFS code, which allows the kernel to mount its own root filesystem during the boot process.

In this section, you'll learn how to configure tbdev1 to act as an NFS server and configure the target board's kernel options for network-mounting their root filesystems.

Configuring the NFS Server

tbdev1 serves as the Project Trailblazer target root filesystem NFS server. You can configure it to serve the i386 files to the i386 target (MZ104 and COTS PC), the ARM files to the ARM target (MediaEngine), and the PowerPC files to the PowerPC target (RPX-CLLF). As you can tell, it's important to serve the correct files to each architecture. Figure 5.2 shows the Project Trailblazer development computers and their IP addresses.

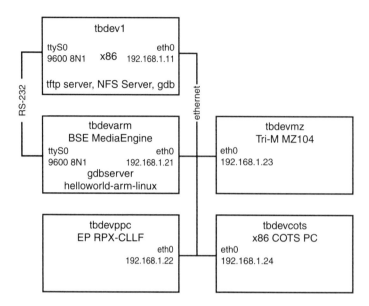

FIGURE 5.2   The Project Trailblazer development stations and their IP addresses.

Here are the steps to install, configure, and run the NFS server on tbdev1:

1. Install the NFS server on tbdev1:

   ```
   root@tbdev1[501]: apt-get install nfs-server
   ```

2. Configure tbdev1's NFS server by adding an entry to its configuration file, /etc/exports, for each target platform. Each entry contains a directory, an IP address, and mounting permission options. To do so, add these lines to /etc/exports:

   ```
   /tftpboot/arm-rootfs     192.168.1.21(rw,no_root_squash)
   /tftpboot/powerpc-rootfs 192.168.1.22(rw,no_root_squash)
   /tftpboot/i386-rootfs    192.168.1.23(rw,no_root_squash)
   /tftpboot/i386-rootfs    192.168.1.24(rw,no_root_squash)
   ```

   The mounting permissions shown here are rw and no_root_squash. rw allows the clients (the target boards) to mount their root filesystems with read and write permissions. The no_root_squash option allows the clients to mount their root filesystems as user root on tbdev1. See the exports man page for more information.

Line 1 of the /etc/exports configuration file says that the MediaEngine with an ARM processor at IP address 192.168.1.21 now has NFS read and write mounting access to the /tftpboot/arm-rootfs directory. Similarly, the RPX CLLF with a PowerPC processor at IP address 192.168.1.22 has NFS read and write mount access to the /tftpboot/powerpc-rootfs directory. Finally, the Tri-M and COTS PC with i386 processor at IP addresses 192.168.1.23 and 192.168.1.24 have NFS read and write access to the /tftpboot/i386-rootfs directory.

3. Make /etc/exports readable by all:

   root@tbdev1[502]: **chmod 444 /etc/exports**

4. The NFS server reads the /etc/exports configuration file at startup, so you need to tell it to reload its configuration:

   root@tbdev1[503]: **/etc/init.d/nfs-server reload**

The NFS server is now configured and ready for NFS mounting by the targets.

Configuring the Target Kernels

During the boot process, the bootloader passes the root filesystem location to the kernel, using the boot prompt mechanism. The ARM and PowerPC bootloaders are configured during the kernel configuration process. On x86 platforms, the Linux loader (lilo) is configured to pass the root filesystem location to the kernel.

lilo is configured using the /etc/lilo.conf file. Both kernel compilation and lilo configuration result in the root filesystem location being passed to the kernel. Without root filesystem location information, the kernel can't mount its root filesystem and stops, with a "kernel panic."

> **TIP**
>
> You can supercede the root filesystem location by entering new location information at the Linux boot: prompt. See the Linux BootPrompt HOWTO[6] for more information. This section does not use the boot prompt because of the length of the NFS server root filesystem location information.

In the following steps, you'll compile the MediaEngine ARM kernel for NFS mounting of the ARM root filesystem; the other platforms are similarly configured, except that their IP addresses and root filesystem paths are different:

1. Change directory to the ARM kernel source and run make menuconfig:

   root@tbdev1[504]: **cd /usr/src/arm-linux/**
   root@tbdev1[505]: **make menuconfig**

2. Scroll and select General setup, and scroll and select Default kernel command string:. Then, enter the following string in the dialog box (as all one string, with no returns):

```
root=/dev/nfs
➥nfsaddrs=192.168.1.21:192.168.1.11::255.255.255.0:tbdevarm:eth0:off
➥nfsroot=192.168.1.11:/tftpboot/arm-rootfs,rw
```

TIP

The Linux BootPrompt HOWTO[6] fully explains the nfsaddrs parameters.

3. Select OK. Continue to select exit until you're asked to save your configuration; then save it.

4. Make a new kernel by using make zImage:

```
root@tbdev1[510]: make zImage
```

5. Copy the new kernel image to /tftpboot/arm-zImage-NFS and make it readable by all:

```
root@tbdev1[511]: cp arch/arm/boot/zImage /tftpboot/arm-zImage-NFS
root@tbdev1[512]: chmod 444 /tftpboot/arm-zImage-NFS
root@tbdev1[516]: ls -l /tftpboot/arm-zImage*
-r--r--r-- 1 root root      646240 Aug 24 15:16 /tftpboot/arm-zImage
-r--r--r-- 1 root root      646308 Aug 28 22:19 /tftpboot/arm-zImage-NFS
```

6. Rebuild the arm-rootfs directory, using the buildrootfilesystem script:

```
root@tbdev1[529]: cd /root/cross/
root@tbdev1[530]: ./buildrootfilesystem arm
```

7. Check for the arm-rootfs directory. It should be located in /tftpboot:

```
root@tbdev1[527]: cd /tftpboot/
root@tbdev1[528]: ls -l
total 6972
-r--r--r--  1 root      root      1705333 Aug 24 16:16 arm-ramdisk.gz
drwxr-xr-x 10 root      root         4096 Aug 24 16:13 arm-rootfs/
-r--r--r--  1 root      root       646240 Aug 24 15:16 arm-zImage
-r--r--r--  1 root      root       646308 Aug 28 22:19 arm-zImage-NFS
```

8. All the pieces are in place to boot the MediaEngine by using NFS mounting of its root filesystem:

```
/tftpboot/arm-zImage-NFS   the ARM kernel with NFS mounting exists
/tftpboot/arm-rootfs       the ARM root filesystem exists
/etc/exports               the NFS Server on tbdev1 configured
```

9. Reboot the MediaEngine, tbdevarm. Use minicom on tbdev1 to download the arm-zImage-NFS kernel file via TFTP, and then boot the arm-zImage-NFS kernel:

```
root@tbdev1[530]: minicom

Boot: BSE 2001 R1.0 SN# 00:50:15:03:00:19
>load arm-zImage-NFS c0008000
loading ... 646308 bytes loaded cksum 00007361
 done
>go c0008000
Uncompressing Linux.......................... done, booting
 the kernel.
Linux version 2.4.2-rmk1-np2-bse (root@tbdev1) (gcc version 2.95.3
20010315 (release)) #4 Tue Aug 28 22:31:45 MST 2001

Processor: Intel StrongARM-1110 revision 6
Architecture: BSE nanoEngine
On node 0 totalpages: 8192
zone(0): 8192 pages.
zone(1): 0 pages.
zone(2): 0 pages.
Kernel command line: root=/dev/nfs nfsaddrs=192.168.1.21:192.168.1.11::
➥255.255.255.0:tbdevarm:eth0:none nfsroot=192.168.1.11:
➥/tftpboot/arm-rootfs,rw

    . . .

VFS: Mounted root (nfs filesystem) readonly.
Freeing init memory: 52K
INIT: version 2.78 booting
INIT: Entering runlevel: 2
Starting Network
bash-2.04#
```

You are now back at the bash prompt from tbdevarm, whose kernel network mounted the ARM root filesystem. How can you tell this? At tbdevarm's bash prompt, use echo to generate a file in the /tmp directory. Remember that tbdevarm's /tmp directory is the same as tbdev1's /tftpboot/arm-rootfs/tmp directory:

```
bash-2.04# echo "This is a NFS root filesystem test" > /tmp/test
```

10. Switch to the tbdev1 console, change into the directory /tftpboot/arm-rootfs, and look for the file called test:

```
root@tbdev1[545]: cd /tftpboot/arm-rootfs/tmp
root@tbdev1[546]: ls
helloworld-arm-linux  helloworld.c  test
root@tbdev1[547]: cat test
This is a NFS root filesystem test
```

tbdevarm successfully network-mounted its root filesystem with read and write access.

11. Change helloworld.c on tbdev1, cross-compile it, and execute it on tbdevarm:

```
root@tbdev1[549]: cd /tftpboot/arm-rootfs/tmp
root@tbdev1[550]: cp /root/cross/builds/helloworld.c helloworld5.c
```

12. Edit helloworld5.c and change the for loop to count to 5 instead of 10. Cross-compile helloworld5.c, and then verify the cross-compile by using the file program:

```
root@tbdev1[560]: arm-linux-gcc -g -o helloworld5 helloworld5.c
root@tbdev1[561]: ls -l
total 60
-rwxr-xr-x  1 root    root       22266 Aug 28 23:05 helloworld-arm-linux
-rw-r--r--  1 root    root         120 Aug 28 23:05 helloworld.c
-rwxr-xr-x  1 root    root       22272 Aug 28 23:22 helloworld5
-rw-r--r--  1 root    root         120 Aug 28 23:21 helloworld5.c
-rw-r--r--  1 root    root          35 Aug 28 23:16 test
root@tbdev1[562]: file helloworld5
helloworld5: ELF 32-bit LSB executable, Advanced RISC Machines ARM, version 1,
dynamically linked (uses shared libs), not stripped
```

13. Switch back to the `minicom` console, look for the new `helloworld5.c` source file and the cross-compiled `helloworld5`. Now execute helloworld5:

```
bash-2.04# cd /tmp
bash-2.04# ls -l
total 60
-rwxr-xr-x    1 0    0          22266 Aug 29  2001 helloworld-arm-linux
-rw-r--r--    1 0    0            120 Aug 29  2001 helloworld.c
-rwxr-xr-x    1 0    0          22272 Aug 29  2001 helloworld5
-rw-r--r--    1 0    0            120 Aug 29  2001 helloworld5.c
-rw-r--r--    1 0    0             35 Aug 29  2001 test
bash-2.04# ./helloworld5
Hello world 1 times!
Hello world 2 times!
Hello world 3 times!
Hello world 4 times!
bash-2.04#
```

You can now run the cross-compiler and gdb on the host, tbdev1. The target, with an NFS-mounted root filesystem, can run gdbserver and then execute cross-compiled programs. With this combination, you can dramatically reduce development time by decreasing the compile/run/debug cycle time.

Summary

This chapter briefly introduced gdb. You used gdb to start and stop an executable and to examine and alter variables. Using the Project Trailblazer target platforms, the Ethernet network, and cross-compiled versions of helloworld and gdbserver, you performed remote debugging. You configured and tested target boards mounting their root filesystem using NFS. The Project Trailblazer engineers will use this combination of gdb, gdbserver, and an NFS-mounted target root filesystem to reduce their development time and effort.

Additional Reading

1. Richard M. Stallman and Roland H. Pesch, "Debugging with gdb: The Gnu Source-Level Debugger Fifth Edition, for gdb Version," www.gnu.org/manual/gdb-4.17/html_chapter/gdb_toc.html.

2. Stuart Ball, "Debugging Embedded Microprocessor Systems," 1998, Butterworth-Heinemann, http://www.bh.com.

3. Po Cheung and Pierre Willard, "X window system interface to the gdb debugger," `ftp://ftp.x.org/contrib/utilities/xxgdb-1.12.tar.gz`.

4. Free Software Foundation, "GNU Project: DDD, Data Display Debugger," `www.gnu.org/software/ddd`.

5. Red Hat Corporation, "The GDB GUI," `http://sources.redhat.com/insight`.

6. Paul Gortmaker, "The Linux BootPrompt HOWTO," `www.linuxdoc.org/HOWTO/BootPrompt-HOWTO.html`, 2001.

PART II

Interfacing

IN THIS PART

6

Asynchronous Serial Communication Interfacing

Project Trailblazer was proceeding quite nicely. The four target hardware boards had been booted, with bash running and an Ethernet network connection. The engineers were ready to begin tackling hardware interfacing. They decided to start with the guest authentication and lift access design. The Silverjack board wants Project Trailblazer to replace paper lift access tickets with low-cost radio-frequency identification (RFID) technology. Guests receive RFID tags that permit passage through an access point located at the bottom of each lift. These lift access points also display individual guest-specific messages. An RFID tag reader outputs tag information via an asynchronous serial link. The access point display receives commands via an asynchronous serial link. The tag reader and display will connect to the target board's serial ports.

A guest can proceed through an access point after authentication by looking at signaling lights: A red light means permission to pass is denied, and a green light indicates permission to go. The permission signaling circuit requires a single bit of information. This bit of information, the RFID tag reader and access point display communication can be accomplished through the use of a target board's serial ports.

In this chapter, you'll develop three C programs: one that sets the serial port control signal (setSerialSignal), one that queries the control signal (getSerialSignal), and one that sends and receives asynchronous serial communications (querySerial). Ultimately, within the Project Trailblazer design, bash scripts running on the target boards will call these three programs and will provide system integration to the Silverjack server. (Chapter 12, "System Integration," addresses all system integration development.) This chapter discusses how to develop a simple serial interface for the Project Trailblazer access points callable from bash.

The original RS-232 standard, defined by the Electronic Industry Association and the Telecommunications Industry Association (EIA/TIA), in 1962, is a complete standard that specifies electrical, functional, and mechanical characteristics for communications between host and peripheral equipment. RS stands for *recommended standard*. The characters RS have been officially replaced by the characters *EIA/TIA* to identify the source of the standard. Nonetheless, people continue to use the term RS-232. In this chapter, RS-232 is synonymous with EIA/TIA-232.

TIP

Dallas Semiconductor's Application Note 83, "Fundamentals of RS-232 Serial Communications"[1] fully describes RS-232. This application note covers electrical, functional, and mechanical characteristics, explains implementation and signaling, and describes PC/modem communications and limitations.

The Project Trailblazer Asynchronous Serial Hardware Development Environment

The Project Trailblazer serial development environment consists of the development workstation, tbdev1, target platform and the peripheral devices: RFID tag reader, LCD display, and lift access permission signal. Figure 6.1 shows the various electrical connections and signal flows. ESPTech of Lakewood, Colorado, supplies the RFID tag reader. Scott Edwards Electronics supplies the serial LCD display. The access permission circuitry driven by an RS-232 signal illuminates a red light or green light.

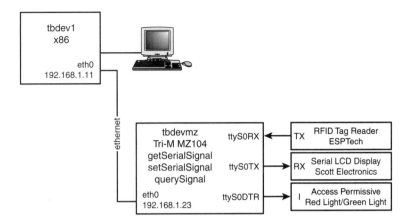

FIGURE 6.1   The Project Trailblazer asynchronous serial hardware development environment.

Target EIA/TIA-232-E Compliance

When you have Linux booted on all platforms, you should be able to develop software for any platform and then port it to another platform by merely cross-compiling. Ideally, the Project Trailblazer engineers could develop and test all the serial communications code on tbdev1 and then cross-compile it for the PowerPC and ARM platforms. Unfortunately, the RPX-CLLF and MediaEngine hardware design does not allow for control of the serial port signal lines.[2,3] The manufacturers state that there is no hardware flow control support on the serial ports. This means that hardware designs can't access the Request to Send (RTS), Data Terminal Ready (DTR), Clear to Send (CTS), Data Set Ready (DSR), and Ring (RI) control signals. These target boards support asynchronous serial communication but don't fully comply with the current EIA/TIA-232-E standard. The Access Permission circuit in Figure 6.1 requires connection to the DTR control signal. Therefore, the RPX-CLLF and MediaEngine can't be used in this hardware design. You will use the x86 target platforms to develop and test the setSerialSignal, getSerialSignal and querySerial programs.

Linux Serial Communications

The Project Trailblazer engineers found three documents specifically addressing Linux asynchronous serial communications:

- Gary Frerking's "Serial Programming HOWTO" (www.linuxdoc.org/HOWTO/Serial-Programming-HOWTO.html)

- David S. Lawyer's "Serial HOWTO" (www.linuxdoc.org/HOWTO/Serial-HOWTO.html)

- Michael Sweet's "Serial Programming Guide for POSIX Operating Systems" (www.easysw.com/~mike/serial)

Using Linux—or, more properly, POSIX—serial communications terminology, they searched for code examples that access the serial port's universal asynchronous receiver transmitter (UART) control signals and send and receive buffers. They discovered that accessing the UART's control signals was straightforward and easy to understand. Manipulating the send and receive buffers requires a more in-depth understanding of the Linux serial device driver capabilities. This device driver contains numerous options, beyond basic UART configuration, for control and processing of modem and terminal communications. Most of these options don't apply for Project Trailblazer. The engineers considered writing their own simplified serial communications driver for UART control, but they decided against that after finding C code examples that resemble the required functionality of setSerialSignal, getSerialSignal, and querySerial.

Linux device files provide access to hardware serial ports. The file open command returns a file descriptor that is used for serial port configuration, control, reading, and writing. The following sections demonstrate this through development of the setSerialSignal, getSerialSignal, and querySerial programs.

Setting the Serial Port Control Signals with setSerialSignal

The Project Trailblazer lift access point receives RFID tag information, performs authentication, and displays a permission signal (that is, a red or green light) permitting or denying guest access to the lift. For the sake of simplicity, the engineers decided to use an RS-232 serial port control signal as the permission signal. There's no need to involve another hardware input/output (I/O) port, such as a parallel port, when the access point serial communications between the target and the RFID reader or display don't use hardware flow control or a DTR signal. The serial port signals RTS or DTR provide this single bit of output, to drive the red light/green light permission signal.

The Linux serial driver provides functionality for modem control through the serial port control signals DTR and RTS. DTR controls the on-hook/off-hook modem status, and RTS controls serial data flow control. In most modem communications applications, the program opens a serial port, makes a dialup connection, performs a task, hangs up the connection, and exits. The Linux serial port driver contains code to handle improperly written or terminated serial communication programs by automatically hanging up the phone line when the port is closed: That is, it "drops DTR." DTR becomes 1, asserted, or an RS-232 negative voltage. This poses an electrical limitation on the lift access point hardware design. Opening and closing the serial port can change the permission signal that is going to the access point—the red light or the green light. Fortunately, the serial driver has an option to disable this automatic hangup activity at port closure. It is settable through changes to the serial ports configuration's c_cflag. The source code in Listing 6.1 disables the automatic hangup activity at port close and sets the serial port's control signals. The setSerialSignal code is shown in Listing 6.1.

LISTING 6.1   The setSerialSignal Program

```
/*
 * setSerialSignal v0.1 9/13/01
 * www.embeddedlinuxinterfacing.com
 *
 *
 * The original location of this source is
 * http://www.embeddedlinuxinterfacing.com/chapters/06/setSerialSignal.c
 *
 * This program is free software; you can redistribute it and/or modify
 * it under the terms of the GNU Library General Public License as
 * published by the Free Software Foundation; either version 2 of the
 * License, or (at your option) any later version.
 *
 * This program is distributed in the hope that it will be useful, but
 * WITHOUT ANY WARRANTY; without even the implied warranty of
 * MERCHANTABILITY or FITNESS FOR A PARTICULAR PURPOSE. See the GNU
 * Library General Public License for more details.
 *
 * You should have received a copy of the GNU Library General Public
 * License along with this program; if not, write to the
 * Free Software Foundation, Inc.,
 * 59 Temple Place, Suite 330, Boston, MA 02111-1307 USA
 */
```

LISTING 6.1   Continued

```
/* setSerialSignal
 * setSerialSignal sets the DTR and RTS serial port control signals.
 * This program queries the serial port status then sets or clears
 * the DTR or RTS bits based on user supplied command line setting.
 *
 * setSerialSignal clears the HUPCL bit. With the HUPCL bit set,
 * when you close the serial port, the Linux serial port driver
 * will drop DTR (assertion level 1, negative RS-232 voltage). By
 * clearing the HUPCL bit, the serial port driver leaves the
 * assertion level of DTR alone when the port is closed.
 */

/*
gcc -o setSerialSignal setSerialSignal.c
*/


#include <sys/ioctl.h>
#include <fcntl.h>
#include <termios.h>

/* we need a termios structure to clear the HUPCL bit */
struct termios tio;

int main(int argc, char *argv[])
{
  int fd;
  int status;

  if (argc != 4)
  {
    printf("Usage: setSerialSignal port                 DTR RTS\n");
    printf("Usage: setSerialSignal /dev/ttyS0|/dev/ttyS1 0|1 0|1\n");
    exit( 1 );
  }

  if ((fd = open(argv[1],O_RDWR)) < 0)
  {
    printf("Couldn't open %s\n",argv[1]);
    exit(1);
  }
```

LISTING 6.1   Continued

```
tcgetattr(fd, &tio);          /* get the termio information */
tio.c_cflag &= ~HUPCL;        /* clear the HUPCL bit */
tcsetattr(fd, TCSANOW, &tio); /* set the termio information */

ioctl(fd, TIOCMGET, &status); /* get the serial port status */

if ( argv[2][0] == '1' )      /* set the DTR line */
  status &= ~TIOCM_DTR;
else
  status |= TIOCM_DTR;

if ( argv[3][0] == '1' )      /* set the RTS line */
  status &= ~TIOCM_RTS;
else
  status |= TIOCM_RTS;

ioctl(fd, TIOCMSET, &status); /* set the serial port status */

close(fd);                    /* close the device file */
}
```

The setSerialSignal program requires three command-line parameters: the serial port to use (/dev/ttyS0 or /dev/ttyS1), the assertion level of DTR (1 or 0), and the assertion level of RTS (1 or 0). Here are the steps to compile and test setSerialSignal:

1. Compile setSerialSignal.c:

   root@tbdev1[505]: **gcc -o setSerialSignal setSerialSignal.c**

2. Connect a voltmeter to ground and to the DTR signal on serial port 0 (ttyS0). DTR is your PC's COM1 DB-9 connector pin 4.

TIP

DB-9 connectors have tiny numbers printed in the connector plastic next to the pins.

3. Run setSerialSignal to set DTR:

   root@tbdev1[506]: **./setSerialSignal /dev/ttyS0 1 0**

4. Your voltmeter should read a negative voltage between –3V and –15V. Setting DTR, using 1 as a command-line parameter, results in a negative RS-232 voltage on the actual DTR pin.

TIP

An RS-232 breakout box simplifies debugging serial communication programs.[6] However, using a RS-232 breakout box with LEDs could lower your signal's voltage. Many RS-232 driver chips can't source enough current to drive the LEDs in the breakout box. If you're experiencing problems, you might want to use a wire to make the DB-9 connections instead of a breakout box.

---

5. Run setSerialSignal to clear DTR:

   root@tbdev1[507]: **./setSerialSignal /dev/ttyS0 0 0**

6. Your voltmeter should read a positive voltage between +3V and +15V. Clearing DTR, using 0 as a command-line parameter, results in a positive RS-232 voltage on the actual DTR pin.

7. Connect a voltmeter to ground and to the RTS signal on serial port 0 (ttyS0). RTS is your PC's COM1 DB-9 connector pin 7.

8. Run setSerialSignal to set RTS:

   root@tbdev1[508]: **./setSerialSignal /dev/ttyS0 0 1**

9. Your voltmeter should read a negative voltage between –3V and –15V. Setting RTS, using 1 as a command-line parameter, results in a negative RS-232 voltage on the actual RTS pin.

10. Run setSerialSignal to clear RTS:

    root@tbdev1[509]: **./setSerialSignal /dev/ttyS0 0 0**

11. Your voltmeter should read a positive voltage between +3V and +15V. Clearing RTS, using 0 as a command-line parameter, results in a positive RS-232 voltage on the actual RTS pin.

Reading the Serial Port Control Signals with getSerialSignal

The getSerialSignal program returns the state, asserted (1) or not asserted (0), of any RS-232 serial port control input signal: DSR, CTS, Data Carrier Detect (DCD), or Ring (RI). getSerialSignal opens a specified serial port, which is supplied as a command-line parameter, and then uses the system call ioctl to determine the serial port control line status and returns an individual signal state, which is also supplied as a command-line parameter. Listing 6.2 shows the getSerialSignal source code.

LISTING 6.2   The getSerialSignal Program

```
/*
 * getSerialSignal v0.1 9/13/01
 * www.embeddedlinuxinterfacing.com
 *
 * The original  location of this source is
 * http://www.embeddedlinuxinterfacing.com/chapters/06/getSerialSignal.c
 *
 *
 * Copyright (C) 2001 by Craig Hollabaugh
 *
 * This program is free software; you can redistribute it and/or modify
 * it under the terms of the GNU Library General Public License as
 * published by the Free Software Foundation; either version 2 of the
 * License, or (at your option) any later version.
 *
 * This program is distributed in the hope that it will be useful, but
 * WITHOUT ANY WARRANTY; without even the implied warranty of
 * MERCHANTABILITY or FITNESS FOR A PARTICULAR PURPOSE. See the GNU
 * Library General Public License for more details.
 *
 * You should have received a copy of the GNU Library General Public
 * License along with this program; if not, write to the
 * Free Software Foundation, Inc.,
 * 59 Temple Place, Suite 330, Boston, MA 02111-1307 USA
 */


/* getSerialSignal
 * getSerialSignal queries the serial port's UART and returns
 * the state of the input control lines. The program requires
 * two command line parameters: which port and the input control
 * line (one of the following: DSR, CTS, DCD, or RI).
 * ioctl is used to get the current status of the serial port's
 * control signals. A simple hash function converts the control
 * command line parameter into an integer.
 */


/*
gcc -o getSerialSignal getSerialSignal.c
*/
```

LISTING 6.2   Continued

```
#include <sys/ioctl.h>
#include <fcntl.h>

/* These are the hash definitions */
#define DSR 'D'+'S'+'R'
#define CTS 'C'+'T'+'S'
#define DCD 'D'+'C'+'D'
#define RI  'R'+'I'

int main(int argc, char *argv[])
{
  int fd;
  int status;
  unsigned int whichSignal;

  if (argc != 3)
    {
    printf("Usage: getSerialSignal /dev/ttyS0|/dev/ttyS1 DSR|CTS|DCD|RI \n");
    exit( 1 );
    }

/* open the serial port device file */
  if ((fd = open(argv[1],O_RDONLY)) < 0) {
    printf("Couldn't open %s\n",argv[1]);
    exit(1);
  }

/* get the serial port's status */
  ioctl(fd, TIOCMGET, &status);

/* compute which serial port signal the user asked for
 * using a simple adding hash function
 */
  whichSignal = argv[2][0]  + argv[2][1] +  argv[2][2];

/* Here we AND the status with a bitmask to get the signal's state
 * These ioctl bitmasks are defined in /usr/include/bits/ioctl-types.h*/
  switch (whichSignal) {
    case  DSR:
      status&TIOCM_DSR ? printf("0"):printf("1");
      break;
```

LISTING 6.2   Continued

```
    case  CTS:
      status&TIOCM_CTS ? printf("0"):printf("1");
      break;
    case  DCD:
      status&TIOCM_CAR ? printf("0"):printf("1");
      break;
    case  RI:
      status&TIOCM_RNG ? printf("0"):printf("1");
      break;
    default:
      printf("signal  %s unknown, use DSR, CTS, DCD or RI",argv[2]);
      break;
  }
  printf("\n");

/* close the device file */
  close(fd);
}
```

The getSerialSignal program requires two command-line parameters: the serial
port to use (/dev/ttyS0 or /dev/ttyS1) and the control signal (DSR, CTS, DCD, or
RI). Here are the steps to compile and test getSerialSignal:

1. Compile getSerialSignal.c:

   root@tbdev1[510]: **gcc -o getSerialSignal getSerialSignal.c**

2. Use the serial port's DTR signal to drive the RI signal. Connect DTR, DB-9 pin
   4, to RI, DB-9 pin 9.

3. Measure the DTR signal voltage; it should be between +3V and +15V. This is
   assertion level 0.

TIP

You might get an open file error if the device file permissions aren't set for read/write access
by everyone. Check the file permissions and give everyone read and write access by using the
chmod command:

chmod a+w+r /dev/ttyS0

4. Use `getSerialSignal` to query the assertion level of the RI signal:

   ```
   root@tbdev1[512]: ./getSerialSignal /dev/ttyS0 RI
   0
   ```

   `getSerialSignal` returns 0, which is correct for a positive voltage on the RI line.

5. Now use the serial port's TX signal to drive the RI signal. Connect TX DB-9 pin 3 to RI DB-9 pin 9.

6. Measure the TX signal voltage; it should be between –3V and –15V. This is assertion level 1.

7. Use `getSerialSignal` to query the assertion level of the RI signal:

   ```
   root@tbdev1[513]: ./getSerialSignal /dev/ttyS0 RI
   1
   ```

   `getSerialSignal` returns 1, which is correct for a negative voltage on the RI line.

How the File open System Call Affects DTR and RTS Signals

While they were debugging, the engineers noticed a peculiar serial driver behavior that required further research. The Linux serial port driver contains functionality for modem control, using the DTR and RTS signals. The serial driver file open system call either asserts or de-asserts both DTR and RTS. You can see this by scanning `/usr/src/linux/drivers/char/serial.c` for the DTR and modem control register (MCR). In particular, these lines in the `startup` function define what gets written to the MCR:

```
info->MCR = 0;
if (info->tty->termios->c_cflag & CBAUD)
        info->MCR = UART_MCR_DTR | UART_MCR_RTS;
```

Why is this important? Obtaining a serial port file descriptor by using the open command results in DTR and RTS either being set or cleared, depending on whether a baud rate is set. The `startup` function doesn't query the MCR to preserve the DTR or RTS status.

Use of DTR and RTS modem control signals allows for two single-bit outputs. Clearing the HUPCL bit in the serial port's `c_cflags` register preserves the individual state of DTR and RTS at file closure. However, the serial port file open system call in `serial.c` either clears or sets both DTR and RTS. This doesn't preserve the state of

DTR or RTS. Applications that require DTR and RTS to operate completely individually should query and set the MCR directly (that is, they should not do so by using the serial port driver) or you can modify serial.c to suit your requirements. Regardless of direct MCR communication or use of the serial port driver, serial communication using the driver requires a file open system call that could change DTR and/or RTS without your knowledge.

This limitation does not affect the Project Trailblazer hardware design for using DTR or RTS control signals to drive the lift access point permission signal. The access point displays a stop indication the majority of the time, and it displays a go indication only momentarily, upon authentication. Using the DTR output signal and clearing the HUPCL bit from serial port's c_cflags variable results in a 0 DTR output state (that is, a positive voltage) across multiple openings and closings of the serial port.

Providing Serial Communication for bash Scripts, Using querySerial

The querySerial program provides serial communication functionality for bash scripts. Project Trailblazer uses querySerial to communicate with the lift access point input and output hardware—the RFID tag reader and the message display. The querySerial command line requires the port, the baud rate, the timeout, and a command to be sent. querySerial performs the following procedures:

1. It opens the requested port.

2. It sets the baud rate.

3. It configures the input buffer.

4. It sets noncanonical mode.

5. It sets the timeout.

6. It sends the user supplied command.

7. It awaits a timeout.

8. It returns the received characters.

9. It exits.

These operations are similar to those for polled serial communications, except for the noncanonical mode setting. As previously mentioned, the Linux serial driver contains code for modem control and terminal operation. To optimize communications over slow serial links, this driver has a mode called canonical that performs various character translations, echoing, command-line processing, and other manipulations. Project Trailblazer doesn't require any serial communications processing. Therefore, the serial port should be configured in noncanonical mode.

querySerial is loosely based on the "Serial Programming HOWTO."[4] It is not opti-mized for high-performance/low-latency communications, but merely shows the simplest way to send a serial command and await a response. The "Serial Programming HOWTO" clearly explains four noncanonical configurations that use VMIN and VTIME. Use of VMIN and VTIME may reduce timeout conditions of a serial communication application. Sweet's "Serial Programming Guide for POSIX Operating Systems"[5] is another excellent document that explains serial communications, port configuration, modem communication, and I/O control. Listing 6.3 shows the querySerial program.

LISTING 6.3   The querySerial Program

```
/*
 * querySerial v0.1 9/17/01
 * www.embeddedlinuxinterfacing.com
 *
 * The original  location of this source is
 * http://www.embeddedlinuxinterfacing.com/chapters/06/querySerial.c
 *
 *
 * Copyright (C) 2001 by Craig Hollabaugh
 *
 * This program is free software; you can redistribute it and/or modify
 * it under the terms of the GNU Library General Public License as
 * published by the Free Software Foundation; either version 2 of the
 * License, or (at your option) any later version.
 *
 * This program is distributed in the hope that it will be useful, but
 * WITHOUT ANY WARRANTY; without even the implied warranty of
 * MERCHANTABILITY or FITNESS FOR A PARTICULAR PURPOSE. See the GNU
 * Library General Public License for more details.
 *
 * You should have received a copy of the GNU Library General Public
 * License along with this program; if not, write to the
 * Free Software Foundation, Inc.,
 * 59 Temple Place, Suite 330, Boston, MA 02111-1307 USA
 */

/* querySerial
 * querySerial provides bash scripts with serial communications. This
 * program sends a query out a serial port and waits a specific amount
 * of time then returns all the characters received. The command line
```

LISTING 6.3   Continued

```
 * parameters allow the user to select the serial port, select the
 * baud rate, select the timeout and the serial command to send.
 * A simple hash function converts the baud rate
 * command line parameter into an integer.  */

/*
gcc -o querySerial querySerial.c
*/


#include <stdio.h>
#include <sys/ioctl.h>
#include <fcntl.h>
#include <termios.h>
#include <stdlib.h>

/* These are the hash definitions */
#define USERBAUD1200 '1'+'2'
#define USERBAUD2400 '2'+'4'
#define USERBAUD9600 '9'+'6'
#define USERBAUD1920 '1'+'9'
#define USERBAUD3840 '3'+'8'

struct termios tio;

int main(int argc, char *argv[])
{
  int fd, status, whichBaud, result;
  long baud;
  char buffer[255];

  if (argc != 5)
  {
    printf("Usage: querySerial port speed timeout(mS) command\n");
    exit( 1 );
  }

/* compute which baud rate the user wants using a simple adding
 * hash function
 */
```

LISTING 6.3   Continued

```
whichBaud = argv[2][0] + argv[2][1];

switch (whichBaud) {
  case USERBAUD1200:
    baud = B1200;
    break;
  case USERBAUD2400:
    baud = B2400;
    break;
  case USERBAUD9600:
    baud = B9600;
    break;
  case USERBAUD1920:
    baud = B19200;
    break;
  case USERBAUD3840:
    baud = B38400;
    break;
  default:
    printf("Baud rate %s is not supported, ");
    printf("use 1200, 2400, 9600, 19200 or 38400.\n", argv[2]);
    exit(1);
    break;
}

/* open the serial port device file
 * O_NDELAY - tells port to operate and ignore the DCD line
 * O_NOCTTY - this process is not to become the controlling
 *            process for the port. The driver will not send
 *            this process signals due to keyboard aborts, etc.
 */
 if ((fd = open(argv[1],O_RDWR | O_NDELAY | O_NOCTTY)) < 0)
 {
   printf("Couldn't open %s\n",argv[1]);
   exit(1);
 }

/* we are not concerned about preserving the old serial port configuration
 * CS8, 8 data bits
 * CREAD, receiver enabled
 * CLOCAL, don't change the port's owner
 */
```

LISTING 6.3   Continued

```
  tio.c_cflag = baud | CS8 | CREAD | CLOCAL;

  tio.c_cflag &= ~HUPCL; /* clear the HUPCL bit, close doesn't change DTR */

  tio.c_lflag = 0;        /* set input flag noncanonical, no processing */

  tio.c_iflag = IGNPAR;  /* ignore parity errors */

  tio.c_oflag = 0;        /* set output flag noncanonical, no processing */

  tio.c_cc[VTIME] = 0;   /* no time delay */
  tio.c_cc[VMIN]  = 0;   /* no char delay */

  tcflush(fd, TCIFLUSH); /* flush the buffer */
  tcsetattr(fd, TCSANOW, &tio); /* set the attributes */

/* Set up for no delay, ie nonblocking reads will occur.
   When we read, we'll get what's in the input buffer or nothing */
  fcntl(fd, F_SETFL, FNDELAY);

/* write the users command out the serial port */
  result = write(fd, argv[4], strlen(argv[4]));
  if (result < 0)
  {
    fputs("write failed\n", stderr);
    close(fd);
    exit(1);
  }

/* wait for awhile, based on the user's timeout value in mS*/
  usleep(atoi(argv[3]) * 1000);

/* read the input buffer and print it */
  result = read(fd,buffer,255);
  buffer[result] = 0; // zero terminate so printf works
  printf("%s\n",buffer);

/* close the device file */
  close(fd);
}
```

The querySerial program requires four command-line parameters: the serial port to use (/dev/ttyS0 or /dev/ttyS1), the baud rate (1200, 2400, 9600, 19200, or 38400), a timeout value in milliseconds, and the command to be sent. querySerial sends the command at the baud rate selected, waits the specified amount of time, and returns all the characters received on the serial port. You can test querySerial directly on tbdev1, without using a target board. Here are the steps to compile and test querySerial:

1. Compile querySerial.c:

   ```
   root@tbdev1[510]: gcc -o querySerial querySerial.c
   ```

2. Physically connect tbdev1's serial ports together, using a null modem adapter and minicom.

3. In one console window, run minicom and configure it by typing **CTRL-a** and then **o**. Then select Serial Port Setup. Set SERIAL DEVICE to /dev/ttyS0 and the Bps/Par/Bits to 1200 8N1.

4. In another console window, run querySerial to send a command out ttyS1 to ttyS0, which then shows up in the minicom window. To do this, issue the following command:

   ```
   root@tbdev1[517]: querySerial /dev/ttyS1 1200 5000 "this is a test"
   ```

   The string "this is a test" should show in the minicom window. The querySerial timeout, which is set to 5000 milliseconds, gives you 5 seconds to type a reply.

5. In the minicom window, type "got it". If you do this within 5 seconds, you should see this at the bash prompt:

   ```
   root@tbdev1[518]: querySerial /dev/ttyS0 1200 5000 "this is a test"
   got it
   root@tbdev1[519]:
   ```

   If you don't finish typing **got it** within 5 seconds, querySerial returns what you did type in 5 seconds.

Summary

You have now developed and tested three programs that set and query serial port control signals and issue serial commands from the bash prompt. That's quite a feat because you had a lot to learn about the internal workings and configuration of the Linux serial device driver. Fortunately, you discovered that the driver provides features that are capable of implementing the input and output Project Trailblazer access point requirements. Future system integration `bash` scripts can call `setSerialSignal`, `getSerialSignal`, and `querySerial` to communicate with the RFID tag reader, the display, and the red light/green light permission display.

Additional Reading

1. Dallas Semiconductor, "Application Note 83, Fundamentals of RS-232 Serial Communications," `http://pdfserv.maxim-ic.com/arpdf/AppNotes/app83.pdf`.

2. Embedded Planet, "Computing Engines, RPX Classic LF (CLLF_BW) User Manual," `www.embeddedplanet.com/PDF/docs/cllf_um.pdf`.

3. Brightstar Engineering, "MediaEngine, Hardware Reference Manual," March 16, 2001.

4. Gary Frerking, "Serial Programming HOWTO," `www.linuxdoc.org/HOWTO/Serial-Programming-HOWTO.html`.

5. Michael Sweet, "Serial Programming Guide for POSIX Operating Systems," `www.easysw.com/~mike/serial`.

6. B&B Electronics, "RS-232 BreakOut Box with 'RS-232 Made Easy' Book," `www.bb-elec.com/product.asp?sku=232BOB1E`.

7

Parallel Port Interfacing

Silverjack maintains its high-quality winter experience with a supplemental snow-making operation. Lift operation monitoring and snow-making equipment control are Project Trailblazer requirements. Lift access point displays inform guests about the current operational status of all mountain lifts. The Silverjack Operations Department will also compile lift uptime statistics for the Marketing Department. Project Trailblazer will allow the Operations Department to centralize and automate the snow-making process. Using mountaintop temperatures, Operations will develop a simple snow-making control algorithm that opens and closes water valves and controls equipment heaters.

The Project Trailblazer engineers discussed lift monitoring and snow-making control with Operations. Together, they determined input and output requirements. Monitoring a single lift requires six inputs, connected to the following alternating current (AC) sources:

- Three-phase AC power for the lift motor

- Lift motor controller output that indicates that the motor is functioning properly

- Lift motor controller output that indicates operation in slow-speed mode

- Lift motor controller output that indicates operation in high-speed mode

- An operator switch that can be closed at lift base

- An operator switch that can be closed at lift top

Controlling a single snow-making branch requires at least four control outputs for this AC equipment:

- Water Valve 1

- Water Valve 2

- Water Valve 3

- Heater 1

Some snow-making branches have six water valves and two heaters. The engineers began to explore options for process control that supported six inputs and four outputs (with the capacity for eight outputs). Numerous input/output (I/O) boards exist, from companies such as Computer Boards (www.computerboards.com), all of which exceed Project Trailblazer requirements for I/O as well as size. The engineers decided that because Project Trailblazer has such modest I/O requirements, the on-board PC parallel port is ideally suited for lift monitoring and snow-making control.

> **TIP**
>
> You should use solid-state relay modules to connect external devices to target boards. Four types exist: input AC (IAC), output AC (OAC), input direct current (IDC), and output direct current (ODC). Both input and output modules provide electrical isolation that protects a target board's sensitive circuitry. Mounting racks have module sockets, fuses, light emitting diodes (LEDs) showing operation, and barrier strips for field connections.

This chapter discusses PC parallel ports, hardware interfacing, and three approaches to parallel port software development for data acquisition and control. The first approach, port I/O, is simple, functional, and clearly demonstrates the low-level hardware control that is necessary for device driver development. The second approach, ppdev, uses Linux's parallel port device driver to control the parallel port. This approach is similar to serial port control through the use of device files and the input/output control (ioctl) system call. The Project Trailblazer engineers could have implemented a solution for lift monitoring and snow-making control using port I/O or ppdev, but they didn't. They decided to take the third approach; they created their own custom device driver that uses the /proc directory. This eloquent solution will simplify their future bash scripting. At first, the engineers were totally intimidated at the thought of device driver development. They're great C programmers, but none knew anything about device drivers, kernel modules, or the process directory. After successfully developing a device driver, they had a new understanding of Linux.

Control Using the Parallel Port

The parallel port, sometimes called a printer port, was originally designed to connect a printer to the computer. Over the years, many other devices, such as scanners, removal drives, and copy protection devices, have been connected to PCs via parallel ports. In today's PCs, this port has eight bidirectional data lines, four bidirectional control lines, and five status input lines, and they are accessed through a DB-25 female connector. Since its inception, the parallel port has evolved into four types:

- The standard parallel port (SPP)

- The PS/2-type (simple bidirectional) port

- The enhanced parallel port (EPP)

- The extended capabilities port (ECP)

The IEEE standard 1284, "IEEE Standard Signaling Method for a Bidirectional Parallel Peripheral Interface for Personal Computers," defines these four types and is summarized in this document:

- Warp Nine Engineering's "Introduction to the IEEE 1284-1994 Standard," www.fapo.com/1284int.htm.

Other online documentation fully explains the similarities and differences between these types and are as follows:

- Jan Axelson's "Parallel Port Complete Programming, Interfacing, & Using the PC's Parallel Printer Port," www.lvr.com/files/ppc1.pdf.

- Craig Peacock's "Interfacing the Standard Parallel Port," www.beyondlogic.org/spp/parallel.pdf.

- Craig Peacock's "Interfacing the Enhanced Parallel Port," www.beyondlogic.org/epp/epp.pdf.

- Craig Peacock's "Interfacing the Extended Capabilities Port," www.beyondlogic.org/ecp/ecp.pdf.

Project Trailblazer requires six inputs and four outputs. Using the online documentation, the engineers determined the bidirectional SPP type of port will suffice. The port does not need to control a high-speed printer—just some simple slow-speed inputs and outputs.

SPP hardware is usually port I/O mapped to the x86 ISA bus (that is, the port isn't memory mapped) at I/O base address 0x378. By using the motherboard BIOS, you can change this address and port type. For this chapter, make sure that your PC's BIOS configures LPT1 as an SPP type at the base address 0x378. The three SPP software registers data, status, and control exist at the base address, base address + 1, and base address +2 (that is, 0x378, 0x379, and 0x37A). Figure 7.1 shows these software registers, their bit definitions, and the hardware connections to the DB-25 parallel port connector.

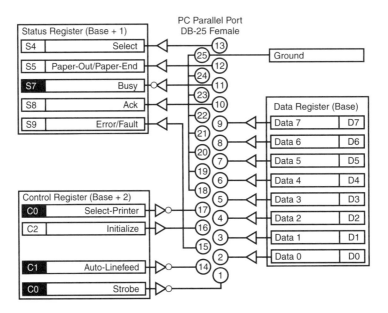

FIGURE 7.1   PC parallel port connection to software registers. The highlighted registers to DB-25 port connections are electrically inverted.

The control register contains two additional bits that are not shown in Figure 7.1. Control bit 5, bidirectional port enable, configures the data bus hardware for input. Control bit 4, IRQ via Ack Line enable, configures the port hardware to generate an interrupt on a low-to-high transition of the Ack line, DB-25 pin 10. Parallel port interrupts are not required for Project Trailblazer acquisition or control. The engineers built a parallel port software development test fixture, shown in Figure 7.2, with switches connected to inputs and LEDs connected to outputs.

TIP

Some PC parallel ports don't actively drive their data and control signals when at Logic Level 1. These open collector/drain signals are pulled high with a resistor located inside the PC. The value of this resistor, which you don't know and can't control, affects the LED's brightness. If you are experiencing problems using LEDs to debug your parallel port programs, you should use a voltmeter or logic probe instead. Also, keep in mind that certain control and status signals are inverted in hardware.

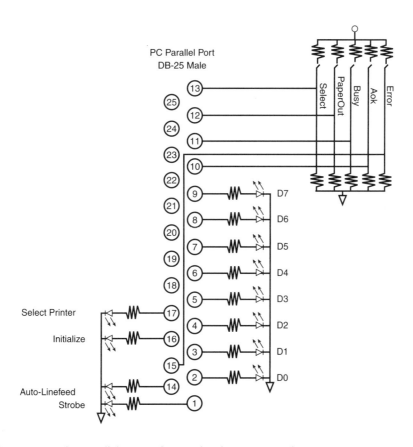

FIGURE 7.2   The parallel port software development test fixture.

An SPP has the six inputs and four outputs Project Trailblazer needs. However, some Silverjack locations will require eight outputs, so the parallel port alone doesn't meet the lift monitoring and snow-making I/O requirements. The engineers designed an interface circuit, shown in Figure 7.3, that connects the PC parallel port to two off-the-shelf Grayhill I/O module boards (www.grayhill.com). This interface circuit consists of an input path that uses an input buffer 74HC244, connected to an Input module rack and an output path that uses an output latch, 74HC533, connected to an output module rack. Both the buffer and the latch data busses connect to the parallel port's data bidirectional data signals, D7–D0. The input buffer's enable (/OE), the output latch's output enable (/OE) and latch enable (/LE) connect to parallel port's control lines. In an output operation, one that turns on or off an AC output module, a byte is placed on the parallel port's data bus and the OUTPUT_LATCH signal is asserted. The latch transfers the data byte from the signal lines D7–D0 to its output signals that in turn drives the output module board. The board's AC output modules

turn on or off corresponding to the bit pattern sent during the output operation. In
an input operation, the parallel port's bidirectional data bus, now configured for
input, reads the D7–D0 signal lines driven by the input buffer. When the
INPUT_ENABLE signal is asserted, the input buffer transfers the eight signals from the
Input module rack and drives the D7–D0 signal lines accordingly. Upon CPU reset,
the parallel port control register contains 0s that results in the OUTPUT_ENABLE signal
to be not asserted. This disables the latch output, turning off all output modules.
Software using this interface circuit will perform input and output operations by
accessing the parallel port's data and control registers. Datasheets for the 74HC244
and 74HC533 are available from Texas Instruments (www.ti.com).

> **TIP**
>
> When you are designing control circuitry, pay close attention to the hardware's startup condi-
> tions. You don't want the interface circuitry turning on or off field devices by itself, before
> your control software starts executing. You should look at register reset values and determine
> their effect on your logic circuitry. Then add pull-up or pull-down resistors to force your inter-
> face logic into a known state. When the control software starts execution, it can take over and
> control your external devices.

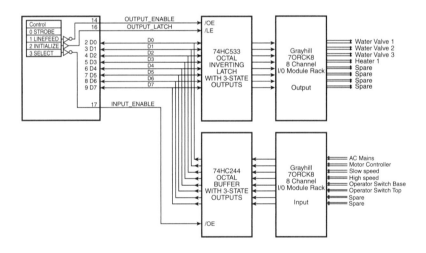

FIGURE 7.3   Project Trailblazer PC parallel port acquisition and control circuit.

Standard Parallel Port Control with Port I/O

I/O port operations with Linux couldn't be simpler. There's one command for
input—inb(*address*)—and one for output—outb(*value*, *address*). C macro expansion implements these two commands without involving any libraries. Use of inb

and outb does require a couple extra lines of code, though. The ioperm command requests and relinquishes port access from the kernel.[1] Writing a byte the parallel port could be as simple as these three lines of code

```
if (ioperm(0x378, 3, 1)) exit(1);
outb(argv[1][0], 0x378);
if (ioperm(0x378, 3, 0)) exit(1);
```

Likewise, reading a byte is simple. You can use the following code to read the parallel port's status lines:

```
if (ioperm(0x378, 3, 1)) exit(1);
putc(inb(0x379));
if (ioperm(0x378, 3, 0)) exit(1);
```

This code may output the ASCII value 0 and is likely to affect bash scripts. Simple additions to these two code fragments allow for lift operation monitoring and control of snow-making equipment.

Monitoring Lift Operation Using Port I/O

Using the inb and outb port I/O calls, the current status of a lift can be read using the interface circuit. liftoperationmonitor.c, shown in Listing 7.1, performs an input operation by configuring the parallel port data port for input, asserting the input buffer's enable signal, INPUT_ENABLE and reading the data lines D7–D0. It outputs a script-friendly version of the data port bits as eight ASCII characters, either 1s or 0s.

> **TIP**
>
> If you experience problems controlling your PC's parallel port, verify its configuration by using your PC's BIOS setup program. For the code in this chapter, you should configure your printer port at address 0x378 and SPP mode (sometimes called output only; bidirectional mode will also work). Also, use the gdb debugger to step through your code while you monitor voltage changes on the parallel port pins with your voltmeter. Verify that the parallel port is functioning correctly one step at a time.

LISTING 7.1   The liftoperationmonitor.c Program

```
/*
 * liftoperationmonitor v0.1 9/25/01
 * www.embeddedlinuxinterfacing.com
 *
 * The original location of this code is
```

LISTING 7.1   Continued

```
* http://www.embeddedlinuxinterfacing.com/chapters/07/liftoperationmonitor.c
*
*
* Copyright (C) 2001 by Craig Hollabaugh
*
* This program is free software; you can redistribute it and/or modify
* it under the terms of the GNU Library General Public License as
* published by the Free Software Foundation; either version 2 of the
* License, or (at your option) any later version.
*
* This program is distributed in the hope that it will be useful, but
* WITHOUT ANY WARRANTY; without even the implied warranty of
* MERCHANTABILITY or FITNESS FOR A PARTICULAR PURPOSE. See the GNU
* Library General Public License for more details.
*
* You should have received a copy of the GNU Library General Public
* License along with this program; if not, write to the
* Free Software Foundation, Inc.,
* 59 Temple Place, Suite 330, Boston, MA 02111-1307 USA
*/

/* liftoperationmonitor
 * liftoperationmonitor uses inb and outb to control an interface
 * circuit connected the PC parallel printer port. The port's
 * control port controls the input/output operation on the
 * interface circuit's data bus.
 */

/*
remember to compile with -O2 for proper inb/outb macro expansion
gcc -O2 -o liftoperationmonitor liftoperationmonitor.c
*/


#include <asm/io.h>

#define SPPDATAPORT     0x378
#define SPPSTATUSPORT  (SPPDATAPORT + 1)
#define SPPCONTROLPORT (SPPDATAPORT + 2)

/* these are the control port bit defs */
```

LISTING 7.1   Continued

```c
#define OUTPUTENABLE 0x02
#define OUTPUTLATCH  0x04
#define INPUTENABLE  0x08
#define SPPPORTREAD  0x20


int main(void)
{
  unsigned char v,i;

/* get permission from the OS to use the
 * data, status and control ports*/
  if (ioperm(SPPDATAPORT, 3, 1))
  {
    perror("ioperm");
    exit(1);
  }

/* this asserts three items.
 * 1. SSPPORTREAD, this configures the bidirectional data port as input
 * 2. INPUTENABLE, this enables the input buffer to drive the data bus
 * 3. OUTPUTENABLE, enable the output latch, driving the output rack
 *                  if you don't assert this, the output modules will
 *                  turn off
 */
  outb(SPPPORTREAD |  INPUTENABLE | OUTPUTENABLE,SPPCONTROLPORT);

/* The input buffer is now driving the bus, so do a read */
  v = inb(SPPSTATUSPORT);

/* Deassert SPPORTREAD and INPUTENABLE.
 * Use OUTPUTENABLE to keep output latch enabled
 */
  outb(OUTPUTENABLE  ,SPPCONTROLPORT);

/* loop through the bits in v and output 8 0s or 1s, like 01000001
 * MSB, D7 is output first
 */
  for (i = 0; i < 8; i++)
  {
    if ( v & 0x80 )
      putchar('1');
```

LISTING 7.1   Continued

```
   else
     putchar('0');

   v <<= 1; /* shift bits */
 }

/* let OS know we're done with the port */
 if (ioperm(SPPDATAPORT, 3, 0))
 {
   perror("ioperm");
   exit(1);
 }
}
```

Snow-Making Control Using Port I/O

By using only `outb` port I/O calls and the interface circuit, the output modules can be turned on or off. snowmakingcontrol.c, shown in Listing 7.2, performs an output operation by outputting a byte on the parallel port data bus then toggling the output latch signal, `OUTPUT_LATCH`. The latch then transfers the data lines, D7–D0, to its output, which turns on or off modules on the output module rack.

LISTING 7.2   The snowmakingcontrol.c Program

```
/*
 * snowmakingcontrol v0.1 9/25/01
 * www.embeddedlinuxinterfacing.com
 *
 * The original location of this code is
 * http://www.embeddedlinuxinterfacing.com/chapters/07/snowmakingcontrol.c
 *
 *
 * Copyright (C) 2001 by Craig Hollabaugh
 *
 * This program is free software; you can redistribute it and/or modify
 * it under the terms of the GNU Library General Public License as
 * published by the Free Software Foundation; either version 2 of the
 * License, or (at your option) any later version.
 *
```

LISTING 7.2   Continued

```
 * This program is distributed in the hope that it will be useful, but
 * WITHOUT ANY WARRANTY; without even the implied warranty of
 * MERCHANTABILITY or FITNESS FOR A PARTICULAR PURPOSE. See the GNU
 * Library General Public License for more details.
 *
 * You should have received a copy of the GNU Library General Public
 * License along with this program; if not, write to the
 * Free Software Foundation, Inc.,
 * 59 Temple Place, Suite 330, Boston, MA 02111-1307 USA
 */

/* snowmakingcontrol
 * snowmakingcontrol uses outb system calls to control an interface
 * circuit connected the PC parallel printer port. The port's
 * control port drives the interface circuit's output latch signals.
 */

/*
remember to compile with -O2 for proper inb/outb macro expansion
gcc -O2 -o snowmakingcontrol snowmakingcontrol.c
*/


#include <asm/io.h>

#define SPPDATAPORT      0x378
#define SPPSTATUSPORT  (SPPDATAPORT + 1)
#define SPPCONTROLPORT (SPPDATAPORT + 2)

/* these are the control port bit defs */
#define OUTPUTENABLE 0x02
#define OUTPUTLATCH  0x04
#define INPUTENABLE  0x08
#define SPPPORTREAD  0x20

int main(int argc, char *argv[])
{
/* get permission from the OS to use the
 * data, status and control ports*/
  if (ioperm(SPPDATAPORT, 3, 1))
  {
```

LISTING 7.2   Continued

```
    perror("ioperm");
    exit(1);
  }


/* Use OUTPUTENABLE to keep output latch enabled */
  outb(OUTPUTENABLE              ,SPPCONTROLPORT);


/* put the first char of command line argument 1 on the data bus */
  outb(argv[1][0],SPPDATAPORT);


/* assert OUTPUTLATCH, this latches the data bus to the latch's
 * outputs, driving the output module rack */
  outb(OUTPUTENABLE | OUTPUTLATCH ,SPPCONTROLPORT); //latch data


/* Use OUTPUTENABLE to keep output latch enabled */
  outb(OUTPUTENABLE              ,SPPCONTROLPORT);


/* let OS know we're done with the port */
  if (ioperm(SPPDATAPORT, 3, 0))
  {
    perror("ioperm");
    exit(1);
  }
}
```

SPP control with port I/O is very simple. The inb and outb commands offer an approach to control the parallel port registers and signals. With the interface circuit shown in Figure 7.3, the engineers can monitor lift operations and control snow-making equipment. There are three drawbacks to this port I/O approach. Developers must always assert the circuit's OUTPUT_ENABLE line to continually drive the output modules. This is a minor nuisance. The second, more difficult, drawback deals with the value of the latch output driving the output modules: There is no electrical mechanism to determine these bit values, other than to keep track of the last byte value written. If multiple bash scripts call the snowmakingcontrol program, somehow these scripts need to store and recall the last written byte value for their bit manipulation. The third drawback deals with use of the ioperm system call. Only the root user can call ioperm. This can affect non-root users' bash access to the parallel port. Accessing the parallel port using inb and outb system calls, with these three drawbacks, is not ideal. Improper control of snow-making equipment could lead to slope closures, operations failure, and expensive repair.

The parallel port control approach described in the next section—using the parallel port device driver (ppdev)—has the same two drawbacks as the port I/O approach. In the following section you'll implement snowmakingcontrol.c functionality using ppdev instead of outb. It's included here for Linux control completeness but isn't considered a viable option for snow-making control. The custom device driver, developed later in this chapter, has no drawbacks and implements a robust and eloquent solution for lift monitoring and snow-making control.

Standard Parallel Port Control Using ppdev

Using inb and outb isn't the only way to query and control the PC parallel port's data, control, and status registers. The Linux parallel port device driver, ppdev, also allows for this control, by using ioctl.[2] This approach is similar to the approach used in Chapter 6, "Asynchronous Serial Communication Interfacing," to control the serial port. A file (/dev/parport0) is opened, and a file descriptor is returned. With this descriptor, calls to ioctl can set individual control bits, query the port status, and read and write to the port's data bus. The program in Listing 7.3, snowmakingcontrolppdev.c, uses ppdev to control the parallel port registers that control the interface circuit in Figure 7.3. ("The Linux 2.4 Parallel Port Subsystem"[2] provides a complete discussion of parport and ppdev.) The following are the steps that the snowmakingcontrolppdev program takes:

1. It opens the /dev/parport0 file.

2. It requests access to the port, by using PPCLAIM.

3. It configures the port for SSP mode, by using IEEE1284_MODE_COMPAT.

4. It sets the OUTPUT_ENABLE line for latch output drive.

5. It writes the command-line argument 1 to the data bus.

6. It toggles the OUTPUT_LATCH line to latch data to the output module.

7. It releases the port.

8. It closes the /dev/parport0 file.

LISTING 7.3   The snowmakingcontrolppdev.c Program

```
/*
 * snowmakingcontrolppdev v0.1 9/25/01
 * www.embeddedlinuxinterfacing.com
 *
 * The original location of this code is
 * http://www.embeddedlinuxinterfacing.com/chapters/07/
```

LISTING 7.3   Continued

```
* snowmakingcontrolppdev.c
*
* Copyright (C) 2001 by Craig Hollabaugh
*
* This program is free software; you can redistribute it and/or modify
* it under the terms of the GNU Library General Public License as
* published by the Free Software Foundation; either version 2 of the
* License, or (at your option) any later version.
*
* This program is distributed in the hope that it will be useful, but
* WITHOUT ANY WARRANTY; without even the implied warranty of
* MERCHANTABILITY or FITNESS FOR A PARTICULAR PURPOSE. See the GNU
* Library General Public License for more details.
*
* You should have received a copy of the GNU Library General Public
* License along with this program; if not, write to the
* Free Software Foundation, Inc.,
* 59 Temple Place, Suite 330, Boston, MA 02111-1307 USA
*/

/* snowmakingcontrolppdev
* snowmakingcontrolppdev uses /dev/parport0 to control an interface
* circuit connected the PC parallel printer port. The port's
* control port drives the interface circuit's output latch signals.
*/

/*
* For more information, see The Linux 2.4 Parallel Port Subsystem, T. Waugh
* http://people.redhat.com/twaugh/parport/html/parportguide.html
*/

/*
gcc -O2 -o snowmakingcontrolppdev snowmakingcontrolppdev.c
*/

#include <stdio.h>
#include <unistd.h>
#include <asm/io.h>
#include <linux/ioctl.h>
#include <linux/parport.h>
#include <linux/ppdev.h>
```

LISTING 7.3   Continued

```c
#include <fcntl.h>

#define SPPDATAPORT     0x378
#define SPPSTATUSPORT  (SPPDATAPORT + 1)
#define SPPCONTROLPORT (SPPDATAPORT + 2)

#define OUTPUTENABLE 0x02
#define OUTPUTLATCH  0x04

struct ppdev_frob_struct frob;

int main(int argc, char *argv[])
{
  int fd, mode;
  unsigned char status, data;

/* 1. get the file descriptor for the parallel port */
  fd = open("/dev/parport0",O_RDWR);
  if (fd == -1)
  {
    perror("open");
    exit(1);
  }

/* 2. request access to the port */
  if (ioctl(fd,PPCLAIM))
  {
    perror("PPCLAIM");
    close(fd);
    exit(1);
  }

/* 3. configure the port for SPP mode */
  mode = IEEE1284_MODE_COMPAT;
  if (ioctl(fd, PPNEGOT, &mode))
  {
    perror ("PPNEGOT");
    close (fd);
    return 1;
  }
```

LISTING 7.3   Continued

```
/* 4. assert the latch's OUTPUTENABLE signal */
  frob.mask = OUTPUTENABLE ;
  frob.val = OUTPUTENABLE;
  ioctl(fd, PPFCONTROL, &frob);



/* 5. put the command line argument 1 on the data bus */
  ioctl(fd,PPWDATA,argv[1][0]);

/* 6. toggle the OUTPUTLATCH signal to latch data */
  frob.mask = OUTPUTENABLE | OUTPUTLATCH ;
  frob.val = OUTPUTENABLE | OUTPUTLATCH;
  ioctl(fd, PPFCONTROL, &frob);

  frob.mask = OUTPUTENABLE ;
  frob.val = OUTPUTENABLE;
  ioctl(fd, PPFCONTROL, &frob);

/* 7. release the port */
  ioctl (fd, PPRELEASE);

/* 8. close the device file */
  close(fd);
}
```

As mentioned previously, using ppdev doesn't solve the two port I/O drawbacks (OUTPUT_ENABLE and latch output value retention). Then why discuss ppdev? Using ppdev gives you another approach to control the parallel port. snowmakingcontrol.c uses inb and outb system calls that require ioperm calls. Use of ioperm requires root operation. SPP control using ppdev doesn't require root operation. Access to the parallel port device driver, /dev/parport0, can be controlled through file permissions. Non-root users can access the parallel port by using ppdev.

Developing a Custom Device Driver

After twiddling parallel port bits using port I/O and ppdev, the Project Trailblazer engineers decided that the potential failures due to drawbacks were unacceptable. Port I/O and ppdev approaches were error prone and risky. They needed a custom device driver for their interface circuit.

Armed with their interface circuit, port I/O, and ppdev knowledge, the Project Trailblazer engineers developed a few requirements for their first device driver:

- The driver should load at startup.

- When loaded, the driver should enable the latch output to drive the output modules.

- The driver should shield software developers from interface logic specifics.

- The driver should offer control of individual pieces of snow-making equipment without requiring the developer to perform bit manipulation.

- The driver should offer monitoring of individual lift signals without requiring the developer to perform bit manipulation.

The engineers started learning about device driver development by reading. Rubini and Corbet's *Linux Device Drivers* (published by O'Reilly) offers a complete discussion of driver development. It covers kernel version 2.4 and new kernel additions. Unfortunately, after reading this book, the engineers still didn't know where to start. Then they found the "Linux Kernel Module Programming Guide,"[3] which steps through kernel module development, character device files, the /proc filesystem, communications with device files, I/O controls, blocking processes, scheduling tasks, and interrupt handlers. The engineers learned the following about device drivers:

- Device drivers are accessed through file operations such as read and write.

- Device drivers run in the kernel space.

- Device drivers can be written as loadable modules.

- Device drivers running in the kernel do not have access to glibc.

- Device drivers that have memory problems (for example, array out of bounds) could crash the kernel.

- Traditionally, accessing device drivers is performed through file operations in the /dev directory.

- Device files in the /dev directory require static or dynamic assignment of major numbers, the general class of the device.

- Static assignment of major numbers creates the potential for device drivers to clash with each other.

- Dynamic assignment of major numbers introduces a small inconvenience in locating the device driver.

- Device drivers can exist in the /proc directory.

- Many Linux processes make available information via files in the /proc directory.

- /proc directory device files are created on-the-fly and do not clash with other device files and can be found easily by filename.

The "Linux Kernel Module Programming Guide"[3] is out of date, and its examples are difficult to compile. The engineers found the "Linux Kernel Procfs Guide,"[4] which applies to kernel 2.4 and is up-to-date. They decided to create the lift monitoring and snow-making control device driver, which would be a loadable kernel module that would use the /proc file system. The engineers planned to be extra careful when writing the device driver, to make sure that array-out-of-bounds conditions never occur. They knew they could not rely on glibc functions. They planned to develop their kernel module device driver around the "Linux Kernel Procfs Guide" program procfs_example.c. They began by writing a helloworld device driver module for the /proc directory. After they were confident in their skills at creating device drivers, they would modify helloworld and create the lift monitoring and snow-making control device driver.

Understanding helloworld_proc_module

Most helloworld programs print "Hello World" and terminate. Kernel module versions of helloworld print "Hello World" to the console or to the system log file when loaded and may print "Goodbye World" when they are unloaded. The helloworld_proc_module will print loading and unloading messages, and it will also store a character string that can be read and written with file operations. This character string offers data persistence across the life of the module. helloworld_proc_module will demonstrate the process of creating the /proc directory file, transferring data from userland to the module, transferring data from the module back to userland, and removing the /proc directory file. Here are the basic steps involved in the execution of helloworld_proc_module:

1. The module is loaded from a script or by hand, with insmod helloworld_proc_module.o.

2. The kernel calls the module's init function. The source code uses a macro define called module_init that declares which function is init. In this case, the statement is module_init(init_helloworld).

3. The module's init function executes and creates a /proc directory file entry called helloworld_file, fills its fields, and then prints a message to the system log. The helloworld_file /proc entry structure contains four fields that the kernel requires for read and write file operations:

- **read_proc**—The read_proc field should contain a pointer to the file's callback function that executes for a read file operation. For example, if a user ran the cat /proc/helloworld_proc_module command at the bash prompt, the kernel would ultimately call the file's read_proc function to handle this file read operation.

- **write_proc**—The write_proc field should contain a pointer to the file's callback function that executes for a write file operation. If a user ran the echo test > /proc/helloworld_proc_module command at the bash prompt, the kernel would call the file's write_proc function to handle this file write operation.

- **data**—The data field contains a pointer to the file's data. During module initialization, a data structure is created and populated. When a read or write callback occurs, using read_proc or write_proc, this data pointer is passed as a parameter. This way, the file's read_proc and write_proc functions can find their associated data.

- **owner**—Because the /proc file entry is used in a module, the owner field should be set to THIS_MODULE.

4. The module is unloaded by a script or by hand, with rmmod helloworld_proc_module.

5. The kernel calls the module's exit function. The source code uses a macro definition called module_exit that declares which function is exit. In this case, the statement is module_exit(cleanup_helloworld);.

6. The exit routine removes the /proc file entry and prints a message to the system log file.

This is quite a bit different from the standard helloworld.c program that you're used to seeing. This helloworld_proc_module program seems complicated, but after you get it running and you understand how to set the helloworld_file fields and how the data pointer is passed to the read and write callback functions, it's pretty simple. Listing 7.4 shows the complete helloworld_proc_module.c program.

LISTING 7.4   The helloworld_proc_module.c Program

```
/*
 * helloworld_proc_module v1.0 9/25/01
 * www.embeddedlinuxinterfacing.com
 *
 * The original location of this code is
 * http://www.embeddedlinuxinterfacing.com/chapters/07/
```

LISTING 7.4   Continued

```
* helloworld_proc_module.c
*
* Copyright (C) 2001 by Craig Hollabaugh
*
* This program is free software; you can redistribute it and/or modify
* it under the terms of the GNU Library General Public License as
* published by the Free Software Foundation; either version 2 of the
* License, or (at your option) any later version.
*
* This program is distributed in the hope that it will be useful, but
* WITHOUT ANY WARRANTY; without even the implied warranty of
* MERCHANTABILITY or FITNESS FOR A PARTICULAR PURPOSE. See the GNU
* Library General Public License for more details.
*
* You should have received a copy of the GNU Library General Public
* License along with this program; if not, write to the
* Free Software Foundation, Inc.,
* 59 Temple Place, Suite 330, Boston, MA 02111-1307 USA
*/

/*
* helloworld_proc_module.c is based on procfs_example.c by Erik Mouw.
* For more information, please see The Linux Kernel Procfs Guide,
* http://kernelnewbies.org/documents/kdoc/procfs-guide/lkprocfsguide.html
*/

/* helloworld_proc_module
* helloworld_proc_module demonstrates the use of a /proc directory entry.
* The init function, init_helloworld, creates /proc/helloworld and
* populates its data, read_proc, write_proc and owner fields. The exit
* function, cleanup_helloworld, removes the /proc/helloworld entry.
* The proc_read function, proc_read_helloworld, is called whenever
* a file read operation occurs on /proc/helloworld. The
* proc_write function, proc_write_helloworld, is called whenever a file
* file write operation occurs on /proc/helloworld.
*
* To demonstrate read and write operations, this module uses data
* structure called helloworld_data containing a char field called value.
* Read and write operations on /proc/helloworld manipulate
* helloworld_data->value. The init function sets value = 'Default'.
*/
```

LISTING 7.4   Continued

```
/*
gcc -O2 -D__KERNEL__ -DMODULE -I/usr/src/linux/include \
    -c helloworld_proc_module.c -o helloworld_proc_module.o

arm-linux-gcc -O2 -D__KERNEL__ -DMODULE -I/usr/src/arm-linux/include \
    -c helloworld_proc_module.c \
    -o /tftpboot/arm-rootfs/helloworld_proc_module.o
*/



#include <linux/module.h>
#include <linux/kernel.h>
#include <linux/init.h>
#include <linux/proc_fs.h>
#include <asm/uaccess.h>

#define MODULE_VERSION "1.0"
#define MODULE_NAME "helloworld proc module"

/* this is how long our data->value char array can be */
#define HW_LEN 8

struct helloworld_data_t {
  char value[HW_LEN + 1];
};

static struct proc_dir_entry *helloworld_file;

struct helloworld_data_t helloworld_data;

/* proc_read - proc_read_helloworld
 * proc_read_helloworld is the callback function that the kernel calls when
 * there's a read file operation on the /proc file (for example,
 * cat /proc/helloworld). The file's data pointer (&helloworld_data) is
 * passed in the data parameter. You first cast it to the helloworld_data_t
 * structure. This proc_read function then uses the sprintf function to
 * create a string that is pointed to by the page pointer. The function then
 * returns the length of page. Because helloworld_data->value is set to
 * "Default", the command cat /proc/helloworld should return
 * helloworld Default
 */
```

LISTING 7.4   Continued

```
static int proc_read_helloworld(char *page, char **start, off_t off,
                                int count, int *eof, void *data)
{
  int len;

/* cast the void pointer of data to helloworld_data_t*/
  struct helloworld_data_t *helloworld_data=(struct helloworld_data_t *)data;

/* use sprintf to fill the page array with a string */
  len = sprintf(page, "helloworld %s\n", helloworld_data->value);

  return len;
}



/* proc_write - proc_write_helloworld
 * proc_write_helloworld is the callback function that the kernel calls
 * when there's a write file operation on the /proc file, (for example,
 * echo test > /proc/helloworld). The file's data pointer
 * (&helloworld_data) is passed in the data parameter. You first cast it to
 * the helloworld_data_t structure. The buffer parameter points to the
 * incoming data. You use the copy_from_user function to copy the buffer
 * contents to the data->value field. Before you do that, though, you check
 * the buffer length, which is stored in count to ensure that you don't
 * overrun the length of data->value. This function then returns the length
 * of the data copied.
 */
static int proc_write_helloworld(struct file *file, const char *buffer,
                                 unsigned long count, void *data)
{
  int len;

/* cast the void pointer of data to helloworld_data_t*/
  struct helloworld_data_t *helloworld_data=(struct helloworld_data_t *)data;

/* do a range checking, don't overflow buffers in kernel modules */
  if(count > HW_LEN)
    len = HW_LEN;
  else
    len = count;
```

LISTING 7.4 Continued

```
/* use the copy_from_user function to copy buffer data to
 * to our helloworld_data->value */
  if(copy_from_user(helloworld_data->value, buffer, len)) {
    return -EFAULT;
  }

/* zero terminate helloworld_data->value */
  helloworld_data->value[len] = '\0';

  return len;
}


/* init - init_helloworld
 * init_helloworld creates the /proc/helloworld entry file and obtains its
 * pointer called helloworld_file. The helloworld_file fields, data,
 * read_proc, write_proc and owner, are filled.  init_helloworld completes
 * by writing an entry to the system log using printk.
 */
static int __init init_helloworld(void)
{
  int rv = 0;

/* Create the proc entry and make it readable and writable by all - 0666 */
  helloworld_file = create_proc_entry("helloworld", 0666, NULL);
  if(helloworld_file == NULL) {
    return -ENOMEM;
  }

/* set the default value of our data to Sam. This way a read operation on
 * /proc/helloworld will return something. */
  strcpy(helloworld_data.value, "Default");

/* Set helloworld_file fields */
  helloworld_file->data = &helloworld_data;
  helloworld_file->read_proc = &proc_read_helloworld;
  helloworld_file->write_proc = &proc_write_helloworld;
  helloworld_file->owner = THIS_MODULE;

/* everything initialize */
  printk(KERN_INFO "%s %s initialized\n",MODULE_NAME, MODULE_VERSION);
  return 0;
```

LISTING 7.4   Continued

```
}

/* exit - cleanup_helloworld
 * cleanup_helloworld removes the /proc file entry helloworld and
 * prints a message to the system log file.
 */
static void __exit cleanup_helloworld(void)
{
  remove_proc_entry("helloworld", NULL);

  printk(KERN_INFO "%s %s removed\n", MODULE_NAME, MODULE_VERSION);
}


/* here are the compiler macros for module operation */
module_init(init_helloworld);
module_exit(cleanup_helloworld);

MODULE_AUTHOR("Craig Hollabaugh");
MODULE_DESCRIPTION("helloworld proc module");

EXPORT_NO_SYMBOLS;
```

TIP

You should use the `helloworld_proc_module.c` source file as a skeleton for interfacing
projects. It compiles, loads, and executes correctly on the x86, ARM, and PowerPC target
boards. You can simply add hardware initialization code to the `init` function, interfacing code
to the `proc_read` and `proc_write` functions, change the names of the `/proc` entries, and
recompile.

Compiling, Inserting, and Testing `helloworld_proc_module` on the MediaEngine

When it is inserted into the kernel, the `helloworld_proc_module` creates a `/proc`
directory entry that bash scripts can read from and write to. Here are the steps to
compile the module using `tbdev1`, and then insert and test the operation of the
`helloworld_proc_module` using `tbdevarm`, the MediaEngine:

1. Compile `helloworld_proc_module.c` by using this command:

```
root@tbdev1[526]: arm-linux-gcc -O2 -D__KERNEL__ -DMODULE
➥-I/usr/src/arm-linux/include -c helloworld_proc_module.c
➥-o /tftpboot/arm-rootfs/helloworld_proc_module.o
root@tbdev1[527]: ls -sh /tftpboot/arm-rootfs/helloworld_proc_module.o
4.0k /tftpboot/arm-rootfs/helloworld_proc_module.o
```

2. Boot `tbdevarm` to gain access using minicom:

```
root@tbdev1[528]: minicom
```

Here's the `tbdevarm` prompt from minicom:

```
bash-2.04#
```

3. Check for the `helloworld_proc_module` object file and to see what modules are loaded:

```
bash-2.04# ls /
bin  dev  etc  helloworld_proc_module.o  lib  proc  sbin  tmp  usr

bash-2.04# cat /proc/modules
bash-2.04#
```

4. Insert `helloworld_proc_module.o`, list the current modules and check the `/proc` directory:

```
bash-2.04# insmod helloworld_proc_module.o
helloworld proc module 1.0 initialized

bash-2.04# cat /proc/modules
helloworld_proc_module    1056    0 (unused)

bash-2.04# ls /proc
1    bus          helloworld   locks        stat
15   cmdline      ide          meminfo      swaps
2    cpuinfo      interrupts   misc         sys
28   devices      iomem        modules      sysvipc
3    dma          ioports      mounts       tty
4    driver       kcore        net          uptime
5    execdomains  kmsg         partitions   version
6    filesystems  ksyms        self
7    fs           loadavg      slabinfo
```

The module initialized, /proc/modules contains an entry for it, and the /proc/helloworld file exists.

5. Check the read_proc function, proc_read_helloworld, by performing a read file operation on the /proc file entry, helloworld:

```
bash-2.04# cat /proc/helloworld
helloworld Default
```

6. Check the write_proc function, proc_write_helloworld, by performing a write file operation on the /proc file entry, helloworld:

```
bash-2.04# echo 1234 > /proc/helloworld
bash-2.04# cat /proc/helloworld
helloworld 1234

bash-2.04#
```

The string 1234 was successfully copied from the proc_write_helloworld function to the data->value field. (You verified that with a read file operation using cat /proc/helloworld.)

7. Remove the module, check the module list in /proc/modules and /proc directory:

```
bash-2.04# rmmod helloworld_proc_module
helloworld proc module 1.0 removed
bash-2.04# cat /proc/modules
bash-2.04# ls /proc/
1    bus          ide         meminfo     swaps
15   cmdline      interrupts  misc        sys
2    cpuinfo      iomem       modules     sysvipc
3    devices      ioports     mounts      tty
36   dma          kcore       net         uptime
4    driver       kmsg        partitions  version
5    execdomains  ksyms       self
6    filesystems  loadavg     slabinfo
7    fs           locks       stat
bash-2.04#
```

You have just compiled, inserted, and tested helloworld_proc_module. This module dynamically creates a /proc directory entry called helloworld. You can read and write to helloworld, and it stores an eight-character value. This seems simple, but this powerful module is the skeleton that the Project Trailblazer engineers needed to create their lift monitoring and snow-making control device driver.

Standard Parallel Port Control Using the Custom Device Driver `liftmon_snowcon`

The Project Trailblazer engineers could barely contain their enthusiasm. They had an interface circuit that connected I/O modules to the parallel port. They had written code using `inb` and `outb` to control their interface board. They had created, compiled, and tested a `proc` module. Now they needed to take a really big step: Combine all these accomplishments and develop the custom lift monitoring and snow-making control device driver, `liftmon_snowcon`.

The engineers created the following requirements for `liftmon_snowcon`:

- **LS1: The driver should load at startup.** This is easily accomplished by adding a line to an `/etc/init.d/rcS` or using the kernel module load file `/etc/modules`.

- **LS2: When it is loaded, the driver should enable the latch output to drive the output modules.** The driver's `module_init` function needs to assert `OUTPUT_ENABLE` and its `module_exit` function should de-assert `OUTPUT_ENABLE`.

- **LS3: The driver should shield software developers from interface logic specifics.** The device driver should provide a hardware control interface so that the developer doesn't need to know about `OUTPUT_ENABLE`, `OUTPUT_LATCH`, data lines, `INPUT_ENABLE`, or assertion levels.

- **LS4: The driver should offer control of individual pieces of snow-making equipment, without requiring the developer to perform bit manipulation.** The device driver should create a `/proc` file for each of the output modules: snowwatervalve1, snowwatervalve2, snowwatervalve3, and snowheater1. Writing 1 or 0 to a specific file should turn the specific module on or off. For example, this turns on the Water Valve 2 output module:

```
echo 1 > /proc/trailblazer/snowwatervalve2
```

  Notice that there is no bit manipulation and the device driver provides actual named files that correspond to the physical world. Internal to the device driver should be an `unsigned char` variable called snowcondata. The driver should perform the necessary bit manipulation within snowcondata.

- **LS5: The driver should offer monitoring of individual lift modules, without requiring the developer to perform bit manipulation.** The device driver should create a `/proc` file for each of the input modules: liftacmains, liftmotorcontroller, liftslowspeed, lifthighspeed, liftoperatorswitchbase, and liftoperatorswitchtop. Reading a specific file should return the status of an input module. For example, this returns either 1 or 0:

```
cat /proc/trailblazer/liftacmains
```

Notice that there is no bit manipulation and that the device driver provides actual named files that correspond to the physical world.

These requirements should simplify system integration using bash scripts. Scripts should work with named lift monitoring and snow-making files in the /proc directory. This device driver overcomes the limitations of port I/O and ppdev by automatically enabling the OUTPUT_ENABLE signal and maintaining the latch output value internally. This approach is more robust and less prone to errors. Code can be added to helloworld_proc_module.c to implement these liftmon_snowcon requirements.

Enhancements to helloworld_proc_module to Create liftmon_snowcon

The liftmon_snowcon module has module_init, module_exit, proc_read, and proc_write routines, just like helloworld_proc_module. The liftmon_snowcon init code doesn't create /proc entries in the /proc directory. Rather, it first creates the directory /proc/trailblazer. Then it creates all the liftmon_snowcon entries—snowwatervalve1, snowwatervalve2, liftacmains, liftmotorcontroller, and so on—in the directory /proc/trailblazer. The init function then fills each of the proc file's data, read_proc, write_proc, and owner fields. init then writes 0 to the latch. This turns off all the output modules. init then asserts the OUTPUT_ENABLE signal. init completes by writing a message to the system log.

TIP

You should separate your /proc file entries from other system entries by making a directory within the /proc directory, using the proc_mkdir function. This makes it easy to identify your project's /proc files.

Notice that in Listing 7.5 there isn't separate proc_read and proc_write functions for each /proc file. The snow-making control files share the same write_proc routine, proc_write_snowcondata, and share the same read_proc routine, proc_read_snowcondata. The data structure liftmon_snowcon_data_t contains a bitmask to distinguish one proc file from another. The bitmask matches up with the hardware bit that is used to control the output port. For example, the snowwatervalve3 proc file's data field contains a pointer to snowwatervalve3_data. snowwatervalve3_data.mask = SNOWWATERVALVE3, which equals 0x04. 0x04 corresponds to D3, which controls the third output module (Water Valve 3). Similarly, the liftmon proc files share the same proc_read function and use data.mask to distinguish one from another.

The `module_exit` routine, `cleanup_liftmon_snowcon`, latches a **0**, disables the latch, removes the proc file entries and the `/proc/trailblazer` directory, and completes by writing a message to the system log file. The `liftmon_snowcon` code is shown in Listing 7.5.

LISTING 7.5   The `liftmon_snowcon.c` Device Driver

```
/*
 * liftmon_snowcon v1.0 9/26/01
 * www.embeddedlinuxinterfacing.com
 *
 * The original location of this code is
 * http://www.embeddedlinuxinterfacing.com/chapters/07/liftmon_snowcon.c
 *
 * Copyright (C) 2001 by Craig Hollabaugh
 *
 * This program is free software; you can redistribute it and/or modify
 * it under the terms of the GNU Library General Public License as
 * published by the Free Software Foundation; either version 2 of the
 * License, or (at your option) any later version.
 *
 * This program is distributed in the hope that it will be useful, but
 * WITHOUT ANY WARRANTY; without even the implied warranty of
 * MERCHANTABILITY or FITNESS FOR A PARTICULAR PURPOSE. See the GNU
 * Library General Public License for more details.
 *
 * You should have received a copy of the GNU Library General Public
 * License along with this program; if not, write to the
 * Free Software Foundation, Inc.,
 * 59 Temple Place, Suite 330, Boston, MA 02111-1307 USA
 */

/*
 * liftmon_snowcon.c is based on procfs_example.c by Erik Mouw.
 * For more information, please see The Linux Kernel Procfs Guide,
 * http://kernelnewbies.org/documents/kdoc/procfs-guide/lkprocfsguide.html
 */


/* liftmon_snowcon
 * liftmon_snowcon uses inb and outp port I/O system calls to control
 * an interface circuit connected the PC parallel printer port. The port's
 * control port drives the interface circuit's output latch signals and
```

LISTING 7.5   Continued

```
 * input buffer. This module performs all bit operations for the data bus.
 * Bash script need only read and write to /proc entry files to determine
 * status or control equipment. In addition, the module's init code asserts
 * the OUTPUT_ENABLE signal and its exit code deasserts the OUTPUT_ENABLE
 * signal.
 *
 * This module creates these /proc entries:
 * Trailblazer directory   /proc/trailblazer
 * Lift Monitoring
 *   AC Mains              /proc/trailblazer/liftacmains
 *   Motor Controller      /proc/trailblazer/liftmotorcontroller
 *   Low Speed Operation   /proc/trailblazer/liftslowspeed
 *   High Speed Operation  /proc/trailblazer/lifthighspeed
 *   Operator Switch Base  /proc/trailblazer/liftoperatorswitchbase
 *   Operator Switch Top   /proc/trailblazer/liftoperatorswitchtop
 * Snow-Making Control
 *   Water Value 1         /proc/trailblazer/snowwatervalve1
 *   Water Value 2         /proc/trailblazer/snowwatervalve2
 *   Water Value 3         /proc/trailblazer/snowwatervalve3
 *   Heater                /proc/trailblazer/snowheater1
 */



/*
gcc -O2 -D__KERNEL__ -DMODULE -I/usr/src/linux/include \
    -c liftmon_snowcon.c -o liftmon_snowcon.o
*/

#include <linux/module.h>
#include <linux/kernel.h>
#include <linux/init.h>
#include <linux/proc_fs.h>
#include <linux/sched.h>
#include <asm/uaccess.h>

#include <asm/io.h>

#define MODULE_VERSION "1.0"
#define MODULE_NAME    "liftmon_snowcon"
```

LISTING 7.5   Continued

```c
/* Standard Parallel Port (SPP) definitions */
#define SPPDATAPORT     0x378
#define SPPSTATUSPORT  (SPPDATAPORT + 1)
#define SPPCONTROLPORT (SPPDATAPORT + 2)

/* SPP control port bit definitions */
#define OUTPUTENABLE         0x02
#define OUTPUTLATCH          0x04
#define INPUTENABLE          0x08
#define SPPPORTREAD          0x20

/* SPP input bit definitions */
#define LIFTACMAINS          0x01
#define LIFTMOTORCONTROLLER  0x02
#define LIFTSLOWSPEED        0x04
#define LIFTHIGHSPEED        0x08
#define LIFTOPERATORSWITCHBASE 0x10
#define LIFTOPERATORSWITCHTOP  0x20

/* SPP output bit definitions */
#define SNOWWATERVALVE1      0x01
#define SNOWWATERVALVE2      0x02
#define SNOWWATERVALVE3      0x04
#define SNOWHEATER1          0x08

/* define a bitmask, each *_file uses this to determine who it is */
struct liftmon_snowcon_data_t {
        unsigned char mask;
};

/* snowcondata is the output latch value stored internally. Control
   changes made by user scripts writing to /proc/trailblazer entries
   result in bits being either cleared or set in snowcondata. We
   write snowcondata to the output latch every time a control change
   occurs */
unsigned char snowcondata;

/* this are the data structures that hold the mask. When a /proc
   file is read or written to, the read_proc or write_proc routine
   receives a pointer to this structure */
struct liftmon_snowcon_data_t liftacmains_data,
```

LISTING 7.5   Continued

```
                                liftmotorcontroller_data,
                                liftslowspeed_data,
                                lifthighspeed_data,
                                liftoperatorswitchbase_data,
                                liftoperatorswitchtop_data,
                                snowwatervalve1_data,
                                snowwatervalve2_data,
                                snowwatervalve3_data,
                                snowheater1_data;

/* These are the pointers to the /proc directory entries */
static struct proc_dir_entry  *tb_dir,
                                *liftacmains_file,
                                *liftmotorcontroller_file,
                                *liftslowspeed_file,
                                *lifthighspeed_file,
                                *liftoperatorswitchbase_file,
                                *liftoperatorswitchtop_file,
                                *snowwatervalve1_file,
                                *snowwatervalve2_file,
                                *snowwatervalve3_file,
                                *snowheater1_file;

/* proc_read - proc_read_liftmon
 * proc_read_liftmon is the callback function that the kernel calls when
 * there's a read file operation on these /proc/trailblazer files:
 * liftacmains, lifthighspeed, liftmotorcontroller, liftoperatorswitchbase
 * liftoperatorswitchtop, and liftslowspeed. The file's data pointer is
 * passed in the data parameter. You first cast it to the
 * liftmon_snowcon_data_t structure. The input module rack values are
 * read by configuring SPP data for input and asserting the input buffer.
 * This places the state of the input modules on the SPP data port. Using
 * inb, the bit values are read then anded with the bitmask value to
 * to determine if the particular input module is on or off. Which
 * particular input module is defined by which /proc/trailblazer/ file
 * is read.
 */
static int proc_read_liftmon(char *page, char **start, off_t off, int count,
                             int *eof, void *data)
{
  unsigned char v;
```

LISTING 7.5   Continued

```
  struct liftmon_snowcon_data_t *liftmon_snowcon_data =
                              (struct liftmon_snowcon_data_t *)data;


  outb(OUTPUTENABLE, SPPCONTROLPORT);
/* this asserts three items.
 * 1. SSPPORTREAD, this configures the bidirectional data port as input
 * 2. INPUTENABLE, this enables the input buffer to drive the data bus
 * 3. OUTPUTENABLE, enable the output latch, driving the output rack
 *                  if you don't assert this, the output modules will
 *                  turn off
 */
  outb(SPPPORTREAD | INPUTENABLE  | OUTPUTENABLE, SPPCONTROLPORT);


/* The input buffer is now driving the bus, so do a read */
  v = inb(SPPDATAPORT);


/* Deassert SPPORTREAD and INPUTENABLE.
 * Use OUTPUTENABLE to keep output latch enabled
 */
  outb(OUTPUTENABLE, SPPCONTROLPORT);


/* mask the input value based on the mask. Each mask is different depending
 * which /proc/trailblazer file was read.
 * Electrical note: returning an inverted value because AC power to an input
 * module pulls outputs a low and the input buffer, 74244, doesn't invert
 */
  if (v & liftmon_snowcon_data->mask)
    page[0] = '0';
  else
    page[0] = '1';


/* return 1 which is the length of page */
  return 1;
}


/* proc_write - proc_write_snowcondata
 * proc_write_snowcondata is the callback function that the kernel calls
 * when there's a write file operation on these /proc/trailblazer files:
 * snowheater1, snowwatervalve1, snowwatervalve2 and snowwatervalve3.
 * The file's data pointer is passed in the data parameter. You first
 * cast it to the liftmon_snowcon_data_t structure. The buffer parameter
```

LISTING 7.5   Continued
_____

```
 * points to the incoming data. If the incoming data is a 1 or a 0,
 * a bit in snowcondata is set or cleared. Which bit is defined by which
 * /proc/trailblazer file is written to. snowcondata is then written to
 * the output latch.
 */
static int proc_write_snowcondata(struct file *file, const char *buffer,
                                  unsigned long count, void *data)
{
  struct liftmon_snowcon_data_t *liftmon_snowcon_data =
                              (struct liftmon_snowcon_data_t *)data;

/* check if the user wrote a 1 or a 0 the /proc/trailblazer file.
   if so, set or clear a bit in snowcondata */
  if (buffer[0] == '1')
    snowcondata |= liftmon_snowcon_data->mask;

  if (buffer[0] == '0')
    snowcondata &= ~liftmon_snowcon_data->mask;


/* Use OUTPUTENABLE to keep output latch enabled */
  outb(OUTPUTENABLE, SPPCONTROLPORT);

/* put snowcondata on the data bus */
  outb(snowcondata , SPPDATAPORT);

/* assert OUTPUTLATCH, this latches the data bus to the latch's
 * outputs, driving the output module rack */
  outb(OUTPUTENABLE | OUTPUTLATCH, SPPCONTROLPORT);

/* Use OUTPUTENABLE to keep output latch enabled */
  outb(OUTPUTENABLE,SPPCONTROLPORT);

  return 1;
}


/* proc_read - proc_read_snowcondata
 * proc_read_snowcondata is the callback function that the kernel calls
 * when there's a read file operation on these /proc/trailblazer files:
 * snowheater1, snowwatervalve1, snowwatervalve2 and snowwatervalve3.
 * The file's data pointer is passed in the data parameter. You first
```

LISTING 7.5   Continued

```
 * cast it to the liftmon_snowcon_data_t structure.  Use snowcondata
 * anded with the bitmask value to determine if the particular output
 * module is on or off. Which particular output module is defined by
 * which /proc/trailblazer/ file is read.
 */
static int proc_read_snowcondata(char *page, char **start, off_t off,
                                 int count, int *eof, void *data)
{
  struct liftmon_snowcon_data_t *liftmon_snowcon_data =
                             (struct liftmon_snowcon_data_t *)data;


/* mask the snowcondata value based on the mask. Each mask is different
 * depending which /proc/trailblazer file was read. */
  if ( snowcondata & liftmon_snowcon_data->mask )
    page[0] = '1';
  else
    page[0] = '0';

/* return the length */
  return 1;
}


/* init - init_liftmon_snowcon
 * init_liftmon_snowcon creates the /proc entry files and obtains
 * their pointers. For each file, the fields, data, read_proc,
 * write_proc and owner, are filled.  init_liftmon_snowcon
 * initializes the output modules in the off state then
 * complete by writing an entry to the system log using printk.
 */
static int __init init_liftmon_snowcon(void)
{
  int rv = 0;

/* Create the trailblazer /proc entry */
  tb_dir = proc_mkdir("trailblazer", NULL);
  if(tb_dir == NULL) {
    rv = -ENOMEM;
    goto out;
  }
  tb_dir->owner = THIS_MODULE;
```

LISTING 7.5   Continued

```
/* Create liftacmains and make it readable by all - 0444 */
  liftacmains_file = create_proc_entry("liftacmains", 0444, tb_dir);
  if(liftacmains_file == NULL) {
    rv = -ENOMEM;
    goto no_liftacmains;
  }
  liftacmains_data.mask = LIFTACMAINS;
  liftacmains_file->data = &liftacmains_data;
  liftacmains_file->read_proc = &proc_read_liftmon;
  liftacmains_file->write_proc = NULL;
  liftacmains_file->owner = THIS_MODULE;


/* Create liftmotorcontroller and make it readable by all - 0444 */
  liftmotorcontroller_file = create_proc_entry("liftmotorcontroller",
                                               0444, tb_dir);
  if(liftmotorcontroller_file == NULL) {
    rv = -ENOMEM;
    goto no_liftmotorcontroller;
  }
  liftmotorcontroller_data.mask = LIFTMOTORCONTROLLER;
  liftmotorcontroller_file->data = &liftmotorcontroller_data;
  liftmotorcontroller_file->read_proc = &proc_read_liftmon;
  liftmotorcontroller_file->write_proc = NULL;
  liftmotorcontroller_file->owner = THIS_MODULE;

/* Create liftslowspeed and make it readable by all - 0444 */
  liftslowspeed_file = create_proc_entry("liftslowspeed", 0444, tb_dir);
  if(liftslowspeed_file == NULL) {
    rv = -ENOMEM;
    goto no_liftslowspeed;
  }
  liftslowspeed_data.mask = LIFTSLOWSPEED;
  liftslowspeed_file->data = &liftslowspeed_data;
  liftslowspeed_file->read_proc = &proc_read_liftmon;
  liftslowspeed_file->write_proc = NULL;
  liftslowspeed_file->owner = THIS_MODULE;

/* Create lifthighspeed and make it readable by all - 0444 */
  lifthighspeed_file = create_proc_entry("lifthighspeed", 0444, tb_dir);
  if(lifthighspeed_file == NULL) {
```

LISTING 7.5 Continued

```
    rv = -ENOMEM;
    goto no_lifthighspeed;
  }
  lifthighspeed_data.mask = LIFTHIGHSPEED;
  lifthighspeed_file->data = &lifthighspeed_data;
  lifthighspeed_file->read_proc = &proc_read_liftmon;
  lifthighspeed_file->write_proc = NULL;
  lifthighspeed_file->owner = THIS_MODULE;

/* Create liftoperatorswitchbase and make it readable by all - 0444 */
  liftoperatorswitchbase_file = create_proc_entry("liftoperatorswitchbase",
                                              0444, tb_dir);
  if(liftoperatorswitchbase_file == NULL) {
    rv = -ENOMEM;
    goto no_liftoperatorswitchbase;
  }
  liftoperatorswitchbase_data.mask = LIFTOPERATORSWITCHBASE;
  liftoperatorswitchbase_file->data = &liftoperatorswitchbase_data;
  liftoperatorswitchbase_file->read_proc = &proc_read_liftmon;
  liftoperatorswitchbase_file->write_proc = NULL;
  liftoperatorswitchbase_file->owner = THIS_MODULE;

/* Create liftoperatorswitchtop and make it readable by all - 0444 */
  liftoperatorswitchtop_file = create_proc_entry("liftoperatorswitchtop",
                                              0444, tb_dir);
  if(liftoperatorswitchtop_file == NULL) {
    rv = -ENOMEM;
    goto no_liftoperatorswitchtop;
  }
  liftoperatorswitchtop_data.mask = LIFTOPERATORSWITCHTOP;
  liftoperatorswitchtop_file->data = &liftoperatorswitchtop_data;
  liftoperatorswitchtop_file->read_proc = &proc_read_liftmon;
  liftoperatorswitchtop_file->write_proc = NULL;
  liftoperatorswitchtop_file->owner = THIS_MODULE;

/* Create snowwatervalve1 and make it root writable, readable by all-0644 */
  snowwatervalve1_file = create_proc_entry("snowwatervalve1", 0644, tb_dir);
  if(snowwatervalve1_file == NULL) {
    rv = -ENOMEM;
    goto no_snowwatervalve1;
  }
```

LISTING 7.5   Continued

```
  snowwatervalve1_data.mask = SNOWWATERVALVE1;
  snowwatervalve1_file->data = &snowwatervalve1_data;
  snowwatervalve1_file->read_proc = &proc_read_snowcondata;
  snowwatervalve1_file->write_proc = &proc_write_snowcondata;
  snowwatervalve1_file->owner = THIS_MODULE;

/* Create snowwatervalve2 and make it root writable, readable by all-0644 */
  snowwatervalve2_file = create_proc_entry("snowwatervalve2", 0644, tb_dir);
  if(snowwatervalve2_file == NULL) {
    rv = -ENOMEM;
    goto no_snowwatervalve2;
  }
  snowwatervalve2_data.mask = SNOWWATERVALVE2;
  snowwatervalve2_file->data = &snowwatervalve2_data;
  snowwatervalve2_file->read_proc = &proc_read_snowcondata;
  snowwatervalve2_file->write_proc = &proc_write_snowcondata;
  snowwatervalve2_file->owner = THIS_MODULE;

/* Create snowwatervalve3 and make it root writable, readable by all-0644 */
  snowwatervalve3_file = create_proc_entry("snowwatervalve3", 0644, tb_dir);
  if(snowwatervalve3_file == NULL) {
    rv = -ENOMEM;
    goto no_snowwatervalve3;
  }
  snowwatervalve3_data.mask = SNOWWATERVALVE3;
  snowwatervalve3_file->data = &snowwatervalve3_data;
  snowwatervalve3_file->read_proc = &proc_read_snowcondata;
  snowwatervalve3_file->write_proc = &proc_write_snowcondata;
  snowwatervalve3_file->owner = THIS_MODULE;

/* Create snowheater1 and make it root writable, readable by all-0644 */
  snowheater1_file = create_proc_entry("snowheater1", 0644, tb_dir);
  if(snowheater1_file == NULL) {
    rv = -ENOMEM;
    goto no_snowheater1;
  }
  snowheater1_data.mask = SNOWHEATER1;
  snowheater1_file->data = &snowheater1_data;
  snowheater1_file->read_proc = &proc_read_snowcondata;
  snowheater1_file->write_proc = &proc_write_snowcondata;
  snowheater1_file->owner = THIS_MODULE;
```

LISTING 7.5 Continued

```
/* initialize snowcondata to 0, all output modules off */
  snowcondata = 0;

/* initialize the control port to know value 0 */
  outb(0, SPPCONTROLPORT);

/* put snowcondata on the data bus */
  outb(snowcondata, SPPDATAPORT);

/* latch it first before we turn on the output modules */
  outb(OUTPUTLATCH, SPPCONTROLPORT);

/* turn on the latch output to drive the output modules */
  outb(OUTPUTENABLE,SPPCONTROLPORT);

/* everything initialed */
  printk(KERN_INFO "%s %s initialized\n", MODULE_NAME, MODULE_VERSION);
  return 0;

/* this removes /proc entries if we have an error along the way */
no_snowheater1:
  remove_proc_entry("snowheater1", tb_dir);
no_snowwatervalve3:
  remove_proc_entry("snowwatervalve3", tb_dir);
no_snowwatervalve2:
  remove_proc_entry("snowwatervalve2", tb_dir);
no_snowwatervalve1:
  remove_proc_entry("snowwatervalve1", tb_dir);
no_liftoperatorswitchtop:
  remove_proc_entry("liftoperatorswitchtop", tb_dir);
no_liftoperatorswitchbase:
  remove_proc_entry("liftoperatorswitchbase", tb_dir);
no_lifthighspeed:
  remove_proc_entry("lifthighspeed", tb_dir);
no_liftslowspeed:
  remove_proc_entry("liftslowspeed", tb_dir);
no_liftmotorcontroller:
  remove_proc_entry("liftmotorcontroller", tb_dir);
no_liftacmains:
  remove_proc_entry("liftacmains", tb_dir);
out:
        return rv;
```

LISTING 7.5   Continued

```
}

/* exit - cleanup_liftmon_snowcon
 * cleanup_liftmon_snowcon turns off the output modules and
 * deasserts the OUTPUT_ENABLE signal. It removes the /proc entry files
 * prints a message to the system log.
 */

static void __exit cleanup_liftmon_snowcon(void)
{

/* this turns off all the output modules */
  outb(0, SPPCONTROLPORT);
  outb(0, SPPDATAPORT);
  outb(OUTPUTLATCH, SPPCONTROLPORT);
  outb(0,SPPCONTROLPORT);

/* removing the /proc entries */
  remove_proc_entry("liftacmains", tb_dir);
  remove_proc_entry("liftmotorcontroller", tb_dir);
  remove_proc_entry("liftslowspeed", tb_dir);
  remove_proc_entry("lifthighspeed", tb_dir);
  remove_proc_entry("liftoperatorswitchbase", tb_dir);
  remove_proc_entry("liftoperatorswitchtop", tb_dir);
  remove_proc_entry("snowwatervalve1", tb_dir);
  remove_proc_entry("snowwatervalve2", tb_dir);
  remove_proc_entry("snowwatervalve3", tb_dir);
  remove_proc_entry("snowheater1", tb_dir);
  remove_proc_entry("trailblazer", NULL);

/* we're done */
  printk(KERN_INFO "%s %s removed\n", MODULE_NAME, MODULE_VERSION);
}


module_init(init_liftmon_snowcon);
module_exit(cleanup_liftmon_snowcon);

MODULE_AUTHOR("Craig Hollabaugh");
MODULE_DESCRIPTION("Trailblazer Lift Monitor and Snow-making Control");

EXPORT_NO_SYMBOLS;
```

Compiling, Inserting, and Testing liftmon_snowcon on the MZ104

When it is inserted into the kernel, liftmon_snowcon creates the /proc/trailblazer
directory and lift-monitoring and snow-making control entries. bash scripts can read
from and write to these entries. Here are the steps to compile the liftmon_snowcon
module, using tbdev1, and then insert and test the operation of liftmon_snowcon,
using tbdevmz, the MZ104:

1. Compile liftmon_snowcon by using this command:

    ```
    root@tbdev1[528]: gcc -O2 -D__KERNEL__ -DMODULE -I/usr/src/linux/include
    ➥-c liftmon_snowcon.c -o /tftpboot/i386-rootfs/liftmon_snowcon.o
    root@tbdev1[529]: ls -sh /tftpboot/i386-rootfs/liftmon_snowcon.o
    8.0k /tftpboot/i386-rootfs/liftmon_snowcon.o
    ```

2. Boot tbdevmz and gain access to it by using its console. Here's the tbdevmz
   prompt:

    ```
    bash-2.04#
    ```

3. Check for the liftmon_snowcon object file and what modules are loaded:

    ```
    bash-2.04# ls /
    bin    etc                lost+found  tmp
    boot   lib                proc        usr
    dev    liftmon_snowcon.o  sbin

    bash-2.04# cat /proc/modules
    bash-2.04#
    ```

4. Insert liftmon_snowcon.o, list the current modules, and then check the /proc
   directory for a trailblazer directory:

    ```
    bash-2.04# insmod liftmon_snowcon.o
    liftmon_snowcon 1.0 initialized

    bash-2.04# cat /proc/modules
    liftmon_snowcon        2106   0 (unused)

    bash-2.04# ls /proc
    1       devices      kcore     pci
    14      dma          kmsg      self
    2       driver       ksyms     slabinfo
    28      execdomains  loadavg   stat
    3       filesystems  locks     swaps
    ```

```
4        fs            meminfo       sys
5        ide           misc          sysvipc
6        interrupts    modules       trailblazer
bus      iomem         mounts        tty
cmdline  ioports       net           uptime
cpuinfo  irq           partitions    version
```

5. Change to the /proc/trailblazer directory and look for the liftmon_snowcon entries:

```
bash-2.04# cd /proc/trailblazer/
bash-2.04# ls
liftacmains              liftslowspeed
lifthighspeed            snowheater1
liftmotorcontroller      snowwatervalve1
liftoperatorswitchbase   snowwatervalve2
liftoperatorswitchtop    snowwatervalve3
```

You have six lift monitoring inputs and four snow-making control outputs.

6. Connect a voltmeter to the ground and to the parallel port control linefeed signal, pin 14, which is the OUTPUT_ENABLE signal. The voltage should read less than +100mV (this is asserted low). init_liftmon_snowcon asserts the OUTPUT_ENABLE signal.

7. Turn on the Heater 1 output module:

```
bash-2.04# echo 1 > snowheater1
```

The data port changes to 0x08, the OUTPUT_LATCH signal toggles, and the latch drives the output module board with 0xF7. The latch inverts 0x08 to get 0xF7. The Heater 1 output module turns on, as well. This verifies the correct operation of the snow-making control outputs. You can check the control outputs—snowwatervalve1, snowwatervalve2, and snowwatervalve3—by echoing a 1 to them.

8. Check a lift-monitoring input:

```
bash-2.04# cat liftacmains
0
bash-2.04#
```

0 means there's no alternating current (AC) applied to the AC Mains input module. Apply AC power to that input module and check again:

```
bash-2.04# cat liftoperatorswitchbase
1
bash-2.04#
```

The monitoring of the AC Mains input modules functions correctly. You can verify the correct operation of the remaining lift monitoring inputs.

9. Remove the module:

```
bash-2.04# rmmod liftmon_snowcon
liftmon_snowcon: Device or resource busy
```

The device is busy because you are currently in the /proc/trailblazer directory.

TIP

When you are in the /proc/trailblazer directory, its in-use counter increases by 1. You can read this counter by using the command cat /proc/modules. Modules that are in use cannot be removed from the kernel.

---

10. Change into another directory, remove the module, and check the /proc/modules file:

```
bash-2.04# cd /
bash-2.04# rmmod liftmon_snowcon
liftmon_snowcon 1.0 removed
bash-2.04# cat /proc/modules
bash-2.04#
bash-2.04# ls /proc
1      cmdline        interrupts     meminfo      stat
14     cpuinfo        iomem          misc         swaps
2      devices        ioports        modules      sys
21     dma            irq            mounts       sysvipc
3      driver         kcore          net          tty
4      execdomains    kmsg           partitions   uptime
5      filesystems    ksyms          pci          version
6      fs             loadavg        self
bus    ide            locks          slabinfo
```

The heater output module goes off. If you check the OUTPUT_ENABLE signal, you will see that it is not asserted (greater than +3V), so the latch outputs are disabled and the output modules are also off. This result shows that the cleanup_liftmon_snowcon code functions correctly.

When it is loaded, this device driver asserts OUTPUT_ENABLE. It shields software developers from interface logic specifics. It provides bash script access to individual lift monitoring and snow-making equipment through a /proc file interface. Use of this device driver eases system integration using bash scripts.

Summary

This chapter covers a tremendous amount of information. The Project Trailblazer engineers started off by establishing their input and output requirements for lift monitoring and snow-making control through discussions with the Operations Department. They investigated I/O boards and decided on PC parallel port use. They then designed an interface circuit to connect a PC parallel port to an input module board and an output module board. When they began writing control software, three approaches evolved: port I/O using inb and outb functions, parallel port control using the Linux ppdev device driver, and development of a custom device driver. The port I/O approach was simple. However, its use had drawbacks that make it too risky. The second approach, using ppdev, didn't solve the drawbacks. The engineers decided to develop a custom device driver, liftmon_snowcon. This driver presented the developers with an easy-to-use interface (that is, files in the /proc directory) for lift monitoring and snow-making control. The driver hides interface circuit-specific knowledge from the developer and provides an eloquent interface for bash scripting. The liftmon_snowcon device driver development was a little more complicated than the use of port I/O, but the benefits far outweigh the costs.

Additional Reading

1. Riku Saikkonen, "Linux I/O port programming mini-HOWTO," www.linuxdoc.org/HOWTO/mini/IO-Port-Programming.html.

2. Tim Waugh, "The Linux 2.4 Parallel Port Subsystem," http://people.redhat.com/twaugh/parport/html/parportguide.html.

3. Ori Pomerantz, "Linux Kernel Module Programming Guide," www.linuxdoc.org/LDP/lkmpg/mpg.html.

4. Erik Mouw, "Linux Kernel Procfs Guide," http://kernelnewbies.org/documents/kdoc/procfs-guide/lkprocfsguide.html.

8

USB Interfacing

Silverjack guests enjoy music and photographs. Whether it's Mozart in the village or Nine Inch Nails in the half pipe, people enjoy outdoor music and continually make positive comments. Project Trailblazer will enhance the mountain's audio capabilities.

Pictures also play an important role at Silverjack. Images are used around the mountain to provide current status information. "How long is the Lift 4 line?" and "Is it snowing at the top of Lift 9?" are common questions that could be immediately answered with pictures. With current mountain images, guests can make decisions about where to go on the mountain in order to avoid long lift lines. Images also enhance safety by allowing guests to view the mountaintop conditions. If it's snowing up high, some people might decide to stay low. Project Trailblazer image collection will enhance both guest enjoyment of Silverjack and their safety.

This chapter follows the Project Trailblazer engineers as they use embedded Linux to play music and collect images.

Linux audio is easy: You install a sound card, recompile the kernel, and reboot. Similarly, for video, you install a video capture card, recompile, and reboot. But these simple processes are possible only if the kernel supports the sound card and video capture card. Many devices don't have Linux support, or the support is via reverse-engineering that provides an unofficial solution.

Cost is a big consideration for Project Trailblazer. Sound cards, which are a commodity item, are inexpensive. Video capture and the associated cameras, on the other hand, are relatively expensive. Project Trailblazer requires image capture at the bottom and top of each lift, as well as in other Silverjack locations. Equipment costs will therefore add up quickly. The engineers need a low-cost solution for audio playback and image capture. Unfortunately, the Project Trailblazer target platforms don't have peripheral component interconnect (PCI) card bus connectors. Therefore, the engineers opted to use universal serial bus (USB) speakers and cameras. The consumer market has driven the price of speakers and cameras very low—in the $30 range. The engineers knew that the majority of USB devices available today ship with Microsoft Windows drivers. They didn't know whether devices and their drivers support Linux. The engineers figured that if the drivers did not exist, they might have to write their own.

Learning About USB

The engineers first found *USB Complete* by Jan Axelson,[1] which claims to tell "everything you need to develop custom USB peripherals." The first half of this book explains USB, data transfers, and device identification (called enumeration). The second half addresses device hardware design using chipsets. The book content isn't an exact match for developing Linux USB device drivers, but it provides a great introduction to USB communications. Here's what the engineers learned:

- The USB bus is asynchronous serial, with differential signaling.

- USB is plug-and-play; the user doesn't configure memory addresses, I/O addresses, interrupts or direct memory access (DMA).

- USB v1.1 supports a 12Mbps data rate.

- USB v2.0, which is relatively new, supports a 480Mbps data rate.

- The USB bus supports up to 127 devices, using a tiered topology of hubs and devices.

- USB devices are self-describing.

- USB supports four transfer modes that address the bandwidth requirements of different devices:

    - Interrupt transfers support periodic bandwidth.

    - Isochronous transfers support guaranteed bandwidth.

    - Control transfers support guaranteed bus access.

    - Bulk transfers support low-priority large data transfer.

- The USB controllers prioritize communications by using the four transfer modes to optimize bus communications.

- In addition to providing electrical and communication protocol specifications, USB defines a number of device classes for common peripherals such as audio devices, modems, mouse devices, keyboards, printers, and mass storage devices. A peripheral device that implements a device class can utilize preexisting host device driver code. Device classes promote interoperability.

- Many USB peripheral devices don't fit into a defined device class, such as scanners, video devices, Ethernet devices, MP3 players, and serial/parallel converters. Manufacturers of these devices must develop host device driver code.

- USB host controllers fall into two categories: universal host controller interface (UHCI) and open host controller interface (OHCI). These controllers are functionally different from one another; a UHCI controller is simpler from a hardware perspective and shifts some communication processing to the host CPU and driver, thus complicating the driver. A variety of vendors offer UHCI and OHCI host controllers.

The engineers continued their USB research and found the Linux USB Project home page (www.linux-usb.org) and The Programming Guide for Linux USB Device Drivers.[2] Browsing through this guide, they discovered the complexities of Linux USB device drivers. The first half of "USB Complete" clearly establishes that USB communications is not simple. "The Linux USB Programming Guide" further confirms this. The engineers decided that Project Trailblazer would not develop any USB device driver code because the steep learning curve would affect the development schedule.

The Linux USB Project home page offers a wealth of USB information. Linux USB device support started in 1996 as the Universal USB Driver (UUSBD). In 1999, Linus Torvalds developed the Alternate USB driver, which was released under the GPL license. As with other Linux code, a group of developers and testers fixed and enhanced the Alternate USB driver. Later that year, a complete driver code rewrite improved the interface and performance. The USB driver code matured and is incorporated into the kernel version 2.4.x configuration process and has been back-ported to kernel version 2.2.18. Drivers for device classes (audio devices, modems, mouse devices, keyboards, and mass storage devices) as well as numerous vendor-specific drivers (scanners, video devices, Ethernet devices, MP3 players, and serial/parallel converters) have been developed. Several vendor-specific drivers are incorporated into the kernel compile process, and the other drivers are compiled separately as loadable modules.

The Project Trailblazer engineers continued learning by reading "The Linux USB Subsystem."[3] This early draft offers an excellent introduction and usage guide for USB at kernel revision 2.4.0-test9. While the engineers were researching USB for Linux, kernel version 2.4.10 was released. They understood that USB driver development continually evolves. This led them to the Linux-USB Device Overview Web site,[4] which acts as a repository for current Linux USB driver information and organizes drivers into these categories: audio, communication, human interface devices, hub, image, keyboard, mass storage, mouse, multifunctional, networking, printer, scanner, serial, vendor, and video. The site offers device and driver overviews, a searchable index, and the ability to add and edit device information. This USB information clearinghouse enabled the engineers to select hardware that had operational Linux USB drivers.

Project Trailblazer USB Hardware

Based on driver functionality, component availability, and cost, the engineers selected the following USB devices for Project Trailblazer:

- Yamaha YST-MS35D USB speakers[5]

- Kensington VideoCAM Super-VGA PC camera, model 67016[6]

- SanDisk USB SmartMedia card reader[7]

One additional product that caught the engineers' attention was the JVC RK-8010VBK AV receiver, with a USB input and five 100-watt output channels.[8] This could be a solution for powering audio at the Silverjack AirPark. The engineers couldn't determine the device's USB specifics from online information, but they assumed that this receiver adheres to the USB Audio Class specification.[9] Therefore, this chapter focuses on using the Yamaha YST-MS35D USB speakers for use around the village. At this point, the engineers threw in an extra side project. They envisioned an image kiosk, where visitors could transfer, view, and send images as email messages from their personal digital cameras. These kiosks would be equipped with SmartMedia card readers (future kiosks are expected to have Compact Flash readers as well), keyboards, monitors, and network connections. Guests would be able to insert their memory cards, view images, and select email options. The remaining sections of this chapter address kernel configuration and supplemental software compilation to get these Project Trailblazer USB devices up and running using tbdev1.

USB Audio: Yamaha YST-MS35D USB Speakers

Configuring Linux for USB audio is simple and straightforward. In 30 minutes, you can perform the following steps on tbdev1:

1. Download the kernel, configure the kernel for USB audio, compile and install the kernel version 2.4.10, and then reboot tbdev1.

2. Connect the USB speakers.

3. Download and compile a console-based MP3 decoder program called `mpg123` and then play an MP3 song.

Downloading, Configuring, Compiling, and Installing Kernel Version 2.4.10

`tbdev1`, as configured in Chapter 3, is running the Debian potato distribution, which uses Linux kernel version 2.2.19. In this section, you will update `tbdev1` to run kernel version 2.4.10. This kernel version has the Project Trailblazer audio, video, and mass storage USB device drivers included within the source distribution. Getting these devices up and running requires simple kernel configurations. In this section, you will configure the kernel to recognize USB audio devices. Here are steps to download, configure, compile, and install kernel version 2.4.10:

1. Log on to `tbdev1` as root, change directory to `/usr/src`, and download and extract the kernel 2.4.10 source, by using these commands:

   ```
   root@tbdev1[550]: cd /usr/src
   root@tbdev1[551]: wget http://www.kernel.org/pub/
   ➥linux/kernel/v2.4/
   ➥linux-2.4.10.tar.gz
   root@tbdev1[552]: tar zxf linux-2.4.10.tar.gz
   ```

TIP

The Linux source code repository, `www.kernel.org`, is an extremely busy Web site. You will experience faster download times if you use a mirror site than if you use `www.kernel.org`. Check `www.kernel.org/mirrors` to find the mirror site closest to you.

---

2. Configure the kernel with USB audio support:

   ```
   root@tbdev1[553]: cd /usr/src/linux
   root@tbdev1[554]: make menuconfig
   ```

3. Configure the kernel options for sound support. Using the up and down arrow keys, scroll to the sound item and press Enter. When you see the Sound configuration menu, select the Sound Card Support item and press the spacebar until a * character appears between < > (that is, <*>). This means that sound card support will be built in to the kernel. If any other items are selected in <*>, scroll to them and use the spacebar to deselect them. Only the Sound Card Support item should be selected for USB audio. Use the left and right arrows to select Exit, and then press Enter. This takes you back to the main menu.

4. Scroll to the USB support item and press Enter. Configure only the following USB support options:

- <*> Support for USB

- [*] USB verbose debug messages

- [*] Preliminary USB device filesystem

- [*] UHCI alternate driver (JE) support

- [*] OHCI (Compaq, iMacs, OPTi, Sis, Ali) support

- [*] USB audio support

TIP

You need to determine your computer's USB host controller type by using the lspci command. Look for the manufacturer of the USB controller. Typically, controllers from Intel and VIA technologies are UHCI devices. CMD, Symbios, OPTi, Lucent, Silicon Integrated Systems, Ali, National Semiconductor, and NEC make OHCI controllers.

Use the left and right arrows to select Exit, and then press Enter. This takes you back to the main menu.

5. Use the left and right arrows to select Exit, and then press Enter. When asked to save the kernel configuration, select Yes and press Enter.

6. Build the new kernel by using this command:

```
root@tbdev1[555]: make dep; make clean; make bzImage
```

7. When the kernel build completes, you need to install the new kernel by copying the kernel image to the /boot directory:

```
root@tbdev1[556]: cp arch/i386/boot/bzImage /boot/usbtest
```

8. With the new kernel image installed, you need to configure lilo to load this kernel when booting instead of loading the potato kernel image. Add this entry to the bottom of /etc/lilo.conf and then run lilo:

```
image=/boot/usbtest
        label=usbtest
        read-only

root@tbdev1[558]: lilo
Added Linux *
Added usbtest
Skipping /vmlinuz.old
root@tbdev1[559]:
```

The * on the Added Linux line means lilo will load this default image. This is kernel 2.2.19, which the potato installation program installed. The new USB kernel is usbtest.

TIP

You can read more about lilo in two places: the LILO mini-HOWTO (www.linuxdoc.org/HOWTO/mini/LILO.html) and the tbdev1 user document's lilo directory, /usr/doc/lilo. These documents fully explain lilo's operation and its configuration file, /etc/lilo.conf.

9. Reboot tbdev1 and press the Alt key when you see lilo. Type usbtest at the boot: prompt, and then press Enter. This boots tbdev1 using the new kernel with USB audio support.

10. Log in as root and check the kernel version by using the uname command:

```
root@tbdev1[500]: uname -r
2.4.10
```

11. Look in the /proc/bus directory for a usb directory. This is the first indication that the kernel has USB support:

```
root@tbdev1[501]: ls /proc/bus/
pci/  usb/
```

12. Mount the usbdevfs filesytem on the /proc/bus/usb directory:

```
root@tbdev1[505]: mount -t usbdevfs usbdevfs /proc/bus/usb/
```

This creates a filesystem that contains human-readable information about the USB subsystem.

13. List the /proc/bus/usb directory contents:

```
root@tbdev1[506]: ls /proc/bus/usb
001/  devices  drivers
```

The devices file contains information about the currently connected USB devices. The drivers file contains a list of currently loaded USB drivers.

tbdev1 is now running kernel version 2.4.10 with USB audio support.

Connecting the USB Speakers

Follow these steps to connect the USB speakers and examine USB information provided by the kernel:

1. Connect the USB speakers and look at the contents of the
    /proc/bus/usb/drivers and /proc/bus/usb/devices:

    ```
    root@tbdev1[519]: cat /proc/bus/usb/drivers
                usbdevfs
                hub
                audio
    ```

    Use cat to check that Linux automatically loaded the USB audio device driver:

    ```
    root@tbdev1[520]: cat /proc/bus/usb/devices
    T:  Bus=01 Lev=00 Prnt=00 Port=00 Cnt=00 Dev#=  1 Spd=12  MxCh= 2
    B:  Alloc=  0/900 us ( 0%), #Int=  0, #Iso=  0
    D:  Ver= 1.00 Cls=09(hub  ) Sub=00 Prot=00 MxPS= 8 #Cfgs=  1
    P:  Vendor=0000 ProdID=0000 Rev= 0.00
    S:  Product=USB UHCI-alt Root Hub
    S:  SerialNumber=e000
    C:* #Ifs= 1 Cfg#= 1 Atr=40 MxPwr=  0mA
    I:  If#= 0 Alt= 0 #EPs= 1 Cls=09(hub  ) Sub=00 Prot=00 Driver=hub
    E:  Ad=81(I) Atr=03(Int.) MxPS=   8 Ivl=255ms
    T:  Bus=01 Lev=01 Prnt=01 Port=00 Cnt=01 Dev#=  2 Spd=12  MxCh= 0
    D:  Ver= 1.00 Cls=00(>ifc ) Sub=00 Prot=00 MxPS= 8 #Cfgs=  1
    P:  Vendor=0499 ProdID=3002 Rev= 1.00
    S:  Manufacturer=YAMAHA
    S:  Product=YAMAHA YST-MS35D USB Speaker
    S:  SerialNumber=Ser 00 em
    C:* #Ifs= 3 Cfg#= 1 Atr=40 MxPwr=  0mA
    I:  If#= 0 Alt= 0 #EPs= 0 Cls=01(audio) Sub=01 Prot=00 Driver=audio
    I:  If#= 1 Alt= 0 #EPs= 0 Cls=01(audio) Sub=02 Prot=00 Driver=audio
    I:  If#= 1 Alt= 1 #EPs= 1 Cls=01(audio) Sub=02 Prot=00 Driver=audio
    . . . some output deleted.
    root@tbdev1[521]:
    ```

    The devices file contains what looks like cryptic information. (See
    /usr/src/linux/Documentation/usb/proc_usb_info.txt for complete description of the /proc/bus/usb/devices output.) You can see the following in the
    lines that start with S:

    ```
    S:  Product=USB UHCI-alt Root Hub
    S:  Manufacturer=YAMAHA
    S:  Product=YAMAHA YST-MS35D USB Speaker
    ```

The USB root hub and the Yamaha USB speakers are running. Also, the I: lines following the Yamaha speaker lines show the device connected to the USB audio driver.

2. The USB subsystem has been loaded, the root hub and the speakers have been found, and the appropriate drivers loaded. Now you need to make two audio devices in the /dev directory. First check for /dev/audio and /dev/dsp, and if they don't exist, create them by using mknod:

```
root@tbdev1[524]: ls -l /dev/audio /dev/dsp
root@tbdev1[525]: mknod -m 666 /dev/dsp   c 14 3
root@tbdev1[526]: mknod -m 666 /dev/audio c 14 4
root@tbdev1[527]: ls -l /dev/audio /dev/dsp
crw-rw-rw- 1 root audio 14, 4 Apr 14 18:44 /dev/audio
crw-rw-rw- 1 root audio 14, 3 Apr 14 18:44 /dev/dsp
```

tbdev1 recognizes the USB speakers, using the kernel's USB subsystem. With the audio device files created, you can now test the USB speakers by using an MP3 decoder.

Downloading and Compiling a Console-Based MP3 Decoder Program

In this section, you will download and compile mpg123, a console-based MP3 decoder. Using mpg123, you will test the USB subsystem and the USB speakers. Here are the steps to download, compile and run mpg123:

1. Download the latest source code for the console-based MP3 decoder mpg123, from www.mpg123.de, extract the source from the tar file, and compile it:

```
root@tbdev1[535]: cd /root
root@tbdev1[536]: wget http://www.mpg123.de/mpg123/mpg123-0.59r.tar.gz
root@tbdev1[537]: tar zxf mpg123-0.59r.tar.gz
root@tbdev1[538]: cd mpg123-0.59r
root@tbdev1[539]: make linux
root@tbdev1[540]: ls -l mpg123
-rwxr-xr-x 1 root root 176049 Oct 7 17:57 mpg123
```

2. Test the USB speakers. To do so, you can play a now-famous Sun Studios recording as the first song:

```
root@tbdev1[555]: mpg123 "Elvis_Presley-Thats_All_Right.mp3"
High Performance MPEG 1.0/2.0/2.5 Audio Player for Layer 1, 2 and 3.
Version 0.59r (1999/Jun/15). Written and copyrights by Michael Hipp.
Uses code from various people. See 'README' for more!
THIS SOFTWARE COMES WITH ABSOLUTELY NO WARRANTY! USE AT YOUR OWN RISK!
Title  : Elvis Presley              Artist: That's All Right
```

```
Album  : The Sun Sessions CD         Year  :
Comment:                             Genre : Rock


Playing MPEG stream from Elvis_Presley-Thats_All_Right.mp3 ...
MPEG 1.0 layer III, 160 kbit/s, 44100 Hz joint-stereo


[1:56] Decoding of Elvis_Presley-Thats_All_Right.mp3 finished.
root@tbdev1[556]:
```

TIP

In addition to playing local MP3 files, mpg123 can also stream files from a URL over the network. Also, the process of decoding MP3 files is CPU intensive. If you experience dropouts during playback, you might want to configure mpg123 to downsample or decode in mono rather than in stereo. Use the command mpg123 --longhelp to show the command options for mpg123.

Elvis comes blasting out of the Yamaha speakers! You can now celebrate your successful configuration, compilation, and test of the Linux USB audio subsystem.

USB Image Capture: Kensington VideoCAM Super-VGA PC Camera

The Kensington VideoCAM is a low-cost USB camera that provides image resolution up to 800×600 pixels. This camera streams video at 24 frames per second. Project Trailblazer doesn't require streaming video—merely image capture. The camera's high resolution will provide excellent-quality images for guest and Silverjack use.

There is no Kensington camera option in the USB support of the kernel configuration program, make menuconfig. The engineers didn't know where to start. So they just plugged in the camera, and the console spewed a couple hundred lines of text. Viewing the system log file, the engineers found these informational lines:

```
Oct  7 19:54:16 tbdev1 kernel: hub.c: USB new device
➥connect on bus1/2, assigned device number 4
Oct  7 19:54:16 tbdev1 kernel: Product: VideoCAM
Oct  7 19:54:16 tbdev1 kernel: usb.c: USB device 4
➥(vend/prod 0x47d/0x5003) is not claimed by
➥any active driver
```

The vend/prod information provides a key. The engineers researched 0x047D and 0x5003 at the Linux-USB device overview Web site and found that the Kensington camera uses the se401 driver. There's a kernel configuration option for se401 under the USB support menu. In this section, you will perform the following steps on tbdev1:

1. Configure the kernel for video operation and se401 use. Compile and install the kernel, and then reboot tbdev1.

2. Connect the Kensington camera.

3. Download and compile a console-based video frame grabber program called vgrabbj, and then capture a video still image.

TIP

The vendor and product information pair identifies a unique USB device. Designs are often licensed to several companies for production and distribution. For example, two companies may offer USB cameras based on the same hardware design. These cameras are identical from an electrical perspective and can use the same USB device driver. If you can't find driver information for your USB device by name, use the vendor and product information pair.

Configuring the Kernel for Video Operation and se401 Use

To use the Kensington camera, you need to configure and rebuild the kernel with support for video and se401. You need to follow these steps:

1. Configure the kernel with video and se401 support by using make menuconfig:

```
root@tbdev1[553]: cd /usr/src/linux
root@tbdev1[554]: make menuconfig
```

2. You need to configure the kernel options for video support. Using the up and down arrow keys, scroll to the Multimedia devices item and press Enter. Select the Video For Linux item and press the spacebar until a * character appears between < > (that is, <*>). Now scroll down to the Video For Linux ---> item and press Enter. With the V4L information in proc filesystem (NEW) item selected, use the spacebar until a * character appears between the [ ] characters (that is, [*]). Select Exit and press Enter. Select Exit and press Enter again. This take you back to the main menu.

3. Scroll to the USB support item and press Enter. Configure this additional USB support option: <*> USB SE401 Camera support.

    Use the left and right arrows to select Exit, and then press Enter. This takes you back to the main menu.

4. Use the left and right arrows to select Exit, and then press Enter. When you are asked to save the kernel configuration, select Yes and press Enter.

5. Build the new kernel by using this command:

```
root@tbdev1[555]: make dep; make clean; make bzImage
```

6. When the kernel build completes, copy the kernel image to the /boot directory and run lilo:

```
root@tbdev1[556]: cp arch/i386/boot/bzImage /boot/usbtest
root@tbdev1[557]: lilo
Added Linux *
Added usbtest
```

7. Reboot and type usbtest at the lilo boot: prompt. Log in as root.

8. Mount usbdevfs on /proc/bus/usb by using this command:

```
root@tbdev1[505]: mount -t usbdevfs usbdevfs /proc/bus/usb/
```

Connecting the Kensington Camera

Follow these steps to connect the Kensington camera and examine USB information provided by the kernel:

1. Plug in the camera and check the /proc/bus/usb/devices file:

```
root@tbdev1[506]: cat /proc/bus/usb/devices
S:  Product=USB UHCI-alt Root Hub
S:  SerialNumber=e000
S:  Manufacturer=YAMAHA
S:  Product=YAMAHA YST-MS35D USB Speaker
S:  SerialNumber=Ser 00 em
C:* #Ifs= 3 Cfg#= 1 Atr=40 MxPwr=  0mA
I:  If#= 0 Alt= 0 #EPs= 0 Cls=01(audio) Sub=01 Prot=00 Driver=audio
P:  Vendor=047d ProdID=5003 Rev=20.50
S:  Product=VideoCAM
C:* #Ifs= 1 Cfg#= 1 Atr=80 MxPwr=500mA
I:  If#= 0 Alt= 0 #EPs= 2 Cls=00(>ifc ) Sub=00 Prot=00 Driver=se401
. . . some lined delete here.
```

The Linux USB subsystem finds the Kensington VideoCAM and loads the se401 driver. Use of the se401 device driver requires the configuration of the Video For Linux Two subsystem.[10] This subsystem creates a /proc directory entry called /proc/video. If you explore that directory, you find these entries:

```
root@tbdev1[515]: cd /proc/video/
root@tbdev1[516]: ls
```

```
dev/  se401/
root@tbdev1[517]: cat /proc/video/dev/video0
name          : Kensington VideoCAM 67016
type          : VID_TYPE_CAPTURE
hardware      : 0x1e
root@tbdev1[518]: cat /proc/video/se401/video0
driver_version : 0.23
model         : Kensington VideoCAM 67016
in use        : no
streaming     : no
button state  : no
button pressed : no
num_frames    : 2
Sizes         : 160x120 200x152 176x144
➥320x240 352x288 400x300 640x480 704x576 800x600
Frames total  : 0
Frames read   : 0
Packets dropped : 0
Decoding Errors : 0
```

That's the camera!

2. Get an image from the camera. First, you need to check for these video device entries in the /dev directory: video and video0. If they don't exist, you need to create them:

```
root@tbdev1[521]: ls -l /dev/video*
root@tbdev1[522]: mknod -m 644 /dev/video0 c 81 0
root@tbdev1[522]: ln -s /dev/video0 /dev/video
root@tbdev1[527]: ls -l /dev/video*
lrwxrwxrwx 1 root root 11 Oct 7 20:42 /dev/video
➥-> /dev/video0
crw-r--r-- 1 root root 81, 0 Oct 7 20:42 /dev/video0
```

Downloading and Compiling a Console-Based Video Frame Grabber

If you were to use cat /dev/video0, an RGB image byte stream would fill the monitor with text characters. That wouldn't do you any good. You can use a program called vgrabbj (http://vgrabbj.gecius.de) to convert the RGB byte stream to a JPEG image. vgrabbj allows you to periodically grab an image, overlay a timestamp on the image, and save it in JPEG format. Here are the steps to download, compile, and run vgrabbj:

1. Get the latest source code for vgrabbj and compile it on tbdev1:

```
root@tbdev1[541]: wget http://vgrabbj.gecius.de/
➥vgrabbj/vgrabbj-latest.tar.gz
root@tbdev1[542]: tar zxvf vgrabbj-latest.tar.gz
root@tbdev1[543]: cd vgrabbj-0.7.4/
root@tbdev1[549]: ./configure
. . . lines removed
checking for jpeg_set_defaults in -ljpeg... no
configure: error: *** jpeg library not found!
Please install the appropriate library ***
```

You can see that tbdev1 is missing some libraries. vgrabbj requires these
libraries and their header files: libjpeg, libpng, and freetype. You need to
install them on tbdev1 and rerun the vgrabbj configure:

```
root@tbdev1[550]: apt-get install libjpeg62-dev
root@tbdev1[551]: apt-get install libpng2-dev
root@tbdev1[552]: apt-get install freetype2-dev
root@tbdev1[553]: ./configure
root@tbdev1[556]: make
gcc -DHAVE_CONFIG_H -I. -I. -I.     -g -O2 -Wall -c vgrabbj.c
gcc -DHAVE_CONFIG_H -I. -I. -I.     -g -O2 -Wall -c font.c
gcc -DHAVE_CONFIG_H -I. -I. -I.     -g -O2 -Wall -c ccvt_c.c
gcc -g -O2 -Wall -o vgrabbj vgrabbj.o font.o ccvt_c.o -lz
➥-lttf -lpng -lm -ljpeg
root@tbdev1[558]: ls -l vgrabbj
-rwxr-xr-x 1 root  root   109463 Oct  7 21:23 vgrabbj
```

2. Run vgrabbj to see what you get:

```
root@tbdev1[559]: vgrabbj -f /tmp/firstpicture.jpeg
Reading image from /dev/video
root@tbdev1[560]: ls -l /tmp/firstpicture.jpeg
-rw-r--r-- 1 root root 6818 Oct 7 21:24 /tmp/firstpicture.jpeg
```

The result is a JPEG image file in the /tmp directory. tbdev1 doesn't
have a JPEG viewer or graphics support, so you have to transfer
/tmp/firstpicture.jpeg to another computer to view it. Sure enough,
it is a JPEG image file, and it is shown in Figure 8.1.

3. The vgrabbj program has many features, such as text overlays, image time-
stamping, and an automatic frame-grabbing time interval. This command line
best suits the Project Trailblazer Lift 9 settings:

```
vgrabbj -e -i vga -f /temp/image.jpg
➥-p "Silverjack Lift 9 Top - %A, %D, %r"
➥-T 20 -a 5 -m 50 -l 30
```

Table 8.1 explains each of these vgrabbj command-line parameters in more detail.

FIGURE 8.1   The vgrabbj image captured from the Kensington VideoCAM Super-VGA USB camera.

TABLE 8.1   vgrabbj Command-Line Options

Command-Line option	Description
-e	Enables the timestamp
-i vga	Sets the image size to 640×480
-f	Writes to an output file instead of to stdout
-p	Defines the overlay in timestamp format
-T	Sets the overlay font size
-a	Sets the overlay alignment on the image
-m	Sets the overlay blending with the original image
-l 30	Tells vgrabbj to become a daemon and write an image file every 30 seconds

4. When you enable vgrabbj's timestamp functionality, you get this error:

```
root@tbdev1[566]: vgrabbj -f /tmp/a.jpg -e
Reading image from /dev/video
Font not found: /usr/share/fonts/truetype/Arialn.ttf,
timestamp disabled Could not initialize font-engine
```

The TrueType font file Arialn.ttf is missing. You can transfer that font file from a Windows machine to the /usr/share/fonts/truetype directory. vgrabbj then runs without errors, and it time-stamps the image correctly.

You have now successfully configured, compiled, and tested music playback and image capture. One USB project remains: the image kiosk that uses a SmartMedia card reader.

USB Mass Storage: SanDisk USB SmartMedia Card Reader

Most digital cameras have removable storage media. By using additional memory cards, the user can increase the number of photographs between computer downloads. An image kiosk that transfers and then emails images from memory cards could provide the same result. Besides, guests would love to email their co-workers shots from the slopes with captions like "Having a Great Time!"

The Project Trailblazer engineers selected the SmartMedia memory reader over Compact Flash or Memory Stick primarily because that's what their personal cameras use. This section outlines the tbdev1 configuration steps to read the contents of a SmartMedia card. Linux USB also supports other removal memory readers. See the Linux-USB device overview Web site for more information.[4]

Kernel version 2.4.10 includes driver source code for the SanDisk USB SmartMedia card reader, model number SDDR-09. USB mass storage device drivers are merely interfaces to the Linux SCSI layer.[3] This means that, in addition to USB options, you also need to configure certain SCSI options within the kernel configuration. In this section, you will configure and build a new kernel that will access the USB SmartMedia card reader as a SCSI device. Here are the steps you will perform on tbdev1:

1. Configure the kernel for SCSI operation and SDDR-09 use. Compile and install the kernel. Then reboot tbdev1.

2. Connect the SanDisk USB SmartMedia card reader.

3. Mount and test the card reader operation.

Configuring the Kernel for SCSI Operation and SDDR-09 Use

To use the SanDisk USB SmartMedia card reader, you will need to configure and rebuild the kernel with support for SCSI and SDDR-09. Follow these steps to configure and compile the kernel:

1. Configure the kernel with SCSI and SDDR-09 support, by using make menuconfig:

```
root@tbdev1[553]: cd /usr/src/linux
root@tbdev1[554]: make menuconfig
```

2. You need to configure the kernel options for SCSI support. Using the up and down arrow keys, scroll to the SCSI support item and press Enter. Select the SCSI support item and press the spacebar until a * character appears between < > (that is, <*>). Select and configure these three SCSI support items:

    - <*> SCSI support

    - <*> SCSI disk support

    - <*> SCSI generic support

    Select Exit and press Enter. This takes you back to the main menu.

3. The SDDR-09 driver is considered new. You will not see an option for it in the USB support menu unless you configure the kernel to prompt for development drivers. Using the up and down arrow keys, scroll to the Code Maturity Level options item and press Enter. Select the Prompt for Development and/or Incomplete Code/Drivers item and press the spacebar until a * character appears between < >. Select Exit and press Enter. This takes you back to the main menu.

4. Configure the USB support options. Using the up and down arrow keys, scroll to the USB support item and press Enter. Configure these USB support items:

    - <*> USB Mass Storage support

    - [*] SanDisk SDDR-09 (and other SmartMedia) support (NEW)

    Select Exit and press Enter. This takes you back to the main menu.

5. SmartMedia cards use the DOS FAT filesystem. You need to configure the kernel for DOS FAT filesystem support. Using the up and down arrow keys, scroll to the File Systems item and press Enter. Configure these file system items:

    - <*> DOS FAT fs support

    - <*> MSDOS fs support

    Select Exit and press Enter. This takes you back to the main menu.

6. Use the left and right arrows to select Exit, and then press Enter. When you are asked to save the kernel configuration, select Yes and press Enter.

7. Build the new kernel by using this command:

```
root@tbdev1[555]: make dep; make clean; make bzImage
```

8. When the kernel build completes, copy the kernel image to the /boot directory and run lilo:

```
root@tbdev1[556]: cp arch/i386/boot/bzImage /boot/usbtest
root@tbdev1[557]: lilo
Added Linux *
Added usbtest
```

9. Reboot and type usbtest at the lilo boot: prompt. Log in as root.

10. Mount usbdevfs on /proc/bus/usb, using this command:

```
root@tbdev1[501]: mount -t usbdevfs usbdevfs /proc/bus/usb/
```

Connecting the SanDisk USB SmartMedia Card Reader

Follow these steps to connect the SanDisk USB SmartMedia card reader and examine USB information provided by the kernel:

1. Plug in the SmartMedia card reader and check the /proc/bus/usb/devices file:

```
root@tbdev1[508]: cat /proc/bus/usb/devices
S:   Product=USB UHCI-alt Root Hub
S:   SerialNumber=e000
S:   Manufacturer=YAMAHA
S:   Product=YAMAHA YST-MS35D USB Speaker
S:   SerialNumber=Ser 00 em
S:   Manufacturer=SanDisk
S:   Product=USB SSFDC
C:* #Ifs= 1 Cfg#= 1 Atr=a0 MxPwr=100mA
I:   If#= 0 Alt= 0 #EPs= 3 Cls=ff(vend.) Sub=01 Prot=01 Driver=usb-storage
```

2. The USB subsystem finds the SmartMedia card reader, USB SSFDC, and loads the usb-storage driver for it. The /proc directory has several SCSI entries now, and the system log file also contains information:

```
root@tbdev1[518]: cat /proc/scsi/scsi
Attached devices:
Host: scsi0 Channel: 00 Id: 00 Lun: 00
  Vendor: Sandisk  Model: ImageMate SDDR-0 Rev: 0208
```

```
     Type:  Direct-Access                 ANSI SCSI revision: 02


root@tbdev1[519]: cat /proc/scsi/usb-storage-0/0
   Host scsi0: usb-storage
       Vendor: SanDisk
      Product: USB SSFDC
Serial Number: None
     Protocol: Transparent SCSI
    Transport: EUSB/SDDR09
         GUID: 078102000000000000000000
     Attached: 1


root@tbdev1[523]: tail /var/log/messages
Oct 8 00:13:01 tbdev1 kernel: hub.c: USB new device
connect on bus1/2, assigned device number 4
Oct 8 00:13:02 tbdev1 kernel: Manufacturer: SanDisk
Oct 8 00:13:02 tbdev1 kernel: Product: USB SSFDC
Oct 8 00:13:02 tbdev1 kernel: scsi0 : SCSI emulation
➥for USB Mass Storage devices
Oct 8 00:13:02 tbdev1 kernel: Vendor: Sandisk Model:
➥ImageMate SDDR-0 Rev: 0208
Oct 8 00:13:02 tbdev1 kernel:    Type:
➥Direct-Access  ANSI SCSI revision: 02
Oct 8 00:13:02 tbdev1 kernel: Attached scsi
➥cremovable disk sda at scsi0, channel 0, id 0, lun 0
Oct 8 00:13:02 tbdev1 kernel: SCSI device
➥sda: 32768 512-byte hdwr sectors (17 MB)
Oct 8 00:13:02 tbdev1 kernel: sda: Write Protect is on
Oct 8 00:13:02 tbdev1 kernel:  sda: sda1
```

This means that a removable SCSI disk partition exists on /dev/sda1.

Mounting and Testing the SanDisk USB SmartMedia Card Reader Operation

Follow these steps to mount the SCSI disk partition, /dev/sda1, and then test the operation of the card reader by copying files from its card to tbdev1:

1. Mount the removable SCSI partition, remembering that SmartMedia cards contain MS-DOS filesystems:

```
root@tbdev1[535]: mount -t msdos /dev/sda1 /mnt
mount: block device /dev/sda1 is write-protected,
➥mounting read-only
root@tbdev1[536]: ls -lR /mnt
```

```
/mnt:
total 16
drwxr-xr-x  3 root  root   16384 Sep 23 18:08 dcim

/mnt/dcim:
total 16
drwxr-xr-x  2 root  root   16384 Sep 29 23:04 100olymp

/mnt/dcim/100olymp:
total 12688
-rwxr-xr-x  1 root  root  416207 Sep 30 13:14 p9301565.jpg
-rwxr-xr-x  1 root  root  418108 Sep 30 13:16 p9301566.jpg
-rwxr-xr-x  1 root  root  433757 Sep 30 13:18 p9301567.jpg
```

You can see that there is one image directory called dcim/100olymp, and it contains three JPEG image files.

2. Copy these three JPEG files to the /tmp directory. Use the cmp command to compare the original files on the card to the new files in the /tmp directory:

```
root@tbdev1[537]: cp -v /mnt/dcim/100olymp/* /tmp
/mnt/dcim/100olymp/p9301565.jpg -> /tmp/p9301565.jpg
/mnt/dcim/100olymp/p9301566.jpg -> /tmp/p9301566.jpg
/mnt/dcim/100olymp/p9301567.jpg -> /tmp/p9301567.jpg
root@tbdev1[538]: cmp /mnt/dcim/100olymp/p9301565.jpg /tmp/p9301565.jpg
root@tbdev1[539]:
```

There's no difference between the SmartMedia file /mnt/dcim/100olymp/p9301565.jpg and the copy in the /tmp directory. This proves that the USB SmartMedia card reader is functioning correctly.

TIP

The card reader driver may not handle removable media correctly or gracefully. To avoid system problems, unmount the card reader drive with umount /dev/sda1 before removing the storage card.

You have now properly configured, compiled, and tested a USB mass storage device in addition to the music playback and image capture devices.

Summary

Project Trailblazer can now play Mozart and Nine Inch Nails, capture mountaintop images for display elsewhere on the mountain, capture lift-line images, and provide an email service for guests' photographs. USB provides connectivity for low-cost consumer-grade equipment that is perfectly suitable for the Silverjack engineers' purposes. The engineers discovered that USB communications are not simple and decided that the device driver development learning curve would dramatically affect their development schedule. The engineers decided on USB devices for audio play-back, image capture, and memory transfer. These devices had kernel version 2.4.10 support, and the engineers merely configured, compiled, and installed the kernel, then rebooted to begin using these USB devices.

Additional Reading

1. Jan Axelson, "USB Complete", Lakeview Research, 2001.

2. Detlef Fliegl, "Programming guide for Linux USB device drivers," `http://usb.cs.tum.edu/usbdoc`.

3. Brad Hards, "The Linux USB sub-system," `www.linux-usb.org/USB-guide/book1.html`.

4. Markus Schlup, "Linux-USB device overview," `www.qbik.ch/usb/devices`.

5. Yamaha Corporation, "Yamaha YSTMS35D," `www.yamaha.com/cgi-win/webcgi.exe/DsplyModel/?gSPK00007YSTMS35D`.

6. Kensington Corporation, "Kensington VideoCAM Super-VGA PC Camera Model #67016," `www.kensington.com/products/pro_cam_d1006.html`.

7. SanDisk Corporation, "SanDisk USB SmartMedia Card Reader," `www.sandisk.com/consumer/im.asp`.

8. JVC Corporation, "RX-8010VBK Description," `www.jvc.com/product.jsp?modelId=MODL026350&page=2`.

9. Ashour, Brackenridge, Tirosh, Todd, Zimmermann, and Knapen "Universal serial bus device class definition for audio devices," `www.usb.org/developers/data/devclass/audio10.pdf`.

10. Bill Dirks, "Video for Linux Two," `www.thedirks.org/v4l2`.

9

Memory I/O Interfacing

Skiers and snowboarders want snow and short lift lines. Silverjack supplements natural snowfall by using snow-making equipment. The Project Trailblazer engineers want to provide guests with lift status information. In Chapter 7, "Parallel Port Interfacing," the engineers interfaced lift monitoring and snow-making equipment to the x86 parallel printer port, using an interface circuit connected to six input and four output modules. The ARM and PowerPC target boards also have the capability to monitor the lifts and control the snow-making equipment. The MediaEngine and the RPX-CLLF don't have parallel printer ports, but they do offer expansion connectors that are perfect for memory-mapped input/output (I/O).

This chapter discusses how the Project Trailblazer engineers redesigned the lift monitoring and snow-making control interface circuit and device driver software module. This chapter steps through the process of designing memory-mapped I/O hardware, configuring the CPU registers, and developing the driver software for the ARM and PowerPC target boards.

The Hardware Design Process

The hardware design process can be broken down into eight phases:

1. Design the external interface hardware.
2. Find space in the memory map.
3. Find the CPU configuration register base address.
4. Configure the memory controller.
5. Assign the output module enable signal.

6. Configure the I/O port controller.

7. Write the `helloworldbit` testing device driver.

8. Write the `liftmon_snowcon` device driver.

Using memory-mapped I/O requires the interface circuit to appear as though it is a static RAM device. The circuit should respond to memory chip selection, write enabling, output enabling, and the bidirectional data bus, and it should perform address decoding. The I/O requirements of six inputs and eight outputs can be implemented by using bytewide data transfers. Upon reset, the interface circuit must not energize any output control module. When the `liftmon_snowcon` device driver initializes (that is, when the module loads), it should turn off all the output control modules and enable output module driving circuit.

Memory-mapped I/O hardware connects to the CPU bus and acts like static RAM memory. The I/O interface circuit needs to be placed in the memory map where no other memory or device (such as an Ethernet controller) exists. Using manufacturers' documentation, the Project Trailblazer engineers need to find a place in memory to locate the I/O circuit.

The ARM and PowerPC processors configure their internal controllers and peripherals by using special configuration registers that are located at a specific memory address upon reset. Using memory-mapped I/O requires determining the register address base location. With this location and predefined offsets from this memory location, the CPU memory controller and general-purpose I/O port configurations can be modified.

Some board designs and operating systems move the register base location after reset. It's possible to find the register base address either in CPU documentation, in Linux source code, or by making a software system call.

When the I/O circuit is physically mapped to a memory location, the CPU's memory controller needs to be configured. The ARM and PowerPC memory controllers offer interfaces to SRAM, EPROM, Flash EPROM, DRAM, SDRAM, and SRAM-like devices in burst and nonburst modes. The Project Trailblazer engineers need to configure the ARM and PowerPC processors to access the I/O circuit as an SRAM-like device.

The interface circuitdesign requires a signal—called `OutputModuleEnable`—to control the output enable for the output control modules. The device driver asserts `OutputModuleEnable` during initialization. Both the ARM and PowerPC processors have many pins that could serve as this control line. The Project Trailblazer engineers need to determine which unused pin, that's available on an expansion connector, should be used.

Before the Project Trailblazer engineers can access the OutputModuleEnable, the CPU's port I/O controller must be configured. Many I/O pins on both the ARM and PowerPC processors have an alternate function for on-chip peripherals, such as serial port signals. The Project Trailblazer engineers need to configure the I/O controller so that the OutputModuleEnable signal doesn't use an alternate function and so that it is an output.

Configuring CPU registers is easy. It's a good idea to test the configuration with a simple program. The Project Trailblazer engineers need to write a simple device driver to test their ARM and PowerPC CPU configuration. This simple device driver, helloworldbit, should configure the CPU memory and I/O controllers and then access a memory location and toggle the OutputModuleEnable signal. By using a logic probe or oscilloscope, the Project Trailblazer engineers need to verify proper configuration of the CPU registers.

With the hardware design complete and tested, the Project Trailblazer engineers need to write the lift monitoring and snow-making control device driver for the ARM and PowerPC processors. Using the liftmon_snowcon.c device driver source code from Chapter 7, the engineers can develop lift monitoring and snow-making control device drivers for the MediaEngine and the RPX-CLLF.

Developing Lift Monitoring and Snow-Making Control for the MediaEngine

This section details the MediaEngine interface hardware design. After the engineers find space in the memory map for the I/O circuit, they configure the CPU registers and test the circuit by using the helloworldbit program. They then develop the MediaEngine liftmon_snowcon device driver, which enables the MediaEngine target board to monitor lifts and control snow-making equipment.

Designing the External Interface Hardware for the MediaEngine

In order for the MediaEngine to monitor lifts and control snow making, it needs to read six inputs and control four outputs. In this design, an output latch and an input buffer connect directly to the MediaEngine's CPU bus. The MediaEngine features external interface connectors that permit buffered access to various CPU signals. The bus expansion header, JP1, provides the signals listed in Table 9.1.

TABLE 9.1   MediaEngine JP1 Signals

Description	Signals
Address lines	A0–A15
Data lines	D0–D15
Chip select	/CS5

TABLE 9.1   Continued

Description	Signals
I/O line	GPIO14
Write enable	/WE
Output enable	/OE
Data ready	RDY
Reset	/RST
Power	+5V, +3V
Ground	GND

Figure 9.1 shows the connections between the output latch (74HC574 Edge Triggered D Flip Flop with three-state outputs), the input buffer (74HC244 Octal Buffer with three-state outputs), and the MediaEngine. Upon reset, GPIO14 is configured as an input pin. A pull-up resistor deasserts the OutputModuleEnable line, which disables the output modules. GPIO14 is then configured as an output pin. It controls the OutputModuleEnable line, which in turn enables or disables the I/O modules. Signals A0, /OE, /WE, and /CS5 control the three to eight line decoder, 74HC138, which performs address and read/write signal decoding.

Here's the write operation of 1 byte (see Figure 10-17, "Variable Latency I/O Write Timing Diagram," in *SA-1110 Developer's Manual*[1] for more information):

1. Deassert A0, /OE and /WE.

2. Set D0–D7.

3. Assert CS5, this enables the HC138.

4. Assert /WE. The HC138's Y2 output asserts the HC574's CLK because /WE = C = L, /OE = B = H, and A0 = A = L.

5. Deassert /WE. The HC138's Y2 deasserts HC574 CLK because /WE = C = H, /OE = B = H, and A0 = A = L. Data D0–D7 enters HC574's flip-flops.

6. Deassert /CS5.

Here's the read operation of 1 byte (see Figure 10-16, "Variable Latency I/O Read Timing Diagram," in *SA-1110 Developer's Manual*[1] for more information):

1. Deassert A0, /OE and /WE.

2. Assert /CS5, this enables the HC138.

3. Assert /OE. The HC138's Y4 asserts the HC244's /OE because /WE = C = H, /OE = B = L, and A0 = A = L. Data D0–D7 enters CPU.

4. Deassert /OE. The HC138's Y4 deasserts HC244 /OE because /WE = C = H, /OE = B = H, and A0 = A = L.

5. Deassert /CS5.

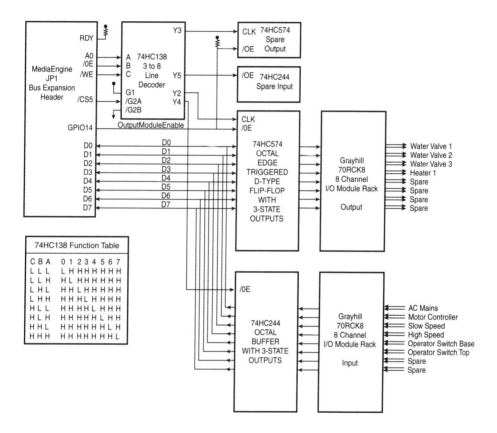

FIGURE 9.1   The MediaEngine `liftmon_snowcon` interface circuit.

Driving the HC138's A signal with A0 permits a spare set of eight inputs and eight outputs to be connected to the MediaEngine bus. GPIO14 asserts the OutputModuleEnable line, which enables the HC574's output buffers. The HC574's output can then turn the output modules on or off. The ready input signal, RDY, slows CPU read and write operations for use with slow memory devices.

TIP

The MediaEngine's ARM clock speed is 200MHz. This design's High-speed CMOS (HC) logic components are fast, but the Project Trailblazer engineers need to configure the CPU to access the interface circuit as slowly as possible because the I/O board trace capacitance could affect performance and reliability.

Finding Space in the Memory Map for the MediaEngine

The MediaEngine has 4MB Boot Flash memory, an Ethernet controller, optional Flash memory, an optional internal modem, an expansion port, and 32MB SDRAM. Table 9.2, which is a reprint of Table 3-1 from the *MediaEngine Hardware Reference Manual*[2], shows device memory mappings. The MediaEngine bus expansion port contains Chip Select 5 (/CS5), which the ARM processor maps to address 0x48000000. Section 2.4, "Memory Map," of the *SA-1110 Developer's Manual*[1], explains that Chip Select 5 is mapped to an 128MB memory block for static-memory or variable-latency I/O devices.

TABLE 9.2   MediaEngine Memory Map

Address Range	Description
0x00000000–0x003FFFFF	4MB Boot Flash
0x08000300–0x0800030F	CS8900A Ethernet Controller
0x10000000–0x11000000	16MB Flash (Optional)
0x18000000–0x18000000	Board Control Reg 0
0x19000000–0x19000000	Board Control Reg 1
0x40000000–0x4000001F	Internal Modem (Optional)
0x48000000–0x4FFFFFFF	Expansion Port
0xC0000000–0xC1FFFFFF	32MB SDRAM

The MediaEngine hardware design makes available chip select 5, /CS5, the expansion port through the JP1 connector. The liftmon_snowcon interface should use /CS5, which is mapped to address 0x48000000.

Finding the Register Base Address for the MediaEngine

The ARM SA-1110 peripheral, system, memory, and expansion on-chip registers are mapped to physical addresses between 0x80000000 and 0xBFFFFFFF (see Section 2.4, "Memory Map," of *SA-1110 Developer's Manual*[1]). Here are the register base addresses for memory and general-purpose I/O:

- Memory interface control registers: 0xA0000000

- General-purpose I/O control registers: 0x90040000

Configuring the Memory Controller for the MediaEngine

The static memory control register, MSC2 (see Section 10.2.4, "Static Memory Control Registers," of *SA-1110 Developer's Manual*[1]), configures control bits for Chip Select 4 and Chip Select 5. MSC2 configures the ROM type, bus width, first access delay, next access delay, and recovery time. Remember that the ARM needs to be configured for the slowest possible configuration of MSC2 for the liftmon_snowcon interface circuit. Table 9.3 shows the MSC2 bit field descriptions and the values used in this design.

TABLE 9.3   MSC2 Bit Field Descriptions and Design Values

Bits	Name	Value	Description
1..0	RT5 1.0	01	ROM Type: Nonburst variable-latency I/O
2	RBW5	1	ROM bus width: 16 bits
7..3	RDF5 4.0	11111	ROM delay first access: delay set to maximum
12..8	RDN5 4.0	11111	ROM delay next access: delay set to maximum
15..13	RRR5 2.0	111	ROM recovery time: recovery time set to maximum

The liftmon_snowcon interface design requires MSC2 to be 0b1111111111111101 or 0xFFF5.

Assigning the Output Module Enable Signal for the MediaEngine

The MediaEngine bus expansion interface connector offers only GPIO14. Therefore, the Project Trailblazer engineers assigned GPIO14 to control the OutputModuleEnable signal.

Configuring the I/O Port Controller for the MediaEngine

GPIO14 is a general-purpose I/O pin and has an alternate function: It can also be the transmit pin for UART 1. The Project Trailblazer engineers need to configure the ARM I/O port controller registers shown in Table 9.4 for GPIO14 output with no alternate function.

TABLE 9.4   Additional ARM register settings to make GPIO14 an output pin

Register	Description	Bit Setting	Description
GAFR	GPIO Alternate Function Register	AF14 = 0	No alternate function
GPDR	GPIO Pin Direction Register	PD14 = 1	Output

Writing the helloworldbit Testing Device Driver for the MediaEngine

Now that the Project Trailblazer engineers have defined the memory space, and determined the register base addresses, assigned the OutputModuleEnable signal, and determined the configuration of the memory and I/O controllers, it's time for them to write a helloworld program. Instead of printing "Hello world", this program should control signal lines. They decide to write a simple device driver to configure the ARM I/O and memory controllers and then control the GPIO14 and /CS5 signals.

The initialization code for the `helloworldbit_mediaengine.c` device driver, which is shown in Listing 9.1, configures the ARM's GPDR and GAFR registers for GPIO14 output, and then it sets and clears GPIO14. The code then configures the MSC2 register for Chip Select 5 operation, and then it reads and writes to physical memory address `0x48000000`. The code uses the `ioremap_nocache` function, which returns virtual addresses for the configuration registers. By using a oscilloscope, the Project Trailblazer engineers then verify the proper operation of GPIO14 and /CS5, as shown in Figure 9.2. The 200MHz MediaEngine clock frequency pushes their oscilloscope's capture capability.

LISTING 9.1   The `helloworldbit_mediaengine.c` Device Driver

```
/*
 * helloworld_bit_mediaengine v1.0 11/03/01
 * www.embeddedlinuxinterfacing.com
 *
 * The original location of this code is
 * http://www.embeddedlinuxinterfacing.com/chapters/09/
 *
 * Copyright (C) 2001 by Craig Hollabaugh
 *
 * This program is free software; you can redistribute it and/or modify
 * it under the terms of the GNU Library General Public License as
 * published by the Free Software Foundation; either version 2 of the
 * License, or (at your option) any later version.
 *
 * This program is distributed in the hope that it will be useful, but
 * WITHOUT ANY WARRANTY; without even the implied warranty of
 * MERCHANTABILITY or FITNESS FOR A PARTICULAR PURPOSE. See the GNU
 * Library General Public License for more details.
 *
 * You should have received a copy of the GNU Library General Public
 * License along with this program; if not, write to the
 * Free Software Foundation, Inc.,
 * 59 Temple Place, Suite 330, Boston, MA 02111-1307 USA
 */

/* helloworld_bit_mediaengine
 * This device driver demonstrates SA-1110 I/O and memory controller
 * register configuration. GPIO14 is configured as an output pin
 * then toggled. CS5 is configured for non burst variable-latency I/O,
 * 16 bit bus with longest read/write delays at memory address
 * 0x48000000. After memory controller configuration, accesses to
```

LISTING 9.1   Continued

```
 * 0x48000000 result in CS5 assertion. Use this device driver and a
 * fast oscilloscope to capture GPIO14 and memory signals. The
 * SA-1110 in the MediaEngine runs at 200MHz, memory access timing is
 * in the nanosecond range.
 */

/*
arm-linux-gcc -O2 -D__KERNEL__ -DMODULE -I/usr/src/arm-linux/include \
-c helloworldbit_mediaengine.c \
-o /tftpboot/arm-rootfs/tmp/helloworldbit_mediaengine.o
*/

#include <linux/module.h>
#include <linux/kernel.h>
#include <linux/init.h>
#include <linux/proc_fs.h>
#include <asm/uaccess.h>
#include <asm/io.h>

#define MODULE_VERSION "1.0"
#define MODULE_NAME "helloworldbit_mediaengine"

/* see section 9.1.1.1 Intel StrongARM SA-1110 Developer's Manual */
#define GPIO                    0x90040000 /* GPIO registers base address */
#define GPLR_OFFSET             0x00
#define GPDR_OFFSET             0x04
#define GPSR_OFFSET             0x08
#define GPCR_OFFSET             0x0C
#define GAFR_OFFSET             0x1C

#define GPIOLEN                 0x20
#define GPIO14                  0x00004000 /* GPIO14 in registers */

#define MEMBASE                 0xA0000000 /* mem controller base address */
#define MSC2_OFFSET             0x2C
#define MEMLENGTH               0x30

#define EXPANSIONPORT           0x48000000 /* expansion port base address */
#define EXPANSIONPORTLEN        2
```

LISTING 9.1   Continued

```
unsigned long int gpdr, gafr, msc2;
static void *io_base, *gpio_base, *mem_base;


/*
 * init_helloworldbit
 *   This function configures the GPDR, GAFR ARM registers for GPIO14 output
 *   Then configures the MCS2 so /CS5 operations are slow as possible
 *   Using a scope or logic probe, load and unload this module to check
 *   /CS5 and CPIO14 operation
 */
static int __init init_helloworldbit(void)
{
  unsigned char i;

/* get the remapped GPIO controller base address register */
  gpio_base = ioremap_nocache(GPIO, GPIOLEN);
  printk("gpio_base = 0x%08X\n",gpio_base);


/* we need to preserve the other bits in gpdr */
  gpdr = readl(gpio_base + GPDR_OFFSET);
  printk("GPDR      = 0x%08X\n",gpdr);

/* we need to preserve the other bits in gafr */
  gafr = readl(gpio_base + GAFR_OFFSET);
  printk("GAFR      = 0x%08X\n",gafr);


  writel(gpdr |  GPIO14, gpio_base + GPDR_OFFSET); /* GPIO14 as output */


  writel(gafr & ~GPIO14, gpio_base + GAFR_OFFSET); /* GPIO14 no alt func */

  writel(        GPIO14, gpio_base + GPCR_OFFSET); /* clear GPIO14 */
  writel(        GPIO14, gpio_base + GPSR_OFFSET); /* set   GPIO14 */

 /* get the remapped memory controller base address register */
  mem_base = ioremap_nocache(MEMBASE, MEMLENGTH);
  printk("mem_base  = 0x%08X\n",mem_base);
```

LISTING 9.1   Continued

```
/* we need to preserve the other bits in msc2 */
  msc2 = readl(mem_base + MSC2_OFFSET);
  printk("MSC2      = 0x%08X\n",msc2);


/* msc2 is for cs5 and cs4, need to mask off the cs3 part */
/* 0xFFF5, non burst SRAM variable, 16 bits, long delays */
  writel((msc2 & 0x0000FFFF) | 0xFFF50000, mem_base + MSC2_OFFSET);

/* read back the new msc2 value and print it */
  msc2 = readl(mem_base + MSC2_OFFSET);
  printk("MSC2      = 0x%08X\n",msc2);

/* get the remapped expansion port base address */
 io_base = ioremap_nocache(EXPANSIONPORT, EXPANSIONPORTLEN);
  printk("io_base   = 0x%08X\n",io_base);

/* read something from and write a test pattern to the expansion port */
  i = readb(io_base);
  writeb(0xAA,io_base);

/* everything initialized */
  printk(KERN_INFO "%s %s initialized\n",MODULE_NAME, MODULE_VERSION);
  return 0;
}


/*
 * cleanup_helloworldbit
 *   This function restores the GPDR, GAFR, MSC2 registers
 */
static void __exit cleanup_helloworldbit(void)
{
  unsigned char i;

/* toggle /CS5 again for testing */
  i = readb(io_base);
  writeb(0xAA,io_base);

/* toggle GPIO14 again for testing */
  writel(       GPIO14, gpio_base + GPCR_OFFSET); /* clear GPIO14 */
  writel(       GPIO14, gpio_base + GPSR_OFFSET); /* set   GPIO14 */
```

LISTING 9.1   Continued

```
  writel(gpdr, gpio_base + GPDR_OFFSET);  /* restore gpdr */
  writel(gafr, gpio_base + GAFR_OFFSET);  /* restore gafr */
  writel(msc2, mem_base  + MSC2_OFFSET);  /* restore msc2 */

/* release the ioremaps */
  iounmap(mem_base);
  iounmap(gpio_base);
  iounmap(io_base);

  printk(KERN_INFO "%s %s removed\n", MODULE_NAME, MODULE_VERSION);
}

module_init(init_helloworldbit);
module_exit(cleanup_helloworldbit);

MODULE_AUTHOR("Craig Hollabaugh");
MODULE_DESCRIPTION("helloworldbit for MediaEngine");

EXPORT_NO_SYMBOLS;
```

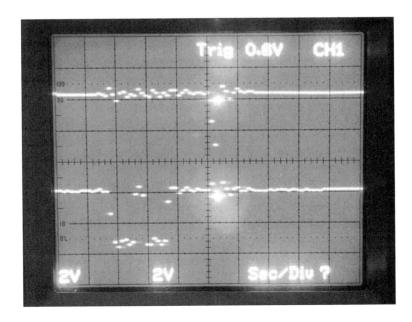

FIGURE 9.2   The oscilloscope output from `rmmod helloworldbit_mediaengine`, in which the top trace shows GPI014 and the bottom trace shows /CS5.

TIP

If your oscilloscope can't capture fast waveform transitions, use an inexpensive digital-logic probe, such as Radio Shack Model 22-303. Its audible tone feature reveals fast transitions to help with high-speed circuit troubleshooting.

Here's the MediaEngine output from inserting and removing the `helloworldbit_mediaengine` module:

```
bash-2.04# insmod helloworldbit_mediaengine.o
gpio_base = 0xC2802000
GPDR      = 0x00000000
GAFR      = 0x00000000
mem_base  = 0xC2804000
MSC2      = 0xFFFCFFFC
MSC2      = 0xFFF5FFFC
io_base   = 0xC2806000
helloworldbit_mediaengine 1.0 initialized
bash-2.04# rmmod helloworldbit_mediaengine
helloworldbit_mediaengine 1.0 removed
```

This output shows the SA-1110 memory and I/O controller configuration registers accepted the `helloworldbit` configuration.

Writing the `liftmon_snowcon` Device Driver for the MediaEngine

All the pieces are in place for the Project Trailblazer engineers to write the MediaEngine version of `liftmon_snowcon`. The interface circuit design connects to the MediaEngine's bus expansion port. The SA-1110 memory and I/O controllers were properly configured and tested, using the `helloworldbit_mediaengine` device driver. Using the `liftmon_snowcon.c` source code, Listing 7.5, as a template, the engineers can replace the parallel port control code with the GPIO14 and /CS5 control code from `helloworldbit_mediaengine.c`. Here's a quick summary of the changes that the engineers need to make to Listing 7.5:

1. Port reads should use the `readb` function instead of `inb`.

2. Port writes should use the `writeb` function instead of `outb`.

3. The `OutputModuleEnable` signal is handled by GPIO14.

Listing 9.2 shows the code for `liftmon_snowcon_mediaengine.c`.

LISTING 9.2   The `liftmon_snowcon_mediaengine.c` Device Driver

```
/*
 * liftmon_snowcon_mediaengine v1.0 11/03/01
 * www.embeddedlinuxinterfacing.com
 *
 * The original location of this code is
 * http://www.embeddedlinuxinterfacing.com/chapters/09/
 *
 * Copyright (C) 2001 by Craig Hollabaugh
 *
 * This program is free software; you can redistribute it and/or modify
 * it under the terms of the GNU Library General Public License as
 * published by the Free Software Foundation; either version 2 of the
 * License, or (at your option) any later version.
 *
 * This program is distributed in the hope that it will be useful, but
 * WITHOUT ANY WARRANTY; without even the implied warranty of
 * MERCHANTABILITY or FITNESS FOR A PARTICULAR PURPOSE. See the GNU
 * Library General Public License for more details.
 *
 * You should have received a copy of the GNU Library General Public
 * License along with this program; if not, write to the
 * Free Software Foundation, Inc.,
 * 59 Temple Place, Suite 330, Boston, MA 02111-1307 USA
 */

/*
arm-linux-gcc -O2 -D__KERNEL__ -DMODULE -I/usr/src/arm-linux/include \
-c liftmon_snowcon_mediaengine.c \
-o /tftpboot/arm-rootfs/tmp/liftmon_snowcon_mediaengine.o
*/

/*
 * liftmon_snowcon_mediaengine.c is based on procfs_example.c by Erik Mouw.
 * For more information, please see, The Linux Kernel Procfs Guide, Erik Mouw
 * http://kernelnewbies.org/documents/kdoc/procfs-guide/lkprocfsguide.html
 */


/* liftmon_snowcon
 * liftmon_snowcon uses read and write system calls to control
 * an interface circuit connected the MediaEngine's expansion port.
```

LISTING 9.2   Continued

```
* This module performs all bit operations for the data bus.
* Bash script need only read and write to /proc entry files to determine
* status or control equipment. In addition, the module's init code asserts
* the OUTPUT_ENABLE signal and its exit code deasserts the OUTPUT_ENABLE
* signal.
*
* This module creates these /proc entries:
* Trailblazer directory   /proc/trailblazer
* Lift Monitoring
*   AC Mains                /proc/trailblazer/liftacmains
*   Motor Controller        /proc/trailblazer/liftmotorcontroller
*   Low Speed Operation     /proc/trailblazer/liftslowspeed
*   High Speed Operation    /proc/trailblazer/lifthighspeed
*   Operator Switch Base    /proc/trailblazer/liftoperatorswitchbase
*   Operator Switch Top     /proc/trailblazer/liftoperatorswitchtop
* Snow-Making Control
*   Water Value 1           /proc/trailblazer/snowwatervalve1
*   Water Value 2           /proc/trailblazer/snowwatervalve2
*   Water Value 3           /proc/trailblazer/snowwatervalve3
*   Heater                  /proc/trailblazer/snowheater1
*/



#include <linux/module.h>
#include <linux/kernel.h>
#include <linux/init.h>
#include <linux/proc_fs.h>
#include <asm/uaccess.h>
#include <asm/io.h>



#define MODULE_VERSION "1.0"
#define MODULE_NAME "liftmon_snowcon_mediaengine"

/* see section 9.1.1.1 Intel StrongARM SA-1110 Developer's Manual */
#define GPIO                 0x90040000 /* GPIO registers base address */
#define GPLR_OFFSET          0x00
#define GPDR_OFFSET          0x04
#define GPSR_OFFSET          0x08
#define GPCR_OFFSET          0x0C
```

LISTING 9.2   Continued

```
#define GAFR_OFFSET             0x1C

#define GPIOLEN                 0x20
#define GPIO14                  0x00004000 /* GPIO14 in registers */

#define MEMBASE                 0xA0000000 /* mem controller base address */
#define MSC2_OFFSET             0x2C
#define MEMLENGTH               0x30

#define EXPANSIONPORT           0x48000000 /* expansion port base address */
#define EXPANSIONPORTLEN        16

unsigned long int gpdr, gafr, msc2;
static void *io_base, *gpio_base, *mem_base;

/* input bit definitions */
#define LIFTACMAINS             0x01
#define LIFTMOTORCONTROLLER     0x02
#define LIFTSLOWSPEED           0x04
#define LIFTHIGHSPEED           0x08
#define LIFTOPERATORSWITCHBASE  0x10
#define LIFTOPERATORSWITCHTOP   0x20

/* output bit definitions */
#define SNOWWATERVALVE1         0x01
#define SNOWWATERVALVE2         0x02
#define SNOWWATERVALVE3         0x04
#define SNOWHEATER1             0x08

/* define a bitmask, each *_file uses this to determine who it is */
struct liftmon_snowcon_data_t {
        unsigned char mask;
};

/* snowcondata is the output latch value stored internally. Control
 * changes made by user scripts writing to /proc/trailblazer entries
 * result in bits being either cleared or set in snowcondata. We
 * write snowcondata to the output latch every time a control change
 * occurs
 */
unsigned char snowcondata;
```

LISTING 9.2   Continued

```
/* this are the data structures that hold the mask. When a /proc
 * file is read or written to, the read_proc or write_proc routine
 * receives a pointer to this structure
 */
struct liftmon_snowcon_data_t liftacmains_data,
                              liftmotorcontroller_data,
                              liftslowspeed_data,
                              lifthighspeed_data,
                              liftoperatorswitchbase_data,
                              liftoperatorswitchtop_data,
                              snowwatervalve1_data,
                              snowwatervalve2_data,
                              snowwatervalve3_data,
                              snowheater1_data;

/* These are the pointers to the /proc directory entries */
static struct proc_dir_entry  *tb_dir,
                              *liftacmains_file,
                              *liftmotorcontroller_file,
                              *liftslowspeed_file,
                              *lifthighspeed_file,
                              *liftoperatorswitchbase_file,
                              *liftoperatorswitchtop_file,
                              *snowwatervalve1_file,
                              *snowwatervalve2_file,
                              *snowwatervalve3_file,
                              *snowheater1_file;

/* proc_read - proc_read_liftmon
 * proc_read_liftmon is the callback function that the kernel calls when
 * there's a read file operation on these /proc/trailblazer files:
 * liftacmains, lifthighspeed, liftmotorcontroller, liftoperatorswitchbase
 * liftoperatorswitchtop, and liftslowspeed. The file's data pointer is
 * passed in the data parameter. You first cast it to the
 * liftmon_snowcon_data_t structure. A read from io_base gets the AC input
 * status module. The result is anded with the bitmask value to
 * to determine if the particular input module is on or off. Which
 * particular input module is defined by which /proc/trailblazer/ file
 * is read.
 */
```

LISTING 9.2   Continued

```c
static int proc_read_liftmon(char *page, char **start, off_t off, int count,
                             int *eof, void *data)
{
  unsigned int v;
  struct liftmon_snowcon_data_t *liftmon_snowcon_data =
                          (struct liftmon_snowcon_data_t *)data;


  v = readb(io_base);

/* mask the input value based on the mask. Each mask is different depending
 * which /proc/trailblazer file was read.
 * Electrical note: returning an inverted value because AC power to an input
 * module pulls outputs a low and the input buffer, 74244, doesn't invert
 */
  if (v & liftmon_snowcon_data->mask)
    page[0] = '0';
  else
    page[0] = '1';

/* return 1 which is the length of page */
  return 1;
}


/* proc_write - proc_write_snowcondata
 * proc_write_snowcondata is the callback function that the kernel calls
 * when there's a write file operation on these /proc/trailblazer files:
 * snowheater1, snowwatervalve1, snowwatervalve2 and snowwatervalve3.
 * The file's data pointer is passed in the data parameter. You first
 * cast it to the liftmon_snowcon_data_t structure. The buffer parameter
 * points to the incoming data. If the incoming data is a 1 or a 0,
 * a bit in snowcondata is set or cleared. Which bit is defined by which
 * /proc/trailblazer file is written to. snowcondata is then written to
 * the output latch.
 */
static int proc_write_snowcondata(struct file *file, const char *buffer,
                                  unsigned long count, void *data)
{
  struct liftmon_snowcon_data_t *liftmon_snowcon_data =
                          (struct liftmon_snowcon_data_t *)data;

/* check if the user wrote a 1 or a 0 the /proc/trailblazer file.
```

LISTING 9.2   Continued

```
   if so, set or clear a bit in snowcondata */
  if (buffer[0] == '0')
    snowcondata |= liftmon_snowcon_data->mask;

  if (buffer[0] == '1')
    snowcondata &= ~liftmon_snowcon_data->mask;

  writeb(snowcondata, io_base);
  return 1;
}


/* proc_read - proc_read_snowcondata
 * proc_read_snowcondata is the callback function that the kernel calls
 * when there's a read file operation on these /proc/trailblazer files:
 * snowheater1, snowwatervalve1, snowwatervalve2 and snowwatervalve3.
 * The file's data pointer is passed in the data parameter. You first
 * cast it to the liftmon_snowcon_data_t structure.  Use snowcondata
 * anded with the bitmask value to determine if the particular output
 * module is on or off. Which particular output module is defined by
 * which /proc/trailblazer/ file is read.
 */
static int proc_read_snowcondata(char *page, char **start, off_t off, int count,
                                 int *eof, void *data)
{
  struct liftmon_snowcon_data_t *liftmon_snowcon_data =
                                 (struct liftmon_snowcon_data_t *)data;

/* mask the snowcondata value based on the mask. Each mask is different
 * depending which /proc/trailblazer file was read. */
  if ( snowcondata & liftmon_snowcon_data->mask )
    page[0] = '0';
  else
    page[0] = '1';

/* return the length */
  return 1;
}



/* init - init_liftmon_snowcon
 * init_liftmon_snowcon creates the /proc entry files and obtains
```

LISTING 9.2   Continued

```
 * their pointers. For each file, the fields, data, read_proc,
 * write_proc and owner, are filled.  Then the I/O controller is configured
 * so GPIO14 is an output and the memory controller works slowly with /CS5.
 * It initializes the output modules in the off state then
 * completes by writing an entry to the system log using printk.
 */
static int __init init_liftmon_snowcon(void)
{
  int rv = 0;

/* Create the trailblazer /proc entry */
  tb_dir = proc_mkdir("trailblazer", NULL);
  if(tb_dir == NULL) {
    rv = -ENOMEM;
    goto out;
  }
  tb_dir->owner = THIS_MODULE;

/* Create liftacmains and make it readable by all - 0444 */
  liftacmains_file = create_proc_entry("liftacmains", 0444, tb_dir);
  if(liftacmains_file == NULL) {
    rv = -ENOMEM;
    goto no_liftacmains;
  }
  liftacmains_data.mask = LIFTACMAINS;
  liftacmains_file->data = &liftacmains_data;
  liftacmains_file->read_proc = &proc_read_liftmon;
  liftacmains_file->write_proc = NULL;
  liftacmains_file->owner = THIS_MODULE;


/* Create liftmotorcontroller and make it readable by all - 0444 */
  liftmotorcontroller_file = create_proc_entry("liftmotorcontroller",
                                        0444, tb_dir);
  if(liftmotorcontroller_file == NULL) {
    rv = -ENOMEM;
    goto no_liftmotorcontroller;
  }
  liftmotorcontroller_data.mask = LIFTMOTORCONTROLLER;
  liftmotorcontroller_file->data = &liftmotorcontroller_data;
  liftmotorcontroller_file->read_proc = &proc_read_liftmon;
```

LISTING 9.2   Continued

```
  liftmotorcontroller_file->write_proc = NULL;
  liftmotorcontroller_file->owner = THIS_MODULE;

/* Create liftslowspeed and make it readable by all - 0444 */
  liftslowspeed_file = create_proc_entry("liftslowspeed", 0444, tb_dir);
  if(liftslowspeed_file == NULL) {
    rv = -ENOMEM;
    goto no_liftslowspeed;
  }
  liftslowspeed_data.mask = LIFTSLOWSPEED;
  liftslowspeed_file->data = &liftslowspeed_data;
  liftslowspeed_file->read_proc = &proc_read_liftmon;
  liftslowspeed_file->write_proc = NULL;
  liftslowspeed_file->owner = THIS_MODULE;

/* Create lifthighspeed and make it readable by all - 0444 */
  lifthighspeed_file = create_proc_entry("lifthighspeed", 0444, tb_dir);
  if(lifthighspeed_file == NULL) {
    rv = -ENOMEM;
    goto no_lifthighspeed;
  }
  lifthighspeed_data.mask = LIFTHIGHSPEED;
  lifthighspeed_file->data = &lifthighspeed_data;
  lifthighspeed_file->read_proc = &proc_read_liftmon;
  lifthighspeed_file->write_proc = NULL;
  lifthighspeed_file->owner = THIS_MODULE;

/* Create liftoperatorswitchbase and make it readable by all - 0444 */
  liftoperatorswitchbase_file = create_proc_entry("liftoperatorswitchbase",
                                          0444, tb_dir);
  if(liftoperatorswitchbase_file == NULL) {
    rv = -ENOMEM;
    goto no_liftoperatorswitchbase;
  }
  liftoperatorswitchbase_data.mask = LIFTOPERATORSWITCHBASE;
  liftoperatorswitchbase_file->data = &liftoperatorswitchbase_data;
  liftoperatorswitchbase_file->read_proc = &proc_read_liftmon;
  liftoperatorswitchbase_file->write_proc = NULL;
  liftoperatorswitchbase_file->owner = THIS_MODULE;

/* Create liftoperatorswitchtop and make it readable by all - 0444 */
```

LISTING 9.2 Continued

```
  liftoperatorswitchtop_file = create_proc_entry("liftoperatorswitchtop",
                                               0444, tb_dir);
  if(liftoperatorswitchtop_file == NULL) {
    rv = -ENOMEM;
    goto no_liftoperatorswitchtop;
  }
  liftoperatorswitchtop_data.mask = LIFTOPERATORSWITCHTOP;
  liftoperatorswitchtop_file->data = &liftoperatorswitchtop_data;
  liftoperatorswitchtop_file->read_proc = &proc_read_liftmon;
  liftoperatorswitchtop_file->write_proc = NULL;
  liftoperatorswitchtop_file->owner = THIS_MODULE;

/* Create snowwatervalve1 and make it root writeable, readable by all-0644 */
  snowwatervalve1_file = create_proc_entry("snowwatervalve1", 0644, tb_dir);
  if(snowwatervalve1_file == NULL) {
    rv = -ENOMEM;
    goto no_snowwatervalve1;
  }
  snowwatervalve1_data.mask = SNOWWATERVALVE1;
  snowwatervalve1_file->data = &snowwatervalve1_data;
  snowwatervalve1_file->read_proc = &proc_read_snowcondata;
  snowwatervalve1_file->write_proc = &proc_write_snowcondata;
  snowwatervalve1_file->owner = THIS_MODULE;

/* Create snowwatervalve2 and make it root writeable, readable by all-0644 */
  snowwatervalve2_file = create_proc_entry("snowwatervalve2", 0644, tb_dir);
  if(snowwatervalve2_file == NULL) {
    rv = -ENOMEM;
    goto no_snowwatervalve2;
  }
  snowwatervalve2_data.mask = SNOWWATERVALVE2;
  snowwatervalve2_file->data = &snowwatervalve2_data;
  snowwatervalve2_file->read_proc = &proc_read_snowcondata;
  snowwatervalve2_file->write_proc = &proc_write_snowcondata;
  snowwatervalve2_file->owner = THIS_MODULE;

/* Create snowwatervalve3 and make it root writeable, readable by all-0644 */
  snowwatervalve3_file = create_proc_entry("snowwatervalve3", 0644, tb_dir);
  if(snowwatervalve3_file == NULL) {
    rv = -ENOMEM;
    goto no_snowwatervalve3;
```

LISTING 9.2   Continued

```
  }
  snowwatervalve3_data.mask = SNOWWATERVALVE3;
  snowwatervalve3_file->data = &snowwatervalve3_data;
  snowwatervalve3_file->read_proc = &proc_read_snowcondata;
  snowwatervalve3_file->write_proc = &proc_write_snowcondata;
  snowwatervalve3_file->owner = THIS_MODULE;

/* Create snowheater1 and make it root writeable, readable by all-0644 */
  snowheater1_file = create_proc_entry("snowheater1", 0644, tb_dir);
  if(snowheater1_file == NULL) {
    rv = -ENOMEM;
    goto no_snowheater1;
  }
  snowheater1_data.mask = SNOWHEATER1;
  snowheater1_file->data = &snowheater1_data;
  snowheater1_file->read_proc = &proc_read_snowcondata;
  snowheater1_file->write_proc = &proc_write_snowcondata;
  snowheater1_file->owner = THIS_MODULE;



/* setting up the memory controller to run slowly with /CS5 */
/* get the remapped memory controller base address register */
  mem_base = ioremap_nocache(MEMBASE, MEMLENGTH);
  printk("mem_base  = 0x%08X\n",mem_base);

/* we need to preserve the other bits in msc2 */
  msc2 = readl(mem_base + MSC2_OFFSET);
  printk("MSC2      = 0x%08X\n",msc2);

/* msc2 is for cs5 and cs4, need to mask off the cs3 part */
/* 0xFFF5, non burst SRAM variable, 16 bits, long delays */
  writel((msc2 & 0x0000FFFF) | 0xFFF50000, mem_base + MSC2_OFFSET);

/* read back the new msc2 value and print it */
  msc2 = readl(mem_base + MSC2_OFFSET);
  printk("MSC2      = 0x%08X\n",msc2);

/* get the remapped GPIO controller base address register */
  io_base = ioremap_nocache(EXPANSIONPORT, EXPANSIONPORTLEN);
  printk("io_base   = 0x%08X\n",io_base);
```

LISTING 9.2   Continued

```
/* set up the I/O controller for GPIO14 output */
/* get the remapped GPIO controller base address register */
  gpio_base = ioremap_nocache(GPIO, GPIOLEN);
  printk("gpio_base = 0x%08X\n",gpio_base);

/* we need to preserve the other bits in gpdr */
  gpdr = readl(gpio_base + GPDR_OFFSET);
  printk("GPDR      = 0x%08X\n",gpdr);

/* we need to preserve the other bits in gafr */
  gafr = readl(gpio_base + GAFR_OFFSET);
  printk("GAFR      = 0x%08X\n",gafr);

/* initialize snowcondata to 0xFF, all output modules off */
/* output modules invert */
  snowcondata = 0xFF;
  writeb(snowcondata, io_base); /* turn off all output modules */
  writel(GPIO14              , gpio_base + GPSR_OFFSET); /* set GPIO14 */
  writel(gpdr | GPIO_GPIO14, gpio_base + GPDR_OFFSET); /* set GPIO14 output*/
  writel(GPIO14              , gpio_base + GPCR_OFFSET); /* clear GPIO14 */
     /* clearing GPIO14 turns on output buffer controlling output modules */

/* everything initialized */
  printk(KERN_INFO "%s %s initialized\n",MODULE_NAME, MODULE_VERSION);
  return 0;

/* this removes /proc entries if we have an error along the way */
no_snowheater1:
  remove_proc_entry("snowheater1", tb_dir);
no_snowwatervalve3:
  remove_proc_entry("snowwatervalve3", tb_dir);
no_snowwatervalve2:
  remove_proc_entry("snowwatervalve2", tb_dir);
no_snowwatervalve1:
  remove_proc_entry("snowwatervalve1", tb_dir);
no_liftoperatorswitchtop:
  remove_proc_entry("liftoperatorswitchtop", tb_dir);
no_liftoperatorswitchbase:
  remove_proc_entry("liftoperatorswitchbase", tb_dir);
```

LISTING 9.2   Continued

```
no_lifthighspeed:
  remove_proc_entry("lifthighspeed", tb_dir);
no_liftslowspeed:
  remove_proc_entry("liftslowspeed", tb_dir);
no_liftmotorcontroller:
  remove_proc_entry("liftmotorcontroller", tb_dir);
no_liftacmains:
  remove_proc_entry("liftacmains", tb_dir);
out:
  return rv;
}



/* exit - cleanup_liftmon_snowcon
 * cleanup_liftmon_snowcon turns off the output modules and
 * deasserts the OUTPUT_ENABLE signal. It removes the /proc entry files
 * prints a message to the system log.
 */
static void __exit cleanup_liftmon_snowcon(void)
{
  writel(gpdr, gpio_base + GPDR_OFFSET); /* restore gpdr */
  writel(gafr, gpio_base + GAFR_OFFSET); /* restore gafr */
  writel(msc2, mem_base  + MSC2_OFFSET); /* restore msc2 */

/* release the ioremaps */
  iounmap(mem_base);
  iounmap(gpio_base);
  iounmap(io_base);

/* removing the /proc entries */
  remove_proc_entry("liftacmains", tb_dir);
  remove_proc_entry("liftmotorcontroller", tb_dir);
  remove_proc_entry("liftslowspeed", tb_dir);
  remove_proc_entry("lifthighspeed", tb_dir);
  remove_proc_entry("liftoperatorswitchbase", tb_dir);
  remove_proc_entry("liftoperatorswitchtop", tb_dir);
  remove_proc_entry("snowwatervalve1", tb_dir);
  remove_proc_entry("snowwatervalve2", tb_dir);
  remove_proc_entry("snowwatervalve3", tb_dir);
  remove_proc_entry("snowheater1", tb_dir);
  remove_proc_entry("trailblazer", NULL);
```

LISTING 9.2   Continued

```
  printk(KERN_INFO "%s %s removed\n", MODULE_NAME, MODULE_VERSION);
}

module_init(init_liftmon_snowcon);
module_exit(cleanup_liftmon_snowcon);

MODULE_AUTHOR("Craig Hollabaugh");
MODULE_DESCRIPTION(
"Trailblazer Lift Monitor and Snowmaking Control for MediaEngine");

EXPORT_NO_SYMBOLS;
```

The engineers have now attached memory-mapped I/O interface hardware to the SA-1110 processor and written a device driver to access it. That's quite a feat.

The MediaEngine design, with its bus expansion port, only allows the use of GPIO14 and /CS5 signals. Although this seems restrictive for other interface projects, the combination of GPIO14, /CS5, and the data lines is a perfect match for the lift monitoring and snow-making control circuit. You'll see in the next section how the RPX-CLLF, using a PowerPC, offers more connectivity options, coupled with additional complexity.

Developing Lift Monitoring and Snow-Making Control for the RPX-CLLF

This section details the phases of the hardware design process for the RPX-CLLF target board. These steps are the same for the MediaEngine and the RPX-CLLF, but architectural differences between these processors warrant detailed coverage for each board.

Designing the External Interface Hardware for the RPX-CLLF

This section details the RPX-CLLF interface hardware design. After the engineers find space in the memory map for the I/O circuit, they configure the CPU registers and test the circuit by using the helloworldbit program. The engineers then develop the RPX-CLLF liftmon_snowcon device driver, which enables the RPX-CLLF target board to monitor lifts and control snow-making equipment.

The RPX-CLLF design offers extensive bus and I/O through two expansion connectors. Table 9.5 shows the CPU signals available for the lift monitoring and snow-making control circuit.

TABLE 9.5   RPX-CLLF Bus and I/O Expansion Connector Signals

Description	Signals
Address lines	A0–A31
Data lines	D0–D31
Chip select	/CS0–/CS7
Write enable	/WE1
Output enable	/OE (GPL1)
Port A	PA0–PA23
Port B	PB0–PB31
Port C	PC0–PC15
Port D	PD3–PD15
Reset	/RST
Power	+5V, +3V
Ground	GND

Figure 9.3 shows the connections between the output latch (74HC574 Edge Triggered D Flip Flop with three-state outputs), the input buffer (74HC244 Octal Buffer with three-state outputs), and the RPX-CLLF. PA0 controls the OutputModuleEnable line. The signals A0, /OE, /WE1, and /CS5 control the three to eight line decoder that performs address and read/write signal decoding. Byte read and byte write operations are similar to those for the MediaEngine (see the section "Designing the External Interface Hardware for the MediaEngine," earlier in this chapter). This design's HC logic components are fast, but the Project Trailblazer engineers want to configure the CPU to access this interface circuit as slowly as possible because the I/O board trace capacitance could affect performance and reliability.

Finding Space in the Memory Map for the RPX-CLLF

The RPX-CLLF has 16MB of DRAM and can accommodate 2MB, 4MB, 8MB, or 16MB Flash memory. Table 9.6, which is a reprint of Table 4-2 from *Embedded Planet PlanetCore Version 1.4 Boot Loader MPC8xx Manual*[3], shows device memory mappings.

TABLE 9.6   RPX-CLLF Memory Map

Chip Enable	Start	Length	Description
N/A	0xFA200000	10000	Internal memory of the CPU
0	0xFC000000	4000000	Flash memory area
1	00000000	Varies	RAM area
2	Varies	Varies	RAM area for second bank
3	0xFA400000	Small	BCSR area
4	0xFA000000	Varies	NVRAM area

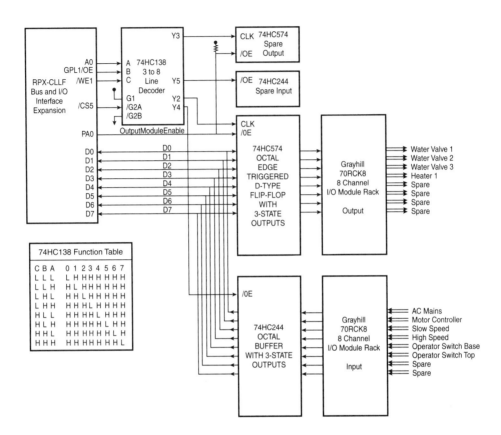

FIGURE 9.3   The RPX-CLLF `liftmon_snowcon` interface circuit.

The PlanetCore boot loader itself can also verify memory-map information. Here's its output from the map command:

```
PlanetCore Boot Loader v1.02
Copyright 2000 Embedded Planet.  All rights reserved.
DRAM available size = 16 MB
wvCV
DRAM OK

Autoboot in 2 seconds.
ESC to abort, SPACE or ENTER to go.

>map
IMMR = 0xFA200000
    Address  Mask    Size WP Mach
```

```
CS0 FC000000 FC000000 Word N  GPCM
CS1 00000000 FF000000 Word N  UPMA
CS2 (not used)
CS3 FA400000 FF7F8000 Word N  GPCM
CS4 FA000000 FFFE0000 Byte N  GPCM
CS5 (not used)
CS6 (not used)
CS7 (not used)
>
```

This output shows that the RPX-CLLF has 16MB of memory, mapped to address `0x00000000` (CS1). This 16MB extends to address `0x01000000`, and there's nothing mapped between `0x01000000` and `0xFA000000`. Note that CS5 is unused. Traditionally, in embedded 8xx designs, RAM is mapped at address 0x00 and I/O devices are mapped above physical address `0x80000000`[4]. That's where the engineers decided to map the lift monitoring and snow-making control interface circuit.

Finding the Register Base Address for the RPX-CLLF

To accommodate a wide variety of designs, the MPC860 CPU uses an internal memory-map register (IMMR) whose memory location can be modified via software control. The PlanetCore Boot Loader output in the preceding section reports that the address of the IMMR is `0xFA200000`. Current or future Linux versions may or may not move the IMMR during the boot process. Device driver code written for the PowerPC 8xx processor family should not hard-code the IMMR location as `0xFA200000`. Rather, it should use the `mfspr` function, which finds the IMMR. Here's a line of kernel code from `arch/ppc/8xx_io/enet.c` using `mfspr`:

```
immap = (immap_t *)(mfspr(IMMR) & 0xFFFF0000);
```

By using IMMR combined with table offsets, the Project Trailblazer engineers can configure all the MPC860 registers.

Configuring the Memory Controller for the RPX-CLLF

The MPC860 features a sophisticated memory controller that is capable of interfacing to SRAM, EPROM, Flash EPROM, regular DRAM devices, self-refresh DRAM devices, extended-data-output DRAM devices, synchronous DRAM devices, and other peripherals. It performs this interfacing through either its general-purpose chip-select machine (GPCM) or a user-programmable machine (UPM). The interface circuit in Figure 9.3 interfaces with the GPCM because it supports nonburstable memory-mapped peripherals. (See Chapter 16, "Memory Controller," in *MPC860 User Manual*[5] for more information.)

NOTE

The PowerPC bit definitions are reversed from those of Intel. With the PowerPC, in a 32-bit word, bit 0 is the most significant bit.

The Project Trailblazer engineers are using Chip Select 5, so they need to configure the Base Register (BR5) and Option Register (OR5) for that chip select. Table 9.7 describes BR5's fields.

TABLE 9.7   BR5 Bit Field Descriptions and Design Values

Bits	Name	Value	Description
0–16	BA	0x80	Base address: 0x80000000
17–19	AT	000	Address type: no access limits
20–21	PS	01	Port size: 01 is 8-bit port size
22	PARE	0	Parity enable: 0 is disabled
23	WP	0	Write protect: 0 is disabled, read and writes allowed
24–25	MS	00	Machine select: 00 is GPCM
26–30		00000	Reserved
31	V	1	Valid: 1 means BR5 and OR5 contents are valid

The `liftmon_snowcon` interface requires BR5 to be
0b1000.0000.0000.0000.0000.0100.0000.0001 which equals 0x80000401.

Table 9.8 describes the OR5's fields.

TABLE 9.8   OR5 Bit Field Descriptions and Design Values

Bits	Name	Value	Description
0–16	AM	0x80	Address mask: 0x80000000
17–19	ATM	000	Address type mask: 000 means no protection desired
20	CSNT	1	Chip select negation time: 1 provides extended hold times
21–22	ACS	11	Address to chip-select setup: 111 provides slowest signals
23	BIH	1	Burst inhibit: 1 means bank doesn't support bursting
24–27	SCY	1111	Select cycle length: 1111 provides slowest signals
28	SETA	0	Select external transfer acknowledgement: 0 means memory doesn't provide acknowledgement
29	TRLX	1	Timing relaxed: 1 means timing provides slowest signals
30	EHTR	1	Extended hold time read: 1 means slowest signals
31		0	Reserved

The `liftmon_snowcon` interface requires OR5 to be
`0b1000.0000.0000.0000.0000.1111.1111.0110`, which equals `0x80000FF6`.

Assigning the Output Module Enable Signal for the RPX-CLLF

The RPX-CLLF bus expansion interface connector offers connections to four CPU I/O ports, A through D. Each port is capable of driving the `OutputModuleEnable` signal. Some port pins support an alternate function of an internal peripheral. The Project Trailblazer engineers identified that Port A Pin 0's alternate function wasn't being used. They selected `PA0` to drive the `OutputModuleEnable` signal.

Configuring the I/O Port Controller for the RPX-CLLF

The Project Trailblazer engineers need to configure the RPX-CLLF I/O port controller registers shown in Table 9.9 for PA0 output with no alternate function. (See Section 34.2, "Parallel I/O Ports," of *MPC860 User Manual*[5] for more general information.)

TABLE 9.9   Additional PowerPC Register Settings to Make `PA0` an Output Pin

Register	Description	Bit Setting	Description
PAPAR	Port A Pin Assignment Register	PAPARDD0 = 0	General I/O
PADIR	Port A Data Direction Register	PADIRDR0 = 1	Selects output

Writing the `helloworldbit` Testing Device Driver for the RPX-CLLF

Now that the Project Trailblazer engineers have defined the memory space, determined the register base addresses, assigned the `OutputModuleEnable` signal, and know the configuration of the memory and I/O controllers, they need to write a `helloworld` program. They write a simple device driver to configure the MPC860 memory and I/O controllers and then control the `/CS5` and `PA0` signals.

The initialization code for the `helloworldbit_rpxcllf.c` device driver, which is shown in Listing 9.3, configures the MPC860's PAPAR and PADIR for `PA0` output, and then it sets and clears `PA0`. The code then configures Chip Select 5's BR5 and OR5 registers, and then it reads and writes to physical memory address `0x80000000`. By using an oscilloscope, the Project Trailblazer engineers then verify the proper operation of `PA0` and `/CS5`, as shown in Figure 9.4.

LISTING 9.3   The `helloworldbit_rpxcllf.c` Device Driver

```
/*
 * helloworld_bit_rpxcllf v1.0 11/03/01
 * www.embeddedlinuxinterfacing.com
 *
```

LISTING 9.3   Continued

```
 * The original location of this code is
 * http://www.embeddedlinuxinterfacing.com/chapters/09/
 *
 * Copyright (C) 2001 by Craig Hollabaugh
 *
 * This program is free software; you can redistribute it and/or modify
 * it under the terms of the GNU Library General Public License as
 * published by the Free Software Foundation; either version 2 of the
 * License, or (at your option) any later version.
 *
 * This program is distributed in the hope that it will be useful, but
 * WITHOUT ANY WARRANTY; without even the implied warranty of
 * MERCHANTABILITY or FITNESS FOR A PARTICULAR PURPOSE. See the GNU
 * Library General Public License for more details.
 *
 * You should have received a copy of the GNU Library General Public
 * License along with this program; if not, write to the
 * Free Software Foundation, Inc.,
 * 59 Temple Place, Suite 330, Boston, MA 02111-1307 USA
 */

/* helloworld_bit_rpxcllf
 * This device driver demonstrates MPC860 I/O and memory controller
 * register configuration. PA0 is configured as an output pin
 * then toggled. CS5 is configured for non burst variable-latency I/O,
 * 8 bus with longest read/write delays at memory address
 * 0x80000000. After memory controller configuration, accesses to
 * 0x8000000 result in CS5 assertion. Use this device driver and a
 * fast oscilloscope to capture PA0 and memory signals.
 */


/*
powerpc-linux-gcc -O2 -D__KERNEL__ -DMODULE -I/usr/src/powerpc-linux/include \
-c helloworldbit_rpxcllf.c \
-o /tftpboot/powerpc-rootfs/tmp/helloworldbit_rpxcllf.o
*/


#include <linux/module.h>
#include <linux/kernel.h>
```

LISTING 9.3   Continued

```
#include <linux/init.h>
#include <linux/proc_fs.h>
#include <asm/uaccess.h>
#include <asm/io.h>

#include <asm/8xx_immap.h>

#define MODULE_VERSION "1.0"
#define MODULE_NAME "helloworldbit_rpxcllf"

volatile immap_t *immap;
static void *io_base;

/* references
 * see section 34.2 Port A MPC860 PowerQUICC User's Manual
 *     section 16.5 General-Purpose Chip-Select Machine (GPCM)
 */

#define EXPANSIONPORT          0x80000000
#define EXPANSIONPORTLEN       16

#define PA0                    0x8000 /* PA0 bit in registers */

/*
 * init_helloworldbit
 * This function configures the PAPAR and PADIR MPC860 registers for PA0
 * output.  Then configures the BR5 and OR5 so /CS5 operations are slow
 * as possible Using a scope or logic probe, load and unload this module
 * to check /CS5 and PA0 operation
 */
static int __init init_helloworldbit(void)
{
  unsigned char i;

/* get immap value */
  immap = (immap_t *)(mfspr(IMMR) & 0xFFFF0000);

/* sets up CS5 for memory at 0x80000000, MPC man Table 16.4.1 BRx Register */
  immap->im_memctl.memc_br5 = 0x80000401;

/* sets up CS5 for memory at 0x80000000, MPC man Table 16.4.2 ORx Register */
```

LISTING 9.3   Continued

```
immap->im_memctl.memc_or5 = 0x80000FF6; /* CS5 slowest */

io_base = ioremap_nocache(EXPANSIONPORT, EXPANSIONPORTLEN);

i = readb(io_base);     /* toggle CS5 and RD */
writeb(0xAA, io_base); /* toggle CS5 and WR */

immap->im_ioport.iop_papar &= ~PA0; /* set PA0 to general I/O */
immap->im_ioport.iop_padir |=  PA0; /* set PA0 as output */

immap->im_ioport.iop_padat &= ~PA0; /* clear PA0, toggle for bit test */
immap->im_ioport.iop_padat |=  PA0; /* set   PA0, toggle for bit test */
/* print out register values */
printk("immr    = 0x%08X\n",immap);
printk("io_base = 0x%08X\n", io_base);
printk("BR5     = 0x%08X\n",immap->im_memctl.memc_br5);
printk("OR5     = 0x%08X\n",immap->im_memctl.memc_or5);
printk("PAPAR   = 0x%04X\n",immap->im_ioport.iop_papar);
printk("PADIR   = 0x%04X\n",immap->im_ioport.iop_padir);

/* everything initialized */
printk(KERN_INFO "%s %s initialized\n",MODULE_NAME, MODULE_VERSION);
return 0;
}


/*
 * cleanup_helloworldbit
 *    This function makes PA0 an input and releases io_base;
 */
static void __exit cleanup_helloworldbit(void)
{

unsigned char i;
/* toggle /CS5 again for testing */
i = readb(io_base);     /* toggle CS5 and RD */
writeb(0xAA, io_base); /* toggle CS5 and WR */

immap->im_ioport.iop_padat &= ~PA0; /* clear PA0, toggle for bit test */
immap->im_ioport.iop_padat |=  PA0; /* set   PA0, toggle for bit test */
```

LISTING 9.3 Continued

```
  immap->im_ioport.iop_padir &= ~PA0; /* set PA0 as input */


/* release the ioremap */
  iounmap(io_base);

  printk(KERN_INFO "%s %s removed\n", MODULE_NAME, MODULE_VERSION);
}

module_init(init_helloworldbit);
module_exit(cleanup_helloworldbit);

MODULE_AUTHOR("Craig Hollabaugh");
MODULE_DESCRIPTION("helloworldbit for RPX-CLLF");

EXPORT_NO_SYMBOLS;
```

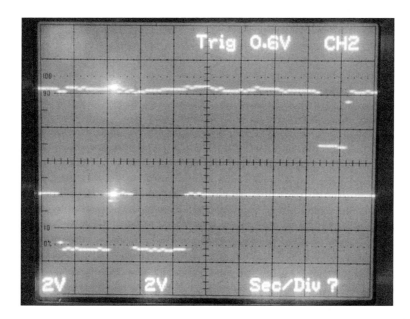

FIGURE 9.4 The scope output from rmmod helloworldbit_rpxcllf, in which the top trace shows PA0 and the bottom trace shows /CS5.

> **TIP**
>
> There's a slight difference between the register configuration of `helloworldbit_rpxcllf.c`
> and that of `helloworldbit_mediaengine.c`. The RPX-CLLF version uses a register structure
> whereas the MediaEngine version uses offsets from a register base address. The PowerPC
> programmers developed the `immap` structure to make coding easier and less error prone (see
> `/usr/src/powerpc-linux/include/asm-ppc/8xx_immap.h`). `helloworldbit_rpxcllf.c` uses
> the immap register structure instead of defining offsets from the base register address, as in
> `helloworldbit_mediaengine.c`.

Here's the output from inserting and removing `helloworldbit_rpxcllf.o`:

```
bash-2.04# insmod helloworldbit_rpxcllf.o
io_base = 0xC2002000
immr    = 0xFA200000
BR5     = 0x80000401
OR5     = 0x80000FF6
PAPAR   = 0x0AFF
PADIR   = 0x8000
helloworldbit_rpxcllf 1.0 initialized
bash-2.04# rmmod helloworldbit_rpxcllf
helloworldbit_rpxcllf 1.0 removed
```

This output shows that the MPC860 memory and I/O controller configuration registers accepted the helloworldbit configuration.

Writing the `liftmon_snowcon` Device Driver for the RPX-CLLF

All the pieces are in place for the Project Trailblazer engineers to write the RPX-CLLF
version of `liftmon_snowcon`. The interface circuit connects to the RPX-CLLF's bus
and I/O expansion connectors. The MPC860 memory and I/O controllers were properly configured and tested, using the `helloworldbit_rpxcllf` device driver. Using the
`liftmon_snowcon.c` source code, Listing 7.5, as a template, the engineer can replace
the parallel port control code with `PA0` and `/CS5` control code from
`helloworldbit_rpx-cllf.c`. Here's a quick summary of the changes that the engineers need to make to Listing 7.5:

1. Port reads use the `readb` function instead of `inb`.

2. Port writes use the `writeb` function instead of `outb`.

3. The `OutputModuleEnable` signal is handled by `PA0`.

Listing 9.4 shows the code for `liftmon_snowcon rpx-cllf.c`.

LISTING 9.4   The `liftmon_snowcon_rpx-cllf.c` Device Driver

```
/*
 * liftmon_snowcon_rpx-cllf v1.0 11/03/01
 * www.embeddedlinuxinterfacing.com
 *
 * The original location of this code is
 * http://www.embeddedlinuxinterfacing.com/chapters/09/
 *
 * Copyright (C) 2001 by Craig Hollabaugh
 *
 * This program is free software; you can redistribute it and/or modify
 * it under the terms of the GNU Library General Public License as
 * published by the Free Software Foundation; either version 2 of the
 * License, or (at your option) any later version.
 *
 * This program is distributed in the hope that it will be useful, but
 * WITHOUT ANY WARRANTY; without even the implied warranty of
 * MERCHANTABILITY or FITNESS FOR A PARTICULAR PURPOSE. See the GNU
 * Library General Public License for more details.
 *
 * You should have received a copy of the GNU Library General Public
 * License along with this program; if not, write to the
 * Free Software Foundation, Inc.,
 * 59 Temple Place, Suite 330, Boston, MA 02111-1307 USA
 */

/*
powerpc-linux-gcc -O2 -D__KERNEL__ -DMODULE -I/usr/src/powerpc-linux/include \
-c liftmon_snowcon_rpxcllf.c \
-o /tftpboot/powerpc-rootfs/tmp/liftmon_snowcon_rpxcllf.o
*/

/*
 * liftmon_snowcon_mediaengine.c is based on procfs_example.c by Erik Mouw.
 * For more information, please see, The Linux Kernel Procfs Guide, Erik Mouw
 * http://kernelnewbies.org/documents/kdoc/procfs-guide/lkprocfsguide.html
 */

/* liftmon_snowcon
 * liftmon_snowcon uses read and write system calls to control
```

LISTING 9.4   Continued

```
* an interface circuit connected the RPX-CLLF's bus and expansion ports.
* This module performs all bit operations for the data bus.
* Bash script need only read and write to /proc entry files to determine
* status or control equipment. In addition, the module's init code asserts
* the OUTPUT_ENABLE signal and its exit code deasserts the OUTPUT_ENABLE
* signal.
*
* This module creates these /proc entries:
* Trailblazer directory  /proc/trailblazer
* Lift Monitoring
*  AC Mains              /proc/trailblazer/liftacmains
*  Motor Controller      /proc/trailblazer/liftmotorcontroller
*  Low Speed Operation   /proc/trailblazer/liftslowspeed
*  High Speed Operation  /proc/trailblazer/lifthighspeed
*  Operator Switch Base  /proc/trailblazer/liftoperatorswitchbase
*  Operator Switch Top   /proc/trailblazer/liftoperatorswitchtop
* Snow-Making Control
*  Water Value 1         /proc/trailblazer/snowwatervalve1
*  Water Value 2         /proc/trailblazer/snowwatervalve2
*  Water Value 3         /proc/trailblazer/snowwatervalve3
*  Heater                /proc/trailblazer/snowheater1
*/

/* references
 * see section 34.2 Port A MPC860 PowerQUICC User's Manual
 *     section 16.5 General-Purpose Chip-Select Machine (GPCM)
 */


#include <linux/module.h>
#include <linux/kernel.h>
#include <linux/init.h>
#include <linux/proc_fs.h>
#include <asm/uaccess.h>
#include <asm/io.h>

#include <asm/8xx_immap.h>


#define MODULE_VERSION "1.0"
#define MODULE_NAME "liftmon_snowcon_cllf"
```

LISTING 9.4   Continued

```
volatile immap_t *immap;
static void *io_base;



#define EXPANSIONPORT           0x80000000
#define EXPANSIONPORTLEN        16


#define PA0                     0x8000



/* input bit definitions */
#define LIFTACMAINS             0x01
#define LIFTMOTORCONTROLLER     0x02
#define LIFTSLOWSPEED           0x04
#define LIFTHIGHSPEED           0x08
#define LIFTOPERATORSWITCHBASE  0x10
#define LIFTOPERATORSWITCHTOP   0x20

/* output bit definitions */
#define SNOWWATERVALVE1         0x01
#define SNOWWATERVALVE2         0x02
#define SNOWWATERVALVE3         0x04
#define SNOWHEATER1             0x08

/* define a bitmask, each *_file uses this to determine who it is */
struct liftmon_snowcon_data_t {
        unsigned char mask;
};

/* snowcondata is the output latch value stored internally. Control
 *  changes made by user scripts writing to /proc/trailblazer entries
 * result in bits being either cleared or set in snowcondata. We
 * write snowcondata to the output latch every time a control change
 * occurs
 */
unsigned char snowcondata;

struct liftmon_snowcon_data_t liftacmains_data,
                              liftmotorcontroller_data,
                              liftslowspeed_data,
                              lifthighspeed_data,
```

LISTING 9.4   Continued

```
                                liftoperatorswitchbase_data,
                                liftoperatorswitchtop_data,
                                snowwatervalve1_data,
                                snowwatervalve2_data,
                                snowwatervalve3_data,
                                snowheater1_data;

static struct proc_dir_entry  *tb_dir,
                                *liftacmains_file,
                                *liftmotorcontroller_file,
                                *liftslowspeed_file,
                                *lifthighspeed_file,
                                *liftoperatorswitchbase_file,
                                *liftoperatorswitchtop_file,
                                *snowwatervalve1_file,
                                *snowwatervalve2_file,
                                *snowwatervalve3_file,
                                *snowheater1_file;

/* proc_read - proc_read_liftmon
 * proc_read_liftmon is the callback function that the kernel calls when
 * there's a read file operation on these /proc/trailblazer files:
 * liftacmains, lifthighspeed, liftmotorcontroller, liftoperatorswitchbase
 * liftoperatorswitchtop, and liftslowspeed. The file's data pointer is
 * passed in the data parameter. You first cast it to the
 * liftmon_snowcon_data_t structure. A read from io_base gets the AC input
 * status module. The result is anded with the bitmask value to
 * to determine if the particular input module is on or off. Which
 * particular input module is defined by which /proc/trailblazer/ file
 * is read.
 */
static int proc_read_liftmon(char *page, char **start, off_t off, int count,
                             int *eof, void *data)
{
  unsigned int v;
  struct liftmon_snowcon_data_t *liftmon_snowcon_data =
                                 (struct liftmon_snowcon_data_t *)data;

  v = readb(io_base);
```

LISTING 9.4   Continued

```
/* mask the input value based on the mask. Each mask is different depending
 * which /proc/trailblazer file was read.
 * Electrical note: returning an inverted value because AC power to an input
 * module pulls outputs a low and the input buffer, 74244, doesn't invert
 */
  if (v & liftmon_snowcon_data->mask)
    page[0] = '0';
  else
    page[0] = '1';

/* return 1 which is the length of page */
  return 1;
}


/* proc_write - proc_write_snowcondata
 * proc_write_snowcondata is the callback function that the kernel calls
 * when there's a write file operation on these /proc/trailblazer files:
 * snowheater1, snowwatervalve1, snowwatervalve2 and snowwatervalve3.
 * The file's data pointer is passed in the data parameter. You first
 * cast it to the liftmon_snowcon_data_t structure. The buffer parameter
 * points to the incoming data. If the incoming data is a 1 or a 0,
 * a bit in snowcondata is set or cleared. Which bit is defined by which
 * /proc/trailblazer file is written to. snowcondata is then written to
 * the output latch.
 */
static int proc_write_snowcondata(struct file *file, const char *buffer,
                                  unsigned long count, void *data)
{
  struct liftmon_snowcon_data_t *liftmon_snowcon_data =
                                 (struct liftmon_snowcon_data_t *)data;

/* check if the user wrote a 1 or a 0 the /proc/trailblazer file.
   if so, set or clear a bit in snowcondata */
  if (buffer[0] == '0')
    snowcondata |= liftmon_snowcon_data->mask;

  if (buffer[0] == '1')
    snowcondata &= ~liftmon_snowcon_data->mask;

  writeb(snowcondata, io_base + 1);
  return 1;
```

LISTING 9.4   Continued

```
}

/* proc_read - proc_read_snowcondata
 * proc_read_snowcondata is the callback function that the kernel calls
 * when there's a read file operation on these /proc/trailblazer files:
 * snowheater1, snowwatervalve1, snowwatervalve2 and snowwatervalve3.
 * The file's data pointer is passed in the data parameter. You first
 * cast it to the liftmon_snowcon_data_t structure.  Use snowcondata
 * anded with the bitmask value to determine if the particular output
 * module is on or off. Which particular output module is defined by
 * which /proc/trailblazer/ file is read.
 */
static int proc_read_snowcondata(char *page, char **start, off_t off,
                                 int count, int *eof, void *data)
{
  struct liftmon_snowcon_data_t *liftmon_snowcon_data =
                          (struct liftmon_snowcon_data_t *)data;

/* mask the snowcondata value based on the mask. Each mask is different
 * depending which /proc/trailblazer file was read. */
  if ( snowcondata & liftmon_snowcon_data->mask )
    page[0] = '0';
  else
    page[0] = '1';

/* return the length */
  return 1;
}

/* init - init_liftmon_snowcon
 * init_liftmon_snowcon creates the /proc entry files and obtains
 * their pointers. For each file, the fields, data, read_proc,
 * write_proc and owner, are filled.  Then the I/O controller is configured
 * so PA0 is an output and the memory controller works slowly with /CS5.
 * It initializes the output modules in the off state then
 * completes by writing an entry to the system log using printk.
 */
static int __init init_liftmon_snowcon(void)
{
  int rv = 0;
```

LISTING 9.4   Continued

```
/* Create the trailblazer /proc entry */
  tb_dir = proc_mkdir("trailblazer", NULL);
  if(tb_dir == NULL) {
          rv = -ENOMEM;
          goto out;
  }
  tb_dir->owner = THIS_MODULE;

/* Create liftacmains and make it readable by all - 0444 */
  liftacmains_file = create_proc_entry("liftacmains", 0444, tb_dir);
  if(liftacmains_file == NULL) {
          rv = -ENOMEM;
          goto no_liftacmains;
  }
  liftacmains_data.mask = LIFTACMAINS;
  liftacmains_file->data = &liftacmains_data;
  liftacmains_file->read_proc = &proc_read_liftmon;
  liftacmains_file->write_proc = NULL;
  liftacmains_file->owner = THIS_MODULE;


/* Create liftmotorcontroller and make it readable by all - 0444 */
  liftmotorcontroller_file = create_proc_entry("liftmotorcontroller",
                                               0444, tb_dir);
  if(liftmotorcontroller_file == NULL) {
          rv = -ENOMEM;
          goto no_liftmotorcontroller;
  }
  liftmotorcontroller_data.mask = LIFTMOTORCONTROLLER;
  liftmotorcontroller_file->data = &liftmotorcontroller_data;
  liftmotorcontroller_file->read_proc = &proc_read_liftmon;
  liftmotorcontroller_file->write_proc = NULL;
  liftmotorcontroller_file->owner = THIS_MODULE;

/* Create liftslowspeed and make it readable by all - 0444 */
  liftslowspeed_file = create_proc_entry("liftslowspeed", 0444, tb_dir);
  if(liftslowspeed_file == NULL) {
          rv = -ENOMEM;
          goto no_liftslowspeed;
  }
  liftslowspeed_data.mask = LIFTSLOWSPEED;
```

LISTING 9.4   Continued

```
    liftslowspeed_file->data = &liftslowspeed_data;
    liftslowspeed_file->read_proc = &proc_read_liftmon;
    liftslowspeed_file->write_proc = NULL;
    liftslowspeed_file->owner = THIS_MODULE;

/* Create lifthighspeed and make it readable by all - 0444 */
    lifthighspeed_file = create_proc_entry("lifthighspeed", 0444, tb_dir);
    if(lifthighspeed_file == NULL) {
            rv = -ENOMEM;
            goto no_lifthighspeed;
    }
    lifthighspeed_data.mask = LIFTHIGHSPEED;
    lifthighspeed_file->data = &lifthighspeed_data;
    lifthighspeed_file->read_proc = &proc_read_liftmon;
    lifthighspeed_file->write_proc = NULL;
    lifthighspeed_file->owner = THIS_MODULE;

/* Create liftoperatorswitchbase and make it readable by all - 0444 */
    liftoperatorswitchbase_file = create_proc_entry("liftoperatorswitchbase",
                                                    0444, tb_dir);
    if(liftoperatorswitchbase_file == NULL) {
            rv = -ENOMEM;
            goto no_liftoperatorswitchbase;
    }
    liftoperatorswitchbase_data.mask = LIFTOPERATORSWITCHBASE;
    liftoperatorswitchbase_file->data = &liftoperatorswitchbase_data;
    liftoperatorswitchbase_file->read_proc = &proc_read_liftmon;
    liftoperatorswitchbase_file->write_proc = NULL;
    liftoperatorswitchbase_file->owner = THIS_MODULE;

/* Create liftoperatorswitchtop and make it readable by all - 0444 */
    liftoperatorswitchtop_file = create_proc_entry("liftoperatorswitchtop",
                                                   0444, tb_dir);
    if(liftoperatorswitchtop_file == NULL) {
            rv = -ENOMEM;
            goto no_liftoperatorswitchtop;
    }
    liftoperatorswitchtop_data.mask = LIFTOPERATORSWITCHTOP;
    liftoperatorswitchtop_file->data = &liftoperatorswitchtop_data;
    liftoperatorswitchtop_file->read_proc = &proc_read_liftmon;
    liftoperatorswitchtop_file->write_proc = NULL;
```

LISTING 9.4 Continued

```
  liftoperatorswitchtop_file->owner = THIS_MODULE;

/* Create snowwatervalve1 and make it root writeable, readable by all-0644 */
  snowwatervalve1_file = create_proc_entry("snowwatervalve1", 0644, tb_dir);
  if(snowwatervalve1_file == NULL) {
          rv = -ENOMEM;
          goto no_snowwatervalve1;
  }
  snowwatervalve1_data.mask = SNOWWATERVALVE1;
  snowwatervalve1_file->data = &snowwatervalve1_data;
  snowwatervalve1_file->read_proc = &proc_read_snowcondata;
  snowwatervalve1_file->write_proc = &proc_write_snowcondata;
  snowwatervalve1_file->owner = THIS_MODULE;

/* Create snowwatervalve2 and make it root writeable, readable by all-0644 */
  snowwatervalve2_file = create_proc_entry("snowwatervalve2", 0644, tb_dir);
  if(snowwatervalve2_file == NULL) {
          rv = -ENOMEM;
          goto no_snowwatervalve2;
  }
  snowwatervalve2_data.mask = SNOWWATERVALVE2;
  snowwatervalve2_file->data = &snowwatervalve2_data;
  snowwatervalve2_file->read_proc = &proc_read_snowcondata;
  snowwatervalve2_file->write_proc = &proc_write_snowcondata;
  snowwatervalve2_file->owner = THIS_MODULE;

/* Create snowwatervalve3 and make it root writeable, readable by all-0644 */
  snowwatervalve3_file = create_proc_entry("snowwatervalve3", 0644, tb_dir);
  if(snowwatervalve3_file == NULL) {
          rv = -ENOMEM;
          goto no_snowwatervalve3;
  }
  snowwatervalve3_data.mask = SNOWWATERVALVE3;
  snowwatervalve3_file->data = &snowwatervalve3_data;
  snowwatervalve3_file->read_proc = &proc_read_snowcondata;
  snowwatervalve3_file->write_proc = &proc_write_snowcondata;
  snowwatervalve3_file->owner = THIS_MODULE;

/* Create snowheater1 and make it root writeable, readable by all-0644 */
  snowheater1_file = create_proc_entry("snowheater1", 0644, tb_dir);
  if(snowheater1_file == NULL) {
```

LISTING 9.4   Continued

```
            rv = -ENOMEM;
            goto no_snowheater1;
  }
  snowheater1_data.mask = SNOWHEATER1;
  snowheater1_file->data = &snowheater1_data;
  snowheater1_file->read_proc = &proc_read_snowcondata;
  snowheater1_file->write_proc = &proc_write_snowcondata;
  snowheater1_file->owner = THIS_MODULE;


/* get the register base address */
  immap = (immap_t *)(mfspr(IMMR) & 0xFFFF0000);

/* set CS5 for memory at 0x80000000, see 16.4.1 Base Registers (BRx)
 * and 16.4.2 Option Registers (ORx) for slow operation
 */
  immap->im_memctl.memc_br5 = 0x80000401;
  immap->im_memctl.memc_or5 = 0x80000FF6;

/* get the remapped GPIO controller base address register */
  io_base = ioremap_nocache(EXPANSIONPORT, EXPANSIONPORTLEN);

/* initialize snowcondata to 0xFF, all output modules off */
/* output modules invert */
  snowcondata = 0xFF;
  writeb(snowcondata, io_base);

  immap->im_ioport.iop_papar &= ~PA0; /* setting PA0 to general I/O */
  immap->im_ioport.iop_padir |=  PA0; /* make PA0 an output         */
  immap->im_ioport.iop_padat &= ~PA0; /* enable the 74HC574 output  */

  printk("immr    = 0x%08X\n",immap);
  printk("io_base = 0x%08X\n", io_base);
  printk("BR5     = 0x%08X\n",immap->im_memctl.memc_br5);
  printk("OR5     = 0x%08X\n",immap->im_memctl.memc_or5);
  printk("PAPAR   = 0x%04X\n",immap->im_ioport.iop_papar);
  printk("PADIR   = 0x%04X\n",immap->im_ioport.iop_padir);

/* everything initialized */
  printk(KERN_INFO "%s %s initialized\n",MODULE_NAME, MODULE_VERSION);
  return 0;
```

LISTING 9.4   Continued

```
/* this removes /proc entries if we have an error along the way */
no_snowheater1:
  remove_proc_entry("snowheater1", tb_dir);
no_snowwatervalve3:
  remove_proc_entry("snowwatervalve3", tb_dir);
no_snowwatervalve2:
  remove_proc_entry("snowwatervalve2", tb_dir);
no_snowwatervalve1:
  remove_proc_entry("snowwatervalve1", tb_dir);
no_liftoperatorswitchtop:
  remove_proc_entry("liftoperatorswitchtop", tb_dir);
no_liftoperatorswitchbase:
  remove_proc_entry("liftoperatorswitchbase", tb_dir);
no_lifthighspeed:
  remove_proc_entry("lifthighspeed", tb_dir);
no_liftslowspeed:
  remove_proc_entry("liftslowspeed", tb_dir);
no_liftmotorcontroller:
  remove_proc_entry("liftmotorcontroller", tb_dir);
no_liftacmains:
  remove_proc_entry("liftacmains", tb_dir);
out:
  return rv;
}


/* exit - cleanup_liftmon_snowcon
 * cleanup_liftmon_snowcon deasserts the OUTPUT_ENABLE signal.
 * It removes the /proc entry files prints a message to the system log.
 */
static void __exit cleanup_liftmon_snowcon(void)
{
  immap->im_ioport.iop_padir &= ~PA0; /* make PA0 an input */

/* release the ioremap */
  iounmap(io_base);

/* removing the /proc entries */
  remove_proc_entry("liftacmains", tb_dir);
  remove_proc_entry("liftmotorcontroller", tb_dir);
  remove_proc_entry("liftslowspeed", tb_dir);
  remove_proc_entry("lifthighspeed", tb_dir);
```

LISTING 9.4   Continued

```
remove_proc_entry("liftoperatorswitchbase", tb_dir);
remove_proc_entry("liftoperatorswitchtop", tb_dir);
remove_proc_entry("snowwatervalve1", tb_dir);
remove_proc_entry("snowwatervalve2", tb_dir);
remove_proc_entry("snowwatervalve3", tb_dir);
remove_proc_entry("snowheater1", tb_dir);
remove_proc_entry("trailblazer", NULL);

printk(KERN_INFO "%s %s removed\n", MODULE_NAME, MODULE_VERSION);
}


module_init(init_liftmon_snowcon);
module_exit(cleanup_liftmon_snowcon);


MODULE_AUTHOR("Craig Hollabaugh");
MODULE_DESCRIPTION(
"Trailblazer Lift Monitor and Snowmaking Control for RPX-CLLF");


EXPORT_NO_SYMBOLS;
```

The engineers have now attached memory-mapped I/O interface hardware to the MPC860 processor and written a device driver to access it.

Summary

This chapter covers a great deal. The Project Trailblazer engineers redesigned the lift monitoring and snow-making control interface for memory-mapped I/O operation on the MediaEngine and RPX-CLLF target boards. They located memory space for the interface board and determined the configuration for the CPU's memory and I/O controllers. The design and configuration passed testing after the helloworldbit device drivers were developed. The engineers used the circuit, the configuration, the helloworldbit source code, and the x86 parallel port liftmon_snowcon device driver code from Chapter 7 to create the lift monitoring and snow-making device drivers for the MediaEngine and the RPX-CLLF. They successfully developed ARM and PowerPC versions of liftmon_snowcon. These target boards can now monitor lifts and control snow-making equipment at Silverjack.

Additional Reading

1. Intel, *SA-1110 Microprocessor Developer's Manual,*
   `http://www.intel.com/design/strong/manuals/278240.htm`.

2. Brightstar Engineering, *MediaEngine Hardware Reference Manual,*
   `http://www.brightstareng.com/pub/mediaman.pdf`.

3. Embedded Planet, *PlanetCore Version 1.4 Boot Loader Manual,*
   `http://www.embeddedplanet.com/pdf/docs/pc_load_20.pdf`.

4. Dan Malek, "Porting PPC," `http://lists.linuxppc.org/linuxppc-embedded/`
   `200005/msg00157.html`.

5. Motorola, *MPC860 User Manual,* `http://e-www.motorola.com/brdata/PDFDB/`
   `docs/MPC860UM.pdf`.

10

Synchronous Serial Communication Interfacing

Months have passed since the inception of Project Trailblazer, and the engineers have experienced success after success while developing with embedded Linux. As fall approaches, the engineers forge ahead with two temperature-related interfacing tasks: temperature sensing and temperature display. Silverjack management wants to provide accurate temperature readings from all key mountain locations and facilities to guests, visitors, employees, and the Operations Department. More than just a convenience, accurate temperature readings serve a safety role, permitting guests and employees to make informed decisions that could affect their well-being. The Project Trailblazer engineers want to acquire temperature readings at all locations and facilities, both outside and in equipment rooms. Management wants a large temperature display at each lift access point. The display should show the temperature in Fahrenheit and Celsius, at both the bottom and top of each lift.

The engineers need to develop cost-effective solutions that connect temperature sensors and large light-emitting diode (LED) displays to their target platforms. They have found inexpensive temperature sensors and LED display drivers that communicate by using synchronous serial communication. More specifically, they have found serial peripheral interface (SPI) and inter-integrated circuit (I2C) devices that connect to microprocessors using clocked serial data communication. In this chapter, we'll follow the engineers as they connect an SPI temperature sensor and I2C LED display drivers to their embedded Linux target boards.

Temperature Sensing and Display

The engineers need a temperature-sensing technology that's inexpensive, accurate and covers an extensive temperature range. They've found the National Semiconductor LM70 SPI digital temperature sensor (www.national.com). For the outdoor temperature display, they've decided to use the Philips Semiconductor I2C SAA1064 four-digit seven-segment LED display driver (www.semiconductors.philips.com).

National Semiconductor's LM70 digital temperature sensor offers 0.25°C resolution over a temperature range of –55°C to +150°C (that is, –67°F to +302°F). The LM70 operates with a supply voltage between +2.65V and +5.5V and consumes 490μA with a temperature accuracy of ±2°C from –40°C to +85°C. It interfaces to microprocessors through an SPI interface. The LM70 is ideal for Project Trailblazer, and each one costs about $1.

Philips Semiconductor specifically designed the SAA1064 with an I2C bus interface capable of driving four seven-segment LED displays. The I2C serial interface permits connection of up to four SAA1064s to a single microprocessor synchronous serial port. One target board connected to four SAA1064s, each driving four seven-segment LEDs, enables display of temperatures at the top and bottom of the lift, in both Fahrenheit and Celsius. For example, a single temperature display with 16 digits can show the lift top temperature of 10°F and –12°C and the lift bottom temperature of 44°F and 6°C. Each SAA1064 costs about $4.

The Project Trailblazer engineers need to connect an LM70 to the x86 parallel port and develop an SPI synchronous serial communication algorithm for a device driver. Embedded developers refer to synchronous serial communication algorithms as "bit-banging" routines. Then the engineers need to connect an LM70 to the MediaEngine's ARM processor. The ARM processor's Serial Port 4 is a synchronous serial port (SSP) that simplifies communications with external SPI devices. Next, the engineers need to connect an SAA1064 to the x86 parallel port and use pre-existing I2C device driver software. Finally, the engineers need to develop an I2C bit-banging routine for the PowerPC, to enable the RPX-CLLF to drive the temperature LED displays. In summary, this chapter outlines the connection and driver development for the devices listed in Table 10.1.

TABLE 10.1   Temperature Device Connectivity and Driver Type

Platform	Software Type
LM70 Temperature Sensor (SPI)	
x86, parallel port	Bit-banging algorithm
SA-1110, SSP	On-chip controller
SAA1064 LED Driver (I2C)	
x86, parallel port	Open-source device driver
MPC860, Port B	Bit-banging algorithm

TIP

The LM70 is one device within an LM temperature sensor family offered by National Semiconductor. Other temperature sensors, such as the LM78, provide additional interfacing capabilities. The LM78 has an on-chip temperature sensor, 7 analog inputs to monitor voltages, 3 tachometer inputs, a watchdog timer, an interrupt controller, and 32 bytes of RAM. See the National Semiconductor Web site (www.national.com) for more information.

SPI Communication and the LM70

The LM70 operates in a continuous temperature conversion mode. In this mode, the LM70 operates as a slave device, accepting communication with a host microprocessor. It is an SPI-compatible device that communicates with the host via three signals: chip select (/CS), serial clock (SC), and bidirectional serial data line (SI/O). Synchronous communication with the LM70 is very simple. Because it continually determines the temperature (continuous conversion mode), the LM70 doesn't require that temperature conversion commands be sent from the host, as do other temperature sensors. Also, the SPI communication bus doesn't support multiple devices; therefore, SPI communication with an LM70 requires no packet formation or address information. An SPI communication consists of the host initiating communication with the assertion of the LM70's /CS line, sending 16 clock pulses while reading the LM70's output on the SI/O signal, and then the host de-asserting the chip select. The LM70 outputs 1 sign bit, 10 temperature bits (most significant bit [MSB] first), 3 high bits, and 2 undefined bits on the falling edge of the serial clock signal. This 11-bit temperature representation is a two's-complement word with a least significant bit (LSB) resolution of 0.25°C.

Let's clarify this temperature value encoding by examining the bits of two examples of temperatures. If the temperature were 25°C, communication with the LM70 would return the binary value 0000 1100 1001 1111, which equals 0x0C9F. The five least significant bits don't contain temperature information, and they affect the magnitude of the temperature value. These bits are removed by dividing the temperature value by 32, which is 2^5. 0x0C9F divided by 32 is 0x64, which is equal to 100. Each least significant bit corresponds to 0.25°C; therefore, 100 times 0.25°C equals 25°C. If the temperature was –25°C, communication with the LM70 would return the binary value 1111 0011 1001 1111, which equals 0xF39F. Dividing by 32 results in a value of 0xFF9C, which corresponds to –100. –100 times 0.25°C equals –25°C.

The LM70 datasheet[1] contains serial bus timing diagrams and switching characteristics. These specifications place an upper limit on communication speed, but that is not a concern in this design. In fact, this design will intentionally slow synchronous communication in order to increase design reliability. Typically, the Project Trailblazer target boards will be located in a communication closet or enclosure. The board's temperature sensor will be close by—within about 20 feet—to measure outside temperatures, for example. Use of slow synchronous communication enables line drivers to overcome the extra capacitance due to long wire lengths.

A device driver communicating with the LM70 temperature sensor performs five steps:

1. It initializes serial communication with SC high and /CS high. It enters the start condition by taking /CS low.

2. It starts data bit transfer by taking SC low. The LM70 then actively drives the SI/O signal with the first bit of information.

3. It takes SC high and then samples the first data bit on the SI/O signal.

4. It continues toggling the SC signal and sampling SI/O until 16 bits are received.

5. It enters the stop condition and terminates communication by taking /CS high.

Connecting the LM70 to the x86 Parallel Printer Port

The LM70 SPI signal lines—/CS, SC, and SI/O—as well as the power line and the ground (GND) connect directly to the parallel port (see Figure 10.1). The parallel port drives /CS and SC but not SI/O. The LM70 drives the SI/O line, which returns the serial data stream. Because of its continuous conversion mode, there's no need to send data to the sensor.

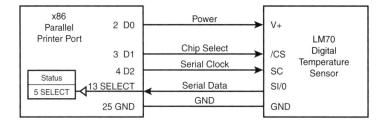

FIGURE 10.1   The LM70 temperature sensor connection to the x86 parallel printer port.

TIP

Check your x86 parallel printer port signal voltages before connecting your interface circuits. Some printer ports operate with +5V, and newer motherboards use +3.3V. You may not be able to power your +5V devices from a +3.3V signal. Or you might destroy your +3.3V devices by connecting them to a +5V signal.

The x86 LM70 device driver implements SPI signaling communication by using parallel printer port connections. This driver provides users with temperature data through /proc directory entries. Listing 10.1 shows the LM70_x86.c device driver code.

LISTING 10.1   The LM70_x86.c Device Driver

```
/*
 * LM70_x86 v1.0 11/05/01
 * www.embeddedlinuxinterfacing.com
 *
 * The original location of this code is
 * http://www.embeddedlinuxinterfacing.com/chapters/10/
 *
 * Copyright (C) 2001 by Craig Hollabaugh
 *
 * This program is free software; you can redistribute it and/or modify
 * it under the terms of the GNU Library General Public License as
 * published by the Free Software Foundation; either version 2 of the
 * License, or (at your option) any later version.
 *
 * This program is distributed in the hope that it will be useful, but
 * WITHOUT ANY WARRANTY; without even the implied warranty of
 * MERCHANTABILITY or FITNESS FOR A PARTICULAR PURPOSE. See the GNU
 * Library General Public License for more details.
 *
 * You should have received a copy of the GNU Library General Public
 * License along with this program; if not, write to the
 * Free Software Foundation, Inc.,
 * 59 Temple Place, Suite 330, Boston, MA 02111-1307 USA
 */

/*
 * LM70_x86.c is based on procfs_example.c by Erik Mouw.
 * For more information, please see The Linux Kernel Procfs Guide, Erik Mouw
 * http://kernelnewbies.org/documents/kdoc/procfs-guide/lkprocfsguide.html
 *
 */

/* LM70_x86
 * This device driver demonstrates communication with a LM70 temperature
 * sensor using SPI signaling. This routine implements SPI communication
 * in software (bit-banging). The driver creates a /proc directory entry
```

LISTING 10.1   Continued

```
 * called /proc/trailblazer/temperature. Scripts can read the current
 * temperature from this file.
 *
 * This device driver communicates with a National Semiconductor
 * LM70CIMM-3 MUA08A connected in the following manner.
 *
 *   Parallel                Temperature
 *    Port      Direction     Sensor
 *     D0    2       ->       V+   5
 *     D1    3       ->       /CS  7
 *     D2    4       ->       SC   2
 *    GND    25      -        GND  4
 *   Select 13       <-       SI/O 1
 */

/*
gcc -O2 -D__KERNEL__ -DMODULE -I/usr/src/linux/include \
-c LM70_x86.c -o LM70_x86.o
*/

#include <linux/module.h>
#include <linux/kernel.h>
#include <linux/init.h>
#include <linux/proc_fs.h>
#include <linux/delay.h>

#include <asm/io.h>

#define MODULE_VERSION "1.0"
#define MODULE_NAME    "LM70_x86"

static struct proc_dir_entry  *tb_dir,
                              *temperature_file;

#define SPPDATAPORT     0x378
#define SPPSTATUSPORT   (SPPDATAPORT + 1)
#define SPPCONTROLPORT  (SPPDATAPORT + 2)

/* status port bit definitions */
#define SIO             0x10
```

LISTING 10.1   Continued

```c
/* data port bit definitions */
#define VCC             0x01
#define nCS             0x02
#define SC              0x04

/* bit delay time, in usecs */
#define DELAY           140

unsigned char data;
#define clkLow()        outb(data & ~SC ,SPPDATAPORT)
#define clkHigh()       outb(data |  SC ,SPPDATAPORT)
#define assertCS()      outb(data & ~nCS,SPPDATAPORT)
#define deassertCS()    outb(data |  nCS,SPPDATAPORT)
#define readBit()       (SIO == (inb(SPPSTATUSPORT) & SIO))

/*
 * function initializeSensor
 * This function initializes the 'data' variable with VCC then
 * applies power to the LM70 by writing 'data' to the parallel
 * port. The /CS and SC lines are then put in an initialization state.
 *
 */
void initializeSensor(void)
{
  data = VCC;
  outb(data ,SPPDATAPORT); /* write the data to the parallel port */
  clkHigh();               /* clock high and /CS are SPI init state */
  deassertCS();
}

/*
 * function powerdownSensor
 * This function removes power from the LM70 by zeroing 'data'
 * and writing it to the parallel port. This function is called
 * when the device driver module is removed
 *
 */
void powerdownSensor(void)
{
  data = 0;
```

LISTING 10.1   Continued

```
  outb(data ,SPPDATAPORT); /* write the data to the parallel port */
}


/*
 * function getTemperature
 * This function perform SPI communications with the LM70. The
 * LM70 clocks serial out on the falling edge of the SC signal.
 * This routine reads the SI/O line for this serial stream after
 * the rising edge of SC signal. The LM70 sends MSB first, this
 * routine performs the bit shifts. The signals, SC and /CS, are
 * intentionally slowed down to allow settling time on long
 * communication lines with extra capacitance.
 *
 * returns
 * getTemperature function returns the temperature in degrees C
 * in 1 degree increments
 *
 * This routine doesn't perform communication error checking or
 * reporting.
 *
 */
int getTemperature(void)
{
  unsigned char i;
  int temperature;

  assertCS();      /* enter the start condition */
  udelay(DELAY);

  temperature = 0;
  for (i = 0; i < 16; i++) {
    clkLow();
    udelay(DELAY);
    clkHigh();
    udelay(DELAY);
    temperature = ((temperature << 1) | readBit());
    /* shift the temperature bits then OR the input bit into the LSB */
  }

  deassertCS();
```

LISTING 10.1   Continued

```
/*
 * Now we to scale the temperature value. Simply shifting the
 * bits right doesn't perform the correct operation if the
 * temperature is below zero. Shifting introduces 0's into the
 * MSB thus losing the negative sign bit. An integer divide by 32
 * preserves the sign bit and eliminates the last unused 5 bits
 *
 * At this point, after the divide by 32. temperature contains
 * the count of LSB bits where 1 LSB equals 0.25C. An additional
 * divide by 4 scales temperature in 1 degree increments.
 */

  temperature /= 128; /* 32 * 4 = 128 */

  return temperature;
}



/*
 * function proc_read_temperature
 * This function is called when the user performs a read operation
 * on /proc/trailblazer/temperature. This function fills the page
 * buffer with a temperature in degrees C.
 *
 */
static int proc_read_temperature(char *page, char **start, off_t off,
                                 int count, int *eof, void *data)
. FIXED ch.
{
  int len, temp;

  temp = getTemperature();
  len = sprintf(page, "%+d", temp); /* temp * 9 / 5 + 32 here for F */

  return len;
}

/*
 * function init_LM70_x86
 * This initialization function creates the /proc/trailblazer
```

LISTING 10.1   Continued

```
 * directory and a temperature entry in it then initializes the
 * LM70 temperature sensor
 *
 */
static int __init init_LM70_x86(void)
{
  int rv = 0;

/* Create the trailblazer /proc entry */
  tb_dir = proc_mkdir("trailblazer", NULL);
  if(tb_dir == NULL) {
    rv = -ENOMEM;
    goto out;
  }
  tb_dir->owner = THIS_MODULE;

/* Create temperature and make it readable by all - 0444 */
  temperature_file = create_proc_entry("temperature", 0444, tb_dir);
  if(temperature_file == NULL) {
    rv = -ENOMEM;
    goto no_temperature;
  }
  temperature_file->data = NULL;
  temperature_file->read_proc = &proc_read_temperature;
  temperature_file->write_proc = NULL;
  temperature_file->owner = THIS_MODULE;

  initializeSensor();

/* everything initialized */
  printk(KERN_INFO "%s %s initialized\n", MODULE_NAME, MODULE_VERSION);
  return 0;

no_temperature:
  remove_proc_entry("trailblazer", NULL);
out:
  return rv;
}


/*
```

LISTING 10.1   Continued

```
 * function cleanup_LM70_x86
 * This clean function powers down the sensor and removes
 * the /proc/trailblazer directory and the temperature entry.
 */
static void __exit cleanup_LM70_x86(void)
{
  powerdownSensor();

  remove_proc_entry("temperature", tb_dir);
  remove_proc_entry("trailblazer", NULL);

  printk(KERN_INFO "%s %s removed\n", MODULE_NAME, MODULE_VERSION);
}


module_init(init_LM70_x86);
module_exit(cleanup_LM70_x86);

MODULE_AUTHOR("Craig Hollabaugh");
MODULE_DESCRIPTION("Trailblazer LM70_x86");

EXPORT_NO_SYMBOLS;
```

The LM70_x86.c device driver contains four main functions:

- **init_LM70_x86**—This is the device driver initialization function, which creates the /proc directory entries trailblazer and trailblazer/temperature and then initializes the temperature sensor.

- **proc_read_temperature**—This function is called whenever the user performs a read operation on /proc/trailblazer/temperature. proc_read_temperature calls getTemperature, which performs the actual SPI communication with the LM70.

- **getTemperature**—This function communicates with the LM70, scales the 11-bit temperature representation, and returns a value in 1-degree-Celcius increments.

- **cleanup_LM70_x86**—This is the device driver cleanup function, which powers down the LM70 and removes the /proc directory entries.

Remember that the LM70 clocks MSB first and then clocks out data bits on the SC falling edge. The SI/O line should be sampled on the SC rising edge. The oscilloscope capture shown in Figure 10.2 shows a bit stream of 0000.1101.1111.1111, which corresponds to 27.75°C. The device driver returns 27°C because the getTemperature function performs an integer division on the value.

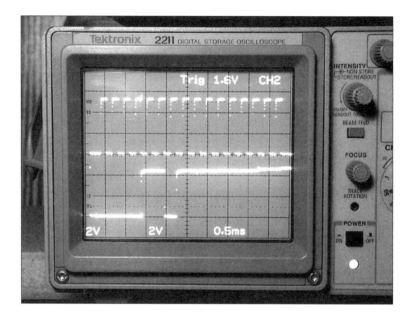

FIGURE 10.2   An oscilloscope capture of SC (top trace) and SI/O (bottom trace) signals during an SPI communication with the LM70.

TIP

The LM70 integrated circuit surface mount packaging has little thermal mass. This means it's very responsive to temperature changes. Merely touching the LM70 affects its temperature reading. You can accurately measure the temperature of an object by gluing the LM70 to it with nonconductive glue.

Here are the commands to compile and get a temperature from an LM70 using tbdev1:

```
root@tbdev1[516]: gcc -O2 -D__KERNEL__ -DMODULE \
➥-I/usr/src/linux/include -c LM70_x86.c -o LM70_x86.o
root@tbdev1[517]: insmod LM70_x86.o
root@tbdev1[518]: cat /proc/trailblazer/temperature
```

```
+27
root@tbdev1[519]:
```

Embedded designs often implement bit-banging routines to communicate with synchronous serial devices. In the interfacing example shown in Listing 10.1, a bit-banging function, getTemperature, communicates with the LM70 that is connected to the x86 parallel printer port. Communication delays can be increased to allow for longer communication signal wires between the host CPU and the temperature sensor.

This example clocks in only 16 temperature data bits. Although it is short, the bit-banging operation requires CPU cycles. Bit-banging operations can be CPU intensive for long serial communication streams. This affects the performance of other programs because the Linux scheduler does not interrupt device driver routines.

Other CPUs can contain dedicated peripherals for synchronous communications, thus alleviating the CPU from having to perform the bit-banging chores. Both the ARM SA-1110 and PowerPC MPC860 contain SPI synchronous communication controllers.

Connecting the LM70 to the MediaEngine

The MediaEngine design allows access to the ARM SA-1110's Serial Port 4 through the J13 connector. Serial Port 4 contains two synchronous serial controllers: the multimedia communication port (MCP) and the SSP. CPU register configuration selects which controller attaches to the pins of Serial Port 4. Selecting neither controller allows these pins to become general input/output (I/O) pins. With general I/O pins, the Project Trailblazer engineers could implement a bit-banging algorithm for the ARM processor, but they don't. The SA-1110's SSP controller supports SPI, which makes it ideal for synchronous communication with the LM70. (See section 11.12.7, "SPP Operation," of *SA-1110 Developer's Manual*[2], for more information on SSP.) Figure 10.3 shows the connection between the MediaEngine and the LM70 temperature sensor.

The MediaEngine LM70 device driver uses programmed I/O operation. That is, it doesn't use CPU interrupts or direct memory access (DMA). Synchronous communication with the LM70 is short and simple; introducing interrupts and DMA channel usage would add unnecessary complications.

Programmed I/O polling is simple. Prior to SPI communication, the SA-1110 SSP receive first in, first out (FIFO) buffer is cleared. The getTemperature function starts SPI communication and then continuously monitors the SSP busy flag Status Register (SSSR) bit. When SPI communication completes, the busy flag bit is cleared and the SSP Data Register (SSDR) contains the 16-bit temperature reading. Programmed I/O using Serial Port 4 with the SSP controller requires configuring the bits in the following two registers:

- SSP Control Register 1 (SSCR1) configuration bit settings:
  - Receive FIFO Interrupt Enable (RIE): 0 masks interrupt
  - Transmit FIFO Interrupt Enable (TIE): 0 masks interrupt
  - Loopback Mode (LBM): 0 disables loopback mode
  - Serial Clock Polarity (SPO): 0 holds SC low during idle
  - Serial Clock Phase (SPH): 0 adds 1 clock cycle delay
  - External Clock Select (ECS): 0 uses internal clock
- SSP Control Register 0 (SSCR0) configuration bit settings:
  - Data Size Select (DSS): 1111 selects 16-bit length
  - Frame Format (FRF): 00 selects Motorola SPI
  - Synchronous Serial Port Enable (SSE): 1 for enable
  - Serial Clock Rate (SCR): 11111111 selects slowest clock

The MediaEngine's `LM70_mediaengine.c` device driver, shown in Listing 10.2, needs to configure the SA-1110's SSCR1 register with 0x0000 and the SSCR0 register with 1111 1111 1000 1111 (0xFF8F).

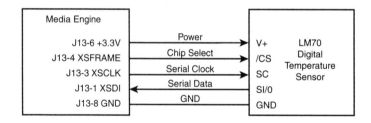

FIGURE 10.3   The LM70 temperature sensor connection to the MediaEngine.

LISTING 10.2   The `LM70_mediaengine.c` Device Driver

```
/*
 * LM70_mediaengine v1.0 11/05/01
 * www.embeddedlinuxinterfacing.com
 *
 * The original location of this code is
 * http://www.embeddedlinuxinterfacing.com/chapters/10/
 *
 * Copyright (C) 2001 by Craig Hollabaugh
 *
 * This program is free software; you can redistribute it and/or modify
 * it under the terms of the GNU Library General Public License as
 * published by the Free Software Foundation; either version 2 of the
 * License, or (at your option) any later version.
 *
 * This program is distributed in the hope that it will be useful, but
 * WITHOUT ANY WARRANTY; without even the implied warranty of
 * MERCHANTABILITY or FITNESS FOR A PARTICULAR PURPOSE. See the GNU
 * Library General Public License for more details.
 *
 * You should have received a copy of the GNU Library General Public
 * License along with this program; if not, write to the
 * Free Software Foundation, Inc.,
 * 59 Temple Place, Suite 330, Boston, MA 02111-1307 USA
 */

/*
 * LM70_mediaengine.c is based on procfs_example.c by Erik Mouw.
 * For more information, please see The Linux Kernel Procfs Guide, Erik Mouw
 * http://kernelnewbies.org/documents/kdoc/procfs-guide/lkprocfsguide.html
 *
 */

/* LM70_mediaengine
 * This device driver demonstrates communication with a LM70 temperature
 * sensor using the SA-1110 SPI controller. The driver uses polled I/O
 * by checking the SSSR's busy flag instead of using interrupts.
 * The driver creates a /proc directory entry called
```

LISTING 10.2   Continued

```
 * /proc/trailblazer/temperature. Scripts can read the current temperature
 * from this file.
 */

/*
arm-linux-gcc -O2 -D__KERNEL__ -DMODULE -I/usr/src/arm-linux/include \
-c LM70_mediaengine.c -o /tftpboot/arm-rootfs/tmp/LM70_mediaengine.o
*/

#include <linux/module.h>
#include <linux/kernel.h>
#include <linux/init.h>
#include <linux/proc_fs.h>
#include <linux/delay.h>

#include <asm/io.h>

#define MODULE_VERSION "1.0"
#define MODULE_NAME    "LM70_mediaengine"


static struct proc_dir_entry  *tb_dir,
                              *temperature_file;


/* see 11.12 Intel StrongARM SA-1110 Microprocessor Developer's Manual */
#define SSP          0x80070000
#define SSCR0_OFFSET 0x60
#define SSCR1_OFFSET 0x64
#define SSDR_OFFSET  0x6C
#define SSSR_OFFSET  0x74

#define SSPLEN       0x78

/* SSP bits */
#define SPP_RNE      0x04
#define SPP_BSY      0x08

static void *ssp_base;

/*
```

LISTING 10.2   Continued

```c
 * function getTemperature
 * This function performs SPI communications with the LM70
 * using programmed I/O (polled mode). Prior to SPI communication,
 * the SA-1110 receive FIFO buffer will be cleared. The getTemperature
 * function will start SPI communication then continuously monitor the
 * SSP busy flag in the SSP Status Register (SSSR). Upon SPI
 * communication completion, the SSP Data Register (SSDR) will contain
 * the 16-bit temperature reading.

 * returns
 * All 16 bits are returned, 11 temperature value bits, 3 1 bits
 * and 2 undefined bits.
 *
 * This routine doesn't perform communication error checking or
 * reporting.
 */
int getTemperature(void)
{
  unsigned char i;
  int temperature, status;

/* need to flush the receive FIFO before we start */
  for (i = 0; i < 16; i++)
  {
    status = readw(ssp_base + SSSR_OFFSET); /* read the status register */
    if ((status & SPP_RNE) == 0) /* is the receive FIFO empty? */
      break;
     temperature = readw(ssp_base + SSDR_OFFSET);
     /* read the receive FIFO to clear out old stuff */
  }

/* start SPI communication, need to feed the transmit FIFO a dummy value */
  writel(0x00, ssp_base + SSDR_OFFSET);

/* now wait until the BSY flag is not set and read the receive FIFO */
  for (i = 0; i < 20; i++)
  {
    status = readw(ssp_base + SSSR_OFFSET); /* read the status register */
    if ((status & SPP_BSY) == 0) /* are we still doing an SPI frame? */
      break;
    udelay(1000); /* wait a little */
```

LISTING 10.2   Continued

```
  }

  temperature = readw(ssp_base + SSDR_OFFSET); /* read the receive FIFO */

/* for debugging uncomment the next line */
/*  printk("temp:  i is %d, temperature is 0x%04X\n",i, temperature); */

/*
 *  Now we to scale the temperature value. Simply shifting the
 *  bits right doesn't perform the correct operation if the
 *  temperature is below zero. Shifting introduces 0's into the
 *  MSB thus losing the negative sign bit. An integer divide by 32
 *  preserves the sign bit and eliminates the last unused 5 bits
 *
 *  At this point, after the divide by 32. temperature contains
 *  the count of LSB bits where 1 lSB equals 0.25C. An additional
 *  divide by 4 scales temperature in 1 degree increments.
 */
  temperature /= 128; /* 32 * 4 = 128 */

  return temperature;
}


/*
 * function proc_read_temperature
 * This function is called when the user performs a read operation
 * on /proc/trailblazer/temperature. This function fills the page
 * buffer with a temperature in degrees C.
 */
static int proc_read_temperature(char *page, char **start, off_t off,
                                 int count, int *eof, void *data)
{
  int len, temp;

  temp = getTemperature();
  len = sprintf(page, "%+d\n", temp); /* temp * 9 / 5 + 32 here for F */

  return len;
}
```

LISTING 10.2   Continued

```
/*
 * function init_LM70_mediaengine
 * This initialization function creates the /proc/trailblazer
 * directory and a temperature entry in it then initializes the
 * LM70 temperature sensor
 */
static int __init init_LM70_mediaengine(void)
{
  unsigned int r;
  int rv = 0;

/* Create the trailblazer /proc entry */
  tb_dir = proc_mkdir("trailblazer", NULL);
  if(tb_dir == NULL) {
    rv = -ENOMEM;
    goto out;
  }
  tb_dir->owner = THIS_MODULE;

/* Create temperature and make it readable by all - 0444 */
  temperature_file = create_proc_entry("temperature", 0444, tb_dir);
  if(temperature_file == NULL) {
    rv = -ENOMEM;
    goto no_temperature;
  }
  temperature_file->data = NULL;
  temperature_file->read_proc = &proc_read_temperature;
  temperature_file->write_proc = NULL;
  temperature_file->owner = THIS_MODULE;

  ssp_base = ioremap_nocache(SSP,SSPLEN);
  printk("ssp_base       = 0x%08X\n",ssp_base);

/*
 * SSCR1 binary value 0000 0000 0000 0000 = 0x0000
 * External Clock Select (ECS),          0 uses internal clock
 * Serial Clock Phase (SPH),             0 adds 1 clock cycle delay
 * Serial Clock Polarity (SPO),          0 holds SC low during idle
 * Loopback Mode (LBM),                  0 disables loopback mode
 * Transmit FIFO Interrupt Enable (TIE), 0 masks interrupt
 * Receive FIFO Interrupt Enable (RIE),  0 masks interrupt
```

LISTING 10.2   Continued

```
 */
  writel(0x0000, ssp_base + SSCR1_OFFSET);

/*
 * SSCR0 binary value 1111 1111 1000 1111 = 0xFF8F
 * Data Size Select (DSS),            1111 selects 16 bit length
 * Frame Format (FRF),                00 selects Motorola SPI
 * Synchronous Serial Port Enable (SSE), 1 for enable
 * Serial Clock Rate (SCR),           11111111 selects slowest clock
 */
  writel(0xFF8F, ssp_base + SSCR0_OFFSET);

/* read the registers and printout results */
  r = readl(ssp_base + SSCR1_OFFSET);
  printk("SSCR1         = 0x%04X\n",r);
  r = readl(ssp_base + SSCR0_OFFSET);
  printk("SSCR0         = 0x%04X\n",r);

/* everything initialized */
  printk(KERN_INFO "%s %s initialized\n", MODULE_NAME, MODULE_VERSION);
  return 0;

no_temperature:
 remove_proc_entry("trailblazer", NULL);
out:
 return rv;
}

/*
 * function cleanup_LM70_mediaengine
 * This clean function powers down the sensor and removes
 * the /proc/trailblazer directory and the temperature entry.
 */
static void __exit cleanup_LM70_mediaengine(void)
{
  iounmap(ssp_base);

  remove_proc_entry("temperature", tb_dir);
  remove_proc_entry("trailblazer", NULL);
```

LISTING 10.2 Continued

```
  printk(KERN_INFO "%s %s removed\n", MODULE_NAME, MODULE_VERSION);
}


module_init(init_LM70_mediaengine);
module_exit(cleanup_LM70_mediaengine);

MODULE_AUTHOR("Craig Hollabaugh");
MODULE_DESCRIPTION("Trailblazer LM70_mediaengine");


EXPORT_NO_SYMBOLS;
```

The LM70_mediaengine.c device driver contains four main functions:

- **init_LM70_mediaEngine**—This is the device driver initialization function, and it creates the /proc directory entries trailblazer and trailblazer/temperature. It then configures the SA-1110's SSCR1 and SSCR0 registers enabling SSP controller operation on Serial Port 4.

- **proc_read_temperature**—This function is called whenever the user performs a read operation on /proc/trailblazer/temperature. proc_read_temperature calls getTemperature.

- **getTemperature**—This function uses the SSP controller that communicates with the LM70. The getTemperature function returns a value in 1-degree-Celcius increments.

- **cleanup_LM70_MediaEngine**—This is the device driver cleanup function, and it removes the /proc directory entries.

The oscilloscope capture shown in Figure 10.4 shows a bit stream of 0000.1011.0011.1111, which corresponds to 22.25°C.

So far the Project Trailblazer engineers have connected the LM70 temperature sensor to the x86 parallel printer port and the MediaEngine's Serial Port 4 with an SSP controller. Synchronous serial signaling permits easy connection of external devices to microprocessors. Communication is simple and fast because there's no need for packet formation or command addressing. Using this type of synchronous serial communication requires a chip select for each external device. CS signals are subject to availability as external SPI device count increases.

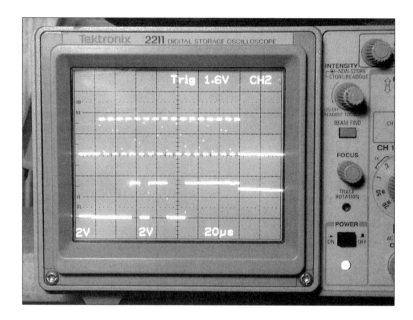

FIGURE 10.4   An oscilloscope capture of *SC* (top trace) and *SI/O* (bottom trace) signals, using the SA-1110 SSP controller for SPI communication with the LM70.

I2C Communication with the Philips Semiconductor SAA1064

The Project Trailblazer engineers plan to use the Philips Semiconductor SAA1064 to interface four seven-segment LED displays to a target board that uses I2C bus signaling. An I2C bus requires only two bidirectional signal lines: serial data (SDA) and serial clock (SCL). This bus supports multiple slave devices through software addressing in which each bus device has a unique address. I2C communication is 8-bit communication, with the data receiver acknowledging the reception of each transferred byte. Bus devices can connect or disconnect at any time, without restarting the master. Philips offers complete and thorough I2C documentation.[3]

Up to four SAA1064 can exist on a single I2C bus. Therefore, the engineers can use them to display the lift top and lift bottom temperatures in both Fahrenheit and Celsius. Each SAA1064 can drive up to four seven-segment LED displays, for a total of 16 LEDs on a single serial bus. The SAA1064 design lowers overall package pin count with two multiplexing LED drive circuits that control two common-anode segments. (See *SAA1064 Datasheet*[4] for more information.)

> **TIP**
>
> The SAA1064 provides direct connection for common-anode seven-segment LED displays without additional circuit components. The SAA1064 can drive common-cathode LED displays with additional circuitry. If you are purchasing LED displays for use with the SAA1064, you should choose common-anode type. This will simplify your interfacing design.

Communication commands can control all LED segments individually on each of the four seven-segment LEDS. The SAA1064 drives the LED segments with a programmable current source that allows for software-controlled brightness without requiring external current limiting resistors. Setting the SAA1064's I2C bus address occurs by applying an analog voltage to the address pin. The SAA1064's industrial temperature range of –40°C to +85°C (–40°F to +185°F) permits unheated operation, which is a definite plus for Silverjack outdoor winter operation.

Connecting the SAA1064 to the x86 Parallel Printer Port

Connecting the SAA1064 to the parallel port requires two signals: SDA and SCL. The display LEDs require more drive current than the parallel port can supply. The power and ground lines must be connected to an external power supply. The PC's power supply can be used. The x86 parallel port doesn't contain a dedicated I2C communications controller. A device driver can implement the I2C protocol in software and then use the parallel port for the SDA and SCL signaling.

An I2C parallel port driver called i2c-pport exists within the lm_sensors project (see www.lm-sensors.nu). This open source project implements the I2C protocol for Linux. The Project Trailblazer engineers decided to use the i2c-pport device driver instead of writing their own. Connecting and communicating with an SAA1064 by using i2c-pport is a five-step process:

1. Download and compile the I2C source code by using these commands:

```
root@tbdev1[501]: cd /root
root@tbdev1[502]: wget www.lm-sensors.nu/archive/
➥i2c-2.6.1.tar.gz
root@tbdev1[503]: tar zxf i2c-2.6.1.tar.gz
root@tbdev1[504]: cd i2c-2.6.1
root@tbdev1[505]: make
    root@tbdev1[506]: ls kernel/*o
kernel/i2c-algo-bit.o  kernel/i2c-elektor.o   kernel/i2c-proc.o
kernel/i2c-algo-pcf.o  kernel/i2c-elv.o       kernel/i2c-velleman.o
kernel/i2c-core.o      kernel/i2c-philips-par.o
kernel/i2c-dev.o       kernel/i2c-pport.o
```

This `ls` output shows that the modules `i2c-core.o`, `i2c-algo-bit.o`, `i2c-dev.o`, and `i2c-pport.o` compiled successfully.

2. Create the character device file with a major number 89 and minor number 0 in the `/dev` directory, by using this command:

```
root@tbdev1[581]: mknod /dev/i2c0 c 89 0
```

3. Load the `i2c-core`, `i2c-algo-bit`, `i2c-pport` and the `i2c-dev` modules:

```
root@tbdev1[515]: cd /root/i2c-2.6.1/kernel
root@tbdev1[516]: insmod i2c-core.o
root@tbdev1[517]: insmod i2c-algo-bit.o
root@tbdev1[518]: insmod i2c-pport.o
root@tbdev1[519]: insmod i2c-dev.o
```

4. Connect the SAA1064 SDA and SCL lines to the x86 printer port and connect the power and ground lines to a floppy disk connector. The author of `i2c-pport` has written instructions for connecting I2C devices to the parallel printer port (see `/root/i2c-2.6.1/doc/i2c-pport`). The parallel port's control lines allow for bidirectional communication. The `i2c-pport` device driver uses the control line auto linefeed signal for SDA and the control line initialize printer signal for SCL. Figure 10.5 shows the complete circuit schematic for connection of four SAA1064s that drive the four seven-segments LEDs.

TIP

You can power an interface circuit from the PC's power supply. The floppy disk connector provides +5VDC, +12VDC, and ground connections. The connector's 0.1-inch pin spacing allows for use of standard headers, thus simplifying the wiring to your interface board. A 250-Watt power supply can typically source more than 20A from the +5V supply and 5A from the +12V supply. See your PC's power supply for actual specifications.

5. Write, compile, and run a program that communicates with the device driver.

The device driver `SAA1064_x86.c` communicates with the SAA1064 via the `i2c-pport` device driver. `SAA1064_x86.c` opens the device file, uses `ioctl` to set the I2C slave address, uses the `write` system call to send a 6-byte stream to the SAA1064, and then closes the device file and exits. The 6-byte stream consists of the following:

- **Byte 1**—The internal starting SAA1064 register address
- **Byte 2**—The configuration register setting
- **Byte 3**—The LED segment 1 value

- **Byte 4**—The LED segment 2 value

- **Byte 5**—The LED segment 3 value

- **Byte 6**—The LED segment 4 value

Listing 10.3 shows the source code for the SAA1064_x86.c device driver. Note that this device driver code only communicates with the SAA1064-#0 at address 0x00.

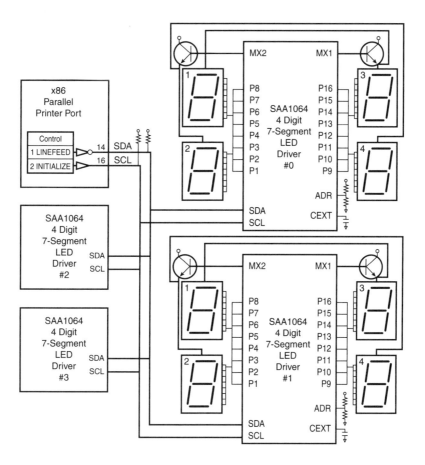

FIGURE 10.5   The SAA1064 seven-segment LED driver connection to the x86 parallel printer port.

LISTING 10.3   The SAA1064_x86.c Device Driver

```
/*
 * SAA1064_x86 v1.0 11/05/01
 * www.embeddedlinuxinterfacing.com
 *
 * The original location of this code is
 * http://www.embeddedlinuxinterfacing.com/chapters/10/
 *
 * Copyright (C) 2001 by Craig Hollabaugh
 *
 * This program is free software; you can redistribute it and/or modify
 * it under the terms of the GNU Library General Public License as
 * published by the Free Software Foundation; either version 2 of the
 * License, or (at your option) any later version.
 *
 * This program is distributed in the hope that it will be useful, but
 * WITHOUT ANY WARRANTY; without even the implied warranty of
 * MERCHANTABILITY or FITNESS FOR A PARTICULAR PURPOSE. See the GNU
 * Library General Public License for more details.
 *
 * You should have received a copy of the GNU Library General Public
 * License along with this program; if not, write to the
 * Free Software Foundation, Inc.,
 * 59 Temple Place, Suite 330, Boston, MA 02111-1307 USA
 */


/* SAA1064_x86
 * This program demonstrates communication with a SAA1064 I2C LED
 * display driver using the i2c-pport x86 parallel port device driver.
 *
 * For more Linux I2C information, visit the lm_sensors site at
 * http://www.lm-sensors.nu/
 *
 * This program opens the I2C device driver file, sets the address for
 * SAA1064-#0 then sends it 6 bytes.
 * byte 1 - internal starting SAA1064 register address
 * byte 2 - configuration register setting
 * byte 3 - LED segment 1 value
 * byte 4 - LED segment 2 value
 * byte 5 - LED segment 3 value
 * byte 6 - LED segment 4 value
 *
```

LISTING 10.3   Continued

```
 * For more SAA1064 or I2C protocol, visit the Philips Semiconductor Web site
 * at http://www.semiconductors.philips.com
 */


/*
 * gcc -I/usr/src/linux/include -o SAA1064_x86 SAA1064_x86.c
 */


#include <fcntl.h>
#include <linux/i2c.h>
#include <linux/i2c-dev.h>


int main(void)
{
  int file;
  int address;
  unsigned char buffer[10], i;


/* seg is a segment mapping table. Element 0, 0xFC, tells the
 * SAA1064 to turn on the segments to display a 0. Likewise,
 * seg's other entries map to 1 through 9 and a through f.
 */
  unsigned char seg[] = { 0xFC, 0x60, 0xDA, 0xF2, 0x66,
                          0xB6, 0xBE, 0xE0, 0xFE, 0xF6,
                          0xEE, 0x3E, 0x9C, 0x7A, 0x9E, 0x8E } ;



  if (( file = open("/dev/i2c0",O_RDWR)) < 0) {
    printf("Can't open /dev/i2c0\n");
    exit(1);
  }


  address = 0x38;

/*
 * Why 0x38? Philip's SAA1064 group address is 0111, the SAA1064-#0 is
 * an address zero, making it's full address 0111.0000 which is 0x70.
 * The I2C driver wants addresses divided by 2, so 0x70 / 2 = 0x38.
 */
  if (ioctl(file,I2C_SLAVE,address) < 0) {
    printf("Can't set address\n");
```

LISTING 10.3   Continued

```
  exit(1);
}

buffer[0] = 0x00;   /* internal starting SAA1064 register address */
buffer[1] = 0x46;   /* 12mA current, all digits on, dynamic mode */
buffer[2] = seg[1]; /* this puts a '1' on the display segment 1 */
buffer[3] = seg[2]; /* this puts a '2' on the display segment 2 */
buffer[4] = seg[3]; /* this puts a '3' on the display segment 3 */
buffer[5] = seg[4]; /* this puts a '4' on the display segment 4 */

if ( write(file,buffer,6) != 6) {
  printf("Write failed\n");
  close(file);
  exit(1);
}

close(file);
}
```

Executing SAA1064_x86 results in 1234 being displayed on SAA1064-#0's LEDs. Figure 10.6 shows the first two characters of an I2C communication with the SAA1064.

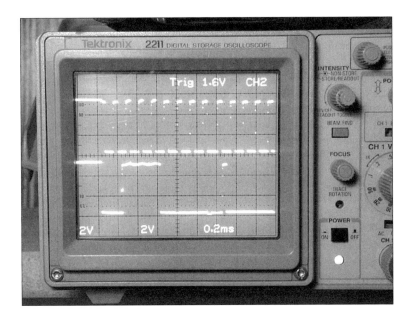

FIGURE 10.6   An oscilloscope capture of *SCL* (top trace) and *SDA* (bottom trace) signals during an I2C communication with an SAA1064.

The SAA1064_x86.c program performs as expected. The four numbers sent to the SAA1064 appear on the seven-segment LEDs. Using code from the lm_sensors project meant that the Project Trailblazer engineers did not have to develop a bit-banged I2C driver for the x86 parallel port. However, the i2c-pport module offers access to the SAA1064 through a /dev directory device file that is not a /proc entry. All the Project Trailblazer interfaces to hardware occur as named /proc entries, and named /proc entries make bash control scripting simple.

It's possible to write an SAA1064 device driver by modifying the SAA1086_x86.c code shown in Listing 10.3 so that it provides named /proc entries. This device driver would access the /dev/i2c0 device file. Using this approach would require loading the i2c-core, i2c-algo-bit, i2c-dev, and i2c-pport modules, as well as the new device driver. It might be easier to write an I2C bit-banging x86 parallel printer port device driver and not use any lm_sensors code. Writing your own I2C bit-banging code is simple. Many I2C source code examples exist to help you understand the communication protocol. In fact, in the next section, you'll see an example because the Project Trailblazer engineers wrote an I2C bit-banging routine for the RPX-CLLF.

Connecting the SAA1064 to the RPX-CLLF

The RPX-CLLF's MPC860 contains a dedicated I2C controller. Use of the controller is more CPU efficient than bit-banging software. The current8xx lm_sensors code utilizes the MPC860's I2C controller. The lm_sensors device drivers provide access to I2C devices through /dev files. Ideally, use of these drivers should reduce Project Trailblazer development time because the engineers don't need a full understanding of MPC860 internals.

At first, the Project Trailblazer engineers were excited about using the lm_sensors code. However, when it came time to cross-compile code for the PowerPC, they changed their minds. Although 8xx files are contained within the lm_sensors project, they aren't kept current and aren't part of its configuration process. Cross-compiling isn't a simple make process. The engineers spent too much time patching and editing make files. They did successfully compile the device drivers. However, inserting modules resulted in errors because some assembly code was missing. Confused, the engineers read more about I2C on the PowerPC mailing list.[5] They decided to abandon the lm_sensors code when they read about the I2C developer discussion concerning the I2C project restructuring: Accounts of unsuccessful compiling, missing assembly, and restructuring led the team to write their own SAA1064 device driver.

Right after successfully using the SA-1110's SSP controller for SPI communication, the engineers decided to investigate using the MPC860's I2C controller. Unfortunately, it wasn't simple. The MPC860's I2C controller uses interrupts, DMA, and memory buffers. The engineers simply didn't have the time or the expertise to figure all this out. Nor did they want to risk making Linux unstable by incorrectly configuring MPC860 registers.

The engineers chose to implement a MPC860 I2C bit-banging device driver for the SAA1064s. This device driver will provide a named /proc directory entry interface, allowing for easy bash scripting. The I2C bus communications will be slowed, to allow for longer bus wire lengths. Their driver will be simple and reliable, and it should provide exactly what the engineers need.

The hardware interface uses the MPC860's Port B because Port B offers open-collector/drain functionality. Remember that both I2C communication lines, SDA and SCL, are bidirectional. The unused lines PB30 and PB31 can serve as the SDA and SCL lines. Figure 10.7 shows the SAA1064 seven-segment LED driver connection to the RPX-CLLF.

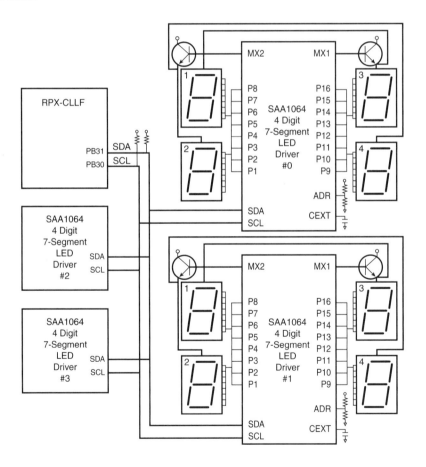

FIGURE 10.7   The SAA1064 seven-segment LED driver connection to the RPX-CLLF.

The SAA1064_rpxcllf.c device driver code shown in Listing 10.4 configures the MPC860 registers and provides access to the SAA1064s through a /proc directory entry. For demonstration proposes, this device driver code only provides access to the SAA1064#0, at address 0x00.

LISTING 10.4   The SAA1064_rpxcllf.c Device Driver

```
/*
 * SAA1064_rpxcllf v1.0 11/10/01
 * www.embeddedlinuxinterfacing.com
 *
 * The original location of this code is
 * http://www.embeddedlinuxinterfacing.com/chapters/10/
 *
 * Copyright (C) 2001 by Craig Hollabaugh
 *
 * This program is free software; you can redistribute it and/or modify
 * it under the terms of the GNU Library General Public License as
 * published by the Free Software Foundation; either version 2 of the
 * License, or (at your option) any later version.
 *
 * This program is distributed in the hope that it will be useful, but
 * WITHOUT ANY WARRANTY; without even the implied warranty of
 * MERCHANTABILITY or FITNESS FOR A PARTICULAR PURPOSE. See the GNU
 * Library General Public License for more details.
 *
 * You should have received a copy of the GNU Library General Public
 * License along with this program; if not, write to the
 * Free Software Foundation, Inc.,
 * 59 Temple Place, Suite 330, Boston, MA 02111-1307 USA
 */

/*
 * SAA1064_rpxcllf.c is based on procfs_example.c by Erik Mouw.
 * For more information, please see The Linux Kernel Procfs Guide, Erik Mouw
 * http://kernelnewbies.org/documents/kdoc/procfs-guide/lkprocfsguide.html
 *
 */

/* SAA1064_rpxcllf
 * This device driver demonstrates I2C communication with a SAA1064 LED
 * display driver. The RPX-CLLF's MPC860 port B is used for I2C data (SDA)
 * and clock (SCL) signals. This routine doesn't use the MPC860's I2C
```

LISTING 10.4   Continued

```
* controller but implements a bit-banging algorithm.
*
* The driver creates a /proc directory entry called
* /proc/trailblazer/temperaturedisplay0. Scripts can write values to
* temperaturedisplay0 which are then displayed on the LED displays.
*
* This driver only communicates with a single SAA1064 at I2C bus address 0.
*/


/*
powerpc-linux-gcc -O2 -D__KERNEL__ -DMODULE -I/usr/src/powerpc-linux/include \
 -c SAA1064_rpxcllf.c -o /tftpboot/powerpc-rootfs/tmp/SAA1064_rpxcllf.o
*/


#include <linux/module.h>
#include <linux/kernel.h>
#include <linux/init.h>
#include <linux/proc_fs.h>
#include <asm/uaccess.h>
#include <asm/io.h>
#include <linux/delay.h>

#include <asm/8xx_immap.h>

#define MODULE_VERSION "1.0"
#define MODULE_NAME "SAA1064_rpxcllf"

#define SDA    0x00000001
#define SCL    0x00000002
#define DELAY 5

#define SAA1064ADDRESS 0x70

volatile immap_t *immap;

/* references
 * see section 34.3 Port B MPC860 PowerQUICC User's Manual
 *
```

LISTING 10.4   Continued

```
* For more SAA1064 or I2C protocol, visit the Philips Semiconductor Web site
 * at http://www.semiconductors.philips.com
 */


static struct proc_dir_entry  *tb_dir,
                              *temperaturedisplay0_file;


/* here are the I2C signaling macros */
#define SCLLow()  immap->im_cpm.cp_pbdat &= ~SCL
#define SCLHigh() immap->im_cpm.cp_pbdat |=  SCL
#define SDALow()  immap->im_cpm.cp_pbdat &= ~SDA
#define SDAHigh() immap->im_cpm.cp_pbdat |=  SDA
#define readSDA() (SDA == (immap->im_cpm.cp_pbdat & SDA))
#define readSCL() (SCL == (immap->im_cpm.cp_pbdat & SCL))



/*
 * function startCommunication
 * This function sets SDA and SCL in the idle state then
 * initiates the 'start' condition
 */
void startCommunication(void)
{
  SDAHigh();      /* put SDA in idle state   */
  SCLHigh();      /* put SCL in idle state   */
  udelay(DELAY);  /* let lines settle        */
  SDALow();       /* initiate start condition */
  udelay(DELAY);  /* let lines settle        */
  SCLLow();       /* initiate start condition */
}


/*
 * function stopCommunication
 * This function sets SDA and SCL in an known state then
 * initiates the 'stop' condition
 */
void stopCommunication(void)
{
  SCLLow();       /* put SCL in known state  */
  SDALow();       /* put SDA in known state  */
  udelay(DELAY);  /* let lines settle        */
```

LISTING 10.4   Continued

```
  SCLHigh();        /* initiate stop condition */
  SDAHigh();        /* initiate stop condition */
}


/*
 * function receiveByte
 * This function toggles the clock line while reading
 * the transmitted data bits. I2C communications sends
 * MSB first.
 */
unsigned char receiveByte(void)
{
  unsigned char i, b;

  SDAHigh();                 /* this tri-states SDA                      */
  b = 0;
  for (i = 0; i < 8; i++)
  {
    udelay(DELAY);           /* let lines settle                        */
    SCLHigh();               /* send the clock                          */
    udelay(DELAY);           /* let lines settle                        */
    b = (b << 1) | readSDA(); /* shift the bits then OR the incoming bit */
    SCLLow();                /* send the clock                          */
  }

  /* this sets up for the next incoming byte */
  udelay(DELAY);
  SCLHigh();
  udelay(DELAY*2);
  SCLLow();
  return b;
}


/*
 * function sendByte
 * This function toggles the clock line while transmitting
 * data bits. I2C communications sends MSB first. This function
 * allows monitors the acknowledge bit (bit 9) asserted by the
 * receiver.
 */
```

LISTING 10.4 Continued

```
unsigned char sendByte(unsigned char b)
{
  unsigned char i;

  for (i = 0; i < 8; i++)
  {
    if (0x80 == (b & 0x80)) /* is the MSB 0 or 1? */
      SDAHigh();
    else
      SDALow();

    udelay(DELAY);          /* let lines settle  */
    SCLHigh();              /* send the clock    */
    udelay(DELAY);          /* let lines settle  */
    SCLLow();               /* send the clock    */

    b = (b << 1);           /* shift to the left */
  }

  /* this sets up for the next outgoing byte       */
  udelay(DELAY);
  SDAHigh();
  SCLHigh();
  udelay(DELAY*2); /* 2 delays help you see acks on a scope */

  /* read the ack here, a sent ack is a 0. */
  i = readSDA();
  SCLLow();

  return i;
}

/*
 * function writei2c
 * This function accepts an address, a character buffer and buffer length.
 * It starts communication, sends the address, then the buffer.
 * If an ack error occurs, it tells you (well it prints to the console).
 */
unsigned char writei2c(unsigned address, unsigned char *buffer,
                       unsigned length)
{
```

LISTING 10.4   Continued

```
  unsigned char i, error;

  startCommunication();

  error = sendByte(address & 0xFE);
    /* 0xFE? The last bit of the I2C address is a read/nWrite bit */

  if (error) /* didn't get an ack at the address */
  {
    stopCommunication();
    printk("no ack at address 0x%2X\n",address);
    return error;
  }

/* sending the buffer here */
  for (i = 0; i < length; i++)
  {
    error = sendByte(buffer[i]);

    if (error) /* didn't get an ack for that byte sent */
    {
      stopCommunication();
      printk("no ack at buffer byte %d\n",i);
      return error;
    }
  }

/* we're done */
  stopCommunication();
  return 0;
}

/*
 * function readi2c
 * This function accepts an address, a character buffer and buffer length.
 * It starts communication, sends the address, then reads the reply into
 * buffer. If an ack error occurs, it tells you (well it prints to the
 * console).
 */
unsigned char readi2c(unsigned address, unsigned char *buffer,
                      unsigned length)
```

LISTING 10.4   Continued

```
{
  unsigned char i, error;
  startCommunication();

  error = sendByte(address | 0x01);

  if (error) /* didn't get an ack at the address */
  {
    stopCommunication();
    printk("no ack at address 0x%2X\n",address);
    return error;
  }

  /* receiving bytes for the buffer here */
  for (i = 0; i < length; i++)
  {
    buffer[i] = receiveByte();
  }

/* we're done */
  stopCommunication();
  return 0;
}


/*
 * function proc_write_display
 * This function gets called when the user writes something to
 * /proc/trailblazer/temperaturedisplay0. It contains a mapping array
 * from numbers (0-9,a-f) to what segments to turn on
 */
static int proc_write_temperaturedisplay0(struct file *file,
                                          const char *buffer,
                                          unsigned long count, void *data)
{
  unsigned char e, displaybuffer[5];

/* seg is a segment mapping table. Element 0, 0xFC, tells the
 * SAA1064 to turn on the segments to display a 0. Likewise,
 * seg's other entries map to 1 through 9 and a through f.
 */
  unsigned char seg[] = { 0xFC, 0x60, 0xDA, 0xF2, 0x66,
```

LISTING 10.4   Continued

```
                          0xB6, 0xBE, 0xE0, 0xFE, 0xF6,
                          0xEE, 0x3E, 0x9C, 0x7A, 0x9E, 0x8E } ;

  if (count >= 4)
  {
    displaybuffer[0] = 0x01;
    displaybuffer[1] = seg[buffer[0]-'0']; /* subtracting '0' shifts the   */
    displaybuffer[2] = seg[buffer[1]-'0']; /* ascii numbers the user wrote */
    displaybuffer[3] = seg[buffer[2]-'0']; /* to the device file to their  */
    displaybuffer[4] = seg[buffer[3]-'0']; /* numeric equivalent           */

    e = writei2c(SAA1064ADDRESS, displaybuffer, 5);
/* for debugging    printk("proc_write_display = %d\n",e); */
  }

  return 1;
}


/*
 * function init_SAA1064_rpxcllf
 * This function creates the /proc directory entries: trailblazer and
 * trailblazer/temperaturedisplay0. It find the IMMR then configures
 * PB30 and PB31 as general I/O, open drain and outputs.
 * It initializes the SAA1064 and has it displays the middle segment '-'
 * as a sign that the driver loaded successfully.
 */
static int __init init_SAA1064_rpxcllf(void)
{
  unsigned char e,buffer[5];

  int rv = 0;

/* Create the trailblazer /proc entry */
  tb_dir = proc_mkdir("trailblazer", NULL);
  if(tb_dir == NULL) {
          rv = -ENOMEM;
          goto out;
  }
  tb_dir->owner = THIS_MODULE;
```

LISTING 10.4   Continued

```
/* Create temperaturedisplay0 and make it readable by all - 0444 */
  temperaturedisplay0_file = create_proc_entry("temperaturedisplay0", 0444,
                                               tb_dir);

  if(temperaturedisplay0_file == NULL) {
          rv = -ENOMEM;
          goto no_temperaturedisplay0;
  }
  temperaturedisplay0_file->data = NULL;
  temperaturedisplay0_file->read_proc = NULL;
  temperaturedisplay0_file->write_proc = &proc_write_temperaturedisplay0;
  temperaturedisplay0_file->owner = THIS_MODULE;


  /* get the IMMR */
  immap = (immap_t *)(mfspr(IMMR) & 0xFFFF0000);

  /* make PB30 and PB31 general I/O */
  immap->im_cpm.cp_pbpar &= ~SDA;
  immap->im_cpm.cp_pbpar &= ~SCL;

  /* make PB30 and PB31 open drain */
  immap->im_cpm.cp_pbodr |= SDA;
  immap->im_cpm.cp_pbodr |= SCL;

  /* make PB30 and PB31 outputs    */
  immap->im_cpm.cp_pbdir |= SDA;
  immap->im_cpm.cp_pbdir |= SCL;

  /* display a little info for the happy module loader */
  printk("immr    = 0x%08X\n",immap);
  printk("PBPAR   = 0x%04X\n",immap->im_cpm.cp_pbpar);
  printk("PBDIR   = 0x%04X\n",immap->im_cpm.cp_pbdir);
  printk("PBODR   = 0x%04X\n",immap->im_cpm.cp_pbodr);
  printk("PBDAT   = 0x%04X\n",immap->im_cpm.cp_pbdat);

  buffer[0] = 0x00; /* internal starting SAA1064 register address */
  buffer[1] = 0x46; /* 12mA current, all digits on, dynamic mode  */
  buffer[2] = 0x02; /* turn on '-' segment on each display         */
  buffer[3] = 0x02;
  buffer[4] = 0x02;
  buffer[5] = 0x02;
```

LISTING 10.4   Continued

```
  if (writei2c(SAA1064ADDRESS, buffer, 6))
  {
    printk("Display initialization failed\n");
    rv = -EREMOTEIO;
    goto no_temperaturedisplay0;
  }
  else
    printk("Display initialization passed\n");

/* everything initialized */
  printk(KERN_INFO "%s %s initialized\n",MODULE_NAME, MODULE_VERSION);
  return 0;

no_temperaturedisplay0:
  remove_proc_entry("temperaturedisplay0", tb_dir);
out:
  return rv;
}

/*
 * function cleanup_SAA1064_rpxcllf
 * This function turns off the SAA1064 display to show that the
 * driver unloaded. It then removes the /proc directory entries
 */
static void __exit cleanup_SAA1064_rpxcllf(void)
{
  unsigned char buffer[5];

  buffer[0] = 0x00;
  buffer[1] = 0x00; /* configuration reg, turn displays off */
  writei2c(SAA1064ADDRESS, buffer, 2);

  remove_proc_entry("temperaturedisplay0", tb_dir);
  remove_proc_entry("trailblazer", NULL);

  printk(KERN_INFO "%s %s removed\n", MODULE_NAME, MODULE_VERSION);
}

module_init(init_SAA1064_rpxcllf);
module_exit(cleanup_SAA1064_rpxcllf);
```

LISTING 10.4   Continued

```
MODULE_AUTHOR("Craig Hollabaugh");
MODULE_DESCRIPTION("SAA1064 driver for RPX-CLLF");


EXPORT_NO_SYMBOLS;
```

The SAA1064_rpxcllf.c device driver contains three main functions:

- **init_SAA1064_RPX-CLLF**—This is the module initialization function, and it creates the /proc directory entries trailblazer and trailblazer/ temperaturedisplay0.

- **proc_write_temperaturedisplay0**—This function is called whenever the user performs a write operation on /proc/trailblazer/temperaturedisplay0. proc_write_temperaturedisplay0 calls writei2c, which performs the actual I2C communication with the SAA1064.

- **cleanup_SAA1064_RPX-CLLF**—This is the module cleanup function, and it removes the /proc directory entries.

You can compile and test the SAA1064_rpxcllf device driver by using these steps:

1. Compile the SAA1064_rpxcllf device driver by using this command:

   ```
   root@tbdev1[520]: powerpc-linux-gcc -O2 -D__KERNEL__ -DMODULE
   -I/usr/src/powerpc-linux/include \
   -c SAA1064_rpxcllf.c \
   -o /tftpboot/powerpc-rootfs/tmp/SAA1064_rpxcllf.o
   ```

2. Load the device driver on the RPX-CLLF by using this command:

   ```
   bash-2.04# insmod SAA1064_rpxcllf.o
   immr    = 0xFA200000
   PBPAR   = 0x1CF0
   PBDIR   = 0x1033
   PBODR   = 0x0033
   PBDAT   = 0x04B3
   Display initialization passed
   SAA1064_rpxcllf 1.0 initialized
   ```

   This console output shows the SAA1064 device driver initialized correctly. The SAA1064#0 LEDs have a dash character displayed.

3. Use this command to write a number to the display:

```
bash-2.04# echo -n 1234 > /proc/trailblazer/temperaturedisplay0
```

The LEDs now display 1234. The first two characters of an I2C communication with the SAA1064 is shown in Figure 10.8. This shows the first byte: address of 0x70 with a receiver acknowledge in bit 9 (the wider clock bit).

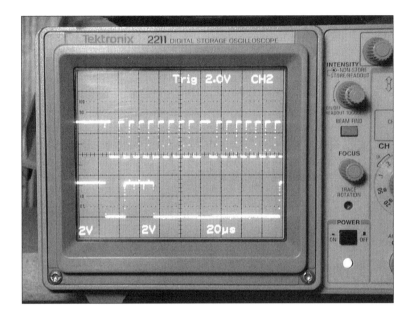

FIGURE 10.8   An oscilloscope capture of *SCL* (top trace) and *SDA* (bottom trace) signals during an RPX-CLLF I2C communication with an SAA1064.

TIP

When debugging I2C hardware and software, you can use an oscilloscope to look for the acknowledge bit of the address byte sent by the receiver. If the bit is there, you have successfully wired the circuit and sent the I2C device the correct start condition and its address. If the bit is not present, you need to check the circuit's wiring, signal and power supply voltage levels, and bus pull-up resistor values, and you need to closely examine the start condition and the data and clock signal timing. Also, while you're debugging the circuit, you should operate your I2C communication at the slowest possible speed. This gives your devices time to properly drive the data and clock signals. When your circuit functions correctly, you can remove delays and increase the communication speed.

Summary

In this chapter the Project Trailblazer engineers connected SPI and I2C devices to their target boards. They developed device drivers that provide access to an SPI temperature sensor and an I2C LED display driver. These drivers utilize bit-banging routines, on-chip controllers, and open-source device drivers. The software/hardware combination presented in this chapter provides a foundation for communication with other SPI and I2C devices connected to the x86, ARM, and PowerPC processors such as EEPROM storage, data converters, digital tuners, and signal processors.

Additional Reading

1. National Semiconductor Corporation, *LM70 datasheet*,
   www.national.com/ds/LM/LM70.pdf.

2. Intel, *SA-1110 Microprocessor Developer's Manual*,
   www.intel.com/design/strong/manuals/278240.htm.

3. Philips Semiconductor, "The I2C-Bus Specification, Version 2.1," www.
   semiconductors.philips.com/acrobat/various/I2C_BUS_SPECIFICATION_3.
   PDF.

4. Philips Semiconductor, *SAA1064 Datasheet*,
   www.semiconductors.philips.com/acrobat/datasheets/SAA1064_CNV_2.pdf.

5. "Additional I2C Support for Embedded PowerPC Systems" discussion thread,
   LinuxPPC-embedded mailing list, http://lists.linuxppc.org/
   linuxppc-embedded.

11

Using Interrupts For Timing

The first snowfall at Silverjack filled the air with excitement. Soon the village would bustle and the slopes would open. As in past years, many skiers and snowboarders would race against the clock on the mountain's racecourse. This year, however, Project Trailblazer wants to collect, display, log, and post race results. Using embedded Linux for Silverjack race timing will reduce data entry errors, increase efficiency, and enhance the racers' experience.

This chapter explores using Linux as an event timer with 1-millisecond resolution. The Project Trailblazer engineers need to develop interrupt handlers for the target boards—the MZ104, the MediaEngine, and the RPX-CLLF. Then they need to use these handlers to measure average interrupt latencies. The engineers need to design a race timer that uses a split interrupt approach with "top half" and "bottom half" handler routines, tasklets, and a self-rescheduling kernel timer.

Linux Timing Sources

Linux provides several mechanisms for event timing, ranging from 1-second down to submicrosecond resolution. This section discusses the following timing sources:

- **date**—The resolution of date is 1s. Using the +%s formatter, date returns the number of seconds that have elapsed since 00:00:00, January 1, 1970.

- **jiffies**—The resolution of jiffies is 10ms. On all platforms, Linux configures a hardware timer that interrupts the processor periodically—typically every

10ms (this value is defined in the kernel source as HZ). The timer interrupt routine increments the kernel variable jiffies by 1. Therefore, the value of jiffies represents the number of 10ms increments that have occurred since booting. It is possible to increase jiffies resolution by altering the HZ source declaration. However, this could ultimately lower overall system performance due to increased interrupt processing. Other mechanisms offer higher resolution.

- **PSR**—The resolution of PSR (which stands for processor-specific registers) is various. Some newer processors contain two 32-bit counters that increment on every system clock cycle. The counters accessed through PSR provide resolutions that are dependent on processor clock speed. Kernel source code provides function calls to access the PSR. For example, the rdtsc function returns the timestamp counter (TSC) on Pentium and newer processors, and the get_tbl function returns the mftb register value on PowerPCs. 486 and ARM processors do not contain system clock counters.

- **get_cycles**—The resolution of get_cycles is various. The get_cycles function, which is defined all on platforms, returns a count of system clock cycles that fit into a single CPU register. Typically this is the lower half of the two 32-bit counters mentioned previously. If the processor doesn't contain a clock counter, get_cycles returns 0. get_cycles returns 0 on 486 and ARM processors.

- **do_gettimeofday**—The resolution of do_gettimeofday is about 1µs. The do_gettimeofday function fills a timeval data structure with the number of seconds and microseconds elapsed since booting. The x86 and PowerPC kernel source claim near-microsecond resolution for do_gettimeofday.

The Project Trailblazer race timer needs to have 1ms resolution. This resolution eliminates using date and jiffies. The MZ104's 486 and the MediaEngine's ARM processors don't contain system clock counters, so the Project Trailblazer engineers also can't use PSR. The get_cycles function returns only a 32-bit counter value. On the slowest clocked target board, the RPX-CLLF (at 70MHz), the get_cycles function can only count 61 seconds' worth of microseconds. A typical race will be longer than 61 seconds, so the get_cycles function won't work for Project Trailblazer. This leaves the do_gettimeofday function. With near-microsecond resolution and a 32-bit counter of seconds (2^{32} seconds = 49,710 days), the do_gettimeofday will provide accuracy for even the longest race. The race timer's interrupt routine can timestamp the race's start and finish by using do_gettimeofday. A scheduled task can later compute the race's overall time.

Interrupt latency is a measure of the time between an event occurring (for example, the race start) and when the processor executes the interrupt handler code. Even with microsecond timing access, race timing won't have millisecond accuracy if the system interrupt latency exceeds a millisecond. The next section examines the Project Trailblazer engineers' development of interrupt handlers within a device driver to measure average interrupt latencies for the MZ104, MediaEngine, and RPX-CLLF target boards.

Measuring Interrupt Latency

Interrupt latency is comprised of hardware propagation time, register saving, and software execution. Propagation time and register saving occur extremely fast—on the order of 10s of nanoseconds. Software execution, on the other hand, can be extremely slow. The Linux kernel allows device drivers to disable interrupts by using the cli system call. While interrupts are disabled, other interrupts can occur, but their service routines are not executed until interrupts are re-enabled. Developers disable interrupts to protect critical sections of their code. For example, a video card driver might disable interrupts for 16ms while waiting for video sync. Or a serial card driver might disable interrupts during a byte transmission. Therefore, *maximum interrupt latency* is a combination of system hardware, peripherals, and the quality of the device driver software. Even with source code availability, this combination and the asynchronous nature of interrupts makes calculating the maximum interrupt latency a difficult, if not impossible, task. On a lightly loaded system with little or no peripherals, it's likely that the average interrupt latency is much smaller than the maximum. Even so, the Project Trailblazer engineers had no idea of the average interrupt latency magnitude. Was it microseconds or milliseconds? They decided to measure it for each target board.

> **TIP**
>
> When you are writing device drivers, you should disable interrupts only when your driver requires absolutely no interruption. While interrupts are disabled, Linux does not update system timers, transfer network packets to and from buffers, or update video information. You should perform your interrupt task as quickly as possible. For lengthy tasks, you should split your handler and use tasklets to perform most of the processing.

Each target board—the MZ104, the MediaEngine, and the RPX-CLLF—has external connections that are capable of generating processor interrupts. In addition, each board can generate an interrupt signal by using one of its own output ports. In the device driver code we're about to discuss, one function asserts the interrupt signal, which causes the interrupt handler to execute. The handler simply deasserts the interrupt signal and exits. The interrupt signal assertion and deassertion can be viewed on an oscilloscope, to determine the average interrupt latency.

To measure the average interrupt latency, the Project Trailblazer engineers need to do the following:

1. Write a device driver that contains the following:

   - Configuration code for the board's interrupt controller, if necessary

   - A request for the interrupt from Linux

   - A function that asserts the interrupt signal

   - An interrupt handler that deasserts the interrupt signal

2. Connect an output port pin to a processor interrupt pin and to the oscilloscope.

3. Load the device driver.

4. Assert the interrupt pin.

5. Watch for the deassertion.

6. Measure the interrupt latency.

7. Repeat steps 4, 5, and 6 to determine the average interrupt latency.

As discussed in the section "Linux Timing Sources," earlier in this chapter, the do_gettimeofday function provides timing information with microsecond resolution. By using two calls to do_gettimeofday, the device driver itself can calculate its own instantaneous interrupt latency. (*Instantaneous* in this case refers to the interrupt latency associated with a single interrupt event.) The instantaneous interrupt latency value will not be the same for interrupt events. The average interrupt latency is the numerical average of several instantaneous interrupt latency values.

The magnitude of the average interrupt latency is what the engineers want to determine for each of their target boards. They need to find out if it is greater than 1ms. A race timer with 1ms accuracy requires a timing source with interrupt latencies of less than 1ms. The engineers need to write an interrupt latency device driver for each of their target boards. They then need to execute this device driver several times, record the instantaneous interrupt latency values, and compute an average interrupt latency value for each board. Using the interrupt latency device driver's output combined with an oscilloscope measurement, the engineers can also verify the microsecond accuracy of the do_gettimeofday function.

The three target board interrupt latency device drivers contain four functions: init, proc_read, interrupt_latency, and cleanup. The init function creates a /proc directory entry called interrupt_latency and configures the processor's interrupt controller and port settings. Reading from the interrupt_latency file calls the function proc_read, which generates an interrupt electrical signal. The device driver handles the interrupt by calling the `interrupt_latency` function. It then computes and prints the instantaneous interrupt latency value. The driver also maintains an interrupt counter to aid in debugging.

Measuring Interrupt Latency on the MZ104

The x86 parallel printer port can generate a processor interrupt. The port's acknowledge (ACK) status signal, pin 10 on the DB-25 connector, is positive-edge triggered and generates interrupt number 7. The Project Trailblazer engineers decide to drive the ACK status line with the printer port's D7 signal (pin 9 on the DB-25 connector). Figure 11.1 shows the MZ104 connection for measuring interrupt latency.

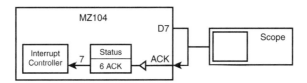

FIGURE 11.1   The MZ104 connection for measuring interrupt latency.

Listing 11.1 shows the source code for the `interrupt_latency_x86.c` device driver for the MZ104.

LISTING 11.1   The `interrupt_latency_x86.c` Device Driver

```
/*
 * interrupt_latency_x86 v1.0 11/25/01
 * www.embeddedlinuxinterfacing.com
 *
 * The original location of this code is
 * http://www.embeddedlinuxinterfacing.com/chapters/11/
 *
 * Copyright (C) 2001 by Craig Hollabaugh
 *
 * This program is free software; you can redistribute it and/or modify
 * it under the terms of the GNU Library General Public License as
 * published by the Free Software Foundation; either version 2 of the
 * License, or (at your option) any later version.
 *
 * This program is distributed in the hope that it will be useful, but
 * WITHOUT ANY WARRANTY; without even the implied warranty of
 * MERCHANTABILITY or FITNESS FOR A PARTICULAR PURPOSE. See the GNU
 * Library General Public License for more details.
```

LISTING 11.1   Continued

```
 *
 * You should have received a copy of the GNU Library General Public
 * License along with this program; if not, write to the
 * Free Software Foundation, Inc.,
 * 59 Temple Place, Suite 330, Boston, MA 02111-1307 USA
 */


/*
 * interrupt_latency_x86.c is based on procfs_example.c by Erik Mouw.
 * For more information, please see, The Linux Kernel Procfs Guide, Erik Mouw
 * http://kernelnewbies.org/documents/kdoc/procfs-guide/lkprocfsguide.html
 */


/*
gcc -O2 -D__KERNEL__ -DMODULE -I/usr/src/linux/include \
-c interrupt_latency_x86.c -o interrupt_latency_x86.o
*/


/* interrupt_latency_x86.c module
 * This module measures interrupt latency of x86 machines by connecting
 * parallel printer port D7 (pin 9) to ACK (pin 10). Enable interrupt
 * generation by status register configuration. Positive going edge on
 * ACK pin generates interrupt 7.
 *
 * Kernel source claims microsecond resolution of do_gettimeofday. Viewing
 * the D7-ACK connection verifies this, well we're close with 10uS.
 *
 * After module insertion, reading /proc/interrupt_latency will assert D7
 * generating the interrupt. The interrupt handler will deassert this signal.
 * View on scope. An interrupt counter is included to help debug a noisy
 * interrupt line.
 */

#include <linux/module.h>
#include <linux/kernel.h>
#include <linux/init.h>
#include <linux/proc_fs.h>

#include <asm/io.h> /* outb */
```

LISTING 11.1 Continued

```
#define MODULE_VERSION "1.0"
#define MODULE_NAME "interrupt_latency_x86"

int interruptcount = 0;
struct timeval tv1, tv2; /* do_gettimeofday fills these */

#define SPPDATAPORT          0x378
#define SPPSTATUSPORT        (SPPDATAPORT + 1)
#define SPPCONTROLPORT       (SPPDATAPORT + 2)
#define SSPINTERRUPTENABLE   0x10

#define INTERRUPT 7

static struct proc_dir_entry *interrupt_latency_file;

/*
 * function interrupt_interrupt_latency
 * This function is the interrupt handler for interrupt 7. It sets the tv2
 * structure using do_gettimeofday. It then deasserts D7.
 */
void interrupt_interrupt_latency(int irq, void *dev_id, struct pt_regs *regs)
{
  do_gettimeofday(&tv2);
  outb(0x00,SPPDATAPORT); /* deassert the interrupt signal */
  interruptcount++;
}

/*
 * function proc_read_interrupt_latency
 * The kernel executes this function when a read operation occurs on
 * /proc/interrupt_latency. This function sets the tv1 structure. It asserts
 * D7 which should immediately cause interrupt 7 to occur. The handler
 * records tv2 and deasserts D7. This function returns the time differential
 * between tv2 and tv1.
 */
static int proc_read_interrupt_latency(char *page, char **start, off_t off,
                                       int count, int *eof, void *data)
{
  int len;
```

LISTING 11.1   Continued

```
  do_gettimeofday(&tv1);
  outb(0x80,SPPDATAPORT); /* assert the interrupt signal */



  len = sprintf(page, "Start   %9i.%06i\nFinish  %9i.%06i\nLatency %17i\n\
Count %19i\n",(int) tv1.tv_sec, (int) tv1.tv_usec,
(int) tv2.tv_sec, (int) tv2.tv_usec, (int) (tv2.tv_usec - tv1.tv_usec),
interruptcount);

  return len;
}

/*
 * function init_interrupt_latency
 * This function creates the /proc directory entry interrupt_latency. It
 * also configures the parallel port then requests interrupt 7 from Linux.
 */
static int __init init_interrupt_latency(void)
{
  int rv = 0;

  interrupt_latency_file = create_proc_entry("interrupt_latency", 0444, NULL);
  if(interrupt_latency_file == NULL) {
    return -ENOMEM;
  }

  interrupt_latency_file->data = NULL;
  interrupt_latency_file->read_proc = &proc_read_interrupt_latency;
  interrupt_latency_file->write_proc = NULL;
  interrupt_latency_file->owner = THIS_MODULE;

  /* request interrupt from linux */
  rv = request_irq(INTERRUPT, interrupt_interrupt_latency, 0,
                  "interrupt_latency",NULL);
  if ( rv ) {
    printk("Can't get interrupt %d\n", INTERRUPT);
    goto no_interrupt_latency;
  }

/* enable parallel port interrupt generation */
  outb(SSPINTERRUPTENABLE,SPPCONTROLPORT);
```

LISTING 11.1   Continued

```c
/* deassert the interrupt signal */
  outb(0x00,SPPDATAPORT);

/* everything initialized */
  printk(KERN_INFO "%s %s initialized\n",MODULE_NAME, MODULE_VERSION);
  return 0;

/* remove the proc entry on error */
no_interrupt_latency:
  remove_proc_entry("interrupt_latency", NULL);
}


/*
 * function cleanup_interrupt_latency
 * This function frees interrupt 7 then removes the /proc directory entry
 * interrupt_latency.
 */
static void __exit cleanup_interrupt_latency(void)
{
/* disable parallel port interrupt reporting */
  outb(0x00,SPPCONTROLPORT);

/* free the interrupt */
  free_irq(INTERRUPT,NULL);

  remove_proc_entry("interrupt_latency", NULL);

  printk(KERN_INFO "%s %s removed\n", MODULE_NAME, MODULE_VERSION);
}

module_init(init_interrupt_latency);
module_exit(cleanup_interrupt_latency);

MODULE_AUTHOR("Craig Hollabaugh");
MODULE_DESCRIPTION("interrupt_latency proc module");

EXPORT_NO_SYMBOLS;
```

The engineers connected the parallel port's D7 signal to the ACK signal with a wire. The following console output shows an instantaneous result for the MZ104 target board:

```
bash-2.04# insmod interrupt_latency_x86.o
interrupt_latency_x86 1.0 initialized
bash-2.04# cat /proc/interrupts
           CPU0
  0:    4188487        XT-PIC  timer
  1:       2057        XT-PIC  keyboard
  2:          0        XT-PIC  cascade
  4:       6016        XT-PIC  serial
  7:          0        XT-PIC  interrupt_latency
 10:      14884        XT-PIC  usb-uhci
 12:     102528        XT-PIC  eth0
 14:       3518        XT-PIC  ide0
 15:       2541        XT-PIC  ide1
NMI:          0
ERR:          0
bash-2.04# cat /proc/interrupt_latency
Start    1006763905.483513
Finish   1006763905.483566
Latency              53
Count                 1
```

The /proc/interrupts file shows that the interrupt_latency routine is registered on Interrupt 7. Reading from the /proc/interrupt_latency file shows an instantaneous latency of 53µs. Figure 11.2 shows an oscilloscope capture of the interrupt signal.

The oscilloscope interrupt signal measurement shows a latency of 44.75µs, whereas the driver returns a calculated latency of 53µs. Code execution accounts for the 8.25µs discrepancy. This small inaccuracy, 8.25µs, is not an issue because the race timer requires 1ms, or 1000µs resolution. 8.25 is negligible compared to 1000.

By using a interrupt latency device driver and oscilloscope measurements, the Project Trailblazer engineers calculated the MZ104 average interrupt latency to be approximately 50µs. The x86 version of the do_gettimeofday function has near-microsecond accuracy.

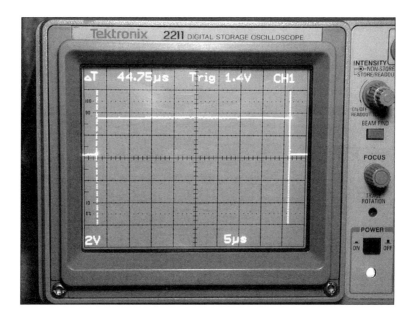

FIGURE 11.2   The MZ104's interrupt signal.

Measuring Interrupt Latency on the MediaEngine

The MediaEngine's general-purpose input/output signal 1 (GPIO01), located on target board's connector J10, can generate SA-1110 Interrupt 1 on the rising edge, on the falling edge, or both. The Project Trailblazer engineers decide to configure the interrupt controller for rising-edge operation. (For more information, see Section 9.2, "Interrupt Controller," of *Intel SA-1110 Developer's Manual*[1].) The SA-1110's interrupt controller is connected to the GPIO01's input, which monitors pin status, regardless of whether the pin is configured as input or output. The engineers set GPIO01 as an output and then generate the interrupt signal. Figure 11.3 shows the internal connection of GPIO01 output register (GPSR/GPCR), the connection of the input level register (GPLR), the connection to the interrupt controller and the external connection to the oscilloscope.

Listing 11.2 shows the source code for the interrupt_latency_mediaengine.c device driver.

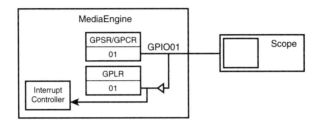

FIGURE 11.3   The MediaEngine connection for measuring interrupt latency.

LISTING 11.2   The `interrupt_latency_mediaengine.c` Device Driver

```
/*
 * interrupt_latency_mediaengine v1.0 11/25/01
 * www.embeddedlinuxinterfacing.com
 *
 * The original location of this code is
 * http://www.embeddedlinuxinterfacing.com/chapters/11/
 *
 * Copyright (C) 2001 by Craig Hollabaugh
 *
 * This program is free software; you can redistribute it and/or modify
 * it under the terms of the GNU Library General Public License as
 * published by the Free Software Foundation; either version 2 of the
 * License, or (at your option) any later version.
 *
 * This program is distributed in the hope that it will be useful, but
 * WITHOUT ANY WARRANTY; without even the implied warranty of
 * MERCHANTABILITY or FITNESS FOR A PARTICULAR PURPOSE. See the GNU
 * Library General Public License for more details.
 *
 * You should have received a copy of the GNU Library General Public
 * License along with this program; if not, write to the
 * Free Software Foundation, Inc.,
 * 59 Temple Place, Suite 330, Boston, MA 02111-1307 USA
 */


/*
 * interrupt_latency_mediaengine.c is based on procfs_example.c by Erik Mouw.
 * For more information, please see, The Linux Kernel Procfs Guide, Erik Mouw
 * http://kernelnewbies.org/documents/kdoc/procfs-guide/lkprocfsguide.html
 */
```

LISTING 11.2   Continued

```
/*
arm-linux-gcc -O2 -D__KERNEL__ -DMODULE -I/usr/src/arm-linux/include \
-c interrupt_latency_mediaengine.c \
-o /tftpboot/arm-rootfs/tmp/interrupt_latency_mediaengine.o
*/


/* interrupt_latency_mediaengine.c module
 * This module measures instantaneous interrupt latency of the MediaEngine
 * using GPIO01. Configure the GRER for GPIO01 rising edge interrupt
 * generation. Setting GPIO01 as an output then setting GPIO01 causes a
 * rising edge that generates the interrupt. GRER is reset by ARM kernel
 * code, therefore just setting the register itself is not enough. Use
 * the set_GPIO_IRQ_edge  ARM-only function. See kernel source for more info.
 *
 * After module insertion, reading /proc/interrupt_latency will assert GPIO01
 * generating the interrupt. The interrupt handler will deassert this signal.
 * View on scope. An interrupt counter is included to help debug noisy a
 * interrupt line.
 */


#include <linux/module.h>
#include <linux/kernel.h>
#include <linux/init.h>
#include <linux/proc_fs.h>


#include <asm/io.h>


#define MODULE_VERSION "1.0"
#define MODULE_NAME "interrupt_latency_mediaengine"


/* see 9.1.1.1 Intel StrongARM SA-1110 Microprocessor Developer's Manual */
/* these are also defined in arch SA-1100.h but differently*/
#define GPIO         0x90040000 /* GPIO registers base address */
#define GPLR_OFFSET  0x00
#define GPDR_OFFSET  0x04
#define GPSR_OFFSET  0x08
#define GPCR_OFFSET  0x0C
#define GAFR_OFFSET  0x1C
#define GRER_OFFSET  0x10
#define GFER_OFFSET  0x14
#define GEDR_OFFSET  0x18
```

LISTING 11.2   Continued

```
#define GPIOLEN      0x20
#define GPIO01       0x00000002

#define IC           0x90050000 /* Interrupt controller register base address */
#define ICIP_OFFSET  0x00
#define ICMR_OFFSET  0x04
#define ICLR_OFFSET  0x08
#define ICFP_OFFSET  0x10
#define ICLEN        0x20

static void *ic_base, *gpio_base;
unsigned long int gpdr, gafr, grer;

int interruptcount = 0;
struct timeval tv1, tv2;

#define INTERRUPT 1

static struct proc_dir_entry *interrupt_latency_file;

/*
 * function interrupt_interrupt_latency
 * This function is the interrupt handler for interrupt 1. It sets the tv2
 * structure using do_gettimeofday. It then clears GPIO01.
 */
void interrupt_interrupt_latency(int irq, void *dev_id, struct pt_regs *regs)
{
  do_gettimeofday(&tv2);
  writel(GPIO01, gpio_base + GPCR_OFFSET); /* deassert the interrupt signal */
  interruptcount++;
}

/*
 * function proc_read_interrupt_latency
 * The kernel executes this function when a read operation occurs on
 * /proc/interrupt_latency. This function sets the tv1 structure. It asserts
 * GPIO01 which should immediately cause interrupt 1 to occur. The handler
 * records tv2 and deasserts GPIO01. This function returns the time
 * differential between tv2 and tv1.
 */
```

LISTING 11.2   Continued

```
static int proc_read_interrupt_latency(char *page, char **start, off_t off,
                                       int count, int *eof, void *data)
{
  int len;

  do_gettimeofday(&tv1);
  writel(GPIO01, gpio_base + GPSR_OFFSET); /* assert the interrupt signal */


 len = sprintf(page,"Start %9i.%06i\nFinish %9i.%06i\nLatency %6i\nCount%i\n",
                    (int) tv1.tv_sec, (int) tv1.tv_usec,
                    (int) tv2.tv_sec, (int) tv2.tv_usec,
                    (int) (tv2.tv_usec - tv1.tv_usec),
                    interruptcount);


  return len;
}

/*
 * function init_interrupt_latency
 * This function creates the /proc directory entry interrupt_latency. It
 * requests interrupt 1 from Linux then configures the interrupt controller.
 */
static int __init init_interrupt_latency(void)
{
  unsigned long r;
  int rv = 0;

  interrupt_latency_file = create_proc_entry("interrupt_latency", 0444, NULL);
  if(interrupt_latency_file == NULL) {
    return -ENOMEM;
  }

  interrupt_latency_file->data = NULL;
  interrupt_latency_file->read_proc = &proc_read_interrupt_latency;
  interrupt_latency_file->write_proc = NULL;
  interrupt_latency_file->owner = THIS_MODULE;

  ic_base = ioremap_nocache(IC,ICLEN);
  printk("ic_base        = 0x%08X\n",ic_base);
```

LISTING 11.2   Continued

```
  /* request interrupt from linux */
  rv = request_irq(INTERRUPT, interrupt_interrupt_latency, 0,
                   "interrupt_latency",NULL);
  if ( rv ) {
    printk("Can't get interrupt %d\n", INTERRUPT);
    goto no_interrupt_latency;
  }

  /* print out interrupt controller status bits */
  r = readl(ic_base + ICIP_OFFSET);
  printk("ICIP        = 0x%08X\n",r);
  r = readl(ic_base + ICMR_OFFSET);
  printk("ICMR        = 0x%08X\n",r); /* bit is set here for INT1 */
  r = readl(ic_base + ICLR_OFFSET);
  printk("ICLR        = 0x%08X\n",r);
  r = readl(ic_base + ICFP_OFFSET);
  printk("ICFP        = 0x%08X\n",r);


  /* get GPIO base for register changing */
  gpio_base = ioremap_nocache(GPIO,GPIOLEN);
  printk("\ngpio_base   = 0x%08X\n",gpio_base);


/* configuring GPIO01 as output */
/* set GPIO01 as output */
  writel(gpdr |  GPIO01, gpio_base + GPDR_OFFSET);

/* set GPIO01 with no alt function */
  writel(gafr & ~GPIO01, gpio_base + GAFR_OFFSET);


  writel(GPIO01              , gpio_base + GPCR_OFFSET);  /* clear GPIO01 */

  gpdr = readl(gpio_base + GPDR_OFFSET); /* preserve the gpdr bits */
  printk("GPDR        = 0x%08X\n",gpdr);

  gafr = readl(gpio_base + GAFR_OFFSET); /* preserve the gafr bits */
  printk("GAFR        = 0x%08X\n",gafr);
```

LISTING 11.2 Continued

```
  r = readl(gpio_base + GPLR_OFFSET);
  printk("GPLR          = 0x%08X\n",r);

  grer = readl(gpio_base + GRER_OFFSET); /* preserve the grer bits */
  printk("GRER          = 0x%08X\n",grer);

/* set GPIO01 to have rising edge int */
  writel(grer | GPIO01, gpio_base + GRER_OFFSET);

/* use ARM-only Linux function requesting edge int */
  set_GPIO_IRQ_edge(GPIO01, GPIO_RISING_EDGE);
  printk("set_GPIO_IRQ_edge\n");

  r = readl(gpio_base + GRER_OFFSET);
  printk("GRER          = 0x%08X\n",r);

  r = readl(gpio_base + GFER_OFFSET);
  printk("GFER          = 0x%08X\n",r);

  r = readl(gpio_base + GEDR_OFFSET);
  printk("GEDR          = 0x%08X\n",r);

  /* everything initialized */
  printk(KERN_INFO "%s %s initialized\n",MODULE_NAME, MODULE_VERSION);
  return 0;

no_interrupt_latency:
  remove_proc_entry("interrupt_latency", NULL);
}



/*
 * function cleanup_interrupt_latency
 * This function frees interrupt 1,  restores registers, then removes the
 * /proc directory entry interrupt_latency.
 */
static void __exit cleanup_interrupt_latency(void)
{
  free_irq(INTERRUPT,NULL); /* free the interrupt */
```

LISTING 11.2   Continued

```
  writel(gpdr, gpio_base + GPDR_OFFSET);   /* restore gpdr */
  writel(gafr, gpio_base + GAFR_OFFSET);   /* restore gafr */
  writel(grer, gpio_base + GRER_OFFSET);   /* restore grer */

  iounmap(ic_base);
  iounmap(gpio_base);

  remove_proc_entry("interrupt_latency", NULL);

  printk(KERN_INFO "%s %s removed\n", MODULE_NAME, MODULE_VERSION);
}


module_init(init_interrupt_latency);
module_exit(cleanup_interrupt_latency);

MODULE_AUTHOR("Craig Hollabaugh");
MODULE_DESCRIPTION("interrupt_latency proc module");


EXPORT_NO_SYMBOLS;
```

The interrupt_latency_mediaengine.c device driver performs steps that are similar to those performed by the interrupt_latency_x86.c device driver. A slight difference exists with the interrupt_latency_mediaengine.c call to set_GPIO_IRQ_edge. The ARM kernel interrupt code maintains an internal copy of the GPIO Rising-Edge Detect Register (GRER) value. Calling set_GPIO_IRQ_edge informs the ARM kernel to include the GPIO01 bit in GRER register manipulations. The following console output shows an instantaneous result for the MediaEngine target board:

```
bash-2.04# insmod interrupt_latency_mediaengine.o
ic_base     = 0xC2802000
ICIP        = 0x00000000
ICMR        = 0xD4008803
ICLR        = 0x00000000
ICFP        = 0x00000000

gpio_base   = 0xC2804000
GPDR        = 0x00000002
GAFR        = 0x00000000
GPLR        = 0x0FF8FBFC
GRER        = 0x00000003
set_GPIO_IRQ_edge
```

```
GRER        = 0x00000003
GFER        = 0x00000000
GEDR        = 0x00000000
interrupt_latency_mediaengine 1.0 initialized

bash-2.04# cat /proc/interrupts
  0:      2205   cs89x0
  1:         0   interrupt_latency
 11:         0   GPIO 11-27
 15:       113   serial
 26:      1455   timer
 28:         0   OST2 - gp
 30:         0   rtc1Hz
 31:         0   rtcAlrm
Err:         0

bash-2.04# cat /proc/interrupt_latency
Start       670.663168
Finish      668.663177
Latency            9
Count              1
```

The /proc/interrupts file shows that the interrupt_latency routine is registered on Interrupt 1. The /proc/interrupt_latency file shows an instantaneous latency of 9μs. Figure 11.4 shows an oscilloscope capture of the interrupt signal.

The interrupt signal measurement shows a latency of 7μs, whereas the driver returns a calculated latency of 9μs. Code execution accounts for this 2μs discrepancy. As with the MZ104, this discrepancy is not a factor in the race timer.

The Project Trailblazer engineers calculated the MediaEngine's average interrupt latency to be approximately 10μs. The StrongARM version of the do_gettimeofday function has near-microsecond accuracy.

Measuring Interrupt Latency on the RPX-CLLF

The RPX-CLLF's MPC860 has seven external interrupt pins. The Project Trailblazers want to drive IRQ2 with PA0, so they configure the interrupt controller for IRQ2 rising-edge operation. Asserting PA0 should generate Interrupt 2. (For more information, see Section 11.5.1, "Interrupt Structure," of *Motorola MPC860 PowerQUICC User's Manual.*[2]) Figure 11.5 shows the interrupt signal connection between the RPX-CLLF's PA0 and IRQ2 and the oscilloscope.

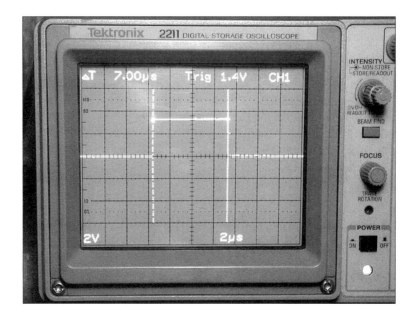

FIGURE 11.4   The MediaEngine's interrupt signal.

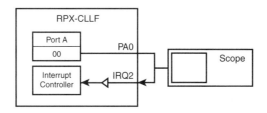

FIGURE 11.5   The RPX-CLLF connection for measuring interrupt latency.

Listing 11.3 shows the source code for the `interrupt_latency_rpxcllf.c` device driver.

LISTING 11.3   The `interrupt_latency_rpxcllf.c` Device Driver

```
/*
 * interrupt_latency_rpxcllf v1.0 11/25/01
 * www.embeddedlinuxinterfacing.com
 *
 * The original location of this code is
 * http://www.embeddedlinuxinterfacing.com/chapters/11/
 *
```

LISTING 11.3   Continued

```
* Copyright (C) 2001 by Craig Hollabaugh
*
* This program is free software; you can redistribute it and/or modify
* it under the terms of the GNU Library General Public License as
* published by the Free Software Foundation; either version 2 of the
* License, or (at your option) any later version.
*
* This program is distributed in the hope that it will be useful, but
* WITHOUT ANY WARRANTY; without even the implied warranty of
* MERCHANTABILITY or FITNESS FOR A PARTICULAR PURPOSE. See the GNU
* Library General Public License for more details.
*
* You should have received a copy of the GNU Library General Public
* License along with this program; if not, write to the
* Free Software Foundation, Inc.,
* 59 Temple Place, Suite 330, Boston, MA 02111-1307 USA
*/

/*
 * interrupt_latency_rpxcllf.c is based on procfs_example.c by Erik Mouw.
 * For more information, please see, The Linux Kernel Procfs Guide, Erik Mouw
 * http://kernelnewbies.org/documents/kdoc/procfs-guide/lkprocfsguide.html
 */

/*
powerpc-linux-gcc -O2 -D__KERNEL__ -DMODULE -I/usr/src/powerpc-linux/include \
-c interrupt_latency_rpxcllf.c \
-o /tftpboot/powerpc-rootfs/tmp/interrupt_latency_rpxcllf.o
*/

/* interrupt_latency_rpxcllf
 * This module measures instantaneous interrupt latency of the RPX-CLLF
 * using PA0 and IRQ2. Configure the SIU for IRQ2 edge interrupt
 * generation. Configure PA0 as an output then setting PA0 causes a
 * rising edge that generates the interrupt.
 *
 * Section 11.5.1 of Motorola MPC860 PowerQUICC User's Manual
 *
 * After module insertion, reading /proc/interrupt_latency will assert PA0
 * generating the interrupt. The interrupt handler will deassert this signal.
 * View on scope. An interrupt counter is included to help debug noisy a
```

LISTING 11.3   Continued

```
 * interrupt line.
 */

#include <linux/module.h>
#include <linux/kernel.h>
#include <linux/init.h>
#include <linux/proc_fs.h>

#include <asm/io.h>

#include <linux/interrupt.h>
#include <asm/irq.h>
#include <asm/mpc8xx.h>
#include <asm/8xx_immap.h>
#include <asm/time.h>

#define MODULE_VERSION "1.0"
#define MODULE_NAME    "interrupt_latency_rpxcllf"

volatile immap_t *immap;
static void *io_base;

#define PA0        0x8000
#define SIEL_ED2   0x08000000

int interruptcount = 0;
#define INTERRUPT SIU_IRQ2

struct timeval tv1, tv2; /* do_gettimeofday fills these */

static struct proc_dir_entry *interrupt_latency_file;

/*
 * function interrupt_interrupt_latency
 * This function is the interrupt handler for interrupt 2. It sets the tv2
 * structure using do_gettimeofday. It then clears PA0.
 */
void interrupt_interrupt_latency(int irq, void *dev_id, struct pt_regs *regs)
{
  do_gettimeofday(&tv2);
  immap->im_ioport.iop_padat |= PA0; /* deassert the interrupt signal */
```

LISTING 11.3   Continued

```
  interruptcount++;
}


/*
 * function proc_read_interrupt_latency
 * The kernel executes this function when a read operation occurs on
 * /proc/interrupt_latency. This function sets the tv1 structure. It asserts
 * PA0 which should immediately cause interrupt 2 to occur. The handler
 * records tv2 and deasserts PA0. This function returns the time
 * differential between tv2 and tv1.
 */
static int proc_read_interrupt_latency(char *page, char **start, off_t off,
                                       int count, int *eof, void *data)
{
  int len;

  do_gettimeofday(&tv1);
  immap->im_ioport.iop_padat &= ~PA0; /* assert the interrupt signal */


 len = sprintf(page, "Start %9i.%06i\nFinish %9i.%06i\nLatency %16i\n\
Count %18i\n",(int) tv1.tv_sec, (int) tv1.tv_usec,
              (int) tv2.tv_sec, (int) tv2.tv_usec,
              (int) (tv2.tv_usec - tv1.tv_usec),
              interruptcount);

  return len;
}


/*
 * function init_interrupt_latency
 * This function creates the /proc directory entry interrupt_latency. It
 * requests interrupt 2 from Linux then configures the interrupt controller.
 */
static int __init init_interrupt_latency(void)
{
  unsigned long r;
  int rv = 0;

  interrupt_latency_file = create_proc_entry("interrupt_latency", 0444, NULL);
  if(interrupt_latency_file == NULL) {
```

LISTING 11.3   Continued

```
    return -ENOMEM;
  }

  interrupt_latency_file->data = NULL;
  interrupt_latency_file->read_proc = &proc_read_interrupt_latency;
  interrupt_latency_file->write_proc = NULL;
  interrupt_latency_file->owner = THIS_MODULE;

  /* request interrupt from linux */
  rv = request_8xxirq(INTERRUPT, interrupt_interrupt_latency, 0,
                      "interrupt_latency",NULL);
  if ( rv ) {
    printk("Can't get interrupt %d\n", INTERRUPT);
    goto no_interrupt_latency;
  }

  /* get the IMMAP register address */
  immap = (immap_t *)(mfspr(IMMR) & 0xFFFF0000);
  immap->im_ioport.iop_papar &= ~PA0; /* set PA0 to general I/O */
  immap->im_ioport.iop_padir |=  PA0; /* set PA0 as output       */

  /* set IRQ2 to edge triggering */
  immap->im_siu_conf.sc_siel |= SIEL_ED2;
  printk("SIEL    = 0x%08X\n",immap->im_siu_conf.sc_siel);

  immap->im_ioport.iop_padat |= PA0; /* deassert the interrupt signal */


/* everything initialized */
  printk(KERN_INFO "%s %s initialized\n",MODULE_NAME, MODULE_VERSION);
  return 0;

no_interrupt_latency:
  remove_proc_entry("interrupt_latency", NULL);
}

/*
 * function cleanup_interrupt_latency
 * This function frees interrupt 2 then removes the
 * /proc directory entry interrupt_latency.
 */
```

LISTING 11.3 Continued

```
static void __exit cleanup_interrupt_latency(void)
{
  free_irq(INTERRUPT,NULL); /* free the interrupt */

  remove_proc_entry("interrupt_latency", NULL);

  printk(KERN_INFO "%s %s removed\n", MODULE_NAME, MODULE_VERSION);
}

module_init(init_interrupt_latency);
module_exit(cleanup_interrupt_latency);

MODULE_AUTHOR("Craig Hollabaugh");
MODULE_DESCRIPTION("interrupt_latency proc module");

EXPORT_NO_SYMBOLS;
```

The interrupt_latency_rpxcllf.c device driver performs steps similar to those of the interrupt_latency_x86.c device driver. However, significant differences exist between the x86 and PowerPC interrupt controllers. The request_8xxirq function is a specialized PowerPC 8xx version of request_irq. request_8xxirq sets all the required MPC860 interrupt registers. When using an 8xx processor, you must explicitly call the request_8xxirq function. The following console output shows an instantaneous latency test result for the RPX-CLLF target board:

```
bash-2.04# insmod interrupt_latency_rpxcllf.o
SIEL    = 0x08000000
interrupt_latency_rpxcllf 1.0 initialized
bash-2.04# cat /proc/interrupts
         CPU0
  3:        0   8xx SIU   Edge      fec
  4:        0   8xx SIU   Edge      interrupt_latency
  5:     3111   8xx SIU   Edge      cpm
 15:        0   8xx SIU   Edge      tbint
BAD:        0
bash-2.04# cat /proc/interrupt_latency
Start        112.477152
Finish       112.477187
Latency             35
Count                1
```

The /proc/interrupts file shows that the interrupt_latency routine is registered on Interrupt 4, not on Interrupt 2. This kernel version incorrectly reports interrupt values. The /proc/interrupt_latency file shows an instantaneous latency of 35μs. Figure 11.6 shows an oscilloscope capture of the interrupt signal.

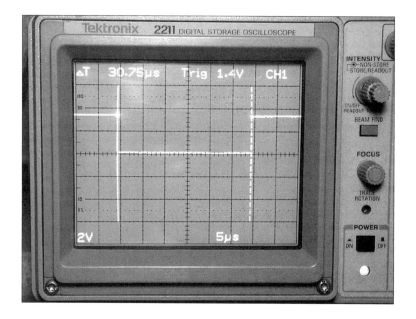

FIGURE 11.6   The RPX-CLLF's interrupt signal.

The interrupt signal measurement shows a latency of 30.75μs, whereas the driver returns a calculated latency of 35μs. Code execution accounts for the 4.25μs discrepancy. As with the x86, this discrepancy is not a factor in the race timer.

The Project Trailblazer engineers calculated the RPX-CLLF's average interrupt latency to be approximately 35μs. The PowerPC version of the do_gettimeofday function has near microsecond accuracy.

Interrupt Latency Test Summary

The MZ104, the MediaEngine, and the RPX-CLLF exhibit fast average interrupt latencies, and their do_gettimeofday functions return near-microsecond accuracy. By using the interrupt latency device drivers and an oscilloscope, the engineers found the average interrupt latency for the MZ104, the MediaEngine, and the RPX-CLLF to be 50μs, 10μs, and 35μs, respectively. With average interrupt latencies at or below 50μs, each target board is capable of providing millisecond timing accuracy for the race timer. The engineers breathe a sign of relief because they feared that they would have to move to a real-time solution, such as RTLinux or Real Time Application Interface (RTAI), which would mean a significant increase in their development time. However, the stock Linux kernel running on the Project Trailblazer target boards provides their required functionality. The engineers are now ready to tackle the design of the race timer.

Implementing the Race Timer

After the Project Trailblazer engineers resolve the average interrupt latency question, they can design the race timer. All the Project Trailblazer target boards have the input/output (I/O) and speed capability to act as the race timer. For this design, the engineers decide to use the MZ104 as the controller. Figure 11.7 shows a schematic of the race timer.

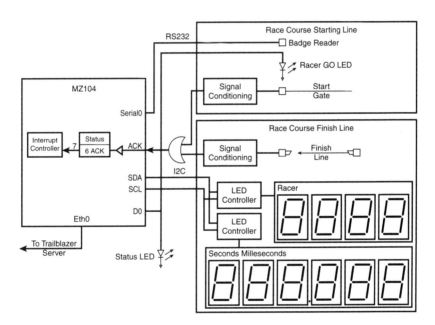

FIGURE 11.7   A schematic of the race timer.

The race timer should have the following functional features:

- It must have 1ms accuracy.
- It should display the current race time at the finish line.
- It should provide a status display to officials operating the timer.

- It should use the racer's pass ID in race information.

- It should provide the racer with a race start indicator.

- It should log race results.

- It should provide access to status, race time, and racer number through /proc directory entries.

Figure 11.8 shows the racer controller state map.

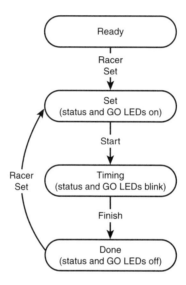

FIGURE 11.8   The race controller state map.

The operational race scenario consists of four states:

- **Ready**—On power-up, the race controller enters the ready state and awaits a racer. The racer gets ready at the starting gate. The radio frequency identification (RFID) tag reader reads the racer's lift pass ID and sends it via the RS-232 serial link. This places the controller in the set state.

- **Set**—The Status LED and Racer Go LEDs turn on. The racer proceeds through the starting gate, which sends a rising-edge signal to the ACK line and generates interrupt 7. The interrupt handler routine executes, records the race start time with do_gettimeofday, schedules the bottom-half tasklet for execution, and puts the controller in the timing state.

- **Timing**—The Status LED and Racer Go LEDs blink at 1-second intervals. When the racer crosses the finish line, the photo detector sends a rising-edge signal to the ACK line and generates interrupt 7. The interrupt handler routine executes, records the race finish time with do_gettimeofday, schedules the bottom-half tasklet for execution, and puts the controller in the done state.

- **Done**—The Status LED and Racer Go LEDs turn off. The controller waits for another racer to enter the starting gate.

The Project Trailblazer engineers have already completed several pieces of this design. Chapter 6, "Asynchronous Serial Communication Interfacing," addresses asynchronous serial communications for the RFID tag reader. Chapter 7, "Parallel Port Interfacing," addresses parallel port operations. Chapter 10, "Synchronous Serial Communication Interfacing," addresses synchronous communications with the Philips SAA1064 I2C LED controller. Earlier in this chapter, the engineers developed the interrupt and timing routines. Chapter 12, "System Integration," addresses system integration with the Project Trailblazer server. Therefore, these details are not covered here. For the remainder of this chapter, we'll concentrate on two areas: interrupt bottom-half processing using tasklets and kernel timers.

Race Timer Interrupt Processing Using Tasklets

Complex or lengthy interrupt processing tasks are often split into two sections. The *top-half routine* executes at interrupt time, performs the minimal amount of work, and schedules the remainder of work, called the *bottom half routine,* to be performed at a later or safer time. The top-half routine can request execution with interrupts disabled; therefore, it should execute and terminate as quickly as possible. The kernel executes bottom-half routines with interrupts enabled. With Linux kernel 2.4 and above, the preferred way to implement bottom-half routine uses tasklets.

Tasklets are declared by using the DECLARE_TASKLET macro. This macro also associates a handler function to the tasklet. The top-half interrupt handler routine should schedule an already declared tasklet for later execution. The kernel executes the scheduled tasklet handler functions after all the interrupt handler routines complete but before execution of the scheduler.

In the race timer design, the interrupt handler, racetimer_interrupt, schedules the race timer tasklet's handler routine, racetimer_do_tasklet, for later execution. The racetimer_do_tasklet function prints race status information to the system log, which is a somewhat lengthy process, and starts a system timer.

Race Timer Status Display Using System Timers

The race timer Status and Racer Go LEDs inform officials, fans, and racers of race activity. A solid on signal means the system is ready for a race to begin. Blinking LEDs mean a race is in progress. When the LEDs are off, a race is complete and the system is ready for another racer to enter the starting gate. The Project Trailblazer engineers need to figure out how to blink the LEDs at a constant 1-second rate.

As you saw at the beginning of this chapter, Linux offers five timing mechanisms, and the engineers chose to use do_gettimeofday for race timing. The race timer driver could sit in a loop calling do_gettimeofday and wait for 1 second to elapse. The race timer driver could also call a system sleep function (usleep, msleep, or sleep) and wait for 1 second to elapse. Both approaches would work, but neither is desirable. The kernel scheduler does not drive code that is executing in the kernel space. A 1-second sleep in the kernel would completely occupy the processor for 1 second, and other processing would not occur during this time. Device drivers that use sleep functions for long delays definitely affect system performance.

Kernel timers solve long time delay problems. By using a timer, device drivers can schedule a function for execution at a future time. A device driver creates a timer, populates the timer's data, function and expires fields and then adds the timer to the kernel's timer list. The x86 kernel scans the timer list approximately 100 times per second. If the kernel's jiffies value is greater than a timer's expires field value, the kernel executes the timer's function handler. Timers operate in a one-shot mode. The kernel executes timer function handlers only once. Drivers that need periodic function execution need to reschedule their kernel timers in the timer's function handler.

In the race timer, the bottom-half tasklet handler, racetimer_do_tasklet, starts the kernel timer called status_timer. One second later, the status_timer expires and the kernel executes the status_timer's function handler, status_timer_timed_out. If the race is in progress (the timing state where the LEDs blink at 1 second intervals), status_timer_timed_out toggles the Status and Racer Go LEDs, sets the status_timer.expires value, and then reschedules (via the add_timer function) status_timer for execution 1 second later. If the race has completed, status_timer_timed_out turns off the LEDs.

Let's look at how the racetimer_x86.c device driver, shown in Listing 11.4, implements bottom-half interrupt processing using a scheduled tasklet and 1-second timing of the Status and Racer GO LEDs.

LISTING 11.4   The racetimer_x86.c Device Driver

```
/*
 * racetimer_x86 v1.0 11/25/01
 * www.embeddedlinuxinterfacing.com
```

LISTING 11.4   Continued

```
 *
 * The original location of this code is
 * http://www.embeddedlinuxinterfacing.com/chapters/11/
 *
 * Copyright (C) 2001 by Craig Hollabaugh
 *
 * This program is free software; you can redistribute it and/or modify
 * it under the terms of the GNU Library General Public License as
 * published by the Free Software Foundation; either version 2 of the
 * License, or (at your option) any later version.
 *
 * This program is distributed in the hope that it will be useful, but
 * WITHOUT ANY WARRANTY; without even the implied warranty of
 * MERCHANTABILITY or FITNESS FOR A PARTICULAR PURPOSE. See the GNU
 * Library General Public License for more details.
 *
 * You should have received a copy of the GNU Library General Public
 * License along with this program; if not, write to the
 * Free Software Foundation, Inc.,
 * 59 Temple Place, Suite 330, Boston, MA 02111-1307 USA
 */

/*
 * racetimer_x86.c is based on procfs_example.c by Erik Mouw.
 * For more information, please see The Linux Kernel Procfs Guide, Erik Mouw
 * http://kernelnewbies.org/documents/kdoc/procfs-guide/lkprocfsguide.html
 */

/*
gcc -O2 -D__KERNEL__ -DMODULE -I/usr/src/linux/include \
-c racetimer_x86.c -o racetimer_x86.o
*/


/* racetimer_x86
 * This module implements a race timer with millisecond accuracy using
 * interrupts and bottom half tasklets. The timer also drives a status
 * indicator line (parallel port DO) showing the timer's current state.
 * Controlling or accessing timer information is provided through /proc
 * directory entries.
 * Here are the timer's states
```

LISTING 11.4   Continued

```
* Ready:  Timer ready for racer number entry
* Set:    Timer ready for racer to start, status indicator ON
* Timing: Timer measuring race time, status indicator blinking 1s intervals
* Done:   Race is done, Timer ready for racer number entry
*
* Interrupts or racer number entry forces a state change.
*
* /proc directory entries
* /proc/trailblazer/racernumber  contains the racer number, timer isn't
*                                ready until a number is written to this
*                                file
* /proc/trailblazer/racetime     contains the current or last race time
* /proc/trailblazer/racestatus   contains the race timer state, R, S, T or D
*/


#include <linux/module.h>
#include <linux/kernel.h>
#include <linux/init.h>
#include <linux/proc_fs.h>
#include <asm/uaccess.h>
#include <asm/io.h>
#include <linux/sched.h>
#include <linux/interrupt.h>
#include <linux/tqueue.h>

#define MODULE_VERSION "1.0"
#define MODULE_NAME "racetimer"

static struct proc_dir_entry *tb_dir,
                        *racer_file, *racestatus_file, *racetime_file;

#define SPPDATAPORT         0x378
#define SPPSTATUSPORT       (SPPDATAPORT + 1)
#define SPPCONTROLPORT      (SPPDATAPORT + 2)
#define SSPINTERRUPTENABLE  0x10
#define STATUSLED           0x01    /* DO on the parallel port */

struct timeval starttime, finishtime;
```

LISTING 11.4 Continued

```
unsigned char state;
#define STATE_Ready  'R'
#define STATE_Set    'S'
#define STATE_Timing 'T'
#define STATE_Done   'D'
/* using letters here instead of numbers, cat /proc/trailblazer/racestatus
 * makes things a little easier to read */


#define INTERRUPT 7

struct timer_list status_timer;
unsigned char toggle;

#define RACERNUMBERLEN 10
unsigned char racernumber[RACERNUMBERLEN+1];

/* status_timer_timed_out
 * This function gets called when the status_timer expires, basically every
 * 1 second during the race (state = STATE_Timing). Its primary purpose is to
 * toggle the status line that blink the LEDs. If we're racing, we need to
 * re-schedule the timer for 1 second in the future.
 */
void status_timer_timed_out(unsigned long ptr)
{
  if (state == STATE_Timing)
  {
    outb(toggle++ & STATUSLED, SPPDATAPORT); /* toggle the statusLED line */
    status_timer.expires = jiffies + HZ;    /* 1 second intervals */
    add_timer(&status_timer);               /* kicks off the next timer */
  }
  else
    outb(0x00, SPPDATAPORT); /* toggle off statusLED line */
}


/* racetimer_do_tasklet
 * This function is the interrupt bottom-half tasklet handler. It performs
 * the lengthy processing that shouldn't be in the interrupt handler. It
 * also starts the status_timer. We only execute this function when an
 * interrupt occurs, either the start of the end of the race.
 */
```

LISTING 11.4   Continued

```
void racetimer_do_tasklet(unsigned long unused)
{
  switch (state) {
  case STATE_Timing: /* got into this state from racetimer_interrupt */
    status_timer.expires = jiffies + HZ; /* 1 second intervals */
    add_timer(&status_timer); /* kicks off the first timer */
    printk(KERN_INFO "RaceTimer: Start  %s %9i.%06i\n",racernumber,
           (int) starttime.tv_sec, (int) starttime.tv_usec);
    break;
  case STATE_Done: /* got into this state from racetimer_interrupt */
    printk(KERN_INFO "RaceTimer: Finish %s %9i.%06i\n",racernumber,
           (int) finishtime.tv_sec, (int) finishtime.tv_usec);
    break;
  }
}


/* DECLARE_TASKLET
 * This macro actually declares the tasklet and associates it handler
 * racetimer_do_tasklet
 */
DECLARE_TASKLET(racetimer_tasklet, racetimer_do_tasklet, 0);

/* racetimer_interrupt
 * Here's the interrupt handler (top-half). It timestamps the race start and
 * finish, changes the state and schedules the bottom half tasklet.
 */
void racetimer_interrupt(int irq, void *dev_id, struct pt_regs *regs)
{
  switch (state) {
  case STATE_Set:
    do_gettimeofday(&starttime);
    state = STATE_Timing; /* change state because now we're racing */
    tasklet_schedule(&racetimer_tasklet);
    break;
  case STATE_Timing:
    do_gettimeofday(&finishtime);
    state = STATE_Done; /* change state because race is over */
    tasklet_schedule(&racetimer_tasklet);
    break;
  }
}
```

LISTING 11.4   Continued

```
/* proc_read_racer
 * This function returns the racer number if the user does a read on
 * /proc/trailblazer/racernumber
 */
static int proc_read_racer(char *page, char **start, off_t off,
                           int count, int *eof, void *data)
{
  int len;

  len = sprintf(page, "%s\n", racernumber);

  return len;
}


/* proc_write_racer
 * This function sets the racer number when the user does a write to
 * /proc/trailblazer/racernumber. Writing to racernumber also changes
 * the state to set.
 */
static int proc_write_racer(struct file *file, const char *buffer,
                            unsigned long count, void *data)
{
  int len;

  if(count > RACERNUMBERLEN) /* array range checking here */
    len = RACERNUMBERLEN;
  else
    len = count;

  if(copy_from_user(racernumber, buffer, len)) {
    return -EFAULT;
  }

  racernumber[len] = '\0';        /* NULL terminate */

  state = STATE_Set;              /* change the state, get set for a new race */

  outb(STATUSLED, SPPDATAPORT); /* turn on status LED, solid on means ready */

  return len;
```

LISTING 11.4   Continued

```
}

/* proc_read_racestatus
 * This function returns the state, R, S, T, or D when user reads from
 * /proc/trailblazer/racestatus
 */
static int proc_read_racestatus(char *page, char **start, off_t off,
                                int count, int *eof, void *data)
{
  int len;

  len = sprintf(page, "%c\n", state);

  return len;
}

/* proc_read_racetime
 * This function returns the current or last race time.
 * do_gettimeofday fills the timeval with current seconds and microseconds.
 * Splitting the time in this way requires a little math because the
 * microseconds value is an integer not fraction, (321423 not .321423) So
 * we do a little fixup below if the microseconds differential requires a
 * carry from the seconds value
 */
static int proc_read_racetime(char *page, char **start, off_t off,
                              int count, int *eof, void *data)
{
  int len;
  long raceseconds, raceuseconds;
  struct timeval currenttime;

  switch (state) {
  case STATE_Ready:
    raceseconds  = 0;
    raceuseconds = 0;
    break;
  case STATE_Set:
    raceseconds  = 0;
    raceuseconds = 0;
    break;
```

LISTING 11.4   Continued

```
  case STATE_Timing:    /* we're racing, give 'em the race time */
    do_gettimeofday(&currenttime);
    raceseconds  = currenttime.tv_sec - starttime.tv_sec;
    raceuseconds = currenttime.tv_usec - starttime.tv_usec;
    break;
  case STATE_Done:      /* race is over, give 'em the race time */
    raceseconds  = finishtime.tv_sec - starttime.tv_sec;
    raceuseconds = finishtime.tv_usec - starttime.tv_usec;
    break;
  }

/* need a little fixup here because tv_sec and tv_usec are individual longs */
  if (raceuseconds < 0) {
    raceuseconds += 1000000;
    raceseconds--;
  }

  len = sprintf(page,"%i.%06i\n", raceseconds, raceuseconds);

  return len;
}

static int __init init_racetimer(void)
{
  int rv = 0;

/* create trailblazer directory */
  tb_dir = proc_mkdir("trailblazer", NULL);
  if(tb_dir == NULL) {
          return -ENOMEM;
  }
  tb_dir->owner = THIS_MODULE;

/* create racer file */
  racer_file = create_proc_entry("racer", 0666, tb_dir);
  if(racer_file == NULL) {
    rv = -ENOMEM;
    goto no_racer;
  }
```

LISTING 11.4   Continued

```
  racer_file->data = NULL;
  racer_file->read_proc = &proc_read_racer;
  racer_file->write_proc = &proc_write_racer;
  racer_file->owner = THIS_MODULE;

/* create racestatus file */
  racestatus_file = create_proc_entry("racestatus", 0444, tb_dir);
  if(racestatus_file == NULL) {
    rv = -ENOMEM;
    goto no_racestatus;
  }

  racestatus_file->data = NULL;
  racestatus_file->read_proc = &proc_read_racestatus;
  racestatus_file->write_proc = NULL;
  racestatus_file->owner = THIS_MODULE;

/* create racetime file */
  racetime_file = create_proc_entry("racetime", 0444, tb_dir);
  if(racestatus_file == NULL) {
    rv = -ENOMEM;
    goto no_racertime;
  }

  racetime_file->data = NULL;
  racetime_file->read_proc = &proc_read_racetime;
  racetime_file->write_proc = NULL;
  racetime_file->owner = THIS_MODULE;

/* get into reset state */
  state = STATE_Ready;

/* turn off the status LED */
  outb(0x00, SPPDATAPORT);

/* Start with a default racer, old number 0 */
  sprintf(racernumber,"0000");

/* request the interrupt, use SA_INTERRUPT to disable other interrupts
 * while we're running
 */
```

LISTING 11.4   Continued

```
  rv = request_irq(INTERRUPT, racetimer_interrupt, SA_INTERRUPT,
                   "racetimer",NULL);
  if ( rv ) {
    printk("Can't get interrupt %d\n", INTERRUPT);
    goto no_interrupt;
  }

/* initialize the status timer but don't start it with add_timer(),
 * let someone else do that */
  init_timer(&status_timer);
  status_timer.function = status_timer_timed_out;
  status_timer.data = (unsigned long)&state;

/* enable parallel port interrupt reporting */
  outb(SSPINTERRUPTENABLE,SPPCONTROLPORT);

  /* everything OK */
  printk(KERN_INFO "%s %s initialized\n",MODULE_NAME, MODULE_VERSION);
  return 0;



/* clean up /proc directory if we got a error along the way */
no_interrupt:
  remove_proc_entry("racetime", tb_dir);
no_racertime:
  remove_proc_entry("racestatus", tb_dir);
no_racestatus:
  remove_proc_entry("racer", tb_dir);
no_racer:
  remove_proc_entry("trailblazer", NULL);
}



static void __exit cleanup_racetimer(void)
{
/* turn off the status LED */
  outb(0x00, SPPDATAPORT);

/* remove the timer */
/* be careful here, if the module is removed and a timer remains
 * in the kernel timer list, the kernel will fault when executing
```

LISTING 11.4   Continued

```
 * the timer's handler (because the handler doesn't exist anymore, you
 * just removed it from memory.) Force the state to done. Then
 * use del_timer_sync, which waits for timer execution completion
 * to occur before deleting the timer. Forcing the state to done tells
 * timer handler status_timer_timed_out to not reschedule the timer.
 */
  state = STATE_Done;
  del_timer_sync(&status_timer);

/* disable parallel port interrupt reporting */
  outb(0x00,SPPCONTROLPORT);

/* free the interrupt */
  free_irq(INTERRUPT,NULL);

/* remove the /proc entries */
  remove_proc_entry("racetime", tb_dir);
  remove_proc_entry("racestatus", tb_dir);
  remove_proc_entry("racer", tb_dir);
  remove_proc_entry("trailblazer", NULL);

  printk(KERN_INFO "%s %s removed\n", MODULE_NAME, MODULE_VERSION);
}

module_init(init_racetimer);
module_exit(cleanup_racetimer);

MODULE_AUTHOR("Craig Hollabaugh");
MODULE_DESCRIPTION("racetimer proc module");

EXPORT_NO_SYMBOLS;
```

You can download, compile, and test the `racetimer_x86` device driver by using tbdev1. Follow these steps:

1. Download the `racetimer_x86.c` source by using wget:

```
root@tbdev1[509]: cd /root
root@tbdev1[510]: wget http://www.embeddedlinuxinterfacing.com/
➥chapters/11/racetimer_x86.c
```

2. Compile the source code by using gcc:

```
root@tbdev1[511]: gcc -O2 -D__KERNEL__ -DMODULE
➥-I/usr/src/linux/include -c racetimer_x86.c
➥-o racetimer_x86.o
```

3. Insert the device driver by using insmod:

```
root@tbdev1[512]: insmod racetimer_x86.o
```

4. Look for interrupt registration on Interrupt 7 and the /proc directory entries by using these commands:

```
root@tbdev1[513]: cat /proc/interrupts
             CPU0
  0:     8163519        XT-PIC  timer
  1:        2195        XT-PIC  keyboard
  2:           0        XT-PIC  cascade
  4:        6016        XT-PIC  serial
  7:           0        XT-PIC  racetimer
 10:       23132        XT-PIC  usb-uhci
 12:      314011        XT-PIC  eth0
 14:       54205        XT-PIC  ide0
 15:        8457        XT-PIC  ide1
NMI:           0
ERR:           0
root@tbdev1[514]: ls /proc/trailblazer/
racer  racestatus  racetime
```

The race timer is registered on Interrupt 7 and the /proc/trailblazer directory contains the race timer files.

5. Check the internal state of the race timer status:

```
root@tbdev1[515]: cat /proc/trailblazer/racestatus
R
```

The output R means that the timer is in the ready state.

6. Start a race by simulating a racer entering the starting gate with this command:

```
root@tbdev1[516]: echo -n "1234" > /proc/trailblazer/racer
```

7. Again check the internal state of the race timer status:

```
root@tbdev1[517]: cat /proc/trailblazer/racestatus
S
```

The output S means that the timer is in the Set state. You can tell from this output that setting the racer number occurred correctly, and it changed the internal state to S, or set. The status LED also came on. Measure the voltage of the parallel port's D0 signal, pin 2 on the DB-25 connector. Your voltmeter should read between +3V and +5V.

8. Now check the race time by using this command:

```
root@tbdev1[518]: cat /proc/trailblazer/racetime
0.000000
```

9. The racer number is entered in the racer file, the race time is 0.00000 and the timer is in the set state. You are set to start the race. Simulate the racer proceeding through the starting gate by generating the interrupt signal on the parallel port ACK line, pin 10 on the DB-25 connector. Use a debounced switch to generate a positive going signal on the ACK line.

TIP

With interrupt latencies in the microsecond range, Linux interrupt routines can easily count mechanical switch bounces. If you would like to see this for yourself, use a toggle switch to generate the interrupt signal on the parallel port's ACK line. Then examine the interrupt count in the /proc/interrupts file. You should see that one switch closure results in more than one interrupt. Mechanical switches alone should not be used to generate interrupt signals in interrupt-based designs or during interrupt driver testing. For testing, use a switch debounce circuit or write a device driver, again for the parallel port, that drives the ACK line from another parallel port pin. The gate_x86 device driver at www.embeddedlinuxinterfacing. com/chapters/11 generates signals for interrupt device driver testing.

10. Again check the internal state of the race timer status:

```
root@tbdev1[519]: cat /proc/trailblazer/racestatus
T
```

The output T means that the timer is in the timing state.

11. Check the race time by using this command:

```
root@tbdev1[520]: cat /proc/trailblazer/racetime
6.331849
```

You are timing a race, and 6.331849 seconds have elapsed.

12. Continue checking the race time:

```
root@tbdev1[521]: cat /proc/trailblazer/racetime
58.101223
```

You are still timing the race. The status LEDs are blinking at 1-second intervals. Figure 11.9 shows an oscilloscope capture of the parallel port's D0 signal. This confirms the Status LED blink rate. As you can see, the system timer works perfectly.

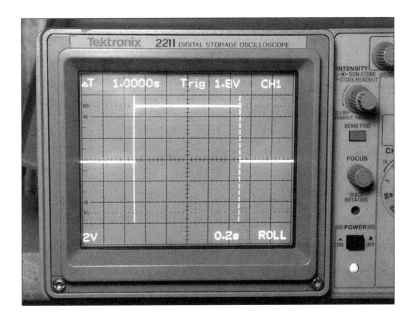

FIGURE 11.9   An oscilloscope reading that confirms the 1-second interval timer performance.

13. Simulate the racer crossing the finish line by using your debounced switch. Again, generate an interrupt signal on the parallel port's ACK line.

14. Check the internal state of the race timer status:

```
root@tbdev1[522]: cat /proc/trailblazer/racestatus
D
```

The output D means the race is done.

15. Check the race time and the system log by using these commands:

```
root@tbdev1[523]: cat /proc/trailblazer/racetime
88.141655
root@tbdev1[524]: grep RaceTime /var/log/messages
Nov 26 22:54:14 tbdev1 kernel: RaceTimer: Start  1234 1006840454.722554
Nov 26 22:55:42 tbdev1 kernel: RaceTimer: Finish 1234 1006840542.864209
```

The race time of your first simulated race was 88.141655 seconds.

16. One last check of /proc/interrupts shows that tbdev1 received two inter-rupts—from the race start and finish:

```
root@tbdev1[525]: cat /proc/interrupts
            CPU0
   0:    8262755        XT-PIC  timer
   1:       2195        XT-PIC  keyboard
   2:          0        XT-PIC  cascade
   4:       6016        XT-PIC  serial
   7:          2        XT-PIC  racetimer
  10:      23132        XT-PIC  usb-uhci
  12:     314556        XT-PIC  eth0
  14:      54257        XT-PIC  ide0
  15:       8457        XT-PIC  ide1
 NMI:          0
 ERR:          0
```

The Project Trailblazer race timer just timed its first race!

Summary

This chapter explores using Linux as an event timer with 1ms resolution. Linux offers several mechanisms for timing, and the do_gettimeofday function with microsecond resolution works best for the three Project Trailblazer target board processors. Whereas determining maximum interrupt latency is difficult, measuring average interrupt latency is relatively easy. Using the interrupt latency device drivers and an oscilloscope, the engineers found the average interrupt latency for the MZ104, the MediaEngine, and the RPX-CLLF to be 50µs, 10µs, and 35µs, respectively. These impressive numbers alleviated the need for the engineers to explore real-time Linux solutions.

The racetimer_x86 device driver implements a split interrupt driver and a 1-second kernel timer. The interrupt top-half routine executes quickly, with interrupts disabled, and schedules the bottom-half tasklet for future execution. The bottom-half tasklet then performs lengthy writes to the system log and starts a 1-second reoccurring kernel timer. By using a kernel timer, the driver avoids using wait loops or sleep functions that dramatically affect system performance.

Additional Reading

1. Intel, *SA-1110 Microprocessor Developer's Manual,*
   `www.intel.com/design/strong/manuals/278240.htm`.

2. Motorola, *MPC860 User Manual,*
   `www.motorola.com/brdata/PDFDB/docs/MPC860UM.pdf`.

12

System Integration

With all the Project Trailblazer field hardware interfaces developed and tested, the engineers were ready to connect everything together. In other words, they were ready to tackle *system integration*. They developed and tested the individual components of Project Trailblazer at the bash prompt on the target boards. However, in the final design, these boards will not function autonomously. Input devices, such as lift-monitoring devices, will collect field information for storage elsewhere. Output devices will control hardware, based on information provided to them. For example, temperature displays will obtain the value to display from a database. Information will be passed between field devices and the database, via the Silverjack network.

Project Trailblazer system integration development needs to take place in two areas: field devices and the Silverjack server. The engineers need to connect field hardware to the database. In this chapter, you will see how the engineers developed the Project Trailblazer system integration by using bash[1,2], an Apache HTTP server[3], a MySQL database[4], gnuplot[5], and a networking connection utility program called netcat (nc).

Integration Overview

The primary integration task is to transfer field data to the server's database and then distribute that data back to the field and to the Web. Although Project Trailblazer has many field devices, the amount of data traveling back and forth consumes a small number of bytes. A variety of network communication protocols exist to connect the field devices to the Silverjack database. Each protocol offers different functionality, complexity, and target board file system usage. The engineers decided to keep the Project

Trailblazer system integration as simple as possible. Their approach uses `bash` scripts wherever possible on the target boards and on the server. Figure 12.1 shows a software block diagram for the Project Trailblazer system integration.

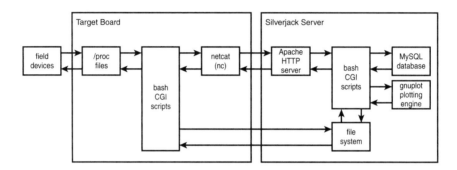

FIGURE 12.1   Target board and Silverjack Server software components.

The engineers' approach includes the following components:

- `bash` scripting is used for field device control and for the Web server Common Gateway Interface (CGI).

- Communication between field devices and the Operations Department uses the Hypertext Transfer Protocol (HTTP).

- The `nc` program provides network communication for `bash` scripts.

- A MySQL database stores all field data except for images, which are stored as files on the server.

- The `gnuplot` program generates any required data plots on demand.

- The Apache HTTP server distributes data to field devices and to the Web.

The remainder of this chapter describes how the Project Trailblazer engineers configured `tbdev1` to act as the Silverjack server and provided system integration functionality for Project Trailblazer. This chapter focuses on three of the Project Trailblazer systems:

- Temperature collection and distribution

- Image collection and distribution

- Guest lift access

The implementation of these three systems provides the integration foundation for all other Project Trailblazer systems.

Installing the System Integration Applications

The engineers needed to install the following applications on tbdev1: MySQL, Apache, and gnuplot. The nc program runs on the target boards. Therefore, the engineers needed to cross-compile an ARM and PowerPC version of nc. These steps are necessary to install the system integration applications and cross-compile nc:

1. Log in as root and install MySQL by using this command:

```
root@tbdev1[504]: apt-get install mysql-server
```

Read the security and update notice and click OK. When asked to remove everything below /var/lib/mysql, click No.

2. Test the MySQL server installation by using the mysql client program:

```
root@tbdev1[505]: mysql
Welcome to the MySQL monitor.  Commands end with ; or \g.
Your MySQL connection id is 2 to server version: 3.22.32-log

Type 'help' for help.
mysql> show databases;
+----------+
| Database |
+----------+
| mysql    |
| test     |
+----------+
2 rows in set (0.00 sec)

mysql> quit
Bye
```

This output shows that the MySQL server is running with access to two databases: mysql and test. We will work more with the MySQL server in the "Creating and Testing the Project Trailblazer Database" section later in this chapter.

3. Install the Apache HTTP server by using this command:

```
root@tbdev1[506]: apt-get install apache
```

4. Test the Apache server by making an HTTP connection to it with this command:

```
root@tbdev1[507]: lynx -dump http://192.168.1.11/ | head -n9


        Welcome to Your New Home in Cyberspace!

This is a placeholder page installed by the Debian
release of the Apache Web server package, because no
home page was installed on this host. You may want to
replace this as soon as possible with your own web
pages, of course....
```

This output means that the Apache HTTP server is running.

5. Install gnuplot by using this command:

```
root@tbdev1[508]: apt-get install gnuplot
```

When asked to install gnuplot setuid root, click No.

6. Test gnuplot by making a sine wave plot, using this command:

```
root@tbdev1[509]: gnuplot

        G N U P L O T
        Linux version 3.7
        patchlevel 1
        last modified Fri Oct 22 18:00:00 BST 1999

        Copyright(C) 1986 - 1993, 1998, 1999
        Thomas Williams, Colin Kelley and many others

        Type `help` to access the on-line reference manual
        The gnuplot FAQ is available from
        <http://www.ucc.ie/gnuplot/gnuplot-faq.html>

        Send comments and requests for help to
        <info-gnuplot@dartmouth.edu>
        Send bugs, suggestions and mods to
        <submit@bugs.debian.org>
```

```
Terminal type set to 'x11'
gnuplot> set terminal dumb
Terminal type set to 'dumb'
Options are 'feed 79 24'
gnuplot> plot sin(x)
```

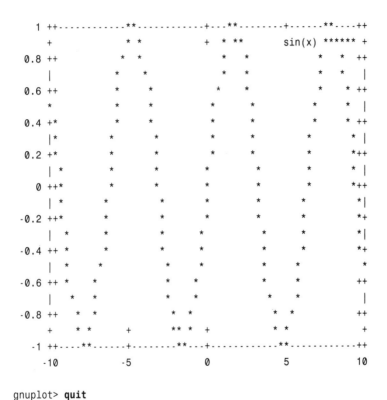

```
gnuplot> quit
```

7. Download and compile the nc program by using these commands:

```
root@tbdev1[510]: cd /root
root@tbdev1[511]: apt-get source netcat
root@tbdev1[512]: cd netcat-1.10/
root@tbdev1[514]: make linux
root@tbdev1[516]: ls -lG nc
-rwxr-xr-x    1 root          17232 Dec 30 19:27 nc
```

This version of nc is an i386 executable. Copy it to the i386 root filesystem directory:

```
root@tbdev1[519]: cp nc /tftpboot/i386-rootfs/usr/bin/
```

8. Now create an ARM cross-compiled version of nc and place it in the corresponding root filesystem for the ARM target board:

```
root@tbdev1[519]: arm-linux-gcc netcat.c
➥-o /tftpboot/arm-rootfs/usr/bin/nc
/tmp/ccb2puO2.o: In function `main':
/tmp/ccb2puO2.o(.text+0x2674): undefined reference to `res_init'
collect2: ld returned 1 exit status
```

This output shows an error in the compilation process. netcat.c requires a slight modification for cross-compiling. Edit netcat.c and search for this line:

```
#define HAVE_BIND /* ASSUMPTION -- seems to work everywhere! */
```

Add the comment characters /* to the line's start. This removes this line from compilation, like this:

```
/*#define HAVE_BIND /* ASSUMPTION -- seems to work everywhere! */
```

9. Now cross-compile nc for the ARM processor again and check the executable by using the file command:

```
root@tbdev1[521]:  arm-linux-gcc netcat.c
➥-o /tftpboot/arm-rootfs/usr/bin/nc
root@tbdev1[522]: file /tftpboot/arm-rootfs/usr/bin/nc
/tftpboot/arm-rootfs/usr/bin/nc: ELF 32-bit LSB executable,
Advanced RISC Machines ARM, version 1, dynamically linked
uses shared libs), not stripped
```

This output shows that an ARM executable called nc exists in the /tftpboot/arm-rootfs/usr/bin directory.

10. Test the ARM version of nc. Boot the MediaEngine and use nc to make an HTTP connection to tbdev1:

```
bash-2.04# echo "GET" | nc 192.168.1.11 80 | head -n15
<!DOCTYPE HTML PUBLIC "-//W3C//DTD HTML 3.2//EN">
<HTML>
<HEAD>
   <META HTTP-EQUIV="Content-Type" CONTENT="text/html;
   charset=iso-8859-1">
   <META NAME="GENERATOR" CONTENT="Mozilla/4.05 [en]
   (X11; I; Linux 2.3.99-pre3 i686) [Netscape]">
   <META NAME="Author" CONTENT="johnie@debian.org
   (Johnie Ingram)">
```

```
   <META NAME="Description" CONTENT="The initial installation of
   Debian/GNU Apache.">
   <TITLE>Welcome to Your New Home Page!</TITLE>
</HEAD>
<BODY TEXT="#000000" BGCOLOR="#FFFFFF" LINK="#0000EF"
  VLINK="#55188A" ALINK="#FF0000">


<BR>

<H1>Welcome to Your New Home in Cyberspace!</H1>
```

echo "GET" | nc 192.168.1.11 80 tells nc to pipe GET to a TCP/IP connection on tbdev1 Port 80. This should return the default Apache server Web page, index.html. As the output shows, nc running on the MediaEngine made an HTTP connection to tbdev1 and retrieved the index.html file.

11. Create a PowerPC cross-compiled version of nc and place it in the corresponding root filesystem for the PowerPC target board:

```
root@tbdev1[523]: powerpc-linux-gcc netcat.c
➥-o˙ /tftpboot/powerpc-rootfs/usr/bin/nc
root@tbdev1[524]: file /tftpboot/powerpc-rootfs/usr/bin/nc
/tftpboot/powerpc-rootfs/usr/bin/nc: ELF 32-bit MSB executable,
PowerPC or cisco 4500, version 1, dynamically linked
uses shared libs), not stripped
```

By following these steps, you have configured tbdev1 with the applications required to develop Project Trailblazer system integration.

Creating and Testing the Project Trailblazer Database

The Project Trailblazer database will store field data from various Silverjack resort locations, for access by field devices and Web services. This database consists of tables that store location, temperature, guest, access, and image information. CGI bash scripts will populate and perform queries on these tables. The trailblazerdbbuild.sql script, shown in Listing 12.1, creates the Project Trailblazer database, grants access to it, creates the database tables, and inserts some testing data.

LISTING 12.1   The trailblazerdbbuild.sql Script

```
# trailblazerdbbuild.sql v1.0 12/31/01
# www.embeddedlinuxinterfacing.com
#
# The original location of this code is
```

LISTING 12.1   Continued

```
# http://www.embeddedlinuxinterfacing.com/chapters/12/
#
# Copyright (C) 2001 by Craig Hollabaugh
#
# This program is free software; you can redistribute it and/or modify
# it under the terms of the GNU Library General Public License as
# published by the Free Software Foundation; either version 2 of the
# License, or (at your option) any later version.
#
# This program is distributed in the hope that it will be useful, but
# WITHOUT ANY WARRANTY; without even the implied warranty of
# MERCHANTABILITY or FITNESS FOR A PARTICULAR PURPOSE. See the GNU
# Library General Public License for more details.
#
# You should have received a copy of the GNU Library General Public
# License along with this program; if not, write to the
# Free Software Foundation, Inc.,
# 59 Temple Place, Suite 330, Boston, MA 02111-1307 USA

# The Project Trailblazer database uses the MySQL database engine. See
# MySQL Documentation at http://www.mysql.com/doc/ for a comprehensive
# discussion of MySQL features and functionality.

#
# As root,
# mysql < trailblazerdbbuild.sql
#

# First, we need to create the database itself
CREATE database trailblazer;

# Now grant privileges.
# grant select, insert and update privileges on all trailblazer database
# tables to a user called trailblazer who must access the database
# from the host running the database. This user, trailblazer, has a
# password tb.
GRANT SELECT, INSERT, UPDATE on trailblazer.*
                                to trailblazer@localhost identified by 'tb';

# start using the trailblazer database
USE trailblazer;
```

LISTING 12.1 Continued

```
# create the locations table
# This table stores Silverjack location information
CREATE TABLE locations (
  location smallint DEFAULT '0' NOT NULL,  # this last IP address octet
  description char(30),                    # text description of location
  PRIMARY KEY (location)                   # the table's key
);

# insert some testing data into locations table
INSERT INTO locations VALUES (30,'Lift 1 Base');
INSERT INTO locations VALUES (31,'Lift 1 Top');
INSERT INTO locations VALUES (32,'Lift 4 Base');
INSERT INTO locations VALUES (33,'Lift 4 Top');
INSERT INTO locations VALUES (34,'Lift 9 Base');
INSERT INTO locations VALUES (35,'Lift 9 Top');

# create the guests table
# This table stores Silverjack guest information
CREATE TABLE guests (
  timestamp timestamp(14),               # record creation timestamp
  first char(20),                        # guest first name
  last char(20),                         # guest last name
  passID char(20) NOT NULL,              # their pass' number
  passValid tinyint,                     # is the pass valid or not?
  PRIMARY KEY (passID)                   # the table's key
);

# insert some testing data into guests table
INSERT INTO guests VALUES (20011227130620,'Melanie','Kline',  1000,1);
INSERT INTO guests VALUES (20011227130649,'Robert','Cort',    1001,1);
INSERT INTO guests VALUES (20011227130720,'John',   'Stephen',1002,1);
INSERT INTO guests VALUES (20011227130729,'Scott',  'Kidner', 1003,1);
INSERT INTO guests VALUES (20011227133729,'Maggi',  'Ann',    1004,0);

# create the accesses table
# This table stores Silverjack access information. For example,
# if a guest accesses lift 1, an entry for that access is stored
# here.
CREATE TABLE accesses (
  timestamp timestamp(14), # timestamp of access
  location smallint,       # the access location
```

LISTING 12.1   Continued

```
  passID char(20)            # the pass that accessed the location
);

# insert some testing data into accesses table
INSERT INTO accesses VALUES (20011227133001,30,1000);
INSERT INTO accesses VALUES (20011227133006,30,1001);
INSERT INTO accesses VALUES (20011227133008,30,1002);
INSERT INTO accesses VALUES (20011227133010,30,1003);
INSERT INTO accesses VALUES (20011227134311,34,1000);
INSERT INTO accesses VALUES (20011227134327,34,1003);
INSERT INTO accesses VALUES (20011227135323,32,1002);
INSERT INTO accesses VALUES (20011227135354,32,1001);

# create the images table
# This table stores Silverjack image information. When a field
# device stores an image file, it will inform the database of
# that storage with location and filename.

CREATE TABLE images (
  timestamp timestamp(14),    # timestamp of image storage
  location smallint,          # the image location
  filename char(30)           # the image filename
);

# create the temperatures table
# This table stores Silverjack temperature information.

CREATE TABLE temperatures (
  timestamp timestamp(14),    # timestamp of temperature storage
  location smallint,          # the temperature location
  temperature tinyint         # the actual temperature
);

# insert some testing data into temperatures table
INSERT INTO temperatures VALUES (20011229000000,30,32);
INSERT INTO temperatures VALUES (20011229040000,30,10);
INSERT INTO temperatures VALUES (20011229080000,30,15);
INSERT INTO temperatures VALUES (20011229120000,30,20);
INSERT INTO temperatures VALUES (20011229160000,30,25);
INSERT INTO temperatures VALUES (20011229200000,30,27);
INSERT INTO temperatures VALUES (20011230000000,30,30);
```

You can use the following steps to create and test the Project Trailblazer database on tbdev1:

1. Log in as root and download the `trailblazerdbbuild.sql` script from the Web site www.embeddedlinuxinterfacing.com:

```
root@tbdev1[503]: cd /root
root@tbdev1[504]: wget http://www.embeddedlinuxinterfacing.com/chapters
➥/12/trailblazerdbbuild.sql
```

2. Using the `trailblazerdbbuild.sql` script, create the Project Trailblazer database:

```
root@tbdev1[505]: mysql < trailblazerdbbuild.sql
```

3. Now perform a simple database query to determine whether the test temperature entries exist with this command:

```
root@tbdev1[506]: echo "select * from temperatures;" | mysql trailblazer
timestamp       location     temperature
20011229000000  30           32
20011229040000  30           10
20011229080000  30           15
20011229120000  30           20
20011229160000  30           25
20011229200000  30           27
20011230000000  30           30
```

This results shows the seven correct test temperatures contained in the database.

4. Now perform a database query with inner joins on multiple tables with this command:

```
root@tbdev1[508]: echo "select \
guests.first, guests.last, locations.description, accesses.timestamp \
from guests,accesses,locations \
where guests.passID = accesses.passID and \
locations.location = accesses.location \
order by accesses.timestamp;" | mysql trailblazer
first    last     description    timestamp
Melanie  Kline    Lift 1 Base    20011227133001
Robert   Cort     Lift 1 Base    20011227133006
John     Stephen  Lift 1 Base    20011227133008
Scott    Kidner   Lift 1 Base    20011227133010
```

```
Melanie Kline   Lift 9 Base   20011227134311
Scott   Kidner  Lift 9 Base   20011227134327
John    Stephen Lift 4 Base   20011227135323
Robert  Cort    Lift 4 Base   20011227135354
```

This query shows four guests accessing three lifts which is also correct.

TIP

You can use the command `mysqldump` to obtain a text file that contains a database's definition and data. You can use this file to back up or re-create a database. The `trailblazerdbbuild.sql` script is an edited version of a `mysqldump` output file.

Developing the Target and CGI Integration Scripts

With the Project Trailblazer database created, populated with test data, and queried, you are ready to move on to developing the Project Trailblazer target and CGI integration scripts.

Collecting and Distributing Temperature Data

The collection and storage of temperature data requires two bash scripts:

- **temperatureReport**—The collection script `temperatureReport`, shown in Listing 12.2, executes continuously on a target board, periodically communicates with an external temperature sensor, and then reports the temperature value via an HTTP connection. The target board's `init` program or a startup script starts the `temperatureReport` script.

- **temperatureRecord**—The database storage script `temperatureRecord`, shown in Listing 12.3, executes as an on-demand CGI script, receives the temperature value, and then sends a formulated database query to the Project Trailblazer database.

LISTING 12.2   The `temperatureReport` Temperature Collection bash Script

```
#!/bin/bash
# temperatureReport v1.0 12/31/01
# www.embeddedlinuxinterfacing.com
#
# The original location of this code is
# http://www.embeddedlinuxinterfacing.com/chapters/12/
#
```

LISTING 12.2   Continued

```
# Copyright (C) 2001 by Craig Hollabaugh
#
# This program is free software; you can redistribute it and/or modify
# it however you want.
#
# temperatureReport
# temperatureReport is a bash script that executes on a target board
# with an external temperature sensor and its module loaded. Loading
# the module, such as LM70_x86.o from Chapter 10 creates the
# /proc/trailblazer/temperature file. This script gets the current
# temperature from /proc/trailblazer/temperature, forms an HTTP GET
# query using temperatureRecord with the temperature as the
# parameter. This query is piped into nc which makes a TCP connection
# to tbdev1's apache HTTP server on port 80. nc is configured with
# the -w flag which sets a connection timeout. If tbdev1's apache
# server doesn't answer, this script will continue to operate.
#
# Call this from inittab using the respawn option as in
# T3:23:respawn:/usr/bin/temperatureReport
# If temperatureReport should die, init will start it again
#
# loop forever
while [ 1 ]
do

# get temp
 temperature=`cat /proc/trailblazer/temperature`

# form the query and pipe to nc
 echo "GET /cgi-bin/temperatureRecord?$temperature" \
     | nc -w 10 192.168.1.11 80

# print out temperature
 echo $temperature

# pause for 5 minutes
 sleep 300
done
```

TIP

You can configure the Linux `init` program to start a target board's bash scripts. If you use the respawn option, `init` restarts the script when it terminates. This is a simple way to ensure that your scripts are always running. Here's an example line from `init`'s configuration file `/etc/inittab` to respawn a bash script:

`T3:23:respawn:/root/temperatureReport`

LISTING 12.3   The `temperatureRecord` Database Storage bash Script

```
#!/bin/bash
# temperatureRecord v1.0 12/31/01
# www.embeddedlinuxinterfacing.com
#
# The original location of this code is
# http://www.embeddedlinuxinterfacing.com/chapters/12/
#
# Copyright (C) 2001 by Craig Hollabaugh
#
# This program is free software; you can redistribute it and/or modify
# it however you want.
#
# temperatureRecord
# temperatureRecord is a CGI script. A field target board sends an
# HTTP request with the temperature as a parameter.
# Apache calls this script setting the $QUERY_STRING variable to the
# temperature and $REMOTE_ADDR variable to the sender's IP address.
# This script extracts the last octet of the IP address using it
# as the location number in an INSERT statement.
#
# Here's the header/content blank separation line required by Apache
echo

# Extract the last octet from the sender's IP address, use this
# as for the location number.
location=`echo $REMOTE_ADDR | cut -f 4 -d '.'`

# Get the temperature sent by the target board
temperature=$QUERY_STRING

# Form the INSERT statement and pipe it to mysql.
# You have to login in to mysql as trailblazer with
```

LISTING 12.3   Continued

```
# password tb because apache will execute this script as
# user www-data not root.
echo "INSERT INTO temperatures (location,temperature) \
    VALUES ($location,$temperature);" | \
    mysql trailblazer --user=trailblazer --pass=tb
```

TIP

The Apache HTTP server sets the following bash environment variables before a CGI script is executed: DOCUMENT_ROOT, HTTP_ACCEPT, HTTP_ACCEPT_ENCODING, HTTP_ACCEPT_LANGUAGE, HTTP_CONNECTION, HTTP_HOST, HTTP_REFERRER, HTTP_USER_AGENT, PATH, REMOTE_ADDR, REMOTE_PORT, SCRIPT_FILENAME, SERVER_ADDR, SERVER_ADMIN, SERVER_NAME, SERVER_PORT, SERVER_SIGNATURE, SERVER_SOFTWARE, SERVER_SOFTWARE, SERVER_PROTOCOL, REQUEST_METHOD, QUERY_STRING, REQUEST_URI, and SCRIPT_NAME. To see some sample values for these variables, go to www.embeddedlinuxinterfacing.com/cgi-bin/environment.

Three bash CGI scripts handle the distribution of stored temperature data via an HTTP connection:

- **temperatureGetLast**—This script, shown in Listing 12.4, accepts a location parameter and returns that location's last recorded temperature.

- **temperatureGetTable**—This script, shown in Listing 12.5, accepts a location parameter and returns a table of that location's recorded temperatures.

- **temperatureGetPlot**—This script, shown in Listing 12.6, accepts a location parameter and returns a portable network graphics (PNG) plot of that location's recorded temperatures.

LISTING 12.4   The temperatureGetLast Temperature Distribution bash Script

```
#!/bin/bash
# temperatureGetLast v1.0 12/31/01
# www.embeddedlinuxinterfacing.com
#
# The original location of this code is
# http://www.embeddedlinuxinterfacing.com/chapters/12/
#
# Copyright (C) 2001 by Craig Hollabaugh
#
```

LISTING 12.4   Continued

```
# This program is free software; you can redistribute it and/or modify
# it however you want.
#
# temperatureGetLast
# temperatureGetLast is a CGI script. A field target board or web service
# sends an HTTP request with a Trailblazer location number
# as a parameter. Apache calls this script setting the $QUERY_STRING
# variable to the location number. This script forms a SELECT statement
# that returns the last recorded temperature for that location.
#
# Here's the header/content blank separation line required by Apache
echo


# Set the location
location=$QUERY_STRING



# Form the SELECT statement and pipe it to mysql.
# You have to login in to mysql as trailblazer with
# password tb because apache will execute this script as
# user www-data not root.
echo "SELECT temperature from temperatures where location = $location \
      order by timestamp desc limit 0,1" | \
      mysql trailblazer --user=trailblazer --pass=tb --silent
```

LISTING 12.5   The temperatureGetTable Temperature Distribution bash Script

```
#!/bin/bash
# temperatureGetTable v1.0 12/31/01
# www.embeddedlinuxinterfacing.com
#
# The original location of this code is
# http://www.embeddedlinuxinterfacing.com/chapters/12/
#
# Copyright (C) 2001 by Craig Hollabaugh
#
# This program is free software; you can redistribute it and/or modify
# it however you want.
#
# temperatureGetTable
```

LISTING 12.5   Continued

```
# temperatureGetTable is a CGI script. A web service sends an HTTP
# request with a Trailblazer location number as a parameter.
# Apache calls this script setting the $QUERY_STRING
# variable to the location number. This script forms a SELECT statement
# that returns a temperature table for that location.
#
# Here's the header/content blank separation line required by Apache
echo

# Set the location
location=$QUERY_STRING

# Form the SELECT statement and pipe it to mysql.
# You have to login in to mysql as trailblazer with
# password tb because apache will execute this script as
# user www-data not root.
echo "SELECT timestamp, temperature from temperatures where \
     location = $location order by timestamp asc;" | \
     mysql trailblazer --user=trailblazer --pass=tb --silent
```

LISTING 12.6   The `temperatureGetPlot` Temperature Distribution bash Script

```
#!/bin/bash
# temperatureGetPlot v1.0 12/31/01
# www.embeddedlinuxinterfacing.com
#
# The original location of this code is
# http://www.embeddedlinuxinterfacing.com/chapters/12/
#
# Copyright (C) 2001 by Craig Hollabaugh
#
# This program is free software; you can redistribute it and/or modify
# it however you want.
#
# temperatureGetPlot
# temperatureGetPlot is a CGI script. A web service sends an HTTP
# request with a Trailblazer location number as a parameter.
# Apache calls this script setting the $QUERY_STRING variable
# to the location number. This script forms a SELECT statement
# that returns a table of record temperatures for the location. The
# script then calls gnuplot to plot these temperatures, creating
```

LISTING 12.6   Continued

```
# and outputting a png image.
#
# Here's the Content-type line to tell the browser that this reply
# is a png image.
echo Content-type: image/png

# Here's the header/content blank separation line required by Apache
echo

# Set the location
location=$QUERY_STRING

# Form the SELECT statement and pipe it to mysql.
# You have to login in to mysql as trailblazer with
# password tb because apache will execute this script as
# user www-data not root. Redirect the output to a temp file.
echo "SELECT timestamp, temperature from temperatures where \
      location = $location order by timestamp asc;" | \
      mysql trailblazer --user=trailblazer --pass=tb --silent > /tmp/tempdata


# Query the database for the location description for use in plot title
locationdes=`echo "SELECT description from locations where \
            location = $location;" | \
            mysql trailblazer --user=trailblazer --pass=tb --silent`

# Execute gnuplot, send various commands to set up plot, then plot
# the temperatures from the temp data file. See http://www.gnuplot.vt.edu/
# for more gnuplot information.
/usr/bin/gnuplot << ENDOFINPUT
set terminal png color
set xdata time
set timefmt "%Y%m%d%H%M%S"
set format x "%m/%d\n%H:%M"
set nokey
set title "$locationdes Temperature"
set ylabel "Temperature (F)"
set xlabel "Date - Time"
set grid
set rmargin 5
plot "/tmp/tempdata" using 1:2 with linespoints
ENDOFINPUT
```

Because the Project Trailblazer database was generated with test data (refer to Listing 12.1), you can test the temperatureGetLast, temperatureGetTable, and temperatureGetPlot scripts. You can use the following commands to download and test these scripts on tbdev1:

```
root@tbdev1[514]: cd /usr/lib/cgi-bin
root@tbdev1[515]: wget http://www.embeddedlinuxinterfacing.com/chapters/12/
➥temperatureGetLast
root@tbdev1[516]: wget http://www.embeddedlinuxinterfacing.com/chapters/12/
➥temperatureGetTable
root@tbdev1[517]: wget http://www.embeddedlinuxinterfacing.com/chapters/12/
➥temperatureGetPlot
root@tbdev1[518]: chmod 755 /usr/lib/cgi-bin/temp*
root@tbdev1[519]: echo "GET /cgi-bin/temperatureGetLast?30" |
➥nc 192.168.1.11 80
30
root@tbdev1[520]: echo "GET /cgi-bin/temperatureGetTable?30" |
➥nc 192.168.1.11 80
20011229000000   32
20011229040000   10
20011229080000   15
20011229120000   20
20011229160000   25
20011229200000   27
20011230000000   30
```

You need to use a browser to test temperatureGetPlot because it returns a PNG plot. Enter this URL in your browser:

http://192.168.1.11/cgi-bin/temperatureGetPlot?30

You should see the plot shown in Figure 12.2. Notice in this figure that when you queried for location 30 (which is Lift 1 Base), the temperatureGetPlot script correctly generated the plot's title, Lift 1 Base Temperature.

Collecting and Distributing Image Data

The Project Trailblazer requirements call for image collection at the base and top of each lift, as well as at other Silverjack locations, for a total of more than 20 target boards with cameras. The image-grabbing software vgrabbj, which is explained in Chapter 8, "USB Interfacing," performs a text overlay operation that labels an image with location and timestamp information. The Project Trailblazer engineers wanted to use this overlay functionality, but it would require individual configuration for each camera-equipped target board. For example, the bash script executing on the target board at the top of Lift 1 would contain the text `Lift 1 Top` as the `vgrabbj` overlay command-line parameter. Likewise, the script executing at the top of Lift 2 would contain `Lift 2 Top`.

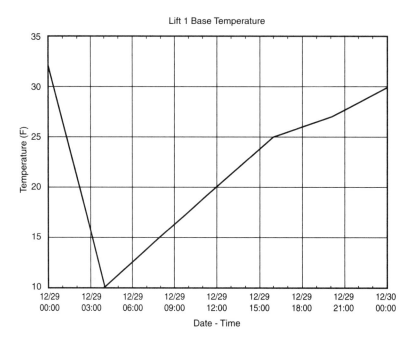

FIGURE 12.2   The Lift 1 Base Temperature Plot, with test data.

You could store location information in a configuration file on each target board's root filesystem. A bash script could open this file to determine what location text to use in the overlay. However, using a file still requires a unique location configuration for each image target board. The engineers wanted to stay away from unique configurations on each board because it is time-consuming and potentially leads to problems. Taking a unique configuration approach requires complete and up-to-date project documentation. The Silverjack technicians who maintain field equipment will require additional training. They will need to learn how to configure the target boards properly before field installation. Image collection is more than a convenience; it's a safety system. Configuration mistakes result in system downtime, which could potentially put guests and employees in dangerous situations. The engineers wanted to design an image collection system that required no unique configuration for each target board.

The engineers decided to use the Project Trailblazer database in an innovative way. They developed a target board bash script called imageReport, shown in Listing 12.7. imageReport queries the Silverjack database for the vgrabbj command. The server returns a unique vgrabbj command that the imageReport script then executes. The Apache HTTP server passes the target board's IP address to CGI scripts in the $REMOTE_ADDR variable. A CGI script called imageGetCommand, shown in Listing 12.8, performs a database query, using the target's IP address, to determine the board's location description. The imageGetCommand CGI script then returns to the target board a complete vgrabbj command with the overlay command-line parameter set to the board's location, current time and date, and the output filename parameter set to a unique filename. The imageReport script executes this unique command and creates a unique image file with the appropriate overlay. Through use of the imageGetCommand CGI script, every camera-equipped target board executes the same imageReport script and therefore, the target boards do not require unique configuration.

LISTING 12.7   The imageReport bash Script

```
#!/bin/bash
# imageReport v1.0 12/31/01
# www.embeddedlinuxinterfacing.com
#
# The original location of this code is
# http://www.embeddedlinuxinterfacing.com/chapters/12/
#
# Copyright (C) 2001 by Craig Hollabaugh
#
# This program is free software; you can redistribute it and/or modify
# it however you want.
#
# imageReport
# imageReport is a bash script that executes on a target board
# with an external video camera and its driver loaded. Loading
# the driver, connects the camera to the /dev/video file.
#
# This script queries the tbdev1's apache HTTP server on port 80
# using nc to obtain the image command. It then executes this command.
# The command is formatted with all the command line parameters
# for the specific target based on based on the target's IP address.
# nc is configured with the -w flag which sets a connection timeout.
# If tbdev1's apache server doesn't answer, this script will continue
# to operate.
#
```

LISTING 12.7   Continued

```
# The image command will also contain a sleep statement to pause
# the main loop.
#
# Call this from inittab using the respawn option as in
# T3:23:respawn:/usr/bin/imageReport
# If imageReport should die, init will start it again
#
# loop forever
while [ 1 ]
do

# get the command
 imageCommand=`echo "GET /cgi-bin/imageGetCommand" \
              | nc -w 10 192.168.1.11 80`

# execute the command and produce no output
 eval $imageCommand > /dev/null 2>&1

done
```

LISTING 12.8   The imageGetCommand bash CGI Script

```
#!/bin/bash
# imageGetCommand v1.0 12/31/01
# www.embeddedlinuxinterfacing.com
#
# The original location of this code is
# http://www.embeddedlinuxinterfacing.com/chapters/12/
#
# Copyright (C) 2001 by Craig Hollabaugh
#
# This program is free software; you can redistribute it and/or modify
# it however you want.
#
# imageGetCommand
# imageGetCommand is a CGI script. A field target board
# sends an HTTP request to retrieve an complete image capture command.
# For Project Trailblazer, we are using the vgrabbj program. This
# script performs a query for location description using the target's
# IP address contained in the $REMOTE_ADDR variable. The script then
```

LISTING 12.8 Continued

```
# returns a completely formatted bash command that includes a unique
# filename for the capture output and an overlay parameter that contains
# location, current time and date information.
#
# The command also contains a sleep statement to pause the script main
# loop running on the target. The sleep value could be changed dynamically
# based on time of day. Here it is set to 300 seconds or 5 minutes.
DELAY=300
#
# This script also logs this request in the Trailblazer database image
# table. Web queries use these image entries to find the latest image
# from a location.
#
# Here's the header/content blank separation line required by Apache
echo

# get the last octet of the target's IP address
location=`echo $REMOTE_ADDR | cut -f 4 -d '.'`

# query the database for the target boards location description
locationdes=`echo "SELECT description from locations where \
            location = $location;" | \
            mysql trailblazer --user=trailblazer --pass=tb --silent`

# output the image command and the sleep statement
filename=`printf "%03d-%s.jpg" $location \`date +%Y%m%d%H%M%S\``
printf "vgrabbj -e -i vga -f /tmp/$filename"
printf " -p \"%s - %s\" -T 20 -a 5 -m 50; sleep $DELAY\n" \
        "$locationdes" "`date +%A\,\ %D\,\ %r`"

# Here's an example output
# vgrabbj -e -i vga -f /tmp/030-20020102000919.jpg -p \
# "Lift 1 Base - Wednesday, 01/02/02, 12:09:19 AM" -T 20 -a 5 -m 50

# Here are the vgrabbj command line options used
#-e       Enables the timestamp
#-i vga   Sets the image size to 640x480
#-f       Writes to an output file instead of to stdout
#-p       Defines the overlay in timestamp format
#-T       Sets the overlay font size
#-a       Sets the overlay alignment on the image
```

LISTING 12.8   Continued

```
#-m      Sets the overlay blending with the original image

# log this query
echo "INSERT INTO images (location,filename) \
     VALUES ($location,\"$filename\");" | \
     mysql trailblazer --user=trailblazer --pass=Trailblazer
```

Using the Network File System (NFS), the target boards mount their root filesystems from the server. (See Chapter 5, "Debugging," for more information about NFS and root filesystem mounting.) When the `imageReport` script evaluates `$imageCommand`, `vgrabbj` writes the image file to the target board's `/tmp` directory, which is also the server's `/tftpboot/i386-rootfs/tmp` directory. When the `imageGetCommand` CGI script is executed, it returns `imageCommand` with a unique filename and also logs this filename in the Project Trailblazer database `images` table. Another CGI script, `imageGetLast`, shown in Listing 12.9, queries the `images` table for the last recorded image at a specific location. The `imageGetLast` script returns the appropriate image file contained in the `/tftpboot/i386-rootfs/tmp` directory.

TIP

If your target board does not mount its root filesystem using NFS, you can use `nc`, `ftp`, `rcp`, `scp`, or `lynx` to copy files from the target board to the server. These programs need to be cross-compiled if the target board doesn't use an x86 processor.

LISTING 12.9   The imageGetLast bash CGI Script

```
#!/bin/bash
# imageGetLast v1.0 12/31/01
# www.embeddedlinuxinterfacing.com
#
# The original location of this code is
# http://www.embeddedlinuxinterfacing.com/chapters/12/
#
# Copyright (C) 2001 by Craig Hollabaugh
#
# This program is free software; you can redistribute it and/or modify
# it however you want.
#
# imageGetLast
# imageGetLast is a CGI script. A web service sends an HTTP
```

LISTING 12.9   Continued

```
# request with a Trailblazer location number as a parameter.
# Apache calls this script setting the $QUERY_STRING variable
# to the location number. This script forms a SELECT statement
# that returns the filename stored in /tftpboot/i386-rootfs/tmp.
#
# Here's the Content-type line to tell the browser that this reply
# is a jpg image.
echo Content-type: image/jpeg

# Here's the header/content blank separation line required by Apache
echo

# Set the location
location=$QUERY_STRING

# Form the SELECT statement and pipe it to mysql.
# You have to login in to mysql as trailblazer with
# password tb because apache will execute this script as
# user www-data not root. Redirect the output to a temp file.
filename=`echo "SELECT filename from images where location = $location \
     order by timestamp desc limit 0,1" | \
     mysql trailblazer --user=trailblazer --pass=tb --silent`

# cat the file out to the browser
cat /tftpboot/i386-rootfs/tmp/$filename
```

You can test the `imageGetCommand` CGI script by using these commands:

```
root@tbdev1[509]: imageCommand=`echo "GET /cgi-bin/imageGetCommand"
➥| nc -w 10 192.168.1.11 80`
root@tbdev1[510]: echo $imageCommand
vgrabbj -e -i vga -f /tmp/011-20020118142244.jpg -p
➥"tbdev1 - Friday, 01/18/02, 02:22:44 PM" -T 20 -a 5 -m 50;
➥sleep 300
```

This shows that the `imageGetCommand` CGI script returned a `vgrabbj` command with unique location identifier, `tbdev1`, in the text overlay parameter and a unique filename, `/tmp/011-20020118142244.jpg`, in the output filename parameter.

You can execute $imageCommand by using this command:

```
root@tbdev1[508]: eval $imageCommand
Reading image from /dev/video
```

vgrabbj captures an image and creates the /tmp/011-20020118142244.jpg image file.

Collecting Guest Pass Identification and Allowing Lift Access

The Project Trailblazer lift access point design uses radio frequency identification (RFID) readers from ESPTech. Each guest's daily or season pass contains an RFID tag that emits a unique 20-character identification string that is read when it is near the RFID reader. When the pass is purchased, a unique ID string is generated and the pass's tag is programmed with the ID. This process also creates an entry in the Project Trailblazer database guests table.

A guest who wants to gain lift access presents his or her pass to the lift access point. The pass's tag emits the guest's unique ID string, which the RFID reader reads and passes via an asynchronous serial link to the access point's target board. The bash script accessPointControl, shown in Listing 12.10, that is executing on the target board reads this unique ID and then queries the Trailblazer database for pass validity. If the pass is valid, the accessPointControl script turns on the access point's green light for 5 seconds, permitting guest access to the lift. If the pass is not valid, the script turns on the access point's red light. The accessAllow CGI script, shown in Listing 12.11, not only returns pass validity information but also logs guest lift access.

LISTING 12.10   The accessPointControl bash Script

```
#!/bin/bash
# accessPointControl v1.0 12/31/01
# www.embeddedlinuxinterfacing.com
#
# The original location of this code is
# http://www.embeddedlinuxinterfacing.com/chapters/12/
#
# Copyright (C) 2001 by Craig Hollabaugh
#
# This program is free software; you can redistribute it and/or modify
# it however you want.
#
# accessPointControl
# accessPointControl is a bash script that executes on a target board
# that controls a lift access point. This script receives the guest
```

LISTING 12.10   Continued

```
# pass ID from the RFID tag reader over serial port 0 (ttyS0). It
# queries the database for pass validity and controls the red light
# green light circuit connected to ttyS0's DTR signal.
#
# Call this from inittab using the respawn option as in
# T3:23:respawn:/usr/bin/accessPointControl
# If accessPointControl should die, init will start it again
#
# loop forever
while [ 1 ]
do

# Get the passID
# The RFID tag reader just outputs the ID when received, no
# need to send it a command to get the ID. This command sets the timeout
# at 2 seconds.
 passID=`querySerial /dev/ttyS0 19200 2000 ''`

 if [ -n "$passID" ] # if passID is not empty. querySerial returned nothing
 then
  # query the database. it will return
  # 1(valid), 0(not valid), or blank (unknown id)
  valid=`echo "GET /cgi-bin/accessAllow?$passID" | nc -w 10 192.168.1.11 80`

  if [ -n "$valid" ] # if valid is not blank
  then
  if [ "$valid" = "1" ] # we have a valid pass, allow access to lift
  then
   # turn green light on for 5 seconds
   setSerialSignal /dev/ttyS0 1 0
   sleep 5
  fi

  # turn red light on
  setSerialSignal /dev/ttyS0 0 0
 fi
 fi
done
```

LISTING 12.11   The accessAllow bash CGI Script

```bash
#!/bin/bash
# accessAllow v1.0 12/31/01
# www.embeddedlinuxinterfacing.com
#
# The original location of this code is
# http://www.embeddedlinuxinterfacing.com/chapters/12/
#
# Copyright (C) 2001 by Craig Hollabaugh
#
# This program is free software; you can redistribute it and/or modify
# it however you want.
#
# accessAllow
# accessAllow is a CGI script. A target board sends an HTTP
# request with a pass RFID as a the parameter.
# Apache calls this script setting the $QUERY_STRING variable
# to the pass RFID. This script forms a SELECT statement
# that returns whether the pass is valid or not (1 or 0). This
# script also logs the access.
#
# Here's the header/content blank separation line required by Apache
echo

# get the location as the last octet of the target board's IP address
location=`echo $REMOTE_ADDR | cut -f 4 -d '.'`

# get the pass ID
passID=$QUERY_STRING

# query the database for the pass valid field for this passID
echo "SELECT guests.passValid from guests where passID = \"$passID\";" \
| mysql trailblazer --user=trailblazer --pass=tb --silent

# log the access
echo "INSERT INTO accesses (location,passID) VALUES ($location,\"$passID\");" \
| mysql trailblazer --user=trailblazer --pass=tb
```

You can test the accessPointControl and accessAllow scripts without having an
ESPTech RFID reader or tags. In Chapter 6, "Asynchronous Serial Communication
Interfacing," you tested the querySerial program, using minicom, ttyS1, and a null

modem cable. That same configuration works here. The Project Trailblazer database contains test data for guests, including pass identification and pass validity information. Of the five guests in the database, four have valid IDs (1000, 1001, 1002, and 1003) and one has an invalid ID (1004). (Refer to Listing 12.1 for more information.)

You can test the `accessPointControl` and `accessAllow` scripts by using the following instructions on `tbdev1`:

1. Connect a null modem cable between COM1 and COM2 on `tbdev1`.

2. Log in as root on two consoles, using Alt+F1 and Alt+F2.

3. On Console 1, download the `accessAllow` CGI script, using these commands:

```
root@tbdev1[508]: cd /usr/lib/cgi-bin/
root@tbdev1[509]: wget http://www.embeddedlinuxinterfacing.com/
↪chapters/12/accessAllow
root@tbdev1[510]: chmod 755 accessAllow
```

4. Now test the `accessAllow` script by querying for the valid user 1003 and the invalid user 1004:

```
root@tbdev1[511]: echo "GET /cgi-bin/accessAllow?1003" |
↪nc 192.168.1.11 80
1
root@tbdev1[512]: echo "GET /cgi-bin/accessAllow?1004" |
↪nc 192.168.1.11 80
0
```

The `accessAllow` CGI script returns 1 for a valid user and 0 for an invalid user. For user IDs that are not in the database, `accessAllow` returns blank:

```
root@tbdev1[513]: echo "GET /cgi-bin/accessAllow?1234" |
↪nc 192.168.1.11 80
root@tbdev1[514]:
```

5. Now download the `accessPointControl` script, using these commands:

```
root@tbdev1[514]: cd /root
root@tbdev1[515]: wget http://www.embeddedlinuxinterfacing.com/
↪chapters/12/accessPointControl
root@tbdev1[516]: chmod 755 accessPointControl
root@tbdev1[517]: ./accessPointControl
```

6. Connect a voltmeter to COM1's DTR signal on DB-9 Connector Pin 4. It should read between +3V and +15V. This is Logic Level 0. Your lift access light should be displaying a red light.

7. Switch to Console 2 (by pressing Alt+F2) and run `minicom`. The `accessPointControl` script executes the `querySerial` command on `ttyS0` at a data rate of 19,200 bits per second. Configure `minicom`'s serial port setting (by pressing Ctrl+A and then O) for operation on `ttyS1` at 19,200 bits per second, 8 data bits, parity none, and 1 stop bit. You will be sending characters from `ttyS1` to `ttyS0`.

8. You are ready to test the lift access system by emulating the RFID reader. In the `minicom` window, quickly type the characters **1000**. The `ttyS1` serial port transmits these characters, to be received by `ttyS0`. The `accessPointControl` script's `querySerial` command should read and return these characters to the `passID` variable. You need to quickly type **1000** because the timeout on the `querySerial` command is set to 2 seconds. The `accessPointControl` script forms and sends a query to the Project Trailblazer database via the `accessAllow` CGI script. The reply, in the case of characters **1000**, should be **1** because a guest with `passID` set to **1000** has a valid pass. The `accessPointControl` script then sets `ttyS0`'s DTR line for 5 seconds, using the `setSerialSignal` command. Your voltmeter should read between –3V and –15V, which is Logic Level 1. Your lift access light should be displaying a green light, allowing access to the lift.

9. After 5 seconds, the `accessPointControl` script clears the DTR signal, and your voltmeter should again read +3V to +15V, meaning Logic Level 0 (that is, the access point's red light would be on).

10. Now try entering an invalid ID. In the `minicom` window, quickly type **1004**. Your voltmeter reading should remain constant, meaning that a valid pass ID was not found.

11. You can query the Project Trailblazer database to check for the access attempts you just simulated, by using this command:

```
root@tbdev1[522]: echo "select * from accesses;" | mysql trailblazer
timestamp       location        passID
20020102205858  11              1000
20020102205909  11              1004
```

This query output shows the access simulations you just performed, using pass IDs 1000 and 1004 from Location 11 (that is, `tbdev1`). Remember that the Silverjack location number is the last octet in the target board's IP address. In this case, `tbdev1` was acting as an access point. Therefore, the location 11 is correct because `tbdev1`'s IP address is 192.168.1.11. Notice also that the access table in the Project Trailblazer database only logs the access timestamp, location, and pass ID; it does not store whether an attempt was successful or unsuccessful.

Summary

The Project Trailblazer engineers started with a collection of high-level requirements. Nine of these addressed safety and the Operations Department's need for automation. In this chapter, the engineers developed a system integration infrastructure using bash, nc, Apache, and MySQL, and then implemented and tested scripts for temperature data, image data, and lift access control. For each solution, the engineers developed an area within the infrastructure.

The temperature collection, storage, and distribution scripts form the foundation for data storage and presentation. Using gnuplot along with database queries forms a powerful visualization tool for representation of field data. The scripts the engineers developed for temperature data can easily be extended to handle lift monitoring, guest messaging, and race timing.

The image collection scripts introduce an innovative mechanism for target board autoconfiguration. Similarly configured field devices coupled to a database can dynamically create location-specific information. Using this approach in applications that have large numbers of field devices dramatically reduces configuration complexity and deployment time.

The access point scripts control field hardware that is based on database data values. These hardware control scripts can be extended to control music playback and snow-making equipment.

The combination of bash scripts, nc, Apache, and MySQL creates a rich system integration development environment. With the database as a centerpiece for integration, implementing system-wide applications is a matter of simple scripting. You can see an example of this by counting the number of executable lines in the access control scripts. In 22 executable lines of code, a complete access control application fulfills the guest authentication system requirement. The other scripts shown in this chapter are similarly simple and short. Simplicity makes systems reliable. Use of bash, nc, Apache, and MySQL greatly simplifies system development, and embedded Linux makes all this possible.

Additional Reading

1. Chet Ramey and Brian Fox, *Bash Reference Manual,* www.gnu.org/manual/bash.

2. Mendel Cooper, *Advanced Bash-Scripting Guide,* www.linuxdoc.org/LDP/abs/html.

3. The Apache Software Foundation Web site, www.apache.org.

4. MySQL Speed, Power and Precision Web site, www.mysql.com.

5. Gnuplot Central Web site, www.gnuplot.vt.edu.

13

Final Thoughts

This book presents a number of embedded Linux topics for use in automation projects. Chapter 2, "System Architecture," introduces you to Project Trailblazer and sets the direction for the book's technical content. Chapters 3, "Selecting a Platform and Installing Tool Sets," 4, "Booting Linux," and 5, "Debugging," help you to build a development workstation, the GNU toolchain, and a cross-platform remote debugging environment. The remaining chapters show you how to interface various hardware field devices to the Project Trailblazer target boards, using Linux for data acquisition and control. All this information forms a foundation for embedded Linux that you can use in your own designs.

This chapter briefly discusses GUI development, real-time capabilities, and embedded Linux vendor offerings. These topics were not used in Project Trailblazer but might be important for your design. The chapter concludes with a discussion that summarizes the performance of the Project Trailblazer hardware.

GUI Development

Your applications will undoubtedly include additional technologies that build on the foundation laid in this book. You might need to use windowing software to develop easy-to-use customer solutions for set-top boxes, point-of-sale systems, human–machine interfaces, and graphical user interfaces.

The X Window system powers the Linux desktop but not embedded devices. Its storage and CPU requirements exceed the capabilities of most embedded hardware designs. Fortunately, numerous solutions exist, each providing a windowing system for embedded Linux GUI development.[1] If your product requires graphics, a variety of options are available for your design (for example, Microwindows, Qt/Embedded, GtkFB, PicoGUI, Micro-X).

Real-time Capabilities

Since its inception as an embedded operating system, Linux has been criticized for its lack of real-time capabilities. Linux and its scheduler were designed for maximum throughput—not for deterministic response. The open-source kernel has enabled developers to offer real-time solutions for Linux.[2] These solutions follow two approaches:

- You can run Linux as a thread within a small real-time operating system.

- You can modify the Linux scheduler and create preemption points within the kernel.

Proponents of the thread approach claim that no modifications to the Linux kernel will ever make it deterministic. The scheduler and preemptable kernel proponents maintain that their modifications are perfectly suitable for the vast majority of applications, thanks to today's high-performance processors. Both arguments have merit. Adopting either approach adds some complexity to your design, thus increasing the development time. Adopting a real-time solution may lock your design into a specific version of the kernel. You earned in Chapter 11, "Using Interrupts for Timing," that the stock Linux kernel has good average interrupt latencies—good enough to develop an event timer with 1ms accuracy—on all the Project Trailblazer target boards. You should seriously consider benchmarking your hardware as described in Chapter 11 before adopting a real-time solution.

Windowing and real-time solutions require interaction between hardware and software. These solutions don't exist for all CPU architectures or graphics hardware. Early in your design phase, you should ensure that software ports exist for your hardware. Also keep in mind that embedded Linux developers are definitely (sometimes fiercely) opinionated, particularly in the areas of windowing and real-time. Their opinions can be of a personal, technical, or business nature. If your design requires either windowing or real-time capabilities, you should thoroughly research and investigate all the options for software and hardware. Many windowing and real-time solutions have licensing requirements that could affect your decisions and the cost of your design.

The Embedded Linux Vendor Offerings

Another criticism of Linux is that it lacks a support structure. However, commercial Linux distribution vendors certainly offer support for desktop, server, and now

embedded systems. There are four predominant commercial embedded Linux
vendors:

Lineo	www.lineo.com
LynuxWorks	www.lynuxworks.com
MontaVista Software	www.mvista.com
Red Hat	www.redhat.com/embedded

These vendors are quick to point out that they offer products based on Linux—that
they are not just packaging and support organizations. This is true. These vendors
offer, as a base product, an embedded Linux toolkit, which at a minimum configures
and compiles the kernel, configures and builds a root filesystem, and offers instruction through documentation.

NOTE

Jerry Epplin reviews these four vendors' toolkits at www.linuxdevices.com.[3]

This embedded Linux toolkit operates on a host computer, typically a Red Hat
machine, and can compile the kernel and other tools for various target platforms,
such as x86, ARM, PowerPC, MIPS, SuperH, and XScale. These vendors offer free
downloads or evaluation versions of their embedded Linux toolkits. Their business
model builds upon their base toolkits to offer products that extend their toolkits'
capabilities (for example, MontaVista's Library Optimizer or Lineo's GPL Compliance
Toolset). In addition to their toolkits and additional product offerings, each vendor
offers design, consulting, and engineering services.

On the surface, these vendors' offerings might seem identical. However, through
conversation or the use of their free or evaluation toolkits, you will learn of their
uniqueness. If you are concerned about vendor assistance with your product design,
you can visit the Web sites and call the vendors. If you have the time, you can
attend an embedded systems conference and visit with the vendors; this will enable
you to meet key people within each organization and allow you to discuss your
design in detail with company engineers. Often at conferences you can meet the
developers who are responsible for the code your design will rely on. If the vendors
can attach your face to your name, you just might get better customer service. If you
need design assistance, these vendors are ready and anxious to help.

Project Trailblazer Hardware

The hardware used in this book was carefully selected to maximize the impact of the
examples. Having three target architectures exposes you to their similarities and

differences. You should realize that the embedded world is not necessarily an x86 world. The interface hardware connected to the Project Trailblazer target boards was selected from among inexpensive chips and devices that are commonly available from local or online electronics suppliers. This interfacing hardware was chosen so that you can duplicate the book's examples on your own bench if you choose to.

For the most part, the Project Trailblazer hardware performed as expected throughout this book. In dealing with hardware designs, however, there are sometimes problems with vendors' products. Project Trailblazer had its share of these problems. Most of these problems were small; some required returning boards and devices to the manufacturers for repair. What's important to know is not that small problems existed but how quickly the manufacturers responded with solutions. Brightstar Engineering, Embedded Planet, Silicon Storage Technology, and Tri-M Systems provided exemplary hardware support for this book.

A key selling point of x86 single-board computers is their binary compatibility with their desktop counterparts: You are supposed to be able to develop an application on your desktop machine, copy it to your target board, and you're done. This book's examples show that working with the MediaEngine and the RPX-CLLF was as easy as working with the MZ104. After you configure your development environment, whether you're compiling or cross-compiling, binary compatibility is no longer a benefit.

Beyond binary compatibility, the relative speed difference between desktops and embedded hardware may mislead you in terms of target board performance. You could develop an application on your desktop machine, only to find out that it doesn't perform adequately on your target board. Also, if you're developing hardware interfaces for an embedded design, developing on your desktop could introduce additional complexity or board turns. Many single-board computers implement the PC104 form factor or other bus and physical board standards. Your desktop machine has PCI slots and might have ISA slots, but it certainly doesn't have a PC104 connector. You can't easily connect PC104 boards to your desktop. You might still opt for the x86 solution where vendor competition spurs competitive pricing. Adherence to form factors offers product alternatives and isolation from sole-source suppliers. Porting issues won't affect your kernel version decisions either. Practically all kernel source development is immediately available for use in x86 designs.

As far as non-x86 boards go, the MediaEngine and the RPX-CLLF have excellent designs and capabilities, via their StrongARM and PowerPC processors. Both the MediaEngine and RPX-CLLF contain bootloader code and a set of onboard diagnostic tools. These tools allow you to configure booting options, program on-board Flash memory, and examine processor registers and memory. These diagnostic tools are invaluable for debugging hardware designs. They allow you to configure CPU registers, which enable you to exercise hardware without booting an operating system.

Most of the Project Trailblazer hardware connected to the MediaEngine or RPX-CLLF was debugged using this capability. These target boards also offer easy interface connectors to the CPU bus. Both the StrongARM 1110 and the PowerPC MPC860 processors contain a variety of on-board peripherals that permit external interfacing without additional external hardware controllers. Your design might require the universal serial bus, inter-integrated circuit (I2C) communications, serial peripheral interface (SPI), or memory-mapped input/output. An ARM or PowerPC processor might contain exactly the peripherals your design requires. This would reduce your design time, part count, physical size, and cost while increasing reliability. Kernel version availability is a potential drawback of selecting an ARM or PowerPC solution. ARM and PowerPC kernel patches require development time. Patch releases for these processors typically lag kernel releases.

Summary

The world wants smart, network-connected devices. This desire will only increase, and these devices will pervade our lives in ways we can only imagine. Processor and memory advances enable developers to concentrate on the application, not the underlying technology. Powerful hardware is not only commonplace but also inexpensive. This combination allows Linux to move into the embedded world. It brings reliability, features, open-source code, and a proven track record.

You now have the tools, the development environment, the hardware examples, and the knowledge you need to build our future. Unencumbered by technology, you can use your imagination, creativity, and expertise to create extraordinary products. Your designs can and will power the world.

Additional Reading

1. Rick Lehrbaum, "The Embedded Linux GUI/Windowing Quick Reference Guide," www.linuxdevices.com/articles/AT9202043619.html.

2. Rick Lehrbaum, "The Real-time Linux Software Quick Reference Guide," www.linuxdevices.com/articles/AT8073314981.html.

3. Jerry Epplin, "A developer's review of the leading Embedded Linux toolkits," www.linuxdevices.com/articles/AT8402180338.html.

Index

A

B

J-K

L

*version
2.4.0 kernal
p. 23*

U

V

W-Z

Web sites

buildrootfilesystem, 73

Computer Boards, 162

Debian, 25

Debian Linux, 72, 86

ELC (Embedded Linux Consortium), 21

ELJ (Embedded Linux Journal), 22

Flash IDE, 109

GNU tool chain, 34

Grayhill, 165

Journeyman (MontaVista), 72

kernels, 209

Lineo, 401

Linux Devices, 22

Linux for PowerPC Embedded Systems, 34

LynuxWorks, 401

MontaVista Software, 401

National Semiconductor, 278-279

parallel ports, 163

Philips Semiconductors, 278

Red Hat, 401

Texas Instruments, 166

toolkits (Linux), 401

USBs (universal serial buses), 207

windowing, 400

workstations

booting

Project Trailblazer, 26

Ethernet cards, 29

tbdevl, 24-26

x86 parallel printer ports

I2C SAA1064 (Philips Semiconductor) LED display drivers, connecting to, 299-301, 305-307, 317

LM70 SPI (National Semiconductor) digital temperature sensors, connecting to, 280, 288